CHILDREN DESIGNERS

Interdisciplinary Constructions for Learning and Knowing Mathematics in a Computer-Rich School

Cognition and Computing Series

Elliot Soloway, Series Editor

CHILDREN DESIGNERS

Interdisciplinary Constructions for Learning and Knowing Mathematics in a Computer-Rich School

Idit Harel

The Media Laboratory
Massachusetts Institute of Technology

ABLEX PUBLISHING CORPORATION
NORWOOD, NEW JERSEY

Cover design by Betsy Chimento and Idit Harel.
Cover photograph by Stephen Sherman.

Photography by Jacqueline Karaaslanian and Stephen Sherman. Teachers and parents of students from Project Headlight gave us their consent to work with, photograph, and videotape the students. The names of the children in this book are not real, but the names of the teachers are. The photographs were taken in the actual research site, but intentionally, they are *not* of the children mentioned in this book.

Figures, illustrations, and replications of children's designs by Idit Harel and Elisabeth Glenwinkle.

Library of Congress Cataloging-in-Publication Data

Harel, Idit.
    Children designers: Interdisciplinary constructions for learning and knowing
mathematics in a computer-rich school / Idit Harel.
      p. cm. — (Cognition and computing series)
    Includes bibliographical references and index.
    ISBN 0-89391-787-7. — ISBN 0-89391-788-5 (pbk.)
    1. Concept learning. 2. Human information processing in children.
3. Computer software—Development. I. Title. II. Series.
LB1062.H3   1991
006.3—dc20   91-15001
                                                  CIP

Ablex Publishing Corporation
355 Chestnut Street
Norwood, New Jersey 07648

to my mother Rachel
with love

TABLE OF CONTENTS

FOREWORD

Seymour Papert

Idit Harel's Instructional Software Design Project began during the time our Epistemology and Learning Group was in the throes of the theoretical labor of birthing the concept for which I have been promoting the name *constructionism*. A strong resonance between her project and this concept reflects a two-way interaction: The project was enriched by the theoretical climate, which in turn gained substantially by having the project as an "object to think with." The resonance also means that each is helpful for explaining the other, and this is what I shall be doing here.

I begin with a simplified preliminary definition of constructionism. The word was chosen to evoke, and put together, two connotations: the psychological term *constructivism* (whose strong meaning for Piaget is sadly diluted in contemporary American educational jargon), and the image of *construction set* (whose reference to things like Tinker Toys or Lego has a natural extension to software construction as in Logo programming or Robot Odyssey). When Piaget describes himself as a constructivist, he is referring to a view that knowledge structures are built by the subject rather than transmitted by a teacher. When we describe ourselves as constructionists, we subscribe to this view but add the idea that building knowledge structures ("in the head") goes especially well when the subject is engaged in building material structures ("in the world") as children do with construction sets.

Of course such statements are at best pointers to a direction of thinking; they leave one, or certainly ought to leave one, with a sense of worry about what all the key words really mean. What does it mean to build a knowledge structure? how do you know when it is happening? and what meaning does "transmitting knowledge" have beyond being anathema to educators with a constructivist bent? One way to dissipate this worry would be to develop formal theoretical models within which the terms could be given precise definitions. Another is to clarify the issues concretely by constructing and examining good instances of constructionism. One might say of the second approach, to which Harel's work makes a very significant contribution, that it is taking a constructionist approach to understanding constructionism.

Piaget often confuses his readers by overly elaborate attempts to take the more formal option. But he more than makes up for it (and this is why he is really so powerful) by also being an accomplished concrete thinker: He has a brilliant way of finding situations that stick in our minds as richly evocative objects to think with. The greatness of the discovery of conservations is reflected in the quantity of thinking it has generated, in its way of coming up in a thousand conversations about children. It matters much less that the conversationalists might think of themselves as refuting Piaget's interpretation of childhood conservations. Even the sceptics think better about children because they have these examples to think with.

For me Piaget's situations have been particularly powerful in giving reality to the idea that much learning, perhaps the best learning and perhaps even all learning, takes place in ways (call them constructivist if you like, or Piagetian, as I did in *Mindstorms*) that are starkly different from the instructionist models underlying contemporary school. It is endemic in school thinking to suppose that learning is facilitated by a process of microdissection of a domain of knowledge into dozens, or hundreds or thousands, of fragments of knowledge that will be strung together as a curriculum. Whether the fragments are old-fashioned "facts" or modern "concepts," hardly matters for the point at issue here; what matters is that knowledge fragments will be fed out in some systematic way under the guidance of The Curriculum. But there is no curriculum for the conservations of quantities. Nor is there much of a curriculum for learning to talk, or to joke, or to manipulate parents or the many other marvelous things children come to be able to do before they go to school. Of course the instructionists say: "That's too bad, that's why children come to have conservation so late and talk nonstandard English. Let's make a curriculum to fix those gaps and deficiencies!" Gee, I say, I'd be more convinced if children in curriculum-driven schools amazed me as much as the younger ones by the the immense amount of learning that seems to be going on.

Yet a doubt arises. Can one be sure that the young children learn so much? How can we measure and compare the amounts of learning needed for the conservation of number, on the one hand, and spoken English on the other? Perhaps the learning children do without school and curriculum is really quite infinitesmal compared with the amount of learning required for such things as multiplication tables. Perhaps the school way really is a more efficient way of learning. Perhaps. How can we make sensible comparisons? Or are we comparing incomparably different kinds of learning?

The comparisons are tricky, because Piaget's studies and school teaching deal with such different domains of knowledge. Enter the Instructional Software Design project, a case study of children working in a domain that squarely overlaps school math but in ways that are discussably much more like Piagetian learning. These children are working with fractions, but without any curriculum and in some cases not doing anything that remotely resembles the microskills identified by the typical school curriculum. Yet in the end they do better at school tests. Why? You can come up with a dozen theories, just as you can explain conservation in many different ways or even explain it away altogether. What makes this project methodologically interesting as an example to emulate goes beyond the particular interpretations its author makes of its results. To a degree that is rare in contemporary "educational experiments," it has a richness that helps one to sink one's teeth more firmly into important concerns.

Harel's work was carried out "in partial fulfillment of the requirements for the degree of Ph.D." Under these circumstances it is customary to ask "What is her thesis? What has she proved?" My job as her thesis superviser (which includes advising her on how to satisfy the academicians as well as on how to advance knowledge) was made much easier by the fact that Harel amply satisfies those whose intellectual methodology attributes value only to enterprises that can be judged by such questions. But for me what is really important about her work is not that she *proved* something but that she *made* something. She made something that will feed thinking and talking for years to come. In some ways, then, it has more in common with the product of an artist than with traditional descriptions of what the product of science ought to be—but perhaps this is true of all of the best science.

OVERVIEW

This book is an inquiry into conditions that could make Papert's Constructionist vision of learning and computer programming possible. During the past six years, a major focus of Papert's research group at the MIT Media Lab has been to define and refine the idea of *programming as a source of learning power,* and to explore *design-based learning environments.*

Papert's *Constructionist* theory (1980, 1991a, 1991b, in press) combined with Perkins's *Knowledge as Design* pedagogy (1986) led me to view technological and computational knowledge as valuable not only in their own right, but also capable of enhancing the learning of many other things such as mathematics, design, and representational structures. As a means of developing and studying Papert's extended notion of programming and its contribution to a child's learning and development, I implemented the "Instructional Software Design Project," through which I explored the learning that takes place when young students develop complete software 'products,' designed for use by other children.

Let's enter the following scene:

It is Wednesday afternoon at the Hennigan Elementary School in Boston. In a large and open area of Project Headlight, 17 fourth-grade students and their teacher are grouped around two large circles, each composed of about a dozen or so desktop computers.

Debbie sits at her computer swinging her legs, her hands poised over the keyboard, completely absorbed in her programming project. To her right, Naomi programs letters on the computer screen in different colors and sizes. Next to her, Michaela debugs a program for a mathematical word-problem involving fractions, comparing thirds and halves by using a representation of measuring cups that are filled with different amounts of orange juice and water. She is very involved with her design, typing with one hand while the other touches the shapes on her computer monitor. A few computers away, the teacher is trying out Tom's program, talking with him about one of his explanations of "what mixed fractions are." In the background, Charlie walks around the second computer circle, holding his notes in one hand chewing on a pencil. He stops suddenly at Sharifa's computer. He chats with her for a moment, presses a key or two on her keyboard, and watches Sharifa's designs as they appear on her computer screen. After looking at her programming code, moving the cursor up and down on the screen, he calls out, "Hey Paul, come see Sharifa's program! It's a fractions clock!"

The noise and movement around the computer area do not seem to bother the students. Back in the other circle, Naomi has completed the title screen for her piece of software, which reads "Welcome to Fractions Land! by Naomi." She stretches her arms and looks around to see what is new in her friends' programs. She then leans over towards Debbie and asks what she is doing.

Debbie shows Naomi her programming code. "It's a long one," she says, running the cursor down the screen, very proud of the 47 lines of code she has programmed for her "HOUSE" procedure. She then exits the LogoWriter editor to run her program to Naomi, who moves her chair closer to Debbie's. In a slow, quiet voice, pointing to the pictures on the screen, Debbie explains to Naomi: "This is my House scene. I designed all these shapes; each one equals one half. In the house, the roof has two halves, the door has two halves, and I will add to this scene two wooden wagons and a sun. I'll divide them into halves too . . . The halves, the shaded parts, are on different sides of the objects. You know, you can use fractions on anything . . . Do you like the colors?"

The idea of representing the halves of different objects, the objects being "regular human things" in a real-life situation, is Debbie's. In the final version of her teaching software, an explanatory text will accompany the pictures on the screen: "This is a house. Almost every shape is one half! I am trying to say that you can use fractions almost every day of your life!" Debbie is the only child in the class who has designed and programmed this particular type of "lesson" to her younger students. She is very clear about why she designed it: to teach other children that fractions are more than strange numbers on school worksheets. She has discovered that fractions can be all around us; they describe objects, experiences, and concepts in everyday life. While Debbie is working on this representation, the only advice she asks of her friend is about the colors: "Do you like the colors?" Naomi tells her: "It's nicer if all the halves are in the same color." They negotiate for a while, but Debbie doesn't agree: "No. It will be boring." Naomi and Debbie continue to work on their projects with their keyboards in their laps.

This book follows a group of fourth-grade students for a whole semester as they wrote instructional software programs to teach other children about *fractions*. We shall see that the overall experience was greater than the sum of the parts: students learned not only about programming and fractions, but also about design, user interface, as well as representational and pedagogical issues.

Software designing represents a new paradigm for computer-based activities in schools. This paradigm of work with children differs radically from traditional use of computer software (and of programming) in schools in several ways. Most important is the *product design component:* The goal of the students' work is to produce a well designed product intended for use by others, to make an educational software package on the model of commercial software products. I have documented quite clearly that awareness of an 'end user' in the process of learning made a significant difference (even in the students' engagement with

Logo Programming in a Computer-Rich Learning Environment (Stephen Sherman Photography)

fractions!). The fourth graders I studied also tested their software (while it was under construction) by meeting with third-grade children who served as test subjects. Here, different concepts and skills in a very different domain of knowledge—namely, the technologically-oriented domains of product design, implementation, and testing—were exercised. Making a product for a real user seemed to motivate a *long period of involvement* (i.e., four months) with one particular project. One of the most solidly documented findings of this work is the importance of this long time period: for example, several of the children who showed the greatest gains from the experience took several weeks to find a voice in which they were comfortably able to engage the subject matter—i.e., rational-number concepts.

The paradigm lends itself particularly well to "whole learning" analogous to the concept of "whole language" that has achieved currency among many educators in the past few years (e.g., Holdaway, 1979). When children were designing software for fractions they were certainly engaged with mathematical ideas and their representations. But they were no less engaged with expression of ideas in words (they did writing and reading), in pictures (they did art), and in moving images (they did animation). They were engaged in thinking about teaching—a subject which touches on the lives of children in very personal ways. They were engaged in thinking about design—a subject that is rarely implemented in schools, and almost never integrated with mathematics learning. Thus the project was essentially transdisciplinary. But while transdisciplinary, the work can be oriented to connect with other subject areas. Fractions, science, grammar, history, poetry, art history—could all lend themselves to this kind of project.

This book attempts to construct an image of "learners as designers." ISDP brings design to education. More specifically, it brings design into **mathematics education.** This paradigm of computer work with children differs from traditional use of computer software (and of programming) in schools in several ways. Let me briefly specify *five reasons* why I think "learners as designers" (or "design for learning") is a rich paradigm for learning and for research on learning mathematics, and in what ways it is different from other approaches. Many of the following reasons are expanded and discussed throughout this book and in other publications (see Appendix and Bibliography). *The integration of these reasons in one learning research enterprise* is the important point I would like to make here. Because the following reasons are interrelated and overlap each other in many ways, it is not natural to list them separately in the way I do here for the purpose of this overview.

First Reason. **Design motivates learning.** Before any learning and productive thinking can occur, people must be motivated. Motivation to learn and think in general, and in mathematics in particular, depends on recognizing that something is important, that it is relevant to oneself. Recognizing relevance depends on cultural background and self-awareness.

We conduct our studies at an inner-city elementary school in Boston. What we see is that many young inner-city people in our age of cultural pluralism and socioeconomic inequities have problems getting to know who they are, what is relevant for their lives, why mathematics and why education (in the ways presented in "typical" American schools) are important and relevant to them. Our present educational system unfortunately offers little help in evoking relevancy, in connecting the learners' outside-of-school cultures with their inside-of-school cultures, and in making education meaningful for students. A great deal of research within the Epistemology & Learning Group at the Media Lab explores the ways design-based education can make education more relevant for students.

In our various activities involving Logo programming and Lego/Logo, we have been observing how, through certain design activities, learners generate concepts, explore ideas, construct products, and appropriate ideas in different voices and in personal ways (e.g., Turkle & Papert, 1990; Harel & Papert, 1990; Resnick & Ocko, 1991). We found that certain design activities allow learners to find relevancy and are excellent vehicles for fostering motivation. Furthermore, in the particular project presented here—ISDP—the act of making a product (for a real user) seemed to motivate students for quite a *long period* of involvement (i.e., four months) with one particular project. The "production process" in ISDP initiates a cycle that begins with the forming of self-awareness: From the very beginning of the project, the young software designers need to face serious questions,

- *What do I know about fractions?*
- *Why do I care about fractions?*
- *What do I want to explore within this domain?*
- *What do I want to communicate and represent for other students?*
- *How am I going to do it?*

When students ask themselves such crucial questions in their process of learning, these questions are leading them to the perceiving of relevance, and especially, to becoming motivated. This leads to professional engagement in the mathematical learning process—and cycling again, to a further and stronger sense of taking a stance, and announcing to the world: *"This is what I think about fractions; these were my problems with fractions; this is how I figured it out; this is how I programmed it; and all of that is embedded in my design."*

So, what are some gains of such a process? Instead of being a victim of the educational system, instead of being a victim of the teacher's agenda and all these math worksheets—design offers students an active and meaningful role. It must be the productive work of the knowing self. Constructionist design activities can encourage motivation and "force" learners to find the relevancy of the learned domain.

Second Reason. **Designers make things happen.** Design substantiates learning in actual accomplishments. For reasons described above, in the ISDP mathematical design project, students learn first-hand that knowing mathematics does not "just happen." They do mathematics, they design representations, and they make it happen. They do this in the form of creating instructional mathematical representations for fractions—creating fractions software, individually and collaboratively—on their computers. Passive learning and voyeurism can hardly exist in such an environment.

Third Reason. **Design evokes self-knowledge. Designers make personal connections between the affective and the cognitive.** The design process is putting people, feelings, things, and situations together (Harel & Papert, 1990). In ISDP this point expressed itself even through children's decisions about the color of shapes, or the size, or the number of the fractions on a computer screen, as well as in choosing what style of representation is appropriate for what concept they wanted to communicate. Therefore, designing as an educational process leads learners towards a productive and a personal (affective and cognitive) contribution to their learning environment. Resnick (e.g., 1991) has documented similar findings in children and adults working in Lego/Logo environments.

Fourth Reason. **Designing a product promotes consideration of intended users, clients, customers—the community of others that designers serve.** Designers learn by teaching (and thinking about) this community. The difference between simply doing something and designing a real product is in the level and quality of commitment and consideration given to the task, and in how one feels while accomplishing it. Too often in schools, it is possible to do things mindlessly while acting as agents for someone else (usually the teacher). Even with high performance, there may be no sense of reward in finishing the job. We found, for example, that designing software (or Lego/Logo constructs) cannot be automatic and mindless. It forces critical thinking, personal judgment, and deep involvement. Our observations of young software designers in ISDP tell us that good designing for other students always evokes feelings of pride and accomplishment.

"Learning by teaching" in design environments is presented in the context of ISDP as another empowering principle. A narrow description of our intention in doing this is that we turn the usual tables by giving the learner the active position of the teacher/explainer rather than passive recipient of knowledge. We also give the learner the position of designer/producer rather than consumer of software. It is a new elaboration of the old idea of learning by doing rather than by being told (or what Papert describes as "Constructionism" rather than "Instructionism," Papert, 1990).

Fifth Reason. **Design is integrative and holistic.** Implementing certain design activities in the school environment can provide an interesting marriage of the "everyday," "real-world" type of activities and the "formal," "school-like" type of activities.

The idea of "designing for learning" as an integrative human capability has been subordinated in our culture in general, and certainly, not valued enough in the culture of our schools. Design activities are not usually integrated into the study of mathematics. Rather, they are left for art classes, woodworking workshops, and so on.

There is a need to take advantage of the transdisciplinary, integrative, and comprehensive nature of any design process, and to explicitly include it into the larger context of human development and schooling. This is because designing has significance beyond the architecting of buildings and the making of enjoyable and effective environments. It is not just another skill we need to learn in school so we can use it when we grow up, to make our society's industry profitable (a common argument among some people who wish to bring design education into schools). Rather, design is viewed here as an **empowering principle,** as a discipline which facilitates other learning, and which marries cultural background, school activites, thought, action, creativity, construction, and reflection.

In this sense, ISDP is a model of holistic and comprehensive learning through design, giving students exciting evidence for how their mathematical schoolwork relates to them, to their lives, and to their community—inside and outside of school. Students can learn to integrate ideas: They experience how math relates to language, how learning relates to teaching, how art relates to science, and how communication relates to understanding. By testing their software (while it is under construction) with third-grade children (who serve as "test subjects"), they can also relate concepts and skills from a different domain of knowledge—namely, the technologically oriented domains of product design, implementation, and testing. Moreover, by designing software for fractions they are certainly engaged with mathematical ideas and their representations; but they are no less engaged with expression of ideas in words (in writing and reading), in pictures (in art), and in moving images (in animation). They are also engaged in thinking about teaching—a subject which touches on the lives of children in very personal ways, and in thinking about design—a subject that is rarely implemented in schools, and almost never integrated with mathematics learning. Thus, ISDP is oriented to connect with other subject areas and skills.

Chapter 1 of this book is divided into four parts. Part 1 describes the general purposes of the study, the research site, and the atmosphere and conditions for the learning that took place in the course of an experiment called the Instructional Software Design Project (ISDP).

Part 2 places the entire study in its intellectual landscape. It presents the rationale and motivations for developing the ISDP approach and for conducting the ISDP research. It discusses the issues in question, and the ways in which the research questions related to previous findings on the learning of fractions and Logo. It also examines how the research method, questions, and objectives were derived from three different but related sources: (a) the experiential motivations for the study, or the ways in which common professional adult experiences—learning-by-teaching as well as learning-by-designing—motivated me to create similar learning experiences for young children; (b) the theoretical motivations for the study, or the way in which the theory of constructionism and other constructivist and cultural learning and cognitive theories led me to create a model learning environment, and to study how children learned and developed in this particular environment; and (c) the technical motivations for the study, or the way in which previous studies and their findings, as well as the issues raised by the existing research in the fields of Logo programming, rational-number knowledge acquisition and understanding, and software designing and programming, motivated me to conduct a study that aimed at *changing the conditions* for learning in these domains, with the goal of solving some of the problems reported by existing research literature.

Part 3 of this Chapter describes a pilot study I conducted in our model school prior to this larger study. The results of the pilot—in the form of case studies of five children—created the foundation for the larger study and was later expanded to the ISDP approach which is presented in this book.

Part 4 describes the research design, method and activities involved in the larger Instructional Software Design Project, providing the reader with a better sense of what is was like to participate in the project. The project's evaluation procedure is described, as well as the pupils involved, their teachers, their math curriculum, the researcher's role, the instruments used, and finally, the data-collection and analysis techniques.

In short, the four parts of this first meta-chapter are meant to create a mental model of the points being addressed in the ISDP approach to learning, and the ways in which the researcher investigated and analyzed them in the context of the study presented in this book.

Chapter 2, entitled Debbie's Case, presents one girl's learning, designing, programming, and thinking processes in the Instructional Software Design Project. A detailed documentation of Debbie's day-by-day microgenetic processes over a four-month period is offered so that the reader can follow Debbie's complex processes of constructing her Fractions Software step-by-step, her learning of fractions and Logo through these processes, her relationship with her (interactive) object as it was developed, and her relationship with her peers and their processes and products. By following Debbie, the reader will better understand the results of the comparative study which are presented in Chapter 3. Several examples of other children's processes and products of ISDP are interlaced into Chapter 2, providing the reader with a broader concept of the context of Debbie's work, as well as illustrating the richness of the ISDP learning environment.

Chapter 3 presents the results of the comparative evaluation. Pre- and post tests and interviews were conducted before and after the experiment with 51 fourth-graders: 17 of these students made up the experimental class (i.e., the instructional software designers), while the other 34 were part of the two control classes. Chapter 3 attempts to familiarize the reader with the results of the experiment and its influence on children's minds and educational practice. The reader will come to realize that the children of the experimental class were able to master fractions and Logo with greater understanding and depth (even in terms of standard school measures) than those in the control classes.

Finally, *Chapter 4* presents eight broad conclusions and integrative discussions of the first three chapters. It presents the ways in which the study did or did not succeed with respect to its major purposes and goals, and explores a number of ideas for further investigation. These conclusions relate to the ISDP culture and its impact on children's learning and thinking and on encouraging diversity in learning styles. Specific attention is given to conclusions regarding educational practice and mathematics curriculum, to the processes of learning programming and fractions, as well as to teaching metacognitive and problem-solving skills. In addition, some conclusions directly relate to research methodology issues, such as implementing an integration of quantitative, qualitative, and comparative methods with an emphasis on studying learners in a context—

specifically, a complex constructionist context, which resembles everyday life and professional experiences more than the typical school life. Emphasis is also placed on the advantages of using video as a research tool in a holistic research enterprise of this kind. Finally, in the last section of Chapter 4, based on the research findings, I shall outline an approach for educationally based technological developments in the form of an integrative and programmable Design-and-Production-Tool for young children's learning.

Children as Software Designers (Jacqueline Karaaslanian Photography)

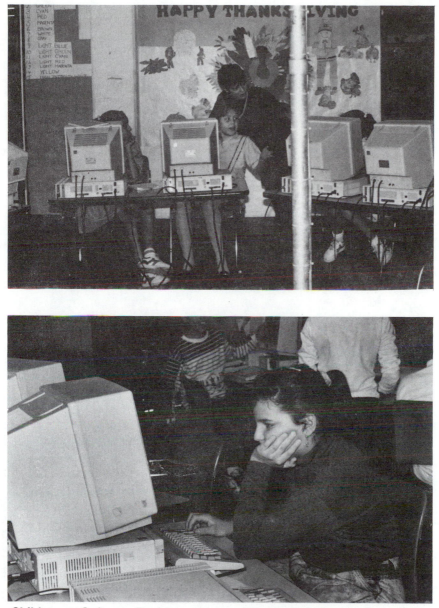

Children as Software Designers (Jacqueline Karaaslanian Photography)

Chapter I

Design For Learning

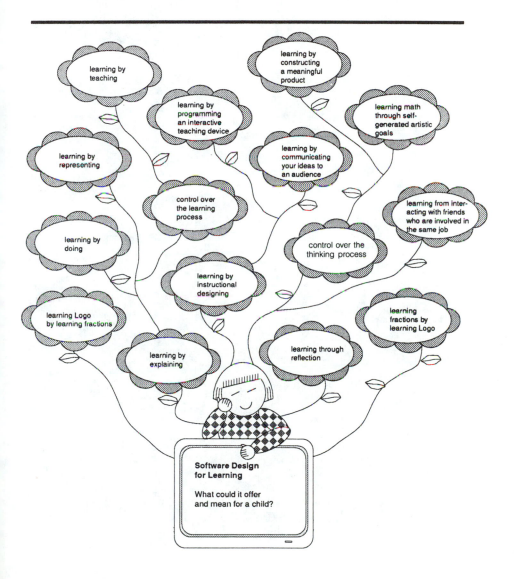

learning by teaching

learning by constructing a meaningful product

learning by programming an interactive teaching device

learning math through self-generated artistic goals

learning by representing

learning by communicating your ideas to an audience

control over the learning process

learning from inter-acting with friends who are involved in the same job

learning by doing

control over the thinking process

learning by instructional designing

learning Logo by learning fractions

learning fractions by learning Logo

learning by explaining

learning through reflection

Software Design for Learning

What could it offer and mean for a child?

(Stephen Sherman Photography)

PART 1
WHY, HOW, & WHERE DESIGN
FOR LEARNING

The aim of this book is to assess and describe an experiment called the Instructional Software Design Project (ISDP). The project involved fourth-grade students in the learning of fractions and Logo by their designing a piece of instructional software about fractions every day, for four months, at their own pace and using their own ideas. In this study I analyze the day-by-day processes these students generated, constructed, or followed, what they gained through ISDP, and how these students differed in predictable ways from others who learned fractions and Logo by methods other than software design.

1.1. SOFTWARE DESIGN AS A LEARNING & RESEARCH ENVIRONMENT

The in-depth studying of children's minds as they learned fractions and Logo through instructional software design (the shaded overlap represented on the left side of Figure 1) had several purposes. Some of the more general goals in conducting this experiment were:

1. To describe, by using both Vygotskian and Piagetian perspectives and the constructionist theory of Papert, what it meant for a child (or a group of students) to learn and be involved in such complex and unusually long problem-solving process related to designing and computer programming.

    The study presented here did not attempt to focus on the kinds of well-defined problems that are usually given to subjects during one observed session. Instead, this study used instructional software design as a *vehicle* for analyzing a child's *total learning* in a rich and complex environment over a long period of time; analyzing a design-based activity and a learning culture that involved many variables (many of which could be considered ill-defined variables); and analyzing what was learned through this complex solution process (but not necessarily focusing just on the solution process itself).

4

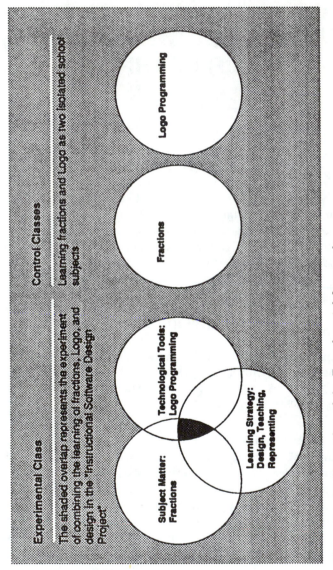

Experimental Class

The shaded overlap represents the experiment of combining the learning of fractions, Logo, and design in the "Instructional Software Design Project"

Technological Tools: Logo Programming

Subject Matter: Fractions

Learning Strategy: Design, Teaching, Representing

Control Classes

Learning fractions and Logo as two isolated school subjects

Fractions

Logo Programming

Figure 1. An Illustration of the Experimental Approach.

2. To understand how students can learn several subject matters and skills at the same time, and how the learning of one can contribute to the other.
3. To experiment with one prototypical activity of this kind, assess what major changes this activity can offer to educational practice, and judge whether or not it reveals any information that might lead to changes in the teaching and learning approaches of fractions and Logo in elementary schools.
4. To investigate in what ways this activity encourages children's learning and understanding of the Logo programming language.
5. To assess in what ways this activity encourages children's learning and understanding of the rational-number representations system.
6. To investigate in what ways this activity encourages children's cognitive awareness (i.e., children's thinking about their own thinking), their cognitive control (i.e., planning, reflection, self-management, and thinking about these cognitive processes), and their metaconceptual thinking (i.e., children's thinking about their own knowledge and understanding of concepts).
7. To gather different kinds of data about the processes of learning through Instructional Software Design and analyze it on several levels:
    • within the individual: the day-by-day microgenetic process of an individual's sequences in creating an interactive teaching software;
    • within the classroom: the process of the whole class who participated in this project;
    • between classes (comparative): the way in which these learning processes compared with those of other students (from two other classrooms in the same school) who learned fractions and Logo through different, more or less conventional approaches.

This set of general goals and purposes makes it clear that the present study will not be formal in the sense of using or producing precise models of mechanisms of learning and thinking. My analyses and inferences from the data are too diverse to permit the creation of functioning models of children's learning, cognitive development, or even software design. I hope to create a comprehensive model of the project itself, to illuminate certain aspects of children's learning and cognition in this constructionist learning environment, of the learning tools they used in this context, and of the learning culture that was created in the project, as well as to make certain advances in understanding a child's cognitive-psychological front.

The project was a construction for me as well as for the students and their teacher. I created this learning environment while participating in it myself in the same way the students did, and I constructed the meanings for this environment and for the children's learning within it as I wrote this document—much like a detective—in an attempt to relate the different pieces of knowledge, functions,

Theoretical goals

Goal 1

Conducting a holistic study combining the theories of Papert, Piaget, Vygostky, and Perkins

Goal 2

Integrating the learning of several subject matters... investigating the contribution of each to another and each to the whole

Goals based on theoretical goals and previous research findings

Goal 3

New apporach for learning Logo programming

Goal 4

New approach for learning fractions

Goal 5

Encouraging meta-cognitive skills, awareness and control: thinking about thinking

Implementation goal

Goal 6

Within the Project Headlight Culture, children were placed beside one another to work on a common instructional software design project, over a long period of time, in view of designing, programming, and using their software for teaching fractions to younger pupils

Data collection and analyses goals

Goal 7a: Individual Assessment

Case studies for building individual models

Goal 7b: Classroom Assessment

17 cases looking at different stage sequences of children, compare and contrast models

Goal 7c: Comparative Assessment

Pre-Post Evaluation

Pre-Post Evaluation

Use Pre/Post-data to investigate individual's progress

Use Pre/Post-data to compare to the 2 other Control classes

Goal 7d: Project Assessment

Describe and analyze the "Project"

Create one prototype

Figure 2.   The study's goals and objectives.

behaviors, processes, and products to one another. In other words, I went through a microgenetic process myself in implementing, analyzing, and writing this study, and did not have well-defined models for implementation or interpretation in advance. What I have produced is: (a) a large body of data that could be used as a springboard for creating such models through better understanding of children's learning and thinking processes in this rare pedagogical situation, and (b) strong evidence for supporting the success of the case under discussion, the ISDP, as a powerful vehicle for children's learning and cognitive development, and for the in-depth studying of children's minds as they learn, think, and produce under these extreme and complex conditions. Since ISDP was based on Papert's constructionist and interdisciplinary approach, this study also offers some evidence and support—a vivid model—for constructionist learning in action. At this point, we do not have many comprehensive models or cases for constructionist learning. Therefore, this study also offers a contribution in this direction.

1.2. THE RESEARCH SITE: PROJECT HEADLIGHT

An inner-city elementary public-school in one of Boston's low SES communities was the site of my study. One-third of this public school, with students from first through fifth grade, of which approximately 40% were black, 40% Hispanic, and 18% white or Asian, had been participating in Project Headlight (Papert, 1985, 1986, 1987b). As part of my work at Project Headlight, I implemented this project, conducting my investigation in one fourth-grade classroom in this school, within the Project Headlight Area during a four-month period. Earlier, during the Spring of 1986, a pilot study had been conducted with fifth graders of Project Headlight, the findings of which revealed the need for further investigations and a more systematic study of the Software Design Project (Harel, 1986). The project was strongly influenced by Project Headlight's educational philosophy and objectives. In the following paragraphs, I shall briefly describe Project Headlight and its educational goals.

During the 1985–1986 academic year, a collaborative project involving Boston Public Schools, the MIT Media Technology Laboratory, and the IBM Corporation laid the foundations for a model school of the future. As I was analyzing the data (Harel, 1988), we were in the third academic year of the running of Project Headlight, and were funded by other organizations such as the National Science Foundation (NSF), the Apple Computer Inc., the Lego Company, the McArthur Foundation, and others. Project Headlight was originated and mainly inspired by Seymour Papert, Professor of Media Technology at the Massachusetts Institute of Technology. It was designed in anticipation of a near future in which technology would be used far more extensively than anything seen today in schools. It anticipated, for example, a system of free access to computers that might eventually involve two computers per student—one at school and one at home. In the model school, the number of computers introduced at the outset was one per three students; and it is to be hoped that this number will gradually increase as more money comes in and as new ways are found to integrate the computers into the educational life of the school. A committee of MIT scholars and school department officials selected this specific inner-city public school as the site for Project Headlight, after inviting proposals from all of Boston's public elementary schools.

Although the project uses technology extensively, it is not defined as a "technology project," but rather as an "education project." It explores new approaches toward learning and teaching in the context of a traditional school that is rich in technology. Its original educational goal was open classrooms, centered around students, integrating the learning of several subjects, and using computers as tools for learning these subjects.

Project Headlight currently operates as a "school-within-a-school," comprising about one-third of the School's students and teachers. The 250 participating students are in grades one through five, and are divided into advanced work classes, regular classes, bilingual classes, and special education classes. The participating teachers learn about computers and the Project's educational methodology during several 3-week-long summer workshops, which, since the summer of 1985, have been repeated each year at progressively more advanced levels and according to the teachers' needs and interests. In addition, there are regular in-service meetings once every week or 2 weeks. Operational decisions are also made in these regular meetings, which are attended by the school's teachers and by the principal of the school, as well as by researchers from the MIT Media Lab. Among the 16 participating teachers, five teach bilingual classes in Spanish, three (including two of the bilingual teachers) are special education teachers, four teach advanced work classes in English, and five teach regular classes in English. The Project uses approximately 120 IBM PCjr computers in classrooms, in teachers' homes, and in the open areas next to the classrooms (see Project Headlight's floor plan). Most of the computers are connected to each other in a local-area network.

The MIT staff participates in several ways. They support and train the teachers, and are responsible for the instruction of teachers and students in computer skills such as Logo, word processing, or using the network. They teach some special courses, conduct a number of projects within several classes (ISDP was one of these), and work towards integrating the computer into the basic curriculum. Finally, MIT researchers conduct an extensive program of observations and documentation of the many projects that have been implemented at the school, and of the teachers' and students' progress.

On the whole, the goals for Project Headlight's first year were to create its technological and conceptual infrastructure, build a team relationship among the various participants, and develop projects and systematic methods of observa-

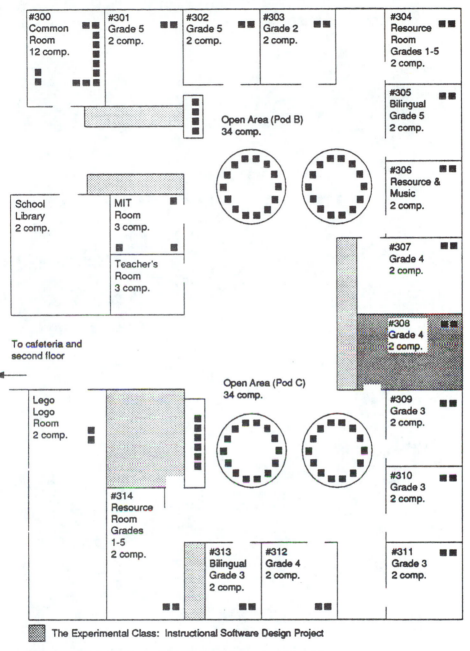

| #300 Common Room 12 comp. | #301 Grade 5 2 comp. | #302 Grade 5 2 comp. | #303 Grade 2 2 comp. | #304 Resource Room Grades 1-5 2 comp. |

Open Area (Pod B) 34 comp.

#305 Bilingual Grade 5 2 comp.

#306 Resource & Music 2 comp.

School Library 2 comp.

MIT Room 3 comp.

Teacher's Room 3 comp.

#307 Grade 4 2 comp.

#308 Grade 4 2 comp.

To cafeteria and second floor

Open Area (Pod C) 34 comp.

Lego Logo Room 2 comp.

#314 Resource Room Grades 1-5 2 comp.

#309 Grade 3 2 comp.

#310 Grade 3 2 comp.

#313 Bilingual Grade 3 2 comp.

#312 Grade 4 2 comp.

#311 Grade 3 2 comp.

The Experimental Class: Instructional Software Design Project

IBM PCjr computers on tables (in the circles or along the walls)

Non-used spaces such as bathrooms

Total number of computers in Project Headlight = 110
(15 other computers are in teacher's homes)

Figure 3.   Project Headlight: Floor Plan and Number of Computers (as of 1986–87).

Scenes from the Research Site: Outside the James Hennigan Public School (Stephen Sherman Photography)

Scenes from the Research Site: Inside the Hennigan School (Jacqueline Karaaslanian Photography)

Scenes from the Research Site: The Hennigan School's Library (on the right, the School's Principal Mrs. Eleanor Perry) (Jacqueline Karaaslanian Photography)

Scenes from the Research Site: The Hennigan School's Cafeteria (the teacher Gilda Keefe and her Students Prepare a Show for the School's "Our Spanish Culture" Celebration (Jacqueline Karaaslanian Photography)

tions. The goals of the second and third years were similar, and many more projects integrating the computer into the basic curriculum were implemented by the teachers and MIT staff. However, the MIT staff concentrated far more than previously on creating among teachers and students a degree of mastery over computers and their use that might support the growth, over a certain period of time, of an educational environment rich in computers.

The following diagram shows Project Headlight's floor plan and the location and number of the computers. Other first- and second-grade classrooms (besides the ones indicated here) participate in the project even though they are located on other floors of the school, and are not shown in the floor plan—the center of Project Headlight.

1.3. DESCRIPTION OF THE INSTRUCTIONAL SOFTWARE DESIGN PROJECT

Seventeen Fourth-Grade Students Placed Beside One Another Worked on a Common Project, One Hour a Day for Four Months.

In the context of ISDP, 17 fourth-grade students (all in one class) each designed, programmed (using the Logowriter programming language), and evaluated a collection of interactive screens (an interactive lesson) to teach third graders about basic concepts of fractions. Each child designed and programmed his or her piece of software for 1 hour each day, for approximately 4 months. On the whole, the students spent close to 70 hours each in this problem-solving enterprise, designing and working on implementing their software.

The Instructional Software Design Project was Open-Ended but Included a Series of Rituals and Activities.

The project was open ended but included a series of activities or routines that all the experimental students followed. Each working day, for 5–7 minutes, the students wrote their plans and drew their designs in their personal designer's notebooks before going to the computer. (The *Designer's Notebook* is a notebook I created especially for this project and will be described in detail later; see Appendix C for a sample.) Then, after completing their writing and drawing of plans and designs, the students worked at their own computers for approximately 45 to 55 minutes. At the computer, the students implemented their plans and designs, created new ones, and revised old ones. When they wished, they were allowed to work with their friends, help each other, or walk around to see what other students were doing. When the computer time was over, each child saved his or her daily files on a special diskette and went back to the classroom. In their Designer's Notebooks, they then wrote and reflected on the problems and changes they had made that day, and sometimes added plans and designs for the next. The students had full freedom in choosing which concepts they wanted to teach, how to design their screens, what the sequence of their lesson should be, and what testing to include, if any. In short, the project was open ended in terms of what the students chose to design, teach, and program. The only two requirements were: (a) that they write in their Designer's Notebooks before and after each working session; and (b) that they spend a specific amount of time at the computer each day. The purpose of this second requirement, regarding the time limitations in using the computer, was to allow the project to fit into the schedule of the class and of the school. This requirement made it possible to estimate and draw generalizations about what students could accomplish in a project of this kind, designed to fit easily into the regular scheduling of any class or school in the future.

**Each Child Used His or Her Personal Designer's Notebook
for Designing and Drawing Screens, Story-Boarding, Planning,
and Reflecting on Changes and Problems.**

The first requirement, writing in the Designer's Notebook, was very important for the project and for children's cognitive development in general. We did not tell the children what to write, how much to write, what or how to plan or draw, or how to reflect or make changes. However, we explained to them that, like professional software designers, they would enjoy keeping track of their ideas and changes, since this could help their implementation, their concentration, their not losing good ideas from one day to the next, and so on. If either of these two limitations became a problem for these children, it was the time requirement at the computer. The students always seemed to be frustrated about having to stop work and leave their computers, and often requested more time. In addition, writing in the Designer's Notebook was a problem at first, since the students were not accustomed to handling in writing such a routine of planning, note taking, and reflecting.

Let us consider for a moment the rituals and skills involved in children's using the Designer's Notebook in the process of designing and programming their software. This routine was essential to the project, and its importance was clear to the teacher as well as to me. The rationale behind teaching children to plan, reflect, and take notes had been documented in several theories and rigorous experiments reported in educational psychology literature, more specifically, in the literature on learning metacognitive, cognitive control, and other related thinking skills (Nickerson, Perkins, & Smith, 1985; Chipman, Segal, & Glaser, 1985; A. L. Brown, Bransford, Ferrara, & Campione, 1983). In none of these experiments, however, were the children required to plan and reflect in writing every day for as long as a period of time as they were in this project (which went on every day for approximately four months). It was therefore expected that, in this context, new insights would be revealed about children's development and abilities in acquiring these executive processes and cognitive control skills.

Writing in their Designer Notebooks during the course of ISDP was clearly a process that the children had to "get used to." It seemed that, after approximately 10 days into the project, the students realized its importance and made it "their own." My assumption is that the length and structure of this project, the fact that the students were in charge of their own learning throughout the project, and the complete integration of these cognitive skills into other kinds of learning, were the crucial factors in encouraging these skills among students (rather than implementing a direct or explicit instruction of them). The Designer's Notebook became a personal and important tool for the children and made them use these skills extensively and grow aware of the benefits of keeping track of their own planning, note taking, and changes. Moreover, they realized that they did not need to implement what they wrote unless they wished to; they realized that the Notebook facilitated their thinking of "new" ideas while still implementing "old" ones; that going back and forth in their Notebooks to "old" drawings and notes was beneficial to them and very useful in their programming processes.

Several "Focus Sessions" About Software Design, Logo Programming, and Fractions Representing were Conducted in the Classroom During the Project.

Several short classroom discussions (10 to 15 minutes each) were conducted during the period of ISDP. In the first one, I briefly introduced, and discussed with the students, the concept of instructional design and educational software. Together, we defined the meaning and purpose of educational or instructional software, and briefly discussed a few pieces of software that the students were familiar with. I showed the students my own designs, plans, flowcharts, and screens from various projects that I had worked on in the past. I also passed among the students the book *Programmers At Work* (Lammer, 1987) and asked them to look at the notes, pieces of programs, and the designs of "real" hardware or software designers and programmers—such as the people who had designed the Macintosh, PacMan, Lotus 1-2-3, and others. In this first session the students also received their personal diskettes and their Designer's Notebooks, and we discussed the ways in which they should and could be used during the Project.

During the other focus sessions we concentrated on issues such as the difficulties of specific fraction concepts and the students' ideas on how they might be explained, represented, or taught. For example, in two of these discussions, we hung two posters, one on each side of the blackboard. On one poster we write,

WHAT IS DIFFICULT ABOUT FRACTIONS? and on the other, WHAT SCREENS OR REPRESENTATIONS COULD BE DESIGNED TO EXPLAIN THESE DIFFICULT CONCEPTS? We asked the students to generate ideas for both posters simultaneously. After long lists of ideas were created, the students could copy all of the listed ideas, or parts of them, into their Designer's Notebook; or, if they wished, they could use these ideas as inspiration for generating new ones. Other discussions focused on specific Logo programming skills. For example, in some of these short sessions about programming, the teacher, the researchers, or one of the students, could stand next to one of the computers that were in the classroom, in front of the whole class or a group of students, and explain about how to use REPEAT, IFELSE, variables, and so on. Again, the students could take notes on such concepts and programming routines in their designer's notebooks or go directly to their computers and write a procedure that included that new programming skill or concept.

The Teacher and the Researcher Collaborated and Actively Participated in all the Children's Software Design and Programming Sessions During the Project.

The teacher, Mrs. Linda Moriarty, and I collaborated and were present during *all* the Software Design Project working hours. We walked around the students, sat next to them, looked at their programs, helped them when needed, and discussed with them their designs, programming, and problems in a friendly and informal way. In general, we had no specific plans for the project's sequence, or for our presentations and focus discussions; rather, they were initiated by the teacher or by me at times when they were relevant to the students' work or problems, or at the students' request.

Seventeen Personal Software-Design-Portfolios were Created.

Finally, these daily activities resulted in 17 products (i.e., 17 different pieces of instructional software about fractions) and 17 personal portfolios—one for each experimental child—consisting of their daily sets of written plans, designs, the pieces of Logo code they programmed, and their written reflections on problems and changes for each working day.

Observations in the Classroom, During the Regular Math Lesson. (Jacqueline Karaaslanian Photography)

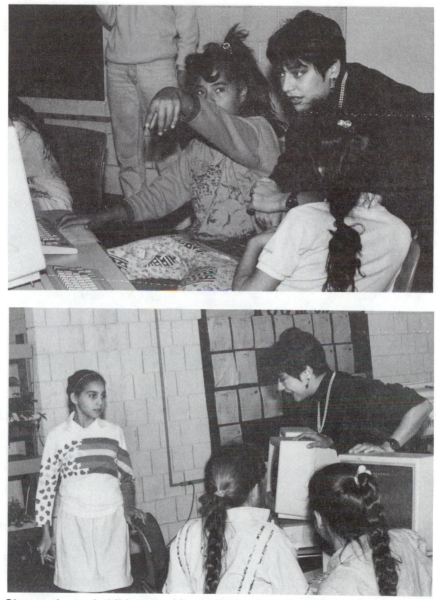

Observations of children working at their computers (Jacqueline Karaasla-nian Photography)

As Students Work on their Projects, I Walk Around the Computer Pods, Observe their Process of Individual Work and Social Interaction, Answer their Questions, and Ask my Questions. The Goal is to Become Very Familiar with the Children, with their Projects, and with their Development Throughout the Project (Jacqueline Karaaslanian Photography)

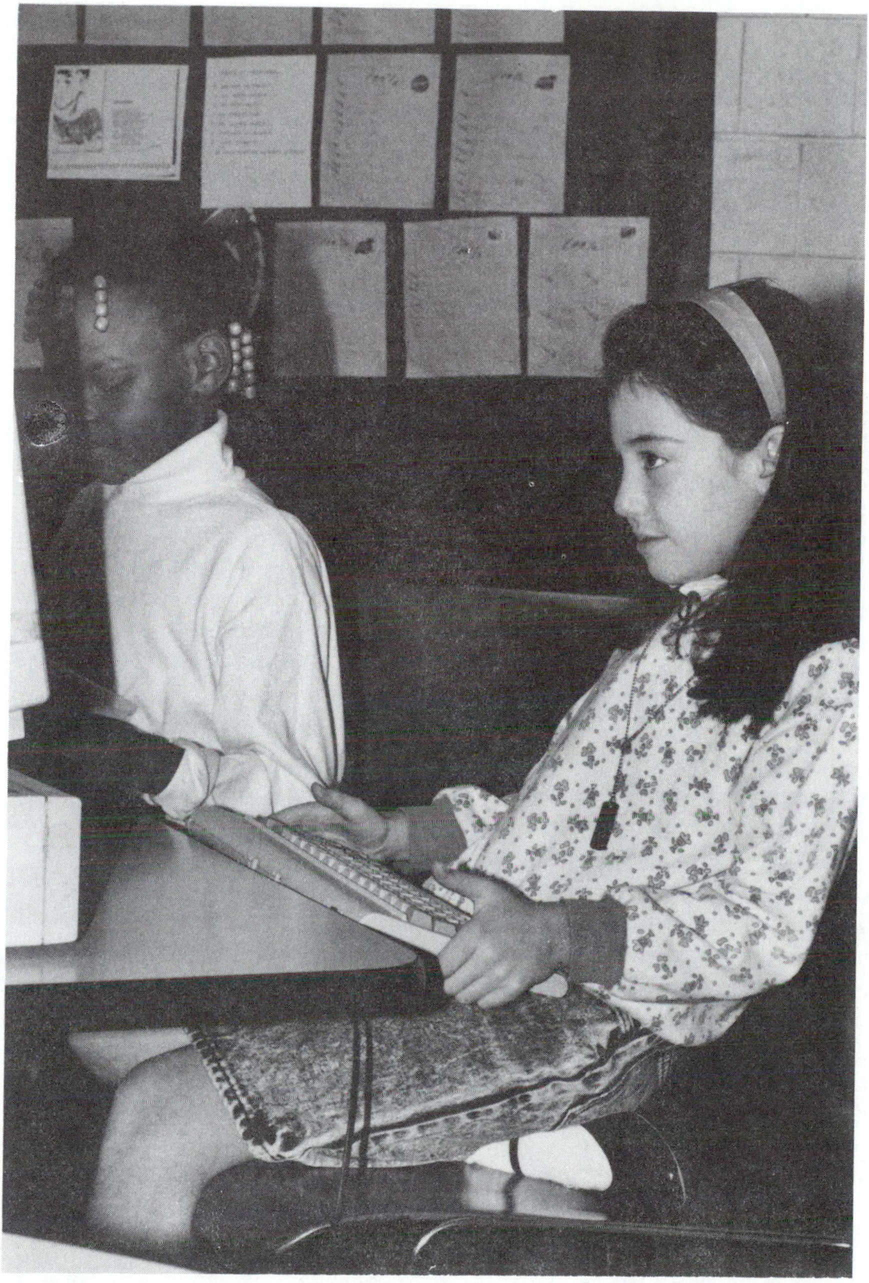

PART 2

THE RESEARCH RATIONALE, THEORETICAL BACKGROUND, AND EDUCATIONAL PHILOSOPHY

Three motivating factors came into play in the rationale for conducting this research:

First, some of my design-based learning experiences, as well as those of certain professionals, incited me to create similar professional-like learning experiences for young students of learning through design and learning by teaching.

Secondly, Piaget's constructivist theory about the characteristics of cognitive development, Papert's constructionism, Vygotsky's social vision of cognitive development—as well as Perkins' ideas about the nature of knowledge and its construction through design—led me to create a model learning environment and to investigate (by using these and other related theories) the children's minds as they learned and thought in this particular environment.

Finally, relevant research literature and previous findings in the fields of Logo, fractions, software, and design incited me to conduct a study that was aimed at changing the conditions of students' learning, as well as researchers' methods of studying students as they learned—thereby attempting to solve some of the problems reported by that research literature.

These three "motivators" are briefly described in the following sections, 2.1., 2.2., and 2.3. When considered together, they form the rationale for designing and implementing ISDP and for conducting research on children's cognition, design processes, problem solving, and learning fractions and Logo under this particular conditions.

2.1. THE EXPERIENTIAL MOTIVATORS FOR THE STUDY

As educators or teachers, producers, computer programmers, software developers—or professional people in general—we are rarely encouraged to draw on our own learning experiences, within our special domains, in order to better understand the reasons, purposes, and processes of learning and teaching in our fields. Too often we tend to forget what was really difficult for us to understand, or why one learning experience was more or less valuable for us than others in the course of our own learning and professional development. I believe, however, that a self-experiential rationale, and all the ordinary personal experiences we, or our friends and colleagues, have gone through, offer strong heuristic reasons for the things we do—especially in education—since we are dealing with our own and other people's personal and professional education throughout our lifetime.

Learning by teaching/learning through design. My learning experiences as an elementary and high-school student, my graduate studies, and my professional work, revealed to me two major things. The first was that I learn most effectively from teaching or explaining something to another person. The concepts, articles, or papers I remember and understand best are the ones I had to present and explain to others in a seminar, rather than the ones that required my completing worksheets or taking conventional tests. In the summer of 1984, for example, I took a 3-month-long intensive course in Harvard's Computer Science Department, "Computer Science and Its Applications Using Pascal Programming." It was almost impossible to fully master all the programming concepts and applications presented in that "crash" course (although I did spent at least 6 hours a day programming, in addition to the lectures and exercises, which were given by excellent instructors). However, it was only after I was asked to give a 2-month-long introductory course to *other* graduate students at the Harvard Graduate School of Education that I realized what I *did* understand about programming in Pascal, what I did know, and especially what I *did not* understand. It was through teaching and explaining the material to others, preparing handouts, drawing diagrams, creating exercises and tests, and answering the students' questions that I really came to understand the material myself. When I was the teacher—rather than the learner—I spent a great deal of time thinking about why something was difficult and how I could clearly explain it to others, or what might be a good exercise to master such and such a programming concept, and so on. I realized that the hands-on experience I had as a tutee, together with the kind of thinking I did as a tutor, helped me to acquire a deeper understanding of the material.

The second thing I experienced as a learner is in some ways related to the first: it was my experience as one of the instructional designers for "Seeing The Unseen," a science videodisc for middle-school students—my work as part of the Harvard Technology Group (see ETC, 1986). My group was involved in designing interactive lessons about basic scientific concepts and processes. I realized that the amount of understanding and knowledge I had gained on the scientific concepts and skills involved in that videodisc was probably greater than that of any future user of that videodisc system. My struggling with the raw materials, my discussions with the group, my thoughts about different ways of presenting a concept, the selections of video-clips and representations, the production of instructional sentences and feedbacks, my decisions about the sequence of screens, the design of graphic displays, an so on forced me and my group to learn, understand, and become involved in all aspects of the content and skills presented in the videodisc and the interactive software.

In brief, whenever I was engaged in a learning activity that combined (a) my action upon the materials, the manipulation of it, and the building with it; and in addition, (b) communication, constructing an argument, and representing, teaching, or explaining my ideas about a given concept *to others,* I was also able to assess, confirm, and broaden my own knowledge and understanding of these ideas. What made a learning experience most valuable to me was the combination of learning-through-doing with learning-through-communicating, while working independently on ideas I generated and sharing my ideas (and products) with others—as we all worked towards accomplishing a challenging, meaningful, and complex task over a long period of time.

For the time being, I will leave aside such issues as the learner's motivation, intentionality, or interest in a specific content or specific process. Let us instead consider for a moment, and in the same way, the experiences of certain professional people in their everyday work or professional training. For example, teachers have occasionally told me that they had "finally understood something today for the first time" when a student asked for an explanation of something he did not understand. Some of my friends (professional computer programmers) at MIT have told me that they "really" learned how to program when they had to teach it to someone else—or when they were involved in a real, complex, long, and meaningful programming job. Many university professors choose to teach a course on the theory or topic of their research *while* they are actually working on it; through their processes of teaching and discussing their work with their students, they also identify and revise their own ideas and theories.

We can also find similar examples in professions that require even more precise skills and expertise. All Israeli fighter pilots, for instance, are required to serve for two years as instructors in the Air Force Academy as part of their intensive training. They come to the Academy as instructors only one year after they have finished their own training in the Academy, because the Air Force believes that these pilots gain new perspectives and understanding about flying by flying with, establishing relationships with, and teaching less experienced cadets how to fly. In fact, the pilots/instructors are reevaluated while actively working at the Air Force Academy, and in many cases, through their teaching, they show greater ability than they did as cadets in the Academy. In such cases, after gaining and demonstrating their new expertise as pilots during their period as instructors, they are later asked to fly a more complex jet (switching, for instance, from a helicopter to a Phantom, or from the latter to an F-16), and to be part of a higher-level squadron from the one they served in before coming to teach at the Academy.

To take other examples from different fields, TV producers have told me that the number of things they learned about a topic or about production while involved in the production process itself was sometimes far greater than their target viewers learned. Furthermore, and highly relevant for the present study, it seems to me that, in the educational software field, the people who are having the most fun and are learning the most are the software designers and programmers. Most educational software today, especially of the drill-and-practice kind, is only used once or twice by the student. The software users rarely gain deep understanding of the concepts taught, unless the software is supplemented by the quality of their teachers' instruction and explanations. But the designer, who has spent a long and intensive period of time designing, learning, and thinking of ways to build explanations and graphical representations for given concepts (even for the simplest form of educational software), has probably mastered these concepts and gained deeper understanding of them.

To summarize, the experiences described above led me to conduct an experiment that would provide children with similar *conditions for learning* as those of the MIT computer programmers, Israeli fighter pilots, university professors, TV producers, or professional software designers. These people gain expertise and learn concepts and skills by actually experiencing and exercising them in long-term, professional, meaningful, and complex contexts; they acquire a deeper understanding of their knowledge and of their professions by communicating their knowledge to less experienced people; they learn about their own theories by teaching them; they learn about flying by instructing less experienced pilots how to fly; they learn about production by producing; and they learn about a topic by designing a videodisc or a piece of software for it.

2.2. THE THEORETICAL MOTIVATORS FOR THE STUDY

The theoretical perspectives, ideologies, and images of learners, such as they are seen in the theories of Piaget, Vygotsky, Papert, and Perkins, were strong motivating factors in my creation of ISDP model learning environment for elementary school children, and in my construction of the image of the learner, whom I placed and studied within this complex environment. The reasons for coming these theories, the ways in which I created the ISDP learning environment, and the image of the learner whom I also attempted to study by using these theories, are described in this section.

Integrating social and individualist aspects of learning. On the whole, ISDP aimed at integrating the social aspects of learning (e.g., Vygotsky, 1962, 1978; Perkins, 1986), with the individualist and constructivist aspects of learning and cognitive growth (e.g., Piaget, 1955, 1972, 1976; Papert, 1980, 1986). It aimed at studying children's learning and cognitive development as a total activity, of which some aspects could be influenced by the "scaffolding" of a guiding adult, a helpful peer, or a probing researcher, while others could be a result of the child's interaction with his or her learning tools, own thoughts, or own spontaneous inventions and constructions.

Piaget's constructivism. For Piaget, the "truly" psychological development of the child, as opposed to his or her school or family development, is spontaneous in nature:

> I will above all stress the spontaneous aspect of development, though I will limit myself to the purely intellectual and cognitive development . . . the development of intelligence itself—what the child learns by himself, what none can teach him and he must discover alone; and it is essentially this development which takes time . . . it is precisely this spontaneous development which forms the obvious and necessary condition for the school development. (Piaget, 1973, pp. 2–4)

In describing the formation of the cognitive stages, Piaget (1973) places central emphasis on constructivism. Although recent theories of mechanism of cognitive development emphasize different aspects of the Piagetian cognitive stages and constructivism, they generally maintain a similar developmental picture (e.g., Case, 1984, 1985; Fischer, cited in Sternberg, 1984).

Papert's constructionism and "objects-to-think-with." Papert (1980) constructs his model of the learner by using Piagetian cognitive theory, artificial intelligence theories (on the society-like mechanisms of the mind), and gender and personality research on the different social and affective facets involved in doing mathematics, computation, and in science education (Papert, 1980; Turkle, 1984; Minsky, 1986). Above all, he emphasizes a constructivist image of learner and of learning. Similar to Piaget, Papert views learning as a child's construction and reconstruction of knowledge rather than as transmission of knowledge from a teacher to a child. Learning means the inventing and the formulating of concepts and rules through an active process of doing and thinking of what one does, how one does it, and what one feels about it at different times during one's intellectual development or at different stages within the problem-solving process. Unlike Piaget, Papert sees learning as particularly effective when it takes place in the context of a rich and concrete activity, which the learner (child as well as adult) experiences while constructing a meaningful product such as a piece of art work, a story, or a research report. For various reasons—related to his personal background, thinking style, and to his beliefs about the future of society—Papert places a great deal of emphasis on "thinking concretely," on learning while constructing a tangible computer program or some kind of a functioning machine (Papert 1980, 1986; Resnick, Ocko, & Papert, 1988).

Although Papert bases himself on Piaget's major ideas on intellectual development, on the mind's psychological structures and mental operations, and on the different stages in a child's cognitive development, he differs from Piaget when considering evocative objects in a child's life. Although his work is based on Piaget's rigorous experiments on children's cognitive development (for example, on the conservation experiments; see Papert's Principle of Learning in Minsky, 1986), Papert is far more involved in cognitive development through the *processes of learning* than Piaget. He creates and emphasizes far richer learning environments than does Piaget in his experiments. While accepting the main principles of Piagetian cognitive progress (i.e., from the sensorimotor period to the preoperational period, to the concrete operational period, and to the formal operational period), Papert is mainly interested in individual differences within the transitional periods, and the role of self-constructed, interactive objects (especially computerized objects) in children's cognitive development. He attempts to understand how these objects might affect children's ways of knowing, thinking, learning, socializing, and how they might affect the (Piagetian) progress in cognitive development. Papert emphasizes that Piaget's theoretical investigations have been on the mind's *internal events,* but that his own perspective, although based on Piaget, is more *interventionist* than Piaget's:

> My goal is education, not just understanding. So in my work I have placed a greater emphasis on two dimensions implicit but not elaborated in Piaget's own work: an interest in intellectual structures *that could develop* as opposed to those that actually at present do develop in the child, and the design of learning environments that are resonant with them . . . [i.e., with the intellectual structures that could develop by the intensive, meaningful and widespread use of Logo. Therefore, Papert believes that cognitive development will eventually be] . . . different in computer-rich cultures of the future. If computer and programming *become a part of the daily life of children,* the conservation-combinatorial gap will surely close and could conceivably be reversed: Children may learn to be systematic before they learn to be quantitative. (Papert, 1980, pp. 156–176; emphasis added)

This particular perspective of Papert's on the important role of self-constructed, concrete, and interactive objects in children's cognitive development, learning, and thinking—and the idea that in many children's and adult's learning and problem-solving situations one could observe the recapitulation of the different Piagetian stages of cognitive development, or even observe new forms of Piagetian progression (of "decalage"), strongly influenced my thinking on the implementation and assessment of the Project.

Vygotsky's social vision. In a slightly different way, Vygotsky (1978, 1962) also looks at the psychological processes of the individual when engaged in "activities," "tasks," or "cultural events" that are far more people oriented, intrapersonal or communication oriented, complex, and stimulating than in Piaget's experiments. Vygotsky places a great emphasis, far more than Piaget, on the role of language, and on the integrative relations between speech and intelligence, or between speech and cognitive development:

> The independence of intelligent action from speech [i.e., Piaget's theoretical position] runs contrary to our own findings, which reveal the integration of speech and

practical thinking in the course of development . . . A child's speech is as important as the role of action in attaining any goal . . . Speech and action are part of one and the same complex psychological function, directed toward the solution of the problem at hand . . . *The more complex the action demanded by the situation and the less direct its solution, the greater importance played by speech in the operation as a whole.* Sometimes speech becomes of such vital importance that, if not permitted to use it, young children cannot accomplish the given task . . . language enables children . . . to overcome impulsive action, to plan a solution to a problem prior to its execution, and to master their own behavior . . . The cognitive and communicative functions of language then become the basis of a new and superior form of activity in children. (Vygotsky, 1978, pp. 24–30; emphasis added)

In my project here described, these ideas were implemented according to a slightly different method: children's were asked to *think about* communicating and explaining their knowledge of fractions to younger students; they were also required to use language intensively in their planning, designing, and reflection processes for their designer's notebooks. These language-based or communication-based tools were expected to affect children's learning and cognitive development in the present context.

Most of the studies in the Vygotskian framework (e.g., Wertsch, 1985; Rogoff & Wertsch, 1984; A. L. Brown et al., 1983; Collins & Brown 1985) focus on the role of language in learning and cognitive development, and on its role in the child's "moving" within the zone of proximal development (the region of skills that lies between the child's independent cognitions and inventions and his or her functioning with sociolingual support). These researchers believe that intelligence develops as a collective activity, jointly accomplished by a child and by an adult through the use of language, and emphasize that, for effective development and learning, the joint sociolingual intellectual action should occur even *before* a child functions intelligently on his own. Rogoff and Wertsch, for example, quoted Vygotsky, whose position was that

Instruction is only good when it proceeds ahead of development. It then awakens and rouses to life those functions which are in a stage of maturing, which lie in the zone of proximal development. It is in this way that instruction plays an extremely important role in development. (Rogoff & Wertsch, 1984, p. 3)

Stressing this social vision of cognition and learning and the highly integrative relations between language and intelligence, Vygotskian researchers focus exclusively on the important role and processes of scaffolding (by the use of language), the role of adult mediation in children's learning, or the imitation and internalization processes in children's cognitive growth. These researchers usually do not collect data or describe, even as a possibility, the learner as someone who sometimes acts as a constructive and efficient independent inventor and builder of his or her own knowledge, without the help of the "scaffolder" adult.

The social-vision studies mainly concentrate on describing the interesting and complex processes of adult guidance, what types of interactions between the adult and the learner result in what types of learnings, and what learning could result by imitation and internalization of culturally appropriate kinds of behavior.

The Vygotskian theorists offer us several important pedagogical ideas, but no technical substructure related to the mechanisms of internalization or of the mind in cognitive development. For my part, while I believe in Piaget's constructivism, in his theoretical substructure, and in his theory of the mechanisms of mind and cognitive development, I also feel that Vygotsky offers an important addition to the Piagetian theory. In other words, I believe that his views on the human, people-oriented cultural and lingual aspects of cognitive development are of great importance and could be used in conjunction with Piagetian perspectives.

To my knowledge, during the time of the present study's conceptualization, no problem-solving studies have so far provided us with a detailed description of a learning or cognitive process by systematically using and analyzing a *combination of both perspectives*. This is why, in the Project here described, my aim was (a) to create an environment that offered students *both* an opportunity for individualistic constructivism and for intensive use of language in a social and cultural interaction, and (b) to study and analyze all of these aspects of learning in children.

Image of the learner/tools for learning and thinking. The notion of intentionality is important to the images of the learner constructed by Vygotsky and Papert. Both see the learner, rather than being a creature of experience, as one who chooses which particular to "enter" or construct. They also try to capture and interpret the learner's intentions in particular learning situations. However, the particular mechanisms that generate, select, and organize what gets through the senses into the mind, and the manner in which the learner makes sense of these experiences and uses them in other learning situations, are slightly different for each theorist. Vygotsky stresses the role of language and the role of scaffolding through the use of language, while Papert, as previously stated, stresses the relationship between the learner and the interactive objects he constructs. Both Papert and Vygotsky see culture as the context for human cognitive development. Papert (unlike many of his interpreters) always urges concentrating attention on culture rather than on technology (Papert, 1985). However, Vygotsky, much more than Papert, emphasizes the acquisition of culturally appropriate types of behavior as a process of interaction between children and adults, in which the adults guide or mediate the children's learning processes (Vygotsky, 1978, 1962; Wertsch, 1985). In this sense, Papert places greater emphasis on the nature of the activity (the Logo programming culture, for example) as the mediator and cultural guide. Vygotsky describes the adult as leading the child on, ahead of his or her development, while Papert believes that, when technological constructivist-based activities become accessible and widely used by society, they could be the major leading factors in the child's learning and cognitive development. Both emphasize the role of dialogue in problem solving: the former emphasizes dialogue with a knowledgeable adult; the latter, dialogue with the computer.

I think that both aspects of learning are important: the child's dialogue with the computer, or with the interactive objects he or she invents and constructs—as well as with his or her teacher, peers, and the various people, objects, knowledge, and other support systems of his or her culture. Bruner (1985) gives an excellent summary of these aspects of learning:

> The world is a symbolic world in the sense that it consists of conceptually organized, rule-bound belief systems about what exists, about how to get to goals, about what is to be valued. There is no way, none, in which a human being could possibly master the world without an aid and assistance of others for, in fact, the world *is* others. The culture stores an extraordinarily rich file of concepts, techniques, and other prosthetic devices that are available . . . [These devices] require for their use certain fundamental skills, notable among them the ability to use language as an instrument of thought—natural language, and eventually, such artificial languages as mathematics, Polish logic, Fortran [or the Logo language], . . . and especially written languages . . . It is a matter of using whatever one has learned before to get higher ground next. What is obvious and, perhaps, "given" in this account is that there must needs be at any given stage of voyaging into the zone of proximal development a support system [internal and/or external] that helps learners get there. (pp. 32–33)

Beyond cognitive deveopment, all of the above theorists' ideas on learning and thinking are based on exceptional learning situations that correspond best to the ideal of each one. They talk about the need for a "support system," or "mediators," but use different types of mediation. They discuss epistemology, abstractions, reflections, concrete and formal knowledge, or zone of proximal development, but use different terminology and describe their processes in slightly different ways. Piagetians, for example, think that children must first construct their own knowledge, and that, on their own (when "ready"), they might occasionally reach or "touch" their own zone of proximal development. Vygotskians, on the other hand, believe that children could do this most effectively with the guidance of a knowledgeable adult. I believe that one should consider both these aspects in the child's process of learning and in "moving" in his or her zone of proximal development, rather than choose one over the other.

In addition, these theorists place an emphasis on "conceptual tools," yet each speculates about different kinds of tools—interactive, self-constructed, technological, lingual, or cultural—depending on his personal background, own culture, beliefs, and interests. In the present study I offer a learning situation that combines and explores the child's interactions and learning through the use of a combination of these conceptual tools.

Knowledge as design. In fact, Perkins's (1986) analytical framework and his theory of knowledge and its construction suggest, to my mind, an interesting combination of the Piagetian, Papertian, and Vygotskian perspectives. His "Knowledge As Design" theory on the *design character* of knowledge, of constructing one's own knowledge, and of the giving and receiving of knowledge, strongly influenced me in the implementation and assessment of my project.

Perkins combines epistemology and social and cognitive psychology in a theory of constructivism that is not based just on what is happening in the learner's head; rather, what is constructed must be done so socially—in an overt way—before, at the same time, or after it is constructed internally. If we consider the design character of knowledge, we realize that the building of one's own knowledge should take place internally by one's own construction and designs—as well as externally, through being scaffolded by a knowledgeable adult who also uses the design framework in his or her mediation and guidance of the child's learning.

In this way, Perkins's social vision is not purely Vygotskian and therefore requires that the relationships between the adult and the learner be of a constructivist nature. The adult's role in the learning process is in allowing the child to construct his or her designs (i.e., pieces of knowledge) but also in guiding and advising him or her in this construction by offering an appropriate design-based learning environment, or design-based intellectual tasks and discussions. Learners can attain a new level of insight when the learning highlights the constructed and constructive character of knowledge. A knowledgable adult, a helpful peer, or a particular design-tool are equally essential in this framework, in that they probe the learner and prompt in him or her the purpose, structures, and arguments of pieces of knowledge (or designs) at times when he or she is not able to construct them effectively on his or her own. Similarly to Papert, Perkins also places a great emphasis on the role of complex products in the child's cognitive development and learning. Perkins believes that the child ought to learn large, complex, and meaningful chunks of information and should not be involved in isolated exercises or learn subject matters as isolated and nonrelated entities. Designing and producing complex products naturally focus the child on the interrelations between different components of any system of knowledge.

Papert values the concrete. While we can find multiple similarities among these theoreticians, I wish to emphasize one major difference among them. Maybe one of the main differences between Papert and the other three theoreticians (Piaget, Vygotsky, and Perkins) is that Papert questions the high value the other three place on abstract and formal thinking. One of his goals is to find ways for concrete and soft thinkers to blossom in learning cultures. Unlike the other three, Papert is *not* attempting to find "best methods" for facilitating abstract thinking or for helping learners reach the formal and the abstract; rather, he wishes to create learning environments where both abstract and concrete (or soft, relational) thinkers could develop within and feel successful about their cognitive achievements.

Integrative and complex learning experience. Taking the idea of the learner's intentionality very seriously, I attempted in my project to provide students with an environment in which they could choose to enter complex cultural learning experiences of design and imitate and use the help of an adult or peer when needed, but could also choose not to interact with society at times when they were involved and satisfied with their own constructions and inventions of designs. Allowing the students to use language intensively, and to combine and move back and forth from a social learning situation to an independent one, was a necessary thing for discovering what students could learn or sort out on their own, and how they did it—as opposed to what and how they would learn through their interactions with their culture. In other words, for my Project, with all of its related rituals and activities, I tried to integrate the ideas of a *conceptual support-system,* to use Bruner's terminology, of a *dialogue* (Vygotsky's term), of *constructionism* (Papert's term), and of *knowledge as design* (Perkins's term). I experimented with specific new conditions of one type of idealized learning, based on the synthesis of the above theorists' image of the learner, and was inspired by their views on the most effective learning processes. In reality, according to Papert's more recent writings constructionism is, in fact, a synthesis of these views.

> Constructionism is a synthesis of the constructivist theory of developmental psychology [Piaget's theory], and the opportunities offered by technology to base education for science and mathematics on activities in which students work towards the construction of an intelligible entity rather than on the acquisition of knowledge and facts without a context in which they can be immediately used and understood. A central feature of constructionism is that *it goes beyond what is usually called "the cognitive" to include social and affective facets of mathematics and science education.* . . . Constructionism goes beyond (while) including hands-on . . . but the fact that [several] children are working to make something, and especially the fact that they are making something they believe in, adds extra dimensions. (1986, p. 8; emphasis added)

ISDP aimed at developing a model for Papert's constructionism by allowing each child to learn concepts in fractions and Logo through his or her (concrete and abstract) own construction of an interactive teaching device—at the same time allowing this process of building and abstractions to be influenced by the child's interactions and conversations with the peers who were around him or her, doing the same job and involved in similar processes. These relations, dialogues, and interactions between one child's spontaneous inventions and thoughts and his or her environment or culture—people, objects, knowledge, and thought—are depicted in the Figure 4.

In the following paragraphs I shall briefly explain the meaning of this diagram and what major ideas and processes it attempted to capture.

- The illustration of the "child's mind" and the black-shaded overlap at the center of the three circles represent the child's own constructions and crea-

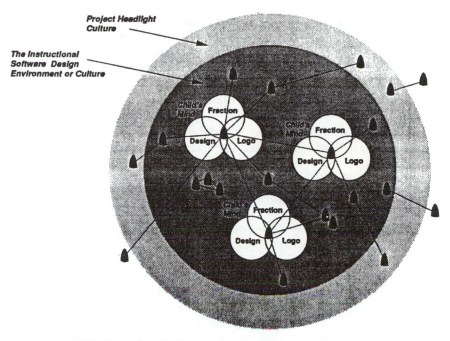

Figure 4.   ISDP Learning Culture.

tions, as well as his or her state of mind while he or she is in the process of *integrating the knowledge or the learning of fractions, Logo, and design* into the Instructional Software Design activity (with all of its routines, rituals, and processes). It indicates the requirement that each child design and implement a piece of software to teach third graders about fractions. The interactions between children's minds are shown in the diagram by straight lines ending in a square node, representing the *complex relations between 17 minds involved in the same job, and their knowledge, objects, and products*. In other words, these nodes stand, not only for the relationship between the *internal and external knowledge* of each child, but for the *relationship between all the experimental children and the other people, objects, and knowledge forming their culture.*

- The dark-grey shaded area represents *the ISDP culture created within the Experimental class as a whole.* It is the environment of each child at the time he was working on his or her Project. It includes interactions, connections, and reciprocal relations among many of the following: other *objects* such as computers, computer tools, designer's notebooks; other *people* such as other students, the teacher, the researcher (myself), and members of the MIT staff (such as Harry Nelson, Mario Bourgoin, and Seymour Papert)—all of whom walked around the computer area, talked together, helped each other, expressed their feelings on various subjects and issues, or worked on different programming projects; and finally, *knowledge* of fractions, Logo, and design as communicated by those involved, or knowledge inherent in other people's projects (which the students could observe simply by walking around and looking at the various computer screens or the different plans and designs in the designer's notebooks).

- The light-grey area represents the *culture of Project Headlight*. As mentioned before, ISDP was my work within Project Headlight and was very much inspired by Headlight's philosophy and routines. This area represents, among other things, Headlight students and teachers from other classes who were working on other computer projects. The experimental students interacted with them before and after each computer session, and sometimes throughout each school day. This area also represents the thoughts and actions of other teachers from Headlight, other people from the MIT staff, and visitors (of which there were many throughout the year).

- In addition, the Project Headlight and its culture (and whatever else it might represent) are *surrounded and interact with other areas* (the rest of the school and its cultural scope), and yet another (the children's homes), and another, and another—ad infinitum. Each child brings with him or her different experiences, feelings, and knowledge from the schoolyard, the school cafeteria, library, field trips, as well as experiences from home and family, and from conversations with family members and friends outside of school. A relevant example is the child's experiences with fractions from stores, from restaurants, movies, games, and so on.

This study does not at all attempt to investigate these complex relationships between individuals and their different cultures (although it takes into account their existence in the child's life). The diagram is also very limited in terms of capturing the interrelations between the different cultures that each child lives in and with. *The diagram's main purpose is to highlight how the conditions for learning in ISDP integrate Piaget's, Papert's, Vygotsky's, and Perkins's theories of learning.* In other words, while the students built their knowledge of fractions, Logo, and software design within this project, some specific interactions were created between the various kinds of knowledge, designs, people, behaviors, objects, technologies, feelings, and products.

Finally, Figure 4, as well as the present study, also attempt to describe how a child, as an instructional software designer, builds his knowledge of fractions, Logo, and instructional design by a recursive process—one might even say a recursive dance—going back and forth between at least three different modes: (a) self-awareness of his or her own knowledge (i.e., metaconceptual thinking, for example, "What do I know about fractions?" or "Can I program this thing in Logo?"); (b) his or her thinking about how another child might come to know it (for example, "What screen should I design to clearly explain how $3/6$ equals $1/2$?" or "Should I use the same or different colors to show that all the objects on my screen are one half?"), and (c) his or her thinking about what other people, such as the other students in his or her class or his or her teacher, think or do about these same concerns regarding fractions, Logo, or design (for example, "Let's see what Debbie did today," or "Gee, Naomi's game about halves and fourths is really cool, and really difficult to program" or "My teacher's explanation of this fractional algorithm was quite confusing" or "Why did Idit (the researcher) ask me that question about my screen?").

During this highly interactive and recursive process, which is described above as the ISDP learning activity, the child, who is at the same time the learner, designer, and computer-program evaluator, comes full circle and becomes aware of his or her own process of learning of a given concept, of the structure of a specific piece of knowledge, and how it relates to other forms of knowing such as a teacher's way of teaching, a friend's knowledge, another child's piece of software, or the conventional final fractions test. And in terms of his or her cognitive development, the child, in this way, will be able to break way from rigidity, concrete, and literal thinking and become more fluent, flexible, and better able to grasp formal knowledge and create complexities.

2.3. THE LOGO PROGRAMMING, FRACTIONS, AND DESIGN RESEARCH AS MOTIVATORS FOR THE STUDY

In the following three subsections I briefly review previous findings from the research on learning computer programming (in Logo), rational-number concepts, and software design. The methodology and findings of previous studies in these three fields, and the questions raised by them, make it clear that new conditions for learning were needed in these domains, as well as new kinds of investigations of children's learning (in this case, Logo programing and basic rational-number concepts). I will later argue, not only that the integrative ISDP was a different and more meaningful way to teach students fractions, Logo, and metacognition, but also that the project suggested a new context for studying students' processes of learning, cognitive development, in addition to assessing their mastery in these domains.

2.3.1. The Research on Logo Programming

Elementary-school children's processes as well as difficulties in learning Logo have been well documented (Pea & Kurland, 1984; Kurland & Pea, 1983; Carver, 1986, 1987; Heller, 1986; Perkins & Martin, 1985; Salomon & Perkins, 1986; Clements, 1985). Many claims have been made about what knowing, learning, and understanding Logo programming means to young students, and about cognitive changes learning to program in Logo is expected to produce (Papert, 1980; Feurzeig, Horowitz, & Nickerson, 1981; Pea & Kurland, 1984).

The very first and most general claim about what learning to program in Logo means was provided by Papert (1980), who stressed the reformulation of knowledge—rethinking and relearning "old" domains to the point that essentially new domains of knowledge would emerge. For example, turtle geometry represented the emergence of a dynamic, computational, and locally described geometry, as against the older, static, paper-and-pencil and globally described geometry. Thus, early in its history, Logo was proposed as a learning tool for learning other things (which involved areas of mathematics, physics, astronomy, robotics, and cybernetics), as a functional tool for acquiring and manipulating other kinds of knowledge, as an "educational philosophy," or as a unique "learning experience," rather than as a set of concepts and skills to be mastered in isolation for their own sake.

Papert also suggested that, once Logo was widely used in society and integrated into many school subjects (like word processors), the particular learning experiences more or less inherent in Logo would bring major changes in learners' attitudes towards learning in general, in their self-images as learners, in their self-esteem, and in their cognitive development. Through Logo programming, students could experience various kinds of thinking, among them creative and impressionistic thinking, as well as the rigorous thinking and precise expression needed to make computers function. Eventually, students could learn how to suit the style of their thinking to the occasion. Programming would also provide an introduction to the use of heuristics (e.g., planning, finding a related problem, exploring alternative solutions, or solving the problem by decomposing it into parts), which they then could apply in other learning situations. Developing a positive and skilled approach to the debugging of errors was particularly stressed, as was modularity, the idea of using small, reusable procedures as building blocks of larger programs or solutions. In the process of programming, students could also learn that there is rarely a single "best" way to do something, but different ways that have comparative costs and benefits with respect to specific goals.

Of course, to get to these larger effects, it is necessary to learn to program in Logo. Thus, specific programming concepts had to be acquired, including use of procedures and subprocedures, variables, conditionals, iteration, and recursion. These concepts, it was claimed, were not just means to a larger end but powerful concepts to learn and understand in their own right.

A review of the major research on children, programming, and cognitive development, reveals an emphasis on issues such as children's difficulties in learning to program, in debugging and modularizing programs, or in how to use inputs, variables, conditionals, recursion, lists, as well as on extent of "transfer" to some other skills (e.g., Carver, 1987; Pea & Kurland, 1984). But the ideas that lay behind Logo's early development have received far less attention, although several attempts have been made to conduct more holistic and constructivist studies about young children and Logo (e.g., Lawler, 1985; Papert, Watt, diSessa, & Weir, 1979; Solomon, 1986; Turkle, 1984; Watt, 1979; Weir, 1986).

The general response to findings that "students had difficulty acquiring Logo skills and concepts, or failed to transfer Logo skills to other domains" has been to create "better instructional techniques." More often than not, these have involved an imposition of traditional instructionistic teaching methods onto Logo, in which Logo was treated as programming per se, isolated from any other subject area (e.g., Carver, 1987; Perkins & Martin, 1985; or several articles in Pea & Sheingold, 1987). Many of the pessimistic interpretations of the findings in the research on children's learning of Logo programming were a result of treating Logo as an object of knowledge in itself, rather than as a tool for acquiring other learning, focusing on short-term incremental changes in the learner, rather than viewing Logo and computers as a trigger for broad changes in a learning culture, which might only be observed over a long period of time. While these issues cannot be addressed in more depth here, they have been considered elsewhere (Papert, 1985, 1987a).

In this ISDP study, Logo was used in a broad and complex situation, was integrated into a larger context of software design and development, and served as a tool for accomplishing other learning. Thus Logo learning was not trivialized in the course of setting out to study it. At the same time, the Logo activity was part of an existing learning community and reflected the everyday concerns of a realistic educational setting.

2.3.2. The Research on Learning Fractions

Elementary-school children's processes as well as difficulties in learning fractions and understanding their representations have also been well documented (Carpenter, Coburn, Reys, & Wilson, 1976; Behr, Lesh, Post, & Silver, 1983; Peck & Jencks, 1981; ETC, 1985; Post, Wachsmuth, Lesh, & Behr, 1985; or Janvier, 1987). Unlike whole numbers, which children largely come to grasp informally and intuitively out of school, learning the rational-number system is confined almost exclusively to school. Because rational-number concepts and algorithms are so difficult for so many pupils, they figure prominently in the curriculum each year from the second grade on. Even so, several national assessments of children's mathematical achievements have found that children's performance on fraction ordering and computation, for example, was low and accompanied by little understanding (Tierney, 1988; Post et al., 1985).

Fractions are ideal tools for learning about number systems and representational systems in mathematics. The understanding of the rational-number representational system is a privileged piece of knowledge among the other pieces of rational-number knowledge. Representations form part of the deep structure of rational-number knowledge, whereas algorithms are the surface structure (e.g., Janvier, 1987). One of the goals of ISDP was to involve students in exploring and learning the system of representations of fractions intensively and in a special way, and then assess their knowledge of basic rational-number concepts and algorithms.

There is a diversity of knowledge about rational numbers, including (a) the subconstructs (e.g., ratio, part-whole, operators, fractions, decimals, or percentages), and (b) the representations for each subconstruct and for the whole rational-number system (e.g., words, mathematical symbols, pictures, or real-life situations). When the child "visits" a particular rational-number subconstruct, he or she will be sensitive to the properties and characteristics of that subconstruct. Several of these subconstructs will be more or less intuitively accessible, and some children might be more familiar with, and think more easily "in the style of" one subconstruct (e.g., fractions), while at the same time they may be less familiar or feel uncomfortable thinking in the style of another (e.g., decimals). In general, the relations between subconstructs are poorly organized and unevenly formalized (e.g., Behr et al., 1983).

The whole rational-number system and its subconstructs derive some meaning from each other, and multiple representations are not just alternative means of understanding but are viewed here as the deep structure of rational-number knowledge. Therefore, it was important to help students move easily from one subconstruct to another, to connect and differentiate between each subconstruct's characteristics and properties, and to express the same ideas using several representations such as sections of circles or rectangles, words, money, food, or time. These kinds of connections are facilitated by understanding the translation processes and relations between the different rational-number representational modes (see Figure 5, which is based on Lesh et al.'s, 1983, and Behr et al.'s, 1983, conceptualization).

A major focus in previous assessments of children's development of rational-number concepts has been the role of manipulative aids, including Pattern Blocks (e.g., Harrison, 1972), Fraction Bars (e.g., Bennett, 1981), Cuisenaire Rods (e.g., Davidson, 1977), or Number-Lines (ETC, 1985), and so on. In these experiments, the materials were used to facilitate the acquisition of rational-number concepts and representations, as the child's understanding moved from the concrete to the abstract (e.g., Davidson, 1977).

The approach in ISDP was very different. The psychological analysis done by Lesh et al. (1983), for example, showed that manipulatives were just *one* form of presentation in the large representational system, and that the other modes of representation (the symbolic, written, or real-life situations) also played a very important and variable role for different thinking styles, and in children's acquisition and use of these concepts. Different materials and activities were found to be useful for making models of different situations, and no single manipulative aid was found to be the "best" for all students, for all rational-number situations, or for translating fractional representations (Behr et al., 1983).

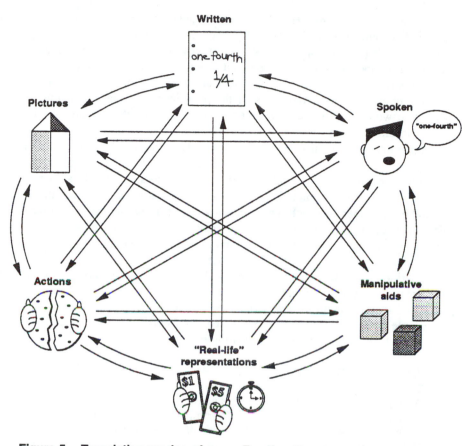

Figure 5.   Translation modes of some Fraction Representations.

Using Logo to represent and combine rational-number representations.
Consistent with Lesh's psychological analysis of representations, ISDP did not
focus on students' working with one subconstruct or any most powerful representation (e.g., as in the Number-Lines or Pattern-Blocks curricula). Instead, ISDP
provided students with an environment in which they could work and explore
relations between several representational modes (e.g., pictures and symbols),
combining the different rational-number subconstructs (e.g., connecting 50%
and ¹/₂), and translating between several representational modes (e.g., designing
a screen that combined both graphical and written representations for the fraction
¹/₂ and the decimal 0.5).

For example, in Logo a child can program a simple picture of a circular region
divided into fourths and, using different flashing colors, shade in two of these
fourths and have them blink on and off in order to show a representation of two-
fourths. The child can add the written words *two-fourths*, which is translating

pictures into written words. He or she can add another picture—a large round clock with an animation of the clock's big hand moving slowly from the number 12 to the number 3—and write, "this is one-fourth of an hour," them move the hand from number 3 to the number 6 and write, "this is another fourth of an hour"; or write on the screen, "one-fourth of an hour is 15 minutes, two-fourths are 30 minutes" (this is a translation of the pictorial representation of time or clocks into words, but it is also a representation of a real-life situation and its translation into fractions).

Another example, taken as these all are from the children's actual projects, is to program a picture showing a one-dollar bill with four quarters underneath. Two of these quarters can be highlighted in different colors, and can be animated to "walk" around the screen and "sit" beside the written words "two-fourths of one dollar." Another approach would be to compose a musical tune, then play half of it, a fourth of it, and so on. We can imagine a variety of representations, from pizzas to gears, from musical rhythms to body movements. As one of the students put it, "Fractions can be put on anything!"

Furthermore, the Logo programming *code* itself becomes a new kind of representation—the writing and the execution of a piece of Logo code being a procedural representation of a pictorial representation. To give an example, a very simple picture of a square region divided into fourths, could be represented in a simple Logo procedure in the following way:

```
TO HALF.SQUARE :NUM
HOME
REPEAT 4 [FD :NUM RT 90]                [drawing a square]
FD NUM/2 RT 90                          [going to the middle of the left
                                         side of the square]

FD NUM                                  [drawing a horizontal line in the
                                         middle]

RT 90 FD :NUM/2 RT 90 FD :NUM/2         [going to the middle on the
                                         bottom side of the square]

RT 90 FD :NUM                           [drawing a vertical line in the
                                         middle]

PR [This is a square]
PR [divided into fourths]               [representing it in words by
                                         printing an instructional
                                         statement on the screen]

HOME
END
```

While this procedure is being executed, the child is able to observe the dynamic and procedural movement of the Turtle on the screen as it follows the Logo instructions given by that child. The execution of this particular procedure will result in the following picture (Figure 6):

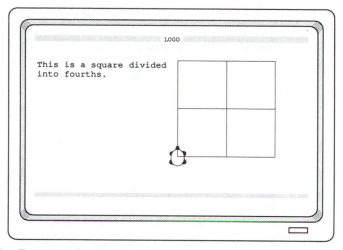

Figure 6. Representing Fractions in Logo.

What is so special about the above picture? A child can draw a square by hand and divide it into fourths, which will result in a similar picture. However, when the same child programs this picture in Logo, he or she must describe his or her actions exactly, step by step. In other words, saying "I am drawing a horizontal line in the middle" is different from saying "I gave instructions to the Logo Turtle go forward :num/2." In the Logo version, the child's involvement with the specifications of the representation is deeper and much more intense. In order to take the Turtle anywhere, the child must be aware, for example, that, in order to characterize this type of representation as a fraction, the parts of the whole must be equal. The quality of the parts idea is manifested in the child's instructions to the Turtle: "Turn RIGHT 90 degrees, and then Go FORWARD :NUM/2," which will result in the Turtle's turning right and going forward for half of the length of one of the square's sides. In the hand-drawn representation, the child can use his or her sense of balance in dividing the line into two pieces. However, in using Logo, the child must understand what dividing the line into two equal pieces means, or dividing a shape into halves. Therefore, the above procedure becomes a programming representation of the pictorial representation. A child can read this Logo code alone (without the printed statement or a view of the final picture) and say: "Aha! This shows four-fourths."

Another example (not in Logo) of the potential richness of a relatively different set of instructions and commands used in computer graphics can be seen in Sachter's (1987) exploratory work. In her system, students were required to manipulate 3-D objects on the screen by giving specific instructions which were in themselves representations of the 3-D objects and of their future rotated movements or scaling.

Sachter studied 11-year-old students from Project Headlight and, among other things, investigated children's development of spatial abilities and their understanding of such concepts as object rotation and scaling while in the process of using her system, giving specific instructions to it, and observing the execution of these instructions. With regard to my previous arguments—dealing with the contribution of the writing of Logo representations for fractions to a child's understanding of the structure of certain fractional representations or of the relationships between representations—some of Sachter's findings were similar to mine: The students who were involved in direct manipulation of the 3-D objects on the computer screen, and who wrote precise and complex instructions and commands, eventually performed much better on other pencil-and-paper spatial tasks than those who did not use her system, and therefore were not able to develop accurate mental representations of the objects' rotations or scalings.

The questions in the Rational-Number Concepts test and in the What Is A Fraction? interview were selected for these very reasons. It was assumed (according to my pilot study; Harel, 1986) that no one in the experimental class would be able to design and program more than maximum of 15 representations during the course of ISDP. In the process of learning fractions in the project, the students did not use any manipulative aids, cover a very wide range of rational-number subconstructs, or translate or manipulate a large number of representations. However, the posttests included a large number of rational-number subconstructs, their multiple representations (in the pencil-and-paper tests), and a variety of manipulative aids (in the interview). These were in fact assessing some kind of transfer.

In summary, my hypothesis was that the experimental students would do well on these tests, not because they actually learned from these materials, but because—through designing representations of fractions, programming representations of fractions with Logo, and explaining and teaching about fractions and their representations on the computer screen—they had the opportunity to think about, reflect upon, revise, and experience (although on a very small scale) the deep principles involved in the relationship between the different rational-number subconstructs and their representational systems. It was clear that the literature on fractions also revealed the need to investigate the following questions: Would designing and programming representations for fractions, and creating graphical displays for equivalence and operations of rational numbers, influence students' thinking and learning about representations of fractions and the relationships between them? Would representing and explaining fractions to another person help students to overcome their own difficulties in understanding fractional representations in the ways that had been reported in the other studies? And if so, in what ways?

To summarize, the ISDP students used Logo to make their own representations of rational-number concepts for teaching. In so doing, they were trying to make the representations that would serve as good pedagogical aids for other students. By becoming designers of instructional software, the students gained distance and perspective in two senses. In the first place, they were dealing, not with the representations themselves, but with a Logo representation of the representations. Moving between representations was subordinated to programming good examples of representations. Secondly, the students programmed, not for themselves, but for others. They had to step outside and think about the other students' reactions. This distance and perspective provided students with control of the process of learning and moving between representations, contrasts with being put through the paces of an externally conceived sequence of learning.

ISDP recast fractions learning in essentially three ways: (a) it emphasized more involvement with the deep structure (representations) over the surface structure (algorithms) of rational-number knowledge; (b) it made fractions learning simultaneously incidental and instrumental to a larger intellectual and social goal, that is, having students think about and explain what they think and learn, in an interactive lesson for younger children; and (c) it encouraged both personal expression and social communication of rational-number knowledge and ideas.

2.3.3. The Computer as a Tool for Instructional Design

In *Knowledge as Design*, Perkins (1986) discusses in detail the instructional philosophy that supports the creation of a design environment for learning, arguing that the act of designing promotes the active and creative use of knowledge by the learner—the designer. In the designing process, Perkins says, the problem's meaning is not given by the problem itself; rather, the designer imposes his or her own meanings and defines his or her own goals before and during the process. The goals and the subgoals may change over that period of time, and keeping track of these changes is a central interest when the design task is not for the purpose of "getting it right," but is instead aimed at learning and developing creative thinking skills.

Schon's work (1987) is also relevant to this theme. He is interested in how different designers (architects, for example) impose their own meaning on a given open-ended problem, and how they overcome constraints (created by themselves, or given as part of the problem they solve) and take advantage of unexpected outcomes. This interactive process requires high levels of reflection and develops the ability to "negotiate" with situations in "as-needed" and creative ways. Gargarian's investigations (1990) of music composition processes reveal similar observations: Composers are designers. They design their own "problem space," and compose while negotiating with constraints and emerging situations in their self-created and open "musical space." I mention Gargarian's work here because he too uses the medium of Logo programming as a design-based learning environment, but, for music composition.

What is the difference between programming as such and designing a piece of instructional software? How does it relate to the "knowledge as design" framework?

A "computer program" is an independent entity consisting of a logically arranged set of programming statements, commands, or instructions that defines the operations to be performed by a computer so that it will achieve specific and desired results. We use the term *instructional software design* to refer to the building of a computer program that has a specific instructional purpose and format—much more is involved than mere programming. In this context, the lessons constructed by children were composed of many computer procedures or routines (i.e., isolated units) that were connected to each other for the purpose of teaching or explaining fractions to younger children. A unit of instructional software is a collection of programs that evolve through consideration of the interface between product and user. The instructional software much facilitate the learning of something by someone.

Designing and creating instructional software on the computer requires more than merely programming it, more than merely presenting content in static pictures or written words, more than managing technical matters. When composing lessons on the computer, the designer combines knowledge of the computer, programming, computer programs and routines, the content, communication, human interface, and instructional design. The communication between the software producers and their medium is *dynamic*. It requires constant goal defining and redefining, planning and replanning, representing, building and rebuilding, blending, reorganizing, evaluating, modifying, and reflecting in similar senses to that described by Perkins and Schon in their work.

In terms of the programming end of it, software designers must constantly move back and forth between the whole lesson and each of its parts, between the overall piece and its subsections and individual screens (e.g., Adelson & Soloway, 1984a, 1984b; Atwood, Jefferies, & Polson, 1980; Jeffries, Turner, Polson, & Atwood, 1981). Because of the computer's branching capabilities, the designer has to consider the multiple routes a user might take, with the result that the nonlinear relationship between the lesson's parts can grow very complex. Moreover, the producer needs to design interactions between learner and computer; designing questions, anticipating users' responses, and providing explanations and feedback—which require sophisticated programming techniques. Finally, the child-producer who wants to design a lesson on the computer must learn about the content, become a tutor, a lesson designer, a pedagogical decision maker, an evaluator, a graphic artist, and so on. The environment we created in ISDP encouraged and facilitated these various processes.

The rare existing literature on the processes of software design or software engineering in no way attempts to investigate what the designers *learn* through the processes of software design. For example, Nickerson's (1986) valuable work focuses, among other things, only on guidelines for "good" software design, and rests on the assumption that an expert software designer is specifying these guidelines. Simon's (Simon & Chase, 1973) relevant research sketches out a theory of the psychological processes involved in reaching a solution for a design task, but only in the context of discussing the distinction between the development of heuristics in well-structured and ill-structured problems (e.g., p. 190).

Other studies are more directly related to the *processes* involved in software design. For example, Guindon and Curtis (1988) collected verbal protocols of professional software designers and revealed "three major design-process control strategies" (pp. 1–5). However, the problem given to their three subjects was still in the well-defined problem framework, "a lift-control problem, that requires their designers to design the logic to move N lifts between M floors, given a set of constraints." The designers were given 2 hours "to produce a solution that was in a form and a level of detail that could be handed off to a competent system programmer to implement." Although the title of this study included the words "processes of software design," this study, in fact, only revealed narrow information about experts' control over the logic design of a complex computer routine, but none on software designing and programming per se, or on what these experts learned through the process about the relationship between their designs and their implementation. In a similar way Adelson and Soloway (1984a, 1984b) studied the way expert designers solved the problem of creating a computerized mailing system. Their observations, as well as others of the same kind (e.g., Guindon, 1987; Guindon, Krasner, & Curtis, 1987; Jefferies, Turner, Polson, & Atwood, 1981), described the very specific cognitive processes of people who were more or less expert designers and performing very logical and well-defined tasks over a short period of time. In fact, very few generalizations could be drawn from the work done by these researchers that might be strongly relevant to my study. Furthermore, besides the collection of verbal protocols and the use of videotaping, few research methods and models existed that might have been directly adopted for the present project, since the problem given to my subjects was broad (though not ill defined!) and was presented in the following manner: "Design a program that teaches a younger child about fractions." The students/designers' processes toward solving the problem took approximately 70 hours of programming, and within this long and complex context each child established his or her own route, goals, and subgoals, which could not be predicted in advance or later analyzed by the researcher—in the sense of "good" or "bad" designs, or "expert" as compared to "novice" approaches.

There are certain drawbacks to implementing instructional software design activity in a school's curriculum. Software design is a time-consuming and complex enterprise, and it is not yet clear how it can fit into the average class schedule. Also, it might cause problems in students' learning of other subjects in the school, and, at the present time, it is not very clear which school subjects would lend themselves best to this complex process of learning. However, my goal in this project was to experiment with one topic (fractions) and make it possible for students to learn through designing and programming instructional software much as they would do in a professional environment. I do not think students can produce "better" quality software than adults, but I believe they could be *involved in the process* of designing and producing instructional software—for their own learning, their own pride, their own fun. I am not suggesting that we have to stop producing educational TV programs, videodiscs, or computer software for children.

What I am saying is that it might be an error to think that the instructional software design process is not suitable or appropriate for children. It is in fact the contrary. In this study I shall not only examine the ways in which children can have fun designing and producing a piece of software, but analyze in detail the ways in which they can learn content and skills through it. Like adults in a professional environment as instructional designers or computer programmers, young children, through instructional software design, can also learn concepts and skills that may be difficult to master in other learning situations. The learning processes of instructional software design offer major changes in the conditions for learning in the ways described by Papert (1986), as quoted below:

> Knowledge about computation [such as programming] and the sciences of information [such as control over one's own processing, metacognition, and constructing of information] have a special role in changing education. Such knowledge is important in its own right. It is doubly important because it has a *reflexive* quality—it facilitates other knowledge. . . The reflexive quality of information science offers a solution to the apparent impossibility of adding another component to an already full school day. If *some knowledge facilitates other knowledge,* then, in a beautifully paradoxical way, more can mean less . . . the idea that learning more science and math means necessarily learning less of something else shows a wrong conception of the integration of these subjects into knowledge and cultures. They should be *supportive* of the other learning. It should be possible to integrate at the same time, blocks, learning of science, mathematical concepts, art, writing, and other subjects. *If two pieces of knowledge are mutually supportive it might be easier to learn both* [at the same time] *than to learn either alone.* (p. 2; emphasis in original)

In my project, with its approach of learning through designing and programming instructional software, these new conditions meant that young children would learn fractions, Logo programming, instructional designing, planning, story boarding, reflection, self-management, and so on—all at the same time and in a synergistic fashion. In the context of the Project, and through the use of the computer, I wanted to integrate different kinds of knowledge and disciplines, because they were mutually supportive of one another and could contribute to each other while the child was in the process of learning them.

I recently heard William Mitchell, Professor of Architecture at the Harvard Graduate School of Design and Principal of the Computer Aided Design Group in Los Angeles, quoting the novelist E. M. Forster, who once asked: "How do I know what I think until I see what I say?" Mitchell emphasized this quote since "it expresses very well the relation of an artist or a designer to his or her medium." He also said that "representations do not merely record, they give

shape to thoughts and mediate the profits of speculation and exploration . . . different representational media, according to their structures, do this
in different ways. Thus when a medium is introduced into a traditional thinking
or design process, that process is likely to change." In his work, Mitchell explores the ways in which the use of computer-aided-design (CAD) technology
changes the traditional architectural design processes. In a very similar spirit, I
explore in this study the ways in which the computer and Logo programming,
and their use for designing fractions software, change students' processes of
learning, thinking, representing, programming, as well as their understanding of
fractions.

. . .

In Part 3 of this chapter, which is following, I shall briefly present an exploratory study I conducted prior to this study, in 1986 (Harel, 1986). The results of
that initial exploratory study contributed to the development of my ideas in the
directions mentioned above, as well as influenced the design of the larger study.

Later, in Part 4 of this chapter, I shall present the research design, describe the
selected pupils and the reasons for selecting them, and outline the different
objectives and questions that guided me (a) in the implementation of ISDP, (b) in
the investigation of the cognitive processes of the individuals who participated in
the experiment, and (c) in the investigation of the learning of the experimental
class as a whole. I shall also describe the research procedure and its instruments,
the data analysis techniques, and how these data will be presented in Chapters II
and III.

PART 3
THE "FRACTIONS PROJECT" PILOT STUDY*

3.1. CHILDREN AS FRACTIONS DESIGNERS

The pilot study focused on the intellectual processes of five children who participated in our very first Fractions Project, a learning project integrating mathematics and computer programming during Project Headlight's first year. As a result
of a short workshop we conducted at the school with several teachers from
Headlight, one teacher, Linda Moriarty, asked her math group of 15 fifth-grade
children to program in Logo representations for fractions equality and fraction
operations for explaining and teaching these to younger children in the school.
Several clinical interviews and observations were conducted with only five of
these children *two months after* they completed their Fractions Projects.

In these interviews, the children were asked to reflect on their final products
(several screens about fractions) and to discuss the processes involved in producing their screens (instructional design strategies, programming processes,
decision-making processes about what to teach, etc). The qualitative results of
the interviews and observations are here described. These suggest that, under the
1986 Fractions Project conditions, these children were able to learn, use, understand, and discuss Logo in different ways from children in other studies in the
field. They gained understanding of mathematical concepts and representations
related to programming and fractions. They generated instructional design strategies making use of advanced programming skills for children of that age,
constructed sophisticated representations for knowledge, learned to think about
their own thinking, and thought about teaching and explaining in a special way.

* This Pilot Study was conducted during Project Headlight's first year of existance. It was then
presented at the LOGO '86 International Conference, Massachusetts Institute of Technology, July
1986. I would like to thank Seymour Papert, Brian Harvey, David Perkins, Sylvia Weir, Sheldon
White, and other reviewers for their critical comments on issues explored and covered in this work.
The teachers, Linda Moriarty and Joanne Ronkin, deserve special thanks for allowing me to observe
their students or take them out of their classrooms when needed. Their openness in discussing issues
related to the Fractions Project is especially appreciated. I thank the software designers: Rosie,
Jessica, Sunny, Damal, and Nicky—Project Headlight's pioneers—for allowing me to keep asking
and asking all these questions. I appreciate the knowledge and insights they provided me and my
colleagues during the Fractions Project period and throughout the first year of our research at the
Hennigan School. I learned a great deal from interacting with them.

Moreover, we found that the project contributed to the children's ability to reflect upon their own learning of fractions and Logo, and to their developing sensitivity about difficulties in understanding fractions, about representation of specific concepts or operations, and about their processes in programming instructional screens.

3.2. RESEARCH OBJECTIVES

The pilot study was designed to assess and describe five children's experiences of learning in the Fractions Project. The project integrated the following three aspects in one learning situation: (a) Logo as a tool for other learning, as well as programming language to be mastered in its own right; (b) fractions as a subject matter; and (c) peer-teaching and instructional design as learning strategies. These three were intertwined. Logo was used as a tool for learning of (b) and (c) above. Logo was used for representing fractions (the subject matter) that integrated the learning of Logo and the learning of fractions. Children's thinking about how to represent knowledge and explain it to others was the technique used for increasing their own understanding of fractions.

The objectives of this study were to qualitatively assess several outcomes of the project: (a) the five children's level of programming in Logo and their own understanding of their Logo programs; (b) their ideas about fractions and their representations; (c) their metacomments on (a) and (b) above—that is, their personal reflections on their math abilities and level of understanding of fractions, Logo programming and instructional design, as well as their ways of thinking critically about their Logo programs, their design ideas, and their teaching objectives.

In addition, the rationale behind this explanatory study was to investigate more closely programming experiences in this particular programming environment. Several questions presented themselves:

- Would intensive use of Logo within the Fractions Project help children to acquire sophisticated programming skills?
- Would integration of Logo into a meaningful context (which provides meaning to programming) help Logo to become flexible tool in the hands of children?
- Would children then pursue a richer route into learning fractions and to metalearning of various kinds?

3.3. THE PARTICIPANTS

Five ethnically diverse, 10- and 11-year-old fifth-grade children—two black boys, one Chinese girl, and two white girls—participated in this study. All these children were members of the advanced math group and studied fractions in their traditional school curriculum with the same math teacher, Mrs. Linda Moriarty, who was also the home-room teacher for three of them. The researcher interacted with and observed all five children prior to the present study (as part of a larger Project Headlight study). Two girls were more intensively observed and studied by the researcher throughout the year, but close relationships were established during the year, prior to this study, with all five children. Additional data on these two girls, and the other three children was available to the researcher and discussed in the context of other Headlight research meetings.

3.4. THE LEARNING CONTEXT

The selected children were fifth graders during the first year of Project Headlight. By the time the Fractions Project started, these children used Logo or Bank-Street Writer almost every day for 8 months. The computer programming and writing projects were integrated into other school subjects, and considered as "computer assignments" or "computer projects."

Sixty percent of the fraction-unit curriculum was traditional. The children were involved in regular classroom learning and completed approximately 40 worksheets on addition, subtraction, multiplication, division, equivalent fractions, and ordering of fractions (from the Spectrum Mathematics Red Book and Blue Book).

The interview with the teacher indicated that she did not present the Fractions Project in a step-by-step fashion, and did not instruct them in how to handle the project:

> I did not present any plan. I asked them what might be some ways to represent fractions or operations on fractions in Logo. . . I wanted them to try their own projects and come up with ideas. We talked about it much more after they got started. I can't remember what were my ideas and what were theirs. . . We discussed their ideas for how to represent fractions in the classroom together after they did some things on the computer. It was a blend.

The teacher also emphasized the discovery approach to learning Logo in her classroom:

> I do not teach them Logo. We have short discussions. We call them 'Logo Tips.' Just new things that they picked up . . . or if, for example, I observe that one kid has discovered something new, I'll talk about those things that I saw happening, and teach them to the rest of the children.

The teacher was the one who suggested to her students the idea of programming screens designed for teaching younger students. She said,

[This was] the first time I did this in my classroom. They were never involved in an activity like this before. I didn't have the right media to do these things before. It is a very effective tool [thinking about teaching others]. Now they really have to think about what they are doing. It is a real good approach because they have to start thinking in terms of teaching someone else. They are so used to teachers always telling them everything. It is important to invite them to think about fractions, about how to represent multiplication or addition, especially because it's such a hard concept to understand.

To summarize, the five children were learning Logo intensively (1 hour every day) during the year using the Headlight interdisciplinary project-based approach. But this was the first time they were involved in representing fractions for other children. The Fractions Project was the first attempt, for the teacher and her students, to integrate mathematics education with Logo programming. It was also the first time they had to develop a longer and coherent Logo program (with opening screens, representations screens, testing screens, etc.) that had an instructional purpose: teaching other children about fractions.

3.5. RESEARCH PROCEDURE AND RATIONALE

The data were gathered in *four situations*. The procedure and rationale for each data-collection situation are described below.

- *Situation 1*. Two months after the Fraction Project was over and the children's instructional screens were completed, each child individually answered the *Reflection-1 Interview Questionnaire*. Each interview was conducted in the MIT room at the Hennigan School, away from the computer. This session lasted approximately 45 to 60 minutes, and was audio recorded.

  The rationale behind this interview was to gather information about: (a) each child's critical thinking about his or her program and the program's general purpose; (b) the children's understanding of fractions and Logo, their teaching objectives, and their reflections on what was learned through the process of creating the program; (c) the children's reflections on the program's sequencing, how the data flows within the program, how the different screens relate to each other, and their notions of aesthetics and strategies for screen designs; and (d) the children's intuitive use of diagrams, plans, or flowcharts. Initiating critical thinking among the children about their own programs, allowed us to assess the children's programming ability and their understanding of data flow within their programs. We were also able to assess children's knowledge of particular fractions concepts which their programs were designed to teach. Within this reflective thinking process we assessed metaunderstandings about learning and teaching, and children's thoughts about their programs' design and educational purposes. Moreover, we hoped that the interview would provide children with a mindful thinking process they would internalize and follow in their future projects.

- *Situation 2.* On another day, each child was asked to present and discuss his or her Logo program with the researcher using a printout of their program. For this session the *Show and Tell Form* was used. This session was conducted while sitting next to a computer, and lasted from 45 to 60 minutes. The researcher took notes of what each child said on the program's printout and also audiotaped the session. The children's screens and Logo code for their programs were analyzed with the children during these sessions. This session started with the child looking at the printout of his or her program and describing the function of each procedure, as well as defining and explaining primitive commands and Logo instructions. Next, the child loaded his or her program on the computer, and the researcher and the child discussed the program. While the children led this session, the researcher worked with them to evaluate the program's title screen, how much control is given to the user, modes of presentation (text, graphics, colors, sound, etc.), techniques for focusing the user's attention, modes of feedback and help, types of remediation, etc. Each of these categories was investigated in the light of the child's way of describing it. What was the child's own terminology when asked to present his or her program? What were the child's comments on the design or the programming of each screen? Did he or she consider how to present feedback, or how to balance text and graphics on the screen? What were the relationships between the child's programming ability and the final design?

  This session was a "reality and quality check" for the children's answers from the first session. The children were talking about some of the same issues in the Reflection-1 Interview. Therefore, the child's descriptions of his or her program capabilities and structure were reassessed in this session by looking and discussing them with the child, and by looking at his or her actual program.

- *Situation 3.* On another day, each child was asked to guide and observe from one to three younger children using the program on the computer. This session was observed by the researcher using the *Children-as-Evaluators Observation Form,* and was also audio recorded. This session lasted approximately 45 minutes.

  This session was designed to acquire more information about the children's ability to discuss their programs with other children, to debug and modify their programs according to other children's requests. The researcher took notes about the following: How do they present their programs to other children? What type of teaching goes on? What comments do they look for? What comments do they get? How do they react to these comments? What ideas do they have at the end for improving their programs? In what ways, if at all, do they implement these ideas for modifications?

- *Situation 4*. In conjunction with these three sessions with each child, the children's math teacher was interviewed twice using the *Teacher Interview Questionnaire*. Information was gathered about: (a) the teacher's own learning experience in the Fractions Project; (b) her views of the fractions-unit as a whole, how she integrated Logo into her traditional unit, and the regular in-classroom activities related to fractions that took place in the same period; (c) her evaluation of the children's understanding and their achievements in the fractions unit; and (d) her description of the children's personalities and learning in general. These two interviews lasted 130 minutes and were audiotaped.

3.6. RESULTS FROM THE PILOT STUDY

The data reveal that the learning experience during the Fractions Project allowed for individual differences in problem solving, programming, design, and learning. Although the Fractions Project was given to the children as an 'assignment,' the children established different approaches in accomplishing it, and each pursued his or her own strategies. Each child thus gained insights into different concepts of fractions and Logo rather than following a common set of 'curricular content and goals.'

The five designers created fairly complex programs. Some of them created more than one program. Their final projects demonstrate their different abilities and styles in Logo programming, knowledge of fractions, and approaches to teaching and design. Their projects reflect individual styles with regard to choosing a concept and representing it: each of the projects was designed and programmed in a different way, even if the designers' educational objectives were similar (e.g., to teach about equivalent fractions or multiplication of fractions).

This section takes a closer look at these individual achievements and individual differences. It emphasizes the richness of the children's reflections on their own processes of creation, their different projects, their views of their own learning and thinking, and their understanding of Logo, fractions, and instructional design. The qualitative and descriptive data that was gathered from each child and on each child, is compared and contrasted by reference to the following eight themes:

1. the children's views of their programs and their teaching objectives;
2. the children's views of their own learning;
3. the children's views on strengths and weaknesses of their programs;
4. the children's mental representations of their programs;
5. the children as planners or nonplanners;
6. the children's learning and understanding of Logo;
7. the children as evaluators and software maintainers; and
8. the children's instructional design strategies.

In the following subsections, the children's own words are quoted, and their ideas and views are described largely by using their terminology. Thereafter, these descriptive results are placed in the larger framework, and their relevance to the research literature will be discussed, focusing on issues related to learning Logo programming, issues related to learning fractions, and issues related to metalearning of various kinds.

3.6.1. The Children's Views of Their Programs and Their Teaching Objectives

Jessica's program was designed to do two things: (a) "to demonstrate equivalent fractions" (showing that $1/2 = 2/4 = 2/8$, and $1/3 = 2/6 = 4/12$, and $1/4 = 2/8 = 4/16$); and (b) "to give you a test about it at the end." Her "demonstrations and explanation part" combines graphics with text because, using her words, "combining words, numbers, and pictures is the best and clearest way for explaining equivalent fractions." And her "test part" includes text only, "because the test should be harder, the pictures make it easier."

Nicky designed two programs. Both of his programs combined text and graphics, and he sees them as "two demonstrations that can back up good explanations." The first program he created was to "demonstrate equivalent fractions, that $4/4 = 1$, and $2/4 = 1/2$. And it gives you a test to see if you [the user] understand it." The second program was designed to "demonstrate multiplication of fractions," showing "how $1/5 * 1/5 = 1/25$," and explaining "how you have to think about it as *a part of a part*." He emphasizes that in the screen representing multiplication he tried "to show the *why*."

Rosie created two programs as well. Neither includes graphics at all. She said: "I was in a phase, you know; it takes too long to wait for these drawings to come up on the screen." She also did not use pictures, since she was designing her programs "as a *test* and not as a demonstration or explanation." Rosie was not explaining the "why" behind the algorithms, to use Nicky's terminology; rather, she wanted to teach her users "how to get better and quicker in solving fractions problems." One of her programs was designed to "teach about addition, subtraction, and multiplication of fractions." And the other program to "teach about fractions decimals and percentages, how to change one to the other." Rosie also included a "help screen," with more detailed explanations (in text only) about the different algorithms, and a "genius screen" that included "the hardest problems of all."

Damal's fractions program was designed to "teach about equivalent fractions, subtraction, and addition of fractions." His program opened with a long introductory "talking part." In this part he asks the user "fun questions about himself, to help them understand, or get used to, how to use the computer," and to decrease the user's computer anxiety . . . so they could, in his words, "concentrate on learning fractions."

Sunny created two programs. The first was designed to "teach about equivalent fractions by using a representation of a balance scale." The second program to "teach about multiplication of fractions." In the second program, Sunny's goal was "to show you how, when you multiply a half with a fourth, you end up with a smaller amount that you had when you began." Both of her programs combine text with graphics, and she emphasizes the game-like design strategy: "so it will be funner and much more interesting to learn like that."

Figures 7–14 are some samples of the children's instructional screens:

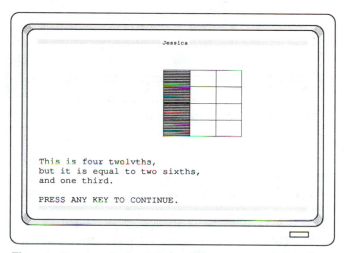

Figure 7. Jessica's First Screen on Equivalent Fractions.

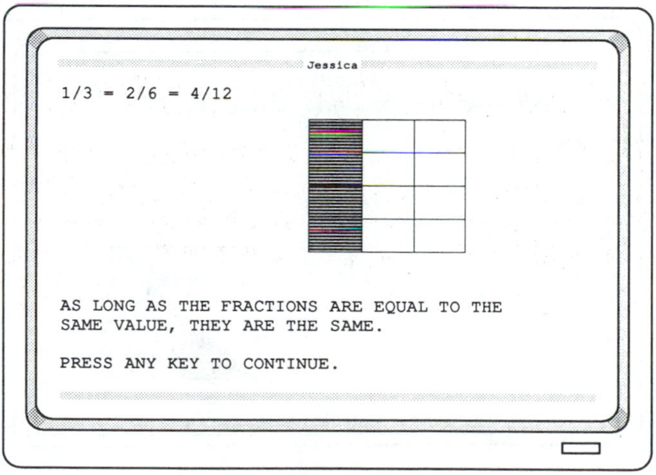

Figure 8. Jessica's Second Screen on Equivalent Fractions.

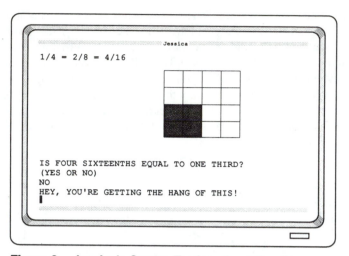

Figure 9.   Jessica's Screen Testing about Fractions.

In her "Testing Part," Jessica first shows her users a representation of equivalent fractions, for example, $1/4 = 2/8 = 4/16$.

Then she clears the graphics off the screen and prints a question on the screen using text only.

In his first program, Nicky taught about equivalent fractions and addition by using the same representation. He shows the user a representation of a square divided into fourths, and asks: "Is the square divided into halves, fifths, or fourths?"

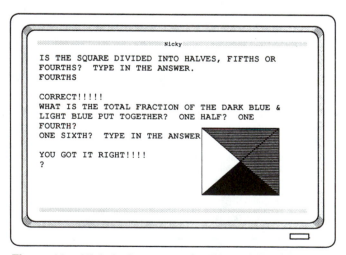

Figure 10.   Nicky's Screen on Addition of Fourths.

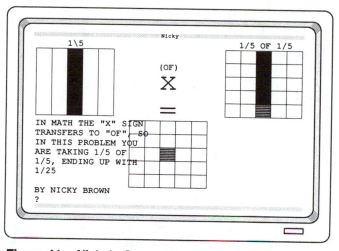

Figure 11.   Nicky's Screen Explaining How to Multiply Fifths.

Then, after the user answers this question, Nicky asks the user: "What is the total fraction of the dark blue and light blue [parts] put together?"

In his second program, Nicky designed a screen to explain multiplication of fractions. Nicky's objective was to demonstrate "why when you multiply frac-

```
                          Rosie
O.k.   Now turn 4/5 into a percentage!!
67
You're a nerd!!
Now try turning 0.7 into a fraction.
7/100
It's so sad BOOOOO HOOOOOOO!!!!
If you turned 0.7 into a percentaage what would
the answer be??
7.10
You're not smart, you are a fart!!
Turn 40% into a fraction.
2/25
you DUMBO!!!!!
Now turn 3/5 into a decimal!!
You're mind is mud!!!
Did you get all these right?
No
To bad for you, try my procedure called..EASY.
?
?
?
```

Figure 12.   Rosie's Program for Testing about Translations between Various Rational-Number Sub-Constructs (Decimals, Percentages, Fractions, etc.).

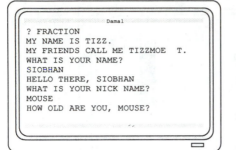

```
              Damal
? FRACTION
MY NAME IS TIZZ.
MY FRIENDS CALL ME TIZZMOE  T.
WHAT IS YOUR NAME?
SIOBHAN
HELLO THERE, SIOBHAN
WHAT IS YOUR NICK NAME?
MOUSE
HOW OLD ARE YOU, MOUSE?
```

```
              Damal
WILL YOU BE MY FRIEND?
YES
MAY I HAVE YOUR NUMBER?
4974826
THANK YOU

DID YOU DO YOUR HOMEWORK?
NO
NO RECESS
I'LL CALL YOU LATER O.K.
```

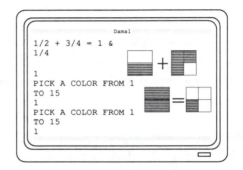

```
              Damal
1/2 + 3/4 = 1 &
1/4

1
PICK A COLOR FROM 1
TO 15
1
PICK A COLOR FROM 1
TO 15
1
```

Figure 13.   Sample Screens from Damal's Project.

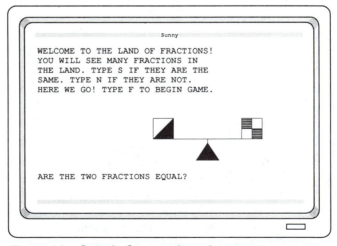

```
                  Sunny
WELCOME TO THE LAND OF FRACTIONS!
YOU WILL SEE MANY FRACTIONS IN
THE LAND. TYPE S IF THEY ARE THE
SAME. TYPE N IF THEY ARE NOT.
HERE WE GO! TYPE F TO BEGIN GAME.




ARE THE TWO FRACTIONS EQUAL?
```

Figure 14.   Sample Screens from Sunny's Project.

tions, the fraction that you multiply decreases not increases." He also wanted to teach his users the "trick of thinking about the operation of multiplication as "taking a part of a part." Therefore, he put the word OF on top of the multiplication sign, and put the sentence "$1/5$ OF $1/5$" on top of the right square (the representation of the other fifth).

Rosie drilled her users about transforming fractions into percentages and decimals. Rosie designed and programmed her screens as an interactive "test" and used text only. Her feedback style is interesting. Also, she sends her users to other subprocedures such as "EASY," which is a help screen, and "GENIUS," which is "the hardest problem of all."

Damal created one program to teach about "addition of fractions parts." Damal's screen includes a pictorial representation of the addition operation combined with the symbolic mathematical statement. He made his program very interactive. The program starts with asking the user "fun questions," Damal said: "This opening part of my program makes the user feel comfortable with the computer." In other parts of the program, Damal gives the user an option to pick up the color for filling in the fractions in the square representations.

Sunny used a representation of the balance scale to teach about equivalent fractions. In the following screen she teaches about $1/2 = 2/4$.

3.6.2. The Children's Views of Their Own Learning During the Project

When asked their reasons for creating their programs, four out of the five children gave as their first reason: "It was our assignment." This was expected, since it was an activity within a school setting. However, the second reason for *all* five of them was: "I wanted to teach [x or y] to show younger kids about fractions." Even though this learning experience was Logo intensive, none of them saw it as a "Logo project." They appropriated the main purpose of the project, which was to design a collection of instructional screens about fractions. Most of their reflections were associated with solving problems related to fractions and their representations, and they often talked about their struggles with the idea of teaching other children, or representing algorithms for younger kids. In other words, the project had a purpose and a meaning beyond being just a "programming project."

Jessica stated that she "didn't learn anything new about equivalent fractions" (which her program was designed to teach). However, it was the first time she had to "think about how to draw it." She talked about her thoughts on how to represent the equivalent fractions in different ways. She also stated she learned new things in Logo such as READCHAR, READLIST, the differences between the two, and how to use RANDOM. She said several times, "How hard it is to teach someone. It's hard to tell someone else who doesn't know anything how to do something and help them understand. You don't know what they know and how to explain it."

Nicky stated that he learned in the project how "the fraction decreases, not increases, after multiplication with another fraction," and that he learned to "think about it [multiplication] as a part of a part." He also said: "I got better in understanding myself what happens when you multiply fractions." His notion about the idea of teaching others was: "It's hard to teach. You have to have a pretty good understanding of something, so you'll be able to explain it well to others. And a lot of times it's really hard to understand what's happening with these fractions." He stated that, before the project started, he "did not really understand the Logo IF and READLIST," but that, since he "used it in his project," he had learned "exactly what it means, and how to use it."

Rosie stated that she is "much quicker about it now." (*It* being adding, subtracting or multiplying fractions, or transforming fractions to decimals or percentages.) In relation to Logo, she "didn't learn anything new," because she had been the first one in her class to use IF and READLIST in a previous programming project. (In fact, she was the one who taught it to others during the Fractions Project.) She does see her program, not as a teaching program, but as a testing program, and said: "It's a very good program for testing other fifth or fourth graders. Too hard for third graders."

Damal stated that he learned mainly about subtraction through this project. "Addition and subtraction are real easy for me now." But "division is what I really have to learn now." He found it pretty difficult to think about teaching younger kids: "It's supposed to be for littler kids, right? But to do it so they can understand it, you have to be sure that you know what you're talking about . . . the teacher has to know more . . . you don't know how the young kid will react to it and all that. It was really hard to get it so they'll like it. Always to think about, and imagine that you're small, and how would you like it." Damal learned in this project to use the SETPC, and to use FILL with SETPAL. He said: "Before, I didn't know how to change the colors real quick." He also learned what he calls "all the talking procedures," meaning IF, READLIST, and so on.

Sunny pushed it to the extreme by stating that "I learned more from my computer than I learned from my teacher . . . because I learned what happens when I multiply fractions. I also learned what a fraction is. It's a part of a whole. And it can be divided into as many parts as you want." She thinks that thinking about teaching others taught her "how to be more careful and clear." She explained: "I used to confuse people, (I would) talk and talk and talk, and no one would understand me. And so, I learned how to explain, little by little, to tell someone how to do something, what they did wrong, and it became easier to talk and make someone listen to you and understand." In terms of learning Logo in the project, Sunny said she learned how to use IF and NAME READCHAR, "so I could let my users press a certain key to continue, or another key to clear the screen or quit."

3.6.3. The Children's Views on Strengths and Weaknesses of Their Programs

The children varied a great deal in their answers to my questions that required to think critically about their programs (i.e., to think about three best things in their programs, or three weaknesses, bugs, or things that needed to be changed and modified in order to make their programs even better and clearer). The data reveal that the children did not have a clear idea of *what it means* to think critically about the projects they did in the past. This is not very surprising, since regular educational practice never leads them to do so. At first, most of their answers were not specific to their programs, but rather more generic reflections about the project as a whole, whether or not it was a worthwhile experience for them, and general ideas about computers and Logo. For example, *Jessica's* critical comments about her program's best things were: "The program is really clear. The testing part is fun." She described in detail why she thinks the feedback she gives for right and wrong answers is appropriately designed.

Nicky thought that his two programs were good, because "it explains it pretty well." He thinks that his first program is "a very good demonstration of equivalent fractions," and that the second is good because "it's explaining the why . . . why when you multiply fractions, it decreases, not increases. It's a part of a part." *Jessica* and *Nicky* also mentioned the colorfulness of their programs as one of the best things.

Damal and *Sunny* both said that the best thing about their programs is that it helped teaching them about fractions. *Damal* also said: "The main thing—it works!" And *Rosie:* "If it's good it's because it's fun!" *Sunny's* most interesting comment was: "It is on the computer, which makes people more eager to learn something new. And I think it is easy to bring it to wherever you go, just take the disk with you." Sunny does not have a computer at home, and she comes from a low-socioeconomic-status family. It seems however, that Project Headlight environment influenced her attitude towards the existance and portability of computers. She has an image of computers being everywhere.

The children were all quite surprised with my question about: "What are the three worst things about your program? or How would you do it differently today, 2 months after your completion?" They usually looked at me as if to say (and some of them actually said): "What do you mean? Is something wrong with it? I was never asked to think about my work in this way. . . Do you want me to change something?" Well, they are not usually involved in a thinking process of this sort in school. But through my explanations and probing, they came to understand that it is only a thinking exercise. After a while, four of them became fully engaged in thinking about ways to make their programs better.

Nicky, for example, was disturbed by the fact that his programs are not interactive enough. He was thinking about how to make it more interactive. "It's not so much fun now, 'cause the user can just see but not type or say to it anything. Especially in my second program. It is sort of boring. . . I should ask some questions after the demonstration, I'll add a procedure that the user can press a key to go on. I know how to do it now." Nicky also thought he should improve the graphics, and much like Sunny, Rosie, and Damal, he also thought he should "add better instructions and add more explanations to the introduction."

Damal really likes his program the way it is. "It's one of my best. It took me a long time, you know." He said that one worst thing about his program might be that someone might think it's not a good job. "It's not so good only if other people think it's not good." For him, the main indication of how to improve it is what other people say. He asked me several times, "Tell me, should I change something? What do you want me to change, or is it perfect?" However, after thinking together for a while, he came to think about more specific issues such as making a better introduction, and "print at the beginning and at the end explanations with big big letters" (i.e., he meant to work on a title and ending pages). Damal also realized the need to improve the representations for his subtraction screen: "I would change the part that is missing after the subtraction." He drew the following (Figure 15):

Figure 15.   Damal's Idea for How to Improve His Representation and Teaching Strategy.

Jessica was not able to deeply criticize her own work, or maybe, like Damal, she was afraid of criticism. The only thing she felt she had to fix was "some misspelled words." My close observation of Jessica indicates that she is usually not very open to criticism of any sort, and she is also very demanding of herself. She usually does not share an idea unless she feels it is perfect. She considered her programs to be "perfect," and a critical thinking exercise such as this one was a great pressure on her.

At the other extreme, *Rosie* offered several constructive comments. She dislikes her programs and thinks she has other, much better, programs as of the day of this interview. She was able to think critically about her programs and list "what is not so exciting about it" and how "to do it differently." She said: "There are no pictures. It's not clear. The only person that could use it is someone my age. It's not interesting 'cause it's only text. . . I also think I should have separated it a little bit. Create spaces. Every question should be a procedure, really. Then, if you get it wrong, I can run that procedure again, and not the whole thing again. It doesn't really teach . . . you know." Rosie was able to comment on how to modify both the structure of her program in terms of Logo, and the instructional purpose of it.

To summarize, some of the children's initial limitations and negative reactions to this thinking task resulted from not being used to think critically or review old projects. But major changes in the children's thinking processes did occur, and rather fast, by my specific intervention and probing. In fact, as we shall later see, when the children were evaluating their pieces of software with younger children, they demonstrated their ability to think critically and make changes. They did not resist it and were flexible in understanding their users' point of view and implement it in their programs—all of which are important metacognitive skills.

3.6.4. The Children's Mental Representations of Their Programs

When the children were asked to draw a diagram of their own programs, a range of answers was given. Four of the children started in describing the *contents* of each screen. Only one of them, Jessica, illustrated the *structure* of her programming code. The other four children could do it after some probing and explanations from the researcher.

Comparing the children's own diagrams with the structure of their actual code reveals that the mental representations they have of their programs are fairly adequate. Their representations, however, were somewhat limited and always presented by them in sequential way.

There are two ways of representing a computer program, the *sequential* way and the *hierarchical* way. The sequential way is much closer to the style in which most people are accustomed to think about computer programming. But the hierarchical way is considered to be more powerful (Harvey, 1985) and creates a better match between the structure of the program and its procedures. Thinking hierarchically is a difficult task for children and for many adults as well. In this study, the children—who were never involved in representing their programs, or taught to think about their programs hierarchically, and had never drawn a diagram like this before—came up only with sequential representations. (In fact, some of the children's programs do not have a complex internal structure and therefore did not require hierarchical representation.) But even the drawings of a sequential diagram was a difficult task for these children. The following paragraphs describe each of the children's diagrams side by side with the hierarchical diagram of their programs (these hierarchical diagrams were created by the researcher, after examining the children's programming codes with the help of Marie Sullivan, an MIT undergraduate student at the Computer Science Department).

Jessica's program is the longest and most complex out of the five children's codes. Although her program includes interactions among so many parts, the diagram she drew was very simple, general, and sequential. She was able to explain the order of her main procedures and the contents of her screens. Her own diagram, however, represents sequentially only the 'top part' of the hierarchical diagram of her program. She only represented her superprocedure and the main subprocedures. In her description she groups Fractions, Fractions2, and Fractions3 as one part which she calls DEMO. And she described "a second part" of her program as "quizzes and tests." She did not describe any of the subprocedures, but included in her diagram the "Press any key to continue" procedure (named TURN), and adequately represented the loop she has in her program—in the test part—with an arrow (which is her procedure ALLDONE).

When *Nicky* was asked to draw a diagram of his two programs, he said: "I can do it for my first program, but not for the second, 'cause my second one is only one screen. So I'll just show you what's on the screen." His first program, however, is also one screen only, but maybe because it includes questions and answers, Nicky could think of it in terms of sequence and was able to write a sequential representation of it.

Rosie's diagrams for both of her programs include three parts, which she called: *Introduction, Questions, Resolution.* She described them as being "all in one long procedure." However, looking at her actual code reveals that that "one long procedure" is the procedure FRACTIONS, in her first program, and F.D.P. in her second (*F* stands for fractions, *D* stands for decimals, and *P* for percentages). Her Introduction and Resolution for both programs are included in separate procedures, and Rosie types these procedure names for her users as she runs the program on the computer. Even during her *Evaluation Sessions* with her younger users, she did not find a need to connect the different parts under one superprocedure.

Other observations of Rosie indicate that she is not a "top-down" designer and programmer. She generates ideas and programs the different parts of her programs as she goes along. In most of her more recent programs, she started to connect procedures and wrote superprocedures for them. But usually, since she is a very impulsive child, when she finishes a program, she will go on to do the next thing that happens to be more exciting for her. She will rarely go back and finish things, put procedures together, delete procedures on the Logo Page that are not used or not related to her main program, or modify her procedures in one way or another. In fact, when asked to do so, she comes up with many ideas for how to change, clean up, or modify her programs, but she does not "feel like doing these things." Rosie is a good example of a child who could benefit from an explicit request to reflect upon what she does every once in a while. She is capable and creative but could learn a lot more from her reflections. She is a tinkerer and functions very well as such, and one should not change her style; however, the data of this study and other observations suggest that she could expand the range of her learning and achievements with a little "afterwards reflections and deeper considerations" on her projects. This issue requires further investigations.

Damal's diagram is sequential as well, but he does not adequately represent the parts of his program and the relationships among his procedures. By contrast, the sequential diagrams of Nicky, Jessica, and Sunny do correspond with the main parts and order of their programs. Damal's diagram is a mixed representation of parts (he separated the "talking" part, for example), and most of his diagram is a description of the text that appears on the screen (i.e., "Before addition, it welcomes you," or "After the addition, it welcomes you to subtraction"). The text on his screen is not separated, but rather included as part of procedures. In addition, Damal's procedure NEXT calls itself again if the user answered it wrongly. But he did not represent the tail-recursive loop in his diagram. The hierarchical diagram we created of his program reveals that his program calls procedures in a "go to" fashion; that is, each procedure calls the next at the end of itself. He does not understand procedures as parts or units of some whole, and as mechanisms that can capture regularity of some sort.

Sunny's diagram is impressive for an 11-year-old child. She adequately captured the five major parts of her program, and the interactions among these parts.

Figures 16–20 present the children's hand-drawn diagrams, side by side to the hierarchical diagrams of their actual programming code (created by the researcher).

During the interview, after the children drew their representations of their programs, they were asked to recall the total number of procedures in each of their programs. Table 1 presents the results of the children's recall.

The examination of the children's code reveals that one of the 'not connected' procedures in each of the children's files is a procedure that they all created for erasing their files from the buffer and saving them on their diskettes. They usually will use this procedure at the end of the "computer time," before they start another activity. The other 'not connected' procedures are procedures that did not work, or procedures that, according to the children, they "got from other children and do not relate to the fractions programs." But most of the 'not connected' procedures are, in fact, procedures that are related to the fractions programs, like Nicky's "title screen" or Rosie's "Help screen." The interesting issue is that they did not erase unrelevant or unfinished procedures from their files, or did not connect the relevant procedures to their superprocedures.

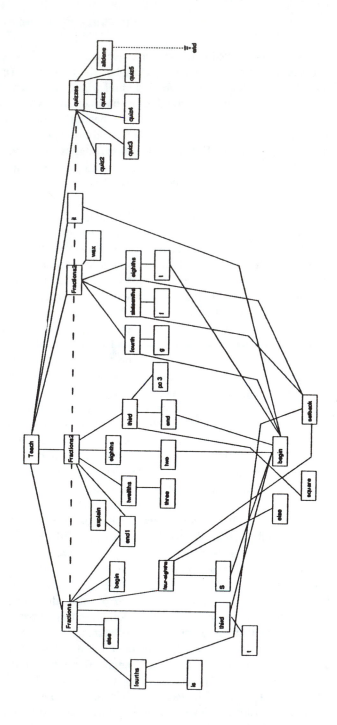

Jessica May 8, 1986

66

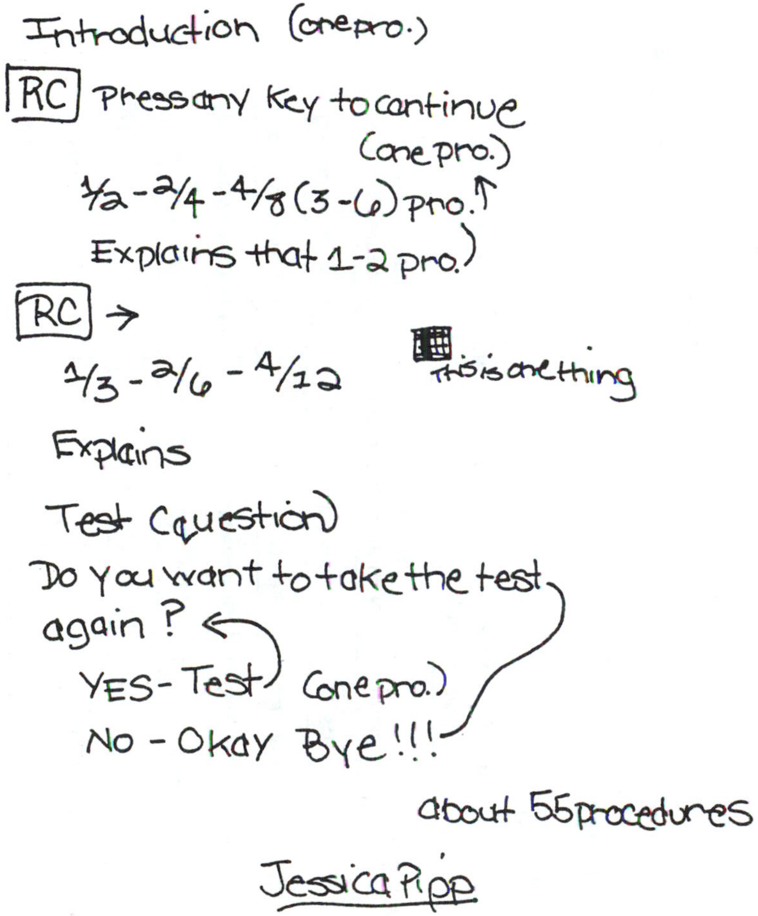

Figure 16. Jessica's Diagram.

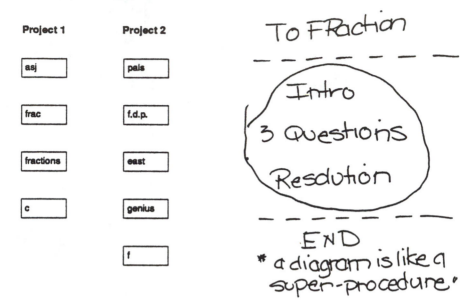

Project 1   **Project 2**

asj

frac

fractions

c

pals

f.d.p.

east

genius

f

Figure 17.   Rosie's Diagram.

Table 1.   Students' Recall of the Number of Procedures Included in Their Programs.

Name	Child's Recall of Number of Procedures	Actual Number of Procedures in Code
Jessica	"55 procedures"	40 (+ 4 not connected)
Nicky Prog. 1	"6 procedures"	7 (+ 3 not connected)
Nicky Prog. 2	"8 procedures"	14 (+ 3 not connected)
Rosie Prog. 1	"1 long procedure"	1 (+ 3 not connected)
Rosie Prog. 2	"1 long procedure"	1 (+ 4 not connected)
Damal	"35 procedures"	13 (+ 4 not connected)
Sunny	"5 procedures"	19 (+ 2 not connected)

The "not connected" procedures are procedures in the children's files that were not structurally integrated into the larger fractions program. These procedures were not included in the superprocedure, or were not called from any other main procedure. These could be unfinished or unrelated procedures, but more often they were very related to the project, and the children would type these procedures' names in order to run them together with the main fractions program.

1. Give instructions
2. Draws square & divides into fourths
3. Fills in each fourt a different color
4. asks a questions about areas filled in
5. If you answer the 1st question correctly it goes on to the second question after telling you you got it right

6. asks a different question and does the same process that it *does* with the 1st question, but it doesn't go or

7. You know the procedure is over when you get the cursor back.

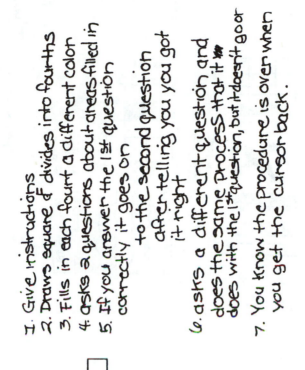

Figure 18. Nicky's Diagrams.

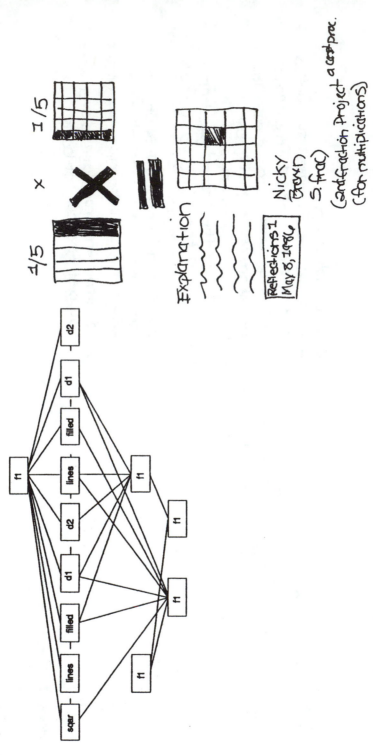

Figure 18. Continued.

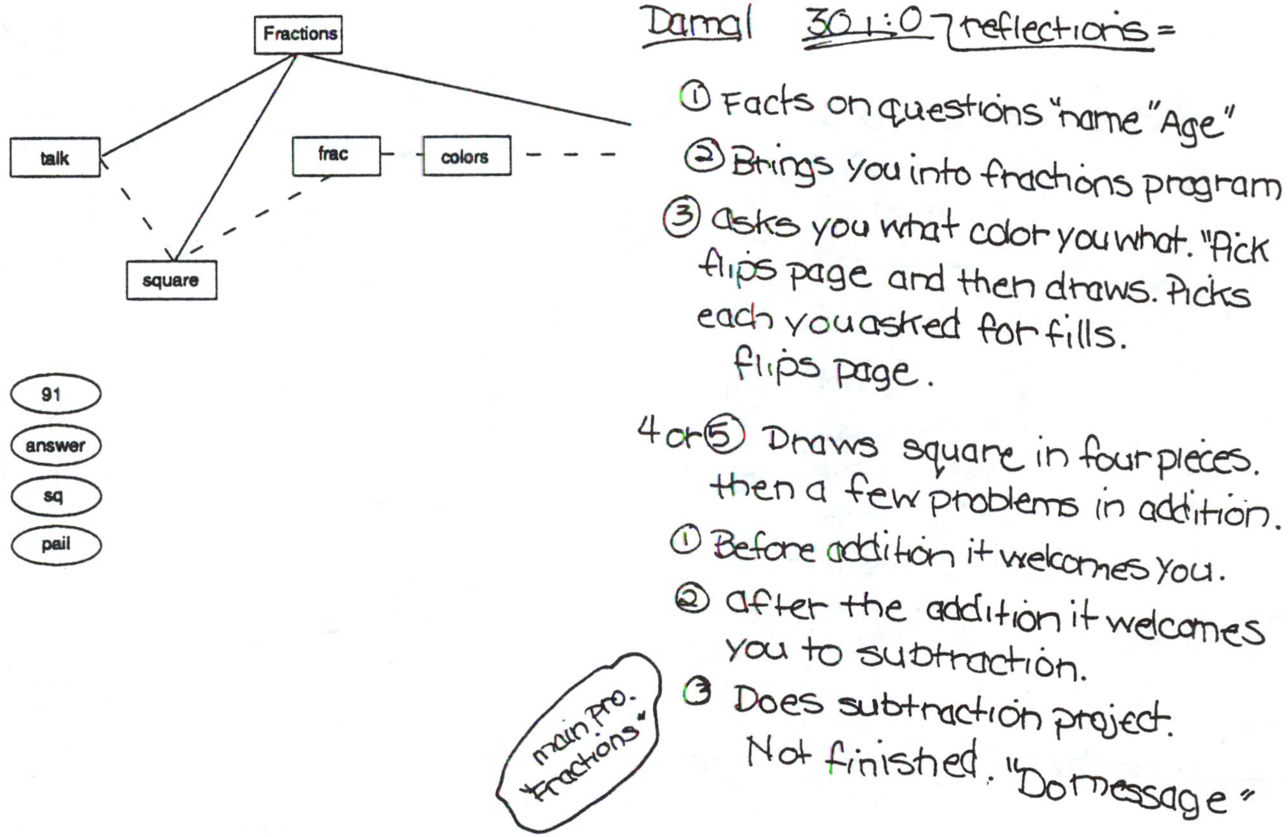

Damal   30↓:0 reflections =

① Facts on questions "name "Age"

② Brings you into fractions program

③ asks you what color you what. "Pick
   flips page and then draws. Picks
   each you asked for fills.
      flips page.

4 or ⑤ Draws square in four pieces.
   then a few problems in addition.

① Before addition it welcomes you.

② after the addition it welcomes
   you to subtraction.

③ Does subtraction project.
   Not finished. "Do message "

main program
fractions

Fractions

frac — colors

talk

square

91   answer   sq   pail

Figure 19. Damal's Diagram.

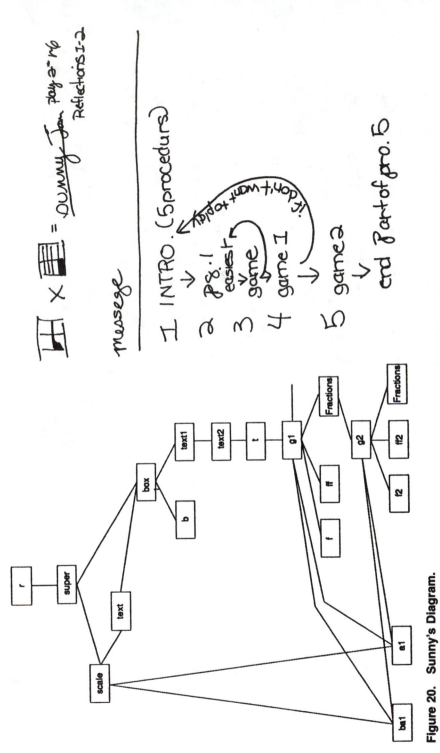

72

Figure 20. Sunny's Diagram.

Later during the interview, when the children were asked to describe the function of each procedure, they were able to do so. Jessica and Nicky were the most accurate about the function of each procedure. Damal, on the other hand, had the impression that his program is "really really long" and stated that it includes 35 procedures, but his code reveals that he actually had 12. His program is indeed long, but composed out of several long procedures. Sunny was also confused between the program's parts and the actual number of procedures. She stated her program had five procedures, but her program really had 21.

To summarize, the above information about the children's mental representations of their programs and procedures raises several research concerns. None of the children found a need to change their diagrams while they were describing their procedures and the functions of these procedures. Their diagrams were satisfactory to them; the children believed that they accurately represented the structure of their programs. These results might be confounded with the children's imperfect memory of the procedures and their lack of familiarity with the task. This issue is open for further investigations. Children might reach a higher level of understanding of Logo programming through being involved in representation activities of this sort.

3.6.5. The Children's Views of Themselves as Planners or Non-Planners

The children's answers to the questions: "Did you plan your program in any way?" Or "Do you usually plan your computer programs, and how?" accurately corresponded to our observations of their actual programming-in-action. Our observations indicate that only one of them, Jessica, is a typical "planner" and a top-down, systematical programmer, and she also views herself as such. The other four children view themselves as "planning along the way," and our observations of them indicate the same. These four children said that they "never have written plans, 'cause it doesn't always work," and that they make decisions about programming and design in an "as needed" or opportunistic fashion, while programming and trying out things on the computer.

Few studies have examined directly the relationship between planning and programming, and learning outcomes. The results are not conclusive (Webb, Ender, & Lewis, 1986). Schneiderman, Mayer, McKay, and Heller (1977), in five studies of programming performance, failed to find an advantage in planning and flowcharting a program in advance. Mandinach (1984), however, did demonstrate that the ability to plan strategically did predict performance in computer-assisted instruction. Bradley (1985) found that a top-down approach toward Logo problem solving tended to relate positively to learning outcomes.

This study did not measure directly the influence of different planning strategies on learning to program. However, Jessica (the planner) did seem to have an advantage in handling a complex program. In addition, we saw how she was the only one who understood the diagramming task right away, and that her diagram represented the structure of her program accurately. But Nicky, not a planner, is almost as good a programmer. Damal's and Rosie's programs, on the other hand, provide some evidence of the result of opportunistic planning. Their programming processes involved making decisions as they went along, in incremental steps. These processes, at the end, did not lead to a coherent and integrated program. It is important to investigate these issues further: Will Rosie and Damal benefit from planning a bit more? Will creating 'action diagrams' for their programming activities, before programming the code on the computer, help the children? In any case, it is important to emphasize that this study, like others (e.g., Webb et al., 1986), suggests that it is not yet clear whether planning would provide learners with better understanding and mastery of programming. For example, Nicky's and Sunny's programs are pretty complex for 11-year-olds, but both these children are nonplanners. Many proposed strategies still need to be tested empirically.

3.6.6. The Children's Use and Understanding of Logo

General issues relating to the children's understanding of Logo and their conceptions about their Logo programs were presented previously. This section presents more specific data about the children's ability to describe and define REPEAT, variables, recursion, procedures, READLIST, and so on.

Understanding and using REPEAT. The children were asked to explain, describe, and give examples for how the Logo command REPEAT is used. All children were able to describe the function of REPEAT in their programs, as well as to define it more generally. For example, *Jessica* said: "I used REPEAT for the drawing of the squares. I use it to repeat the same thing again." *Nicky:* "I use it for squares, lines . . . it's good when you want to repeat something more than once." *Damal:* "I used it for everything. For squares, for colors . . . instead of doing it over and over again. It does it for you." And *Sunny:* "It's telling the computer to do *something* as many times as I want it to."

Understanding and using variables. The data reveal that they all described variables only as inputs to procedures. For example, *Nicky* said: "The outside of my square took a variable, to change the size of it. So one procedure could draw many different squares. I also use variables to change colors." *Sunny* said: "I used variables for the sides and the angles of shapes . . . and when I want to make something change into another thing. I can just use the same procedure to make many things as I need." *Jessica:* "For example, the SETPALs used variables to change the colors of the FILLs, to flash it on the screen."

None of the children referred to their use of MAKE and NAME in this context. That brings up some interesting questions: Do they know the difference between

NAME and MAKE? Do they understand that by using MAKE or NAME they actually change the value of a variable? This complex issue needs to be further investigated and explained to the children.

Understanding and using recursion. The children understood and used tail recursion (see definition in Harvey, 1985). *Jessica* explained: "I use recursion to call the same procedure again." Sunny: "If I want the procedure to repeat itself over and over again." *Nicky* confessed: "I use it. But the problem with it is, that you have to do FUNCTION BREAK when you want to stop it." Nicky does not know about the stop rules in using recursion. *Damal* does not really know the meaning of recursion. He said: "I use IF for that" meaning that the procedure call is embedded in an IF statement.

The children were also asked to explain and define IF *and* READLIST *or* READCHAR. Their explanations reveal that they do not understand the meaning and functions of those very accurately. They seem to have a 'functional template' that gives meaning to each primitive by attaching them together. That is, they can only understand and use them together in a specific and narrow way—to ask questions and get users' answers or inputs. For example, *Nicky* said "READLIST reads what you type . . it's in charge of the answer." *Damal* said that he uses them in his "talking parts. You have to use it when you ask questions and want to give answers or go on to another thing."

During the interviews and while examining the children's programming code with them, several other programming issues came up in relation to the children's programming ability and understanding. Some of their misconceptions were really interesting cognitively, but all raise issues related to educational practice; that is, learning programming through discovery vs. explicit instruction, or more structured discovery.

3.6.7. The Children as Software Evaluators and Maintainers

The evaluation sessions of the five children with several younger kids from the school emphasize the importance of another idea: the children's attitudes and techniques in maintaining their programs. The data from these sessions revealed that the task—of receiving comments from others, modifying a procedure upon request, printing extra information and instructions, or making a program do anything needed—was, unexpectedly, a task that all children could enjoy and handle pretty well.

Pea (1984) reports that children learning Logo did not like to change or debug their programs at all. He found that they prefer instead to rewrite their programs from scratch. The present study suggests the opposite. None of these children have even thought of creating their programs from scratch. Their programs were too long for doing that. Instead, they were acting like professional software maintainers and tried to solve the problems and bugs through thinking about adding on features, and modifying existing procedures.

Jessica was surprised to find out that her program is too easy for a fourth grader, her original target users' age. She therefore tried it with a third grader. The third grader, however, felt the test was too difficult for him, because he could not solve the questions without the graphical representations. Jessica came up with the following conclusion: "I should include a part in my program that asks my users what grade they are in. If they type 'fourth,' they'll get the program the way it is. If they type 'third,' they'll get a different test *with* pictures." During the evaluation session she wrote on a piece of paper how she would modify her program to do so. She also pointed out in the code where the new features should be included.

Nicky's users' (a third-grade girl, and a fourth-grade girl) complaints were about the fact that his program accepts only one form of input (*one-fourth* in words), and when they typed the right answer in numbers ($1/4$), they got feedback, as if their answer was wrong. Nicky agreed this was a problem and attempted to correct it right away. He added three new procedures that can take a list as an input. For this purpose, he used MEMBERP for the first time, which he learned through this session.

He added to his *D3* procedure the following:

```
. . . . . . . .
NAME FIRST READLIST "J
IF (MEMBERP :J [ONE HALF ½ ²/₄ TWO FOURTHS])
[PR (YOU GOT IT RIGHT! ! !]] [PR [Wrong. TRY AGAIN. . .] D3]
END
```

So his users were satisfied and the session went on. But there is a bug in the code. Nicky did not yet know that, even if the user types "one" or "4" or "/", the procedure will treat it too as the right answer. He did not have the strategy of testing how a procedure runs with right and wrong answers . . . an important skill he still needs to learn.

Damal's user, a third-grade girl, complained about his program's pace: "I can't read it. It's too fast." Damal's first reaction was: "But I can read it. It's not too fast for me." And from then on, he read all the screens to her in an affected voice, "as if I'm the computer." His user was still complaining and did not give up: "It's still too fast, Damal!" Damal eventually entered the editor and added WAITS in some of his procedures (upon his user's requests).

His user also complained: "I don't always understand what you are talking about. You must add more directions here and there." Damal's reaction to that was: "There are not supposed to be many directions. That's how I like it. You give them a hint on what to do, and after the hint, they should know what to do. First you go through it, show them, and then let them try it. I do it the hard way, always the hard way!" This fascinating conversation on teaching and learning approaches, and the level of the instructional interactivity, continued as follows:

Damal:	*"The hard way is like you tell, but you give the person an example of what you mean, and then, you set them off to work on their own. . ."*
Siobhan:	*"Oh! no, no, no. . . But your program doesn't do any of that!"*
Damal:	*"Yes it does!"*
Siobhan:	*"No. What I mean, is that you said that the hard way is to give a hint or example, and* then *let me do it all by myself. So, you gave me a hint, but you never let me do anything by myself!"*
Damal:	*"[thinking for awhile] Yes, it's true. . ."*
Siobhan:	*"The other person that is doing it, should come up with the answer, not you."*
Damal:	*"[thinking for awhile]. . . Oh! I know, I know! You want me to put a fraction on the screen, then another fraction, and then to leave an open box for* you *to give me the answer?"*
Siobhan:	*"Yes, yes."*
Damal:	*"I like it. Yeah. It's better. . ."*
Idit:	*"Why is it better, Damal?"*
Damal:	*"Because then you can really learn something. Put one fraction that you do on the computer, and then put one that they, the users can do. I think I have to add a whole new project here. . ."*

A model for the cognitive gains from peer-teaching. This conversation went on into many directions. Other children experienced similar thoughts during their evaluation sessions as well. The methodology of asking children to evaluate their programs with younger children and friends is important for their learning, decentering, and cognitive growth. The example above demonstrates the cognitive gains of peer-teaching or peer-reviewing of someone's work. The quality of the interaction that occurred between Damal and Siobhan is invaluable. They learned something together and contributed to each other's thinking and learning.

These sessions provided opportunity for the five children to talk about fractions and their instructional programs with others, to exchange ideas in a professional way. Their users, naturally, had complaints and requested certain features to be added or changed. The children/designers were able to discuss how to do it and were able to debug their programs and add some of the requested features during the session itself, or write on paper their ideas of how to change it later. In order to do this in the real professional world, software designers must have a clear model of their programs and their teaching objectives. And indeed, these young designers were able to understand their users, to negotiate ideas and strategies, to enter their programs, find the procedures, and modify and change what is needed.

"Hards" and "softs:" different experiences in the evaluation sessions. The data reveal that the "softs" (Turkle, 1984) were more flexible and benefitted more from the evaluation sessions, since they were able to interact and exchange ideas freely and were willing to modify their products according to ideas from people other than themselves. Jessica, the only "hard" of the five, a perfectionist, and a

rigid planner, had quite a difficult time during her evaluation sessions. Right at the beginning of the fractions project, she created top-down written plans for her program. Her goal was always getting the program on the computer to realize her handwritten plans. Moreover, during the process of programming, when she changed something on the computer, she also changed it on her written plans. Jessica, who has very high standards for her work (in all areas in the school), and who worked in a systematic fashion to bring her program to perfection, was not able to be interactive and flexible during the sessions with her younger users. She seemed to be intimidated by their reactions. Although she finally came up with a creative idea for modifying her program, it took her time to accept doing so.

In contrast, the other four children, who were characterized as having soft and interactive personalities, had different experiences in the evaluation sessions. During their processes of programming, they usually let the overall shape of their programs emerge from their interactions with the computer or with their teacher and peers. They are used to thinking in a conversational mode. A session like this was a natural experience for them, because as tinkerers and softs they are used to arranging and rearranging the elements they are working with in a flexible way. These children were more eager to discover new combinations and enjoyed adding (or even thinking about adding) new features to their program. Damal's conversation with Siobhan was an example for that. Rosie's and Nicky's sessions were even better examples, since their pleasure in thinking together and interacting led to changes in their own thinking.

3.6.8. The Children's Instructional Design Strategies

Content analysis of the children's programs prior to the interviews revealed that all children designed programs that are described in the professional software world as "computerized tutorials." Therefore, the categories and guidelines for the Show and Tell Interview were inspired by Allessi and Trollip's (1985) description of "the general structure and components of a tutorial" (pp. 65–133).

According to Allessi and Trollip, the aim of a typical tutorial lesson on the computer is to present information and skills and to guide a student through initial use of these skills. Figure 21 shows the structure and sequence of a typical tutorial (based on Allessi & Trollip, 1985, p. 66).

Not all tutorials engage in all these presentations and activities, and not all of the children's programs contain this particular structure in full. However, this model was selected here as a common base for possible instructional factors relevant to the children's work. The data on the children's instructional design strategies were organized according to the above model.

When asked: "How did you think about the design of your screens?" the five children responded as follows.

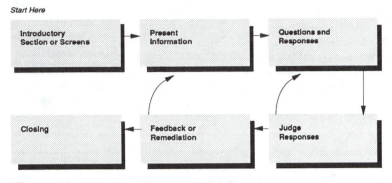

Figure 21.   A Typical Tutorial Structure.

Jessica's instructional theory was reflected in her answer: "First, you have to give a good explanation before you give them a test. That's what I thought about. . . . Because if you don't give good explanations, how are they going to know?" Jessica also had a clear idea of when she chose to use text, and when graphics: "I had to use text and graphics in my first part, the demonstration. But I don't use pictures in the test part. It's harder to solve my questions without the pictures. The pictures in the first part are important, they are explaining (the pictures) what they are supposed to learn. Then in the test, they have to learn how to do it without pictures." She said she used colors because "it's nicer," but also because "it explains the equivalent fractions better . . . you can see that the colored area in two fourths is equal to the area of one half. I flash the colors, too. To make it really clear to them."

I asked Jessica why she had selected squares for her design; she answered: "It's easier to divide. It's easier to see it. More than with circles or triangles." ("Why?") "Because triangles are uneven. You can maybe use them for halves, but it will be really confusing to show with them two-eighths or four-twelfths."

When asked "what type of answers do you give to your users?" Jessica said: "Funny answers. I give a different answer to each question. You can always try it (the question) again if you are wrong. But if you are right, it'll tell you, 'You are hot!' . . . you can always take the test again and again, until you get it right."

Nicky's reasons for using colors in his first program on equivalent fractions were very interesting: "If I use colors, I don't need to ask, 'What fraction is the top part?' That's confusing. They will not understand which top part . . . so it's better to ask, 'What is the *red* part' or 'What are the light blue and the dark blue parts together.' People understand it better. I use colors to emphasize things. To distinguish things. Also, if there are colors on the screen it makes it more interesting to look at. It's good for learning. You can learn lots of things according to colors! You can group things according to colors!" Nicky continued to explain his color philosophy; he became quite animated.

When asked about his strategies for using text or graphics, he answered: "All pictures should be clear. But sometimes you need text to explain the pictures. In fact, most of the time you need pictures to help you explain text. Text alone is usually boring. If you teach somebody something, you should explain it to them with pictures. You could also use the blackboard for that . . . but you have to use pictures that explain what to do and why to do it. Not just doing things on paper, worksheets, and get a grade on it. Seeing is more important, more than just hearing the teacher."

In another context Nicky emphasized his teaching ideas further: "I don't say teachers cannot teach multiplication well, but I think it's good to take a break sometimes, stop listening to all these explanations, and do it yourself on the computer, see the pictures of it, and do it yourself!"

I asked Nicky: "What makes a computer program really good?" He answered: "It has to be an interesting subject. It has to be colorful. Real life colors are good, animation is really good, stuff like that. Also it has to be easy to use. It should ask questions and let them press any key to go on."

During these interviews, Nicky pointed out many important pedagogical and instructional concerns he had, such as the level of student's involvement and of interest in the subject matter, level of the software's interactivity, ease of use, the importance of colors, animation, and simulations, and the idea of building software around interesting subject matter.

Damal was also reflecting on his processes of making decision about design: "First, I was going to have it all in text and numbers. Then I thought it was hard to understand, so I put in a few pictures. I decided that it's good to put pictures in the middle of the screen, and the text at the top." Similarly to Nicky, Damal's reasons for using colors were: "Make it fancy, and help you to see things." He explained: "If they, the users, don't know what you're talking about, you go, 'Look over here,' they can ask, 'Where?' But if you use colors you can say: 'Look at the red or yellow part,' and they will know right away what you're talking about." In another context, Damal said: "When you do something in drawing, and when you have to draw it, automatically you can see subtraction of fractions. They can see the numbers, the pictures, and also how it was done." Damal referred to two important issues. The first is his translation of subtraction to pictures, words, and numbers on the same computer screen. The second was the procedural representation in Logo. All of these together create understanding among his users and himself.

Sunny's approach to the processes of designing screens is: "I'll just picture it in my mind. And then, I'll try to fit everything in. And when I work more with the computer, and put my ideas in it, I'll have more and more ideas. I also try to put text in pictures. It makes it more interesting. I think pictures help you understand more than reading."

Figure 22 presents Sunny's explanations about why she chose to represent the fractions in squares. She also said she "designed her squares as large as possible, so people can really see the fractions."

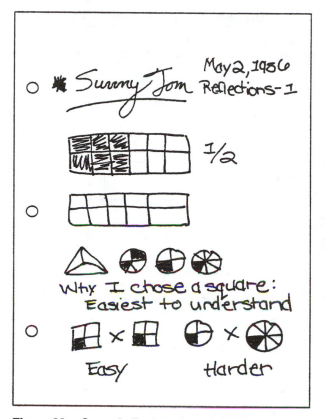

Figure 22. Sunny's Explanations for Why She Chose a Square for Her Representations and Teaching.

In addition, Sunny said she does not use sound in her program since: "sometimes noise distracts you from what you are supposed to be doing." She uses colors because: "With the use of colors you can see that parts are separated from other parts."

When asked: "How do you focus your users' attention?" Sunny answered: "I try to choose a subject that is really interesting, try to make it enjoyable, I used the balance scale game, I try to arrange it so it's really hard, and they have to work to succeed." She continued: "I figured it's important to have introduction and to explain more. Because sometimes, even my teacher doesn't do it. Sometime I don't really know if they'll really enjoy what I'm doing. So only if they feel they want to go on with my program and play the games." Sunny designed her program in a way that gives the user an option to quit after the introduction, and before or after each other part in her program. Another interesting feature was, if you get Game 2 wrong, the program sends you back to Game 1, as Sunny said, "to practice your knowledge a little more."

Table 2.   Pilot Study, Design Analysis of children's programs.

Instructional Design Analysis	Jessica	Nicky	Rosie	Damal	Sunny
Title page	y	y	n	n	y
Presentation of Objectives	y	n	y	n	y
Directions/Instructions	y	n	n	some	y
How much user's control	lots	some	none	none	lots
Forward progression based on user's answers	y	y	n	some	y
Paging capacity	y	n	n	n	y
Menu options	n	n	n	n	n
Time limits	n	n	n	y	n
Any pre-testing	n	n	n	n	n
Any Post-testing	y	y	y	n	y
Text presentations only	n	n	y	n	n
Graphics presentations only	n	n	n	n	n
Combine Test & Graphics	y	y	n	y	y
Animation (SETPAL in Logo)	y	n	n	n	n
Sound	n	n	n	n	n
Feedback for correct answer	y	y	y	y	y
Feedback for wrong	y	y	y	y	y
Remediation by repeating old info. or a question	y	after debugging	y	y	y
Option to quit	n	n	n	n	y
Option for variety of user's responses or inputs	n	after debugging	n.	n	n
Level of interactivity	medium	medium	high	high	low
Linear program	demo is	y	y	y	parts
Branching program	test is	n	n	n	y

(continued)

Table 2—(*Continued*)

Instructional Design Analysis	Jessica	Nicky	Rosie	Damal	Sunny
Criteria for branching	user' ans.	—	—	user' ans.	user' ans.
Directions for branching	y	n	n	n	y
Sequence of screens based on	difficulty	difficulty	difficulty	difficulty	creation
Type of help	none	none	screen	none	screen
Option for re-doing a part	y	n	n	n	y
Option for re-starting	n	n	n	n	n
Final message	y	n	y	n	y
How many questions in all	4	3	8	1	4
Complexity, overall	high	medium	low	medium	high

Rosie, unlike her peers, who were creating graphical representations and explanations, created two "text only" programs and thus was not involved in many of the instructional design considerations and metacognitive processes. She could talk about design and representation issues, or design learning ideas related to her other programming projects, but these other projects are not the scope of this book.

The other four children, who were involved in creating representations combining graphics and text, were involved in many more interesting thinking processes than Rosie. If we are interested in encouraging children's involvement in higher-level thinking processes, we might want to encourage them to create multiple representations that combine graphics, text, and mathematical symbols.

To summarize, the data reveal that a great variety of considerations were interlaced in the children's work, and their decisions about design. The children's instructional design strategies could be grouped into two: (a) appeal and user's attitude considerations—for example, "colors are beautiful," or "people will say 'wow!'" or "It's more interesting," or "they will pay attention to the colors and the parts"; and (b) instructional and learning considerations, that involve thinking about understanding the concepts they wanted to teach, for example, "pictures are good because people can see it and understand," or "my introduction is important because you have to explain them what to do and how," or "colors are good for distinguishing parts and group things." These considerations were derived from the children's learning and teaching theories.

Table 2 presents a comparative summary of the five children's design features and instructional design considerations.

3.7. DISCUSSION OF PILOT STUDY

3.7.1. Issues Related to Learning Logo Programming

Many attempts have been made to evaluate children's ability, difficulties, and the cognitive consequences of learning to program in Logo. The research literature could be divided into two major groups of concerns: (a) studies investigating how much Logo children learned under certain circumstances, and (b) studies investigating the effects of learning Logo on children's cognitive development. Many studies of group 1, above, reported that children performed at low levels on such fundamental aspects of programming as understanding primitive commands. Children in these studies could mainly write chains of commands in direct mode, had great difficulty in using procedures and variables, and were rarely able to debug their programs. Many studies of group 2, above, reported that children who learned to program in Logo failed to demonstrate clear cognitive advantages (e.g., Pea, 1984; Pea & Kurland, 1984; Carver & Klahr, 1986; Heller, 1985; Perkins & Martin, 1985, and others).

However, the conditions under which Logo was learned in most of the research environments reported in the above literature were usually poor. The children did not have time to learn Logo in any depth, and were not provided with activities for learning Logo in a meaningful way. Thus, deeper speculations about reasons for difficulties in programming become almost irrelevant. Because the level of Logo mastery was low among the children, conclusions about cognitive effects must be best interpreted as conclusions about the effects on cognitive development of *small amounts* and of *low-level understanding* of Logo. The feedback provided by these studies about Logo learning and understanding can be misleading. Also, it could make it difficult to study the potential outcomes, as well as to design materials intended for children who are learning in a high-density computer environment and have more intensive and broad computer experiences (Papert, 1984a, 1984b, 1985, 1986; Salomon & Perkins, 1986).

The present study explored some aspects of learning to program and metacognition in the context of Project Headlight—a unique learning environment where children had much larger exposure to Logo. The children who participated in this study used computers 5 days a week, for 1½ hours each day. The computers were integrated into several school subjects (e.g., literature, music, math, reading, writing, social studies, etc.). When using the computer for Logo programming, the children did not learn Logo as an isolated curriculum area, but rather to pursue goals within a larger context (e.g., learning fractions). The topics for projects were given by the teacher, but children themselves initiated ideas for their own programming projects. Collaboration was encouraged in most of the computer activities. In short, the uses that children find for Logo programming at Project Headlight are much more intensive and often have very meaningful and personal quality.

The rationale behind this exploratory study was to investigate more closely programming experiences in a richer and more complex programming environment. It seems that the intensive use of Logo in the Headlight context, and within the Fractions Project (designing instructional screens), helped children to acquire sophisticated programming skills. The integration of Logo into a meaningful context (which provides meaning to programming) made Logo a flexible tool in the hands of children, and they did pursue an interesting route to metalearning of various kinds. Here is a summary of some of these results.

Understanding of Logo. The pilot study raised some concerns with regard to the five children's understanding of procedures, variables, and recursion, their understanding of their program code, and the children's programming styles (e.g., planners vs. opportunistic programmers). Overall, it appears that these children are much better programmers than children of that age in either studies in the field. The children constructed long and complicated programs consistent with their high level of expertise in Logo. They demonstrated their understanding of Logo in three different situations: while talking about it away from the computer, while looking at the printouts of their programs, and while they were working at the computer and running or modifying their programs.

Programming styles. The styles of the children's programs, and of their programming or maintaining processes, were different. In considering the discussions about programming and thinking styles made by Turkle (1984, "hard vs. soft") and by Papert (1980, "planner vs. tinkerer"), the data suggest that Jessica is the only "planner" with the "hard" style, and she also demonstrated high programming ability and high ability in reflection and matacognition. Nicky, Sunny, Rosie, and Damal could be described as "tinkerers" and "softs" in their style of programming. Among these, Nicky and Sunny performed at higher levels with respect to programming ability and metacognitive gains.

Programming skill development within the Fractions Project context and afterwards. The children all think of themselves as better programmers at the time of the interviews, which were conducted two months after the Fractions Project ended. They each had several ideas on how to make their programs better by using new Logo commands that they had learned. They would say, for example, "I didn't know how to do it then, but now I know how to call my question again if the user made a mistake, until they get it right." Or, "Now I know how to ask them [the users] what grade they are in, and give them different questions according to their grade." Or, "I should flash 2/4 and 1/2 on the same side of the square, so they can see it is the same. I know how to use SETPAL now. They can even choose the colors." Some of the children used these techniques already in their Fractions Projects, but others learned about it afterwards (i.e., learned how to use recursion, variables, READLIST, READCHAR, IF statements, SETPAL, RANDOM, etc.).

Putting Logo programming in a meaningful context, and following up with reflections, redesigns, and modifications. The review of the literature revealed that previous investigations of the impact of programming on cognitive skills have yielded only few positive, and more often negative, findings. Salomon and

Perkins (1986) describe conditions for transfer of cognitive skills from programming, and offer a broad characterization of the conditions under which the higher-level cognitive skills tend to develop among children. It seems that the Fractions Project, together with the activities of the data collection for this study, created a learning experience that achieved some of these conditions. Many positive findings (although only gathered qualitatively and presented descriptively) came about in this study when the programming activity integrated the "low" and the "high" roads. Logo was integrated into a larger meaningful context of software design in the fractions domain ("high road"), and the extensive practice and more time on task ("low road") were available to children. The results demonstrate the important interplay between the learning of Logo, fractions, and metacognition. Logo became more meaningful to children, because it was embedded within the fractions and the software-designing context. Children's learning of programming therefore increases when they learn it in a larger meaningful context, and when they work on programs that make sense to them. They learned new Logo operations and commands due to their design considerations, such as wanting their programs to be able to handle a user's input or to be able to flash the colors of the fractions parts on the screen.

3.7.2. Issues Related to Learning Fractions

Behr et al. (1983) report that "school curricula tend to emphasize procedural skills and computational algorithms for rational numbers" rather than providing a "careful development of important functional understanding" (pp. 91–92). Peck and Jencks (1981) express the need to shift the emphasis from the learning of rules for operations on fractions to the awareness of conceptual basis. Wearne-Hilbert and Hilbert (1983) also state that "we need to spend more time in early grades developing foundational concepts . . . we are progressing too rapidly into the operations with fractions without ensuring a full understanding of initial concepts" (p. 105). Their research indicates that children need to understand part–whole relations. Ellenbruch and Payne (1978) and Lesh et al. (1983) also suggest that, for beginners, the introduction to fractions concepts should be made through representations using the part–whole model.

Children's difficulties in understanding part–whole relations is one of the major concerns of the Harvard-based ETC (1985, pp. 5, 87) Fractions Group. They describe how their focus on part–whole relations was a very meaningful starting point for children. In their early pilot studies, they found that children did not realize, for example, that fourths are embedded in eighths.

Post et al. (1985) list many of the reasons why understanding fractional relationships are so cognitively complex: (a) the fraction size depends on the relation between the two whole numbers in the fraction symbol; (b) there is an inverse relation between the numbers of parts into which the whole is divided and the resulting size of each part; (c) when fractions have like denominators, there is a direct relation between the number of parts being considered and the order of fractions; (d) when fractions have like numerators, there is an inverse relation between the denominators and the order of fractions; (e) when fractions have different numerators and denominators, judgments about the order require an extensive and flexible use of fractions equivalence; (f) there is a counterintuitive notion that there is no "next" fraction; and (g) (linguistic consideration) *more* or *greater* can mean to a child more area that is covered by each part. There is a confusion about *greater* as a greater number of parts in the partitioned whole vs. a greater fraction size.

Post (1981) also addresses some features of successful attempts at developing meaning and understanding of fractions. These are: (a) active student involvement, (b) use of manipulative materials, (c) the opportunity for students to share ideas and talk about fractions together, and (d) emphasis should be placed on conceptual meanings and representations prior to algorithms.

Although the research literature emphasizes the understanding of part–whole relations as a prerequisite to understanding fractions by beginners, failure in understanding part–whole relation can only be considered as one obstacle out of many. Thinking in terms of part–whole is a tool to understand some fractions problems such as addition or equivalence. However, it might become an obstacle in understanding division of fractions. In addition, there are many more representations than part–whole in area representations. The problem of representing fractions goes beyond the problem of part–whole. Children's trouble with the part–whole concept might lie in their not being able to deal well enough with the issue of representations of fractions.

The Fractions Project focused on the idea of representing fractions and manipulating these representations through looking at fractions as area. Emphasis was placed on the role of Logo as a tool for representing fractions and explaining these representations. The learner acted as the constructor of these representations (not the teacher), and as epistemologist in the Piagetian sense. The children were engaged in an epistemological activity thinking about what they themselves know (or do not know) and how to explain it to others. This activity was very different from the other worksheet activities they did in the classroom; it emphasized representing fractions rather than algorithms of fractions.

The following is a summary of some of the outcomes of this approach to learning fractions.

Children's knowledge of fractions. This explanatory study does not allow us to come up with significant results on issues such as "Do children know fractions better than other children who did not have this learning experience?" This might be a weak point of this study. As a pilot study, the results do serve, however, as a good measure of outcomes for the Fractions Project experience *itself*. We are now more aware of the *qualities* of this particular learning experience and pedagogy. This study is a hypothesis generator for future studies, and could help us identify which variables we want to control in future studies, or what type of fraction-knowledge tests should be developed. The interviews with the teachers and the pupils at Headlight indicate that Logo helped them understand fractions better and empowered their thinking about them. These observations are important even if not measured quantitatively.

Children's thinking and talking about fractions and their representations. The most interesting data about the children's learning of fractions are related to the ways they *talked* and *thought* about fractions. It is quite special and exciting that 10- and 11-year-old children can talk about how to represent fractions and how to explain operations on fractions in words, mathematical symbols, and drawings. During the interviews, they could verbalize and draw what is difficult about multiplication of fractions, or division, or subtraction, and why. Again, it would be interesting (and much more dramatic) to compare these children with another group of children (who did not go through the same learning experience) and to see whether or not they think about fractions and their representations in a similar way, and in what ways the two groups are different.

Children's learning fractions as epistemologists. The children's perspective was that they learned "a lot" about fractions during this project. They said: "How can you teach it if you don't know it yourself?" They also gained awareness about what they know and do not know about fractions. Damal, for example, said: "I learned about addition, subtraction, and multiplication. I don't teach about division in my programs 'cause I don't understand it myself." In short, the project invited children think epistemologically about their own knowledge, and how they came to know various concepts of fractions, how did they made them "their own." They could also separate what they learned from the process of constructing their programs, and what they see as what other children could learn from their programs. For example, Nicky stated that, through the programming of his multiplication screen, he came to understand that the fraction decreases not increases, and that he learned to think of this operation as taking a part of another part. Moreover, he was also aware that: "That's confusing. A lot of kids know *how to* do it but they don't know the *why.*" But when Nicky was asked whether his program is good for teaching this concept, he said: "No. It's just a demonstration. It should be used to back up good explanations that are given before you use it." In other words, Nicky feels he himself learned to understand the multiplication algorithm through his design and programming process, but he does not view his product as powerful enough to create the same understanding in someone else.

Children's conceptions of the role of the computer in the learning of fractions. It appears that all five children considered the computer better than other media (books or worksheets) for learning about fractions, since "with the computer you can *see it* or *do it* yourself." Sunny said: "It's funner with the computer." Jessica commented on the computer's feedback option that does not exist in school worksheets: "In my program, you can get an answer or the explanation on what you did wrong, and why." Nicky said the computer is a great tool for understanding the presented information "on the computer, with the shapes and the colors, you can *really* see it's a part of a part." And finally, Rosie commented on the importance of learning by doing: "You learn better about fractions 'cause *you* make it happen on the computer."

3.7.3. Issues Related to Metacognition and Metalearning of Various Kinds

Theorists like Vygotsky (1978), Bruner (1966, 1985), Brown (1978, 1984), and others view learning as a profoundly social process and emphasize the roles of language and dialogue in learning and mediated cognitive growth. Daiute (1985, 1986), Bruffee (1984), Perret-Clermont (1980), Cooper (1980), and others emphasize the role of collaboration and peer-teaching in helping learners to learn, develop sophisticated problem-solving strategies and other thinking skills.

In *Mind in Society* (1978), Vygotsky illustrates a general developmental law for the higher mental functions, one that he feels could be applied in its entirety to children's learning processes. He proposes that

> An essential feature of learning is that it creates the zone of proximal development; that is, learning awakens a variety of internal developmental processes that are able to operate only when the child is interacting with his environment and in coopera- tion with his peers. While these processes are internalized, they become part of the child independent developmental achievement. (p. 90)

Piaget has shown in several of his books that higher-level reasoning occurs in a children's group in the form of arguments. These arguments, according to Piaget, help children construct and internalize ideas in the form of thought. Children construct their point of view and check the basis of their thoughts and understandings of a concept by constructing arguments. Such observations prompted Piaget to conclude that communication produces the need for checking and confirming one's own thoughts (e.g., *Language and Thought of the Child*, 1953). Furthermore, in *The Child's Conception of Space* (1967), Piaget also emphasizes young children's difficulty in decentering; that is, to move freely from one point of view to another, either in a literal or metaphorical sense. Increasing socialization and communication develops the child's ability to decen- ter and to come closer to an "objective" view of the whole, and "it is far more general and more fundamental to knowledge in all its forms."

Piaget and Vygotsky have in common the following theoretical position: As children are engaged in an activity that leads them to communicate, argue, or explain their ideas and thoughts to others, they are also assessing, confirming, and broadening their own knowledge of these ideas. This position has been recently transferred into educational practice by designing classroom discourse on a topic, peer-teaching, or collaborative learning situations. Collaborative activities with computers have recently become popular, especially in learning to write (e.g., Rubin & Bruce, in press; Daiute, 1985). Daiute (1985), for example, writes:

> When they are communicating in writing on the computer, children are likely to write about topics that are of interest to *them* . . . they write with interest and authority. These communicative and collaborative writing activities are valuable, because they provide social reasons for writing, and because they offer models the children can internalize as they learn to work autonomously. (p. 174)

> When students write to communicate, they find the activity easier than when they write for the sake of writing. Although writing can be the creation of the work of art and the stimulator of clear thinking, most students discover the joys of writing when they use text to communicate—to others as well as to themselves. The best ways to help someone to learn how to write is to build text creation carefully on communication, so beginning writing at any age should be based on communication, such as writing a letter, persuading someone to do something, reading text aloud, or writing with another person. (p. 5)

The technique of learning to read through reading to others, or learning to write through writing stories to others—writing through interacting, arguing, criticizing, revising, much like professional writers and thinkers—was also used in the Fractions Project, but for learning mathematics. The rationale behind the Fractions Project was to involve children in learning a concept by designing representations and explanations for it to teach others. The assumption was that children's understanding of fractions and Logo would increase when they are involved in designing and programming a piece of software to teach others.

In addition, the development of instructional software required that children explore different design and knowledge-communication strategies, such as the content of their instructions, or the wording of feedback for correct or incorrect answers. Children had to explore issues related to interactivity, comprehension, appeal, and aesthetics of their screens. These explorations added affective- and social-thinking processes to the cognitive processes in the children's learning experiences. In summary, the children in this project externalized their own intelligence into the design and programming of their screens. Through their communication with the surrounding environment—teachers, other pupils, and computers—they had assessed, confirmed, and built their own knowledge. While doing that, the children were thinking about their own knowing.

The following is a summary of the results regarding the contribution of the Fractions Project to the children's metalearning. The results are pretty much interrelated. Again, future studies could include interviewing and testing of other groups of children who did not learn in the same way, so further conclusions could be made on how significant and dramatic are these children's metacognitive and metalearning gains.

Learning through teaching. All the five children referred to the process of thinking about teaching others, what they learned from it, and how interesting and important it was for them. They came up with different teaching and learning theories. They were able to define the pedagogical reasons for their screen designs. They stated why they designed their screen the way they did, in terms of choosing particular shapes, colors, spatial design, and so on. They were clear about when and why they provided instructions and directions, and the rationale behind the types of feedback they gave to the users. They explained when they used graphics and when text, and when and why they decided to use both. Their reasons were always related to the best ways for communicating what they wanted to teach.

Design considerations. A project of this kind invited children to consider their instructional designs on two levels. (a) What could be described as the *appeal and attitude* level of software design; such as, "it has to be colorful in order to focus the users attention," or "it's nicer like this." (b) What could be described as the *knowledge representation* level of software design, such as, "I had to use two different colors in order to show that these are two parts of the same whole," or "it's clearer to understand now, because I used the pictures and not only words and numbers." These comments of the children are metacognitive, and extends the range of what is considered to be doable, thinkable, and learnable by children at this age.

Representing knowledge. The interviews with the teacher and the pupils indicate that the project helped them to mentally illustrate fractions and operations. Using Logo was very important to the process of representing knowledge to oneself and to others. The activity of representing and programming these representations is considered as high-level cognitions.

Critical thinking. At first, the children found it difficult to think critically about their programs. However, the information gathered after probing them, and especially from the children's "evaluation sessions" with younger kids, indicate that they could become more critical of their own products, able to change and modify, and make them clearer and better in many ways. We should encourage children to be involved in more situations of this kind during their learning in schools.

3.7.4. Ideas and Questions for Further Research

This exploratory study revealed the need for future studies about the Fractions Project, or other projects of its kind, a similar learning environment, or pedagogy of learning through design and representation.

Here are some questions that we found to be interesting and valuable for further investigations:

1. Will children who learn fractions in other ways, not through using Logo, be

able to think and talk about fractions representation in similar ways to the children in this study?

2. Do the children in this study actually know fractions better than children who only learned about fractions in the traditional school unit? (It became clear to us that, in order to answer questions of the 1 and 2 kind, there is a need to design research with pre- and posttests and interviews about fractions, and give it to at least one other control group.)

3. Will drawing representations for fractions on paper (or by using the Macintosh, or any other tools that are different than programming) facilitate the growth of the same knowledge of fractions among learners? What would be interesting ways to study this problem (i.e., relations between different representation tools and different kinds of fractions knowledge)?

4. How does the strategy of learning by thinking-about-teaching contribute to these children's understanding of fractions and metacognition? Is there any difference between "thinking about teaching" and "actual peer-teaching?" How could we study that problem?

5. Why were these children good programmers? What variables within the Fractions Project contributed to it mostly? What other projects could be designed for facilitating such understanding and learning of Logo? Maybe . . . software design for teaching Logo to others?

6. What other learning, gains, or changes are possible under these unusual pedagogical conditions? Will, and how, will these intellectual gains be transfered to other learning situations?

7. Finally, this study presented a rich qualitative data that was gathered from five children *after* they completed their projects. It became clear to us that future studies should be designed to also assess the children's development *during* the project. There was a need to collect data about the participants before, during, and after the project. We realized that comparisons to control groups of various kinds (controls for Logo learning or fractions teaching strategies), and techniques for *detailed observations* and support during the children's processes of software design, could help gathering more specific information on the contribution of this approach to children's learning and cognitive development.

PART 4
ISDP RESEARCH DESIGN AND METHOD

As a result of the pilot study, a much larger and more comprehensive study was designed and implemented. This study, which provided the main body of data for this book, aimed at focusing systematically and deeply on: (a) the learning, cognitive processes, and experiences of a whole class during a 4-month period, with close examination of each student who designed, programmed, and evaluated a piece of software about fractions during that prolonged period of time; and (b) the ways in which the software design process contributed to the experimental students' learning of fractions and Logo; in other words, comparing the experimental students' learning with the learning of the students in two control classes.

The sections that follow are organized accordingly. In section 4.1., entitled "The Experimental Treatment," I shall describe my objectives and procedure for the implementation of the project in the experimental class, and the investigation of each child's cognitive and learning processes during the Instructional Software Design Project. In section 4.2., entitled "The Evaluation of the Treatment," I shall describe my objectives and procedure for the evaluation of the project: comparing, pre and post, the experimental class with the two control classes. The general concerns of this study as a whole are represented in Figure 23.

4.1. THE EXPERIMENTAL "TREATMENT": ISDP

As stated previously, the experiment aimed at interlacing students; learning of *basic rational-number concepts* and *Logo programming* in a *software design activity*. It was assumed that, through this integrative approach (means), the experimental students would learn (the ends): basic concepts of fractions, programming concepts and skills in Logo, and thinking skills such as self-management, reflection, planning, revising, and representing (which come together under the term *metalearning* in Figure 24).

For this purpose, I selected a fourth-grade classroom (N = 17) composed of 6 black students (4 girls and 2 boys), 2 Oriental students (1 girl and 1 boy), 1 part-Indian boy, and 8 white students (3 girls and 5 boys). This particular class was

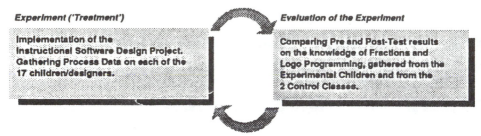

Experiment ('Treatment')

Implementation of the
Instructional Software Design Project.
Gathering Process Data on each of the
17 children/designers.

Evaluation of the Experiment

Comparing Pre and Post-Test results
on the knowledge of Fractions and
Logo Programming, gathered from the
Experimental Children and from the
2 Control Classes.

Figure 23.   The Study's Objectives and Procedure.

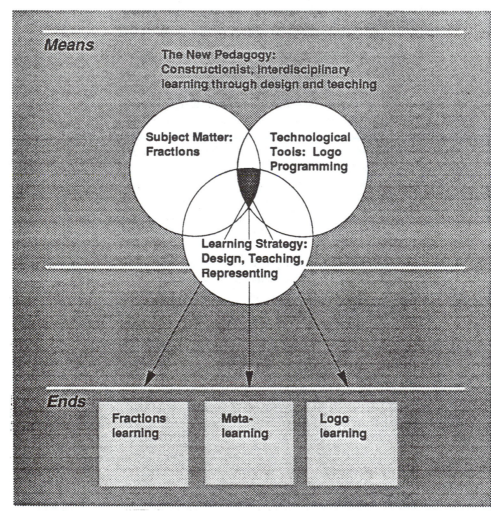

Means

The New Pedagogy:
Constructionist, interdisciplinary
learning through design and teaching

Subject Matter:
Fractions

Technological
Tools: Logo
Programming

Learning Strategy:
Design, Teaching,
Representing

Ends

Fractions
learning

Meta-
learning

Logo
learning

Figure 24.   Means/Ends.

selected for various reasons. The teacher of this class had participated in the studies I had conducted in 1985–1986, when she was teaching a fifth-grade class (e.g., Harel, 1986). She was one of the most active teachers in Project Headlight and was excited and willing to participate again, in Spring 1987 with her fourth-grade pupils, in this long and complex project. This teacher and I had enjoyed a fruitful relationship since 1985; furthermore, she believed in the main ideas embodied in ISDP, and we were both interested in working together on this project. These were major factors in the selection of this class, because it was important, in this kind of project, for the teacher to fully participate, invest a great deal of time and thought into it every day, and constantly collaborate with me on all levels, including the management of this learning environment, the extensive and intensive interaction with the pupils, data collection, and many other aspects of implementation. In addition, most of the students in the selected class were new to the school and had never used a computer until September 1986. We thought that ISDP offered an interesting situation for these pupils to learn about the computer, Logo, and fractions. The teacher was aware that "fractions and Logo are very difficult for so many students," and that "fourth-grade students do not have deep understanding of both." The software design activity, according to her, "could offer a great change" within this class's learning approach; because of her experience in similar projects the year before, she believed that "designing and programming instructional software to teach about fractions could help many of these students to overcome many learning difficulties," such as those reported by the literature on Logo and fractions.

My objectives during the experiment were twofold: (a) to *implement* the Instructional Software Design Project within the selected fourth-grade classroom; and at the same time (b) to *assess* the day-by-day cognitive processes and learning achievements that resulted from the students' designing and programming instructional software. In other words, I was involved in implementing the project, inspiring the teacher and her pupils, being there during all the working sessions, talking to students, and working with them; at the same time, I was involved in collecting data about the ongoing microgenetic processes of each individual of this class during the duration of the project.

The students collected most of the process-data for me. In order to achieve some of the goals of this study (i.e., such as the students' metalearning of various kinds), I wanted the students themselves to keep track of their own work and, much like professional software designers, to have the chance of constantly reflecting upon the different stages of development of their products. In short, I wanted the students themselves to follow, be aware of, and appreciate their own learning and design processes in the same way and at the same time as I was following and studying their processes.

The implementation of the Instructional Software Design Project meant involving students in learning fractions and programming through the teaching of fractions via the use of Logo, and in designing and programming interactive screens for teaching about fractions in their own way for a long period of time. In other words, my goal was to implement software design for students as a long-term process of creation and revision towards a complex product, in a similar way to the working methods of professional software designers; but the emphasis was on the *learning* that took place during these processes.

In order to accomplish these objectives, the students were asked to work on their Projects for one hour a day, four times a week, for four months. This group of students designed instructional fractions software in addition to their regular math curriculum. Throughout the project I was a source of inspiration, a facilitator, an intervener (question-asker), a resource, a manager of the learning environment, and sometimes a teacher (conducting small sessions with teacher and students). Eventually, part of the management and facilitating was taken over by the teacher and her students (see also Harel, 1986). Several of the short (5–15 minute) classroom presentations or discussions (called *Focus Sessions*) were initiated and conducted by the researcher or by the teacher. These discussions and instruction were initiated according to the students' needs, problems, and concerns, without any strict preestablished plan.

For both educational and research purposes, I wanted to create a learning environment in which design, or instructional design, as well as programming processes, would be integrated and overt; to create an environment in which metacognitive and metaconceptual thinking were facilitated and explicit to the greatest possible extent (i.e., very much in the spirit of Perkins's, 1986, *Knowledge as Design* approach). Finally, besides implementing the project, I also had in mind a set of objectives for the assessment of the cognitive and learning processes of the individuals (i.e., I wanted to gather information for the individual case studies). I wanted to examine the processes involved in learning through software design, both on *individual* and *classroom* levels; and to create records of the design and cognitive processes that would benefit the *child,* the *teacher,* and the *researcher* at the same time.

I followed and observed the software designers *every day* while they were working on their programs. Besides these observations, protocols of the students' processes were gathered by videotaping individual students while they were working at the computers and participating in the classroom discussions. In addition, online, daily records of the design, programming, and learning processes were kept *by the students themselves.* After each working period they saved their daily working files from the computer in a special diskette, which resulted in approximately 60 online files per child. Every day, before and after each working session, the software designers' daily ideas, plans, story-boards, and reflections were written *by them* in their Designer's Notebooks. Their daily computer files, the things they wrote in their Designer's Notebooks, the teacher's comments, and the researcher's daily observations and conversations with the students constructed a "holistic" picture of each child's progress in creating his or her product.

The objectives of the Designer's Notebooks were twofold. First of all, they were created for *educational purposes:* to encourage metacognition such as self-management, reflection, and planning, and to foster students' screen designs and reflections in *writing*. Secondly, the Designer's Notebooks were created for *research purposes:* to accumulate records on each designer's process, plans, drawings, changes, problems, and so on. These notebooks included such headings as: "My Plans For Today," with design grids and writing space; "Problems I Had Today," for the students' reflections and ideas for changes; "My Script," with story-boards; "Notes," and so on.

4.2. THE EVALUATION OF THE EXPERIMENTAL TREATMENT: COMPARING THE EXPERIMENTAL CLASS WITH TWO CONTROL CLASSES

The general aim of the evaluation was to find out whether software design could be considered as a process, or tool, as a means of learning concepts and skills in several domains at the same time. Within this context, instructional software design was used, among other things, for integrating the learning of fractions and Logo. The evaluation of the experimental treatment made it possible to go beyond the documentation of the learning and cognitive processes of the individuals in the experimental class, and to find additional and more systematic evidence of whether or not these software designers had mastered the domains integrated into the project.

Moreover, the Software Design Project was *not* taught to all the students of the experimental class in a unified way. On the contrary, its structure was open-ended, and resulted in many *different artifacts* (see also Harel, 1986). It was therefore very important to test the experimental class before and after the experiment was conducted, in order to find out whether the students had mastered the specific concepts in fractions and Logo, or had only found "fun and excitement" in an unusual project. My study attempted to go even further: I wanted, not only to demonstrate that the experimental students were able to *master* these subjects, but to show how, by designing software for teaching fractions, they might find different ways to work with problems given to them *within* these domains.

A comparative study was conducted with the experimental class by means of two other classes. In order to gather information about the growth of the experimental class *as a whole,* and to understand the effects of the Software Design Project on the experimental class' learning of fractions and Logo, these three classes ($n = 51$) were pretested and interviewed on their knowledge of fractions and Logo during the month of January. After this, one class ($n = 17$), was provided with the Instructional Software Design Project (the experimental treatment described above), which meant intervening in the learning and teaching strategies for the fractions and Logo programming curricula. The two other

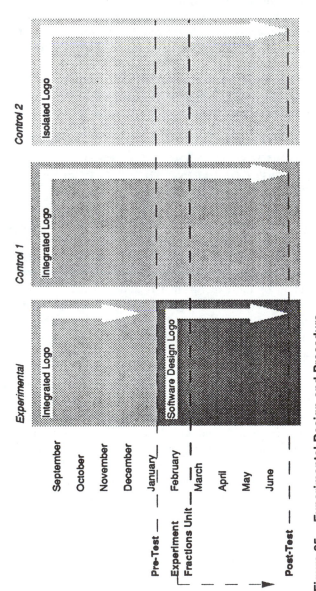

Figure 25. Experimental Design and Procedure.

98

classes ($n = 18$; $n = 16$), were *not* provided with the experimental treatment, and continued to study math and programming in their traditional way. This procedure is shown in Figure 25.

This diagram shows the different Logo learning approaches used in the three selected classes before and during the experiment (these three approaches to learning Logo will be described in the following sections). It also shows the experimental design. The three classes were pretested during January; they began their "Fractions Unit" (their regular math curriculum) in March, and worked on it until the end of April; the Fractions Software Design experiment was worked on by one class only, and lasted from the end of February to the middle of June; the posttests and interviews were conducted during the last three weeks of June. Via the assessment of the control students' knowledge of fractions and Logo, and the pre- and posttests and interviews with the selected 51 pupils, the software designers were compared with other students who had learned fractions and Logo and (according to the school's tests) had also mastered their concepts, though not through software design.

4.2.1. Description of the Pupils

The three classes were selected for several reasons related to their (a) unified grade level and school, (b) unified mathematics learning approaches, and (c) various Logo learning approaches. These reasons are further described below.

1. Grade level and school, ethnicity, and gender. All the selected subjects were fourth graders from the same inner-city public school in one of Boston's lowest SES communities. According to the City of Boston, these three classes were considered advanced work classes (A.W.C). Two of these were "regular A.W.C.," and the third was a "bilingual A.W.C." These fourth-grade students had not been part of an A.W.C. in third grade, and were selected to be part of the fourth-grade A.W.C. according to the following: (a) the students' evaluations and grades given by their teachers in third grade; (b) their final grades in the City of Boston's Public Schools' examination in math, reading, social studies, etc., at the end of the third grade; (c) their parents' motivation to place them in advanced work classes, since all parents had to fill applications and attend interviews after the students' third-grade teacher had recommended that their students apply for A.W.C.

The three selected classes were almost identical in their proportion of boys and girls: the first class (experimental) consisted of 8 girls and 9 boys; the second (control-1), of 11 girls and 7 boys; and the third (control-2), of 9 girls and 7 boys. In terms of their ethnicity, the experimental class was very similar to the control 1 class: the first (experimental), consisted of 6 black, 2 Oriental, 1 part-Indian, and 8 white students; the second (control-1), consisted of 8 black, 3 Oriental, 6 white students, and 1 Hispanic child. However, the third class, the Spanish bilingual

A.W.C, consisted of 16 Hispanic or part-Hispanic boys and girls. Since the regular mathematics and programming curricula and testing were conducted in *English only* and *regularly* in all three classes, it was assumed that the fact that one of these classes was Spanish bilingual would not affect the results of this particular study. The analysis did not attempt to focus on trends related to gender and ethnicity in the results of this study. The results of the pretests indicated that all the students were on a very similar level of understanding fractions and Logo before the experiment started.

The results from the fractions pretests were also compared with those of the students in the Behr et al. national study (1983). This comparison showed that the three selected classes were not very advanced in their knowledge of fractions; therefore the students in the present study would provide us with sufficient evidence for generalizations and conclusions about low-, medium-, and high-level students, and not just A.W.C pupils.

2. Mathematics learning approaches. All the subjects studied math every day and during the same class period. Each of the classes' teachers taught a math group: one teacher taught the *low math group,* another the *medium group,* and the third the *high group* (i.e., the low-level students from the three selected classrooms studied together, as did the medium- and high-level students). The math classes of all levels were handled in a traditional fashion, where the teacher taught and the students completed assignments and exercises from given worksheets, and were usually tested once a week. The three teachers (all females—two white and one Hispanic) had received their teacher training in the United States, had been teaching for several years in this public school, and were very similar in their teaching techniques and procedures. All three were quite informal in their relationships with their pupils. They tended to be creative and tried as much as possible to provide their pupils with small projects in the course of their teaching. They shared their curricula, updated each other on their pupils' progress and difficulties and, according to them, because of the Boston Public School Referenced Tests, they covered almost the same material in most subjects, especially in math, writing, and reading. They continued to do the same while they were teaching the fractions unit, which lasted from March through April 1987.

The three teachers tested their pupils at the beginning of the year, and also considered their pupils' math-test results of the previous year, so as to divide the pupils into *math groups.* The division of the pupils into particular math groups is shown in Table 3.

This division of the students into three math levels quite consistently corresponded with the students' results in the pretests (e.g., all the low-math students scored low in the pretests, and the high-math ones scored high). This division will therefore be used for comparing the students' learning and understanding levels as well as their scores in the various posttests.

Table 3.   Math Levels Three Classes.

Experimental		Control 1		Control 2	
Low Math	N = 4	Low Math	N = 5	Low Math	N = 5
Medium Math	N = 5	Medium Math	N = 6	Medium Math	N = 5
High Math	N = 8	High Math	N = 7	High Math	N = 6
Total in Class	N = 17	Total in Class	N = 18	Total in Class	N = 16

3. Logo learning approaches. The three selected classes began to learn Logo programming during September of 1986 (four months before the research had begun). Three Logo learning approaches were assessed and compared for this study. For this purpose, I named them *Integrated-Logo, Isolated-Logo,* and *Software-Design-Logo.*

In the beginning, two Integrated-Logo classes and one Isolated-Logo class were selected. During the experiment, one of the Integrated-Logo classes switched into the Software-Design-Logo approach (Software-Design-Logo was only one aspect of the Treatment). The two other classes remained constant in their Logo learning approaches (as Integrated-Logo and Isolated-Logo) throughout the experiment, acting as two different Control classes. In this context, it is important to note that all three classes remained constant (between the pre- and posttests) in their regular mathematics curriculum. There were no changes of any kind in the traditional Fractions Unit. However, the students from the experimental class thought about fractions, designed and programmed screens about fractions, and discussed fractions with one another during the Instructional Software Design Experiment. *No didactic teaching of any additional information was given during their software working sessions.* It was therefore possible to investigate exactly how much the experimental students were able to learn by their construction of an interactive teaching device about fractions. The general characteristics of each approach of learning and teaching Logo programming, the reasons for their existence and for naming them thus are described in the following paragraphs.

Integrated-Logo. Two Integrated-Logo classes were originally selected for this study. They were part of MIT's Project Headlight. In general, students in the Integrated-Logo classes programmed from 45 to 60 minutes a day, five days a week, in an open area next to their classes. The teachers of the Integrated-Logo classes who were participating in Project Headlight had been and were being trained by an MIT staff (see Section 1.2). They implemented a project-oriented approach toward programming, which meant that no worksheets or exercises were given by the teachers. Instead, students worked on several Logo programming projects that were integrated into a specific curriculum, such as science or literature. It was the first year in Project Headlight for these two classes, and their first year in learning how to program or use the computer. Therefore, it was assumed that, at the point of starting the experiment, their programming skills would be equal to, and almost as low as, those of the third Isolated-Logo class (which is described below). The Integrated-Logo teachers did not grade their students in Logo, since each child's work was different from the others'. The teachers used a "soft" evaluation system for the students' project, usually relying on their level of involvement in their work, their investment of time and thought, or their amount of learning new Logo skills.

Isolated-Logo. One Isolated-Logo class was selected for this study. Its pupils, like those in the Integrated-Logo classes, began to program in Logo for the first time in September 1986. However, they used the computer only for 30 to 45 minutes a week, in the schools' computer room. The pupils in the Isolated-Logo class neither integrated their learning of programming into the curriculum nor worked on meaningful "projects." Instead, they learned how to program by completing short programming exercises and assignments given by the computerroom coordinator. This Isolated-Logo class was learning Logo as part of a "computer literacy" program—the most common approach used today in elementary schools across the United States. Their teacher was not involved in the computer sessions, which were handled by the computer-room coordinator at all times. The students were graded by their teacher according to the exercises they had completed.

Software-Design-Logo. This Logo learning and teaching approach was one aspect of the Experiment as a whole; it was strongly inspired by, and very similar in nature to, the Integrated-Logo described above. Software-Design-Logo took Integrated-Logo one step further. The major differences between Integrated-Logo and Software-Design-Logo were in the purpose, structure, meaning, characteristics, and length of the "projects."

Software-Design-Logo consisted in students' using Logo for the purpose of designing and programming instructional software. It involved the students in programming something for others rather than just for themselves. It required that the students think about a target audience and construct a program that would work for another, even younger, person. The Integrated-Logo projects (in Project Headlight) usually lasted from a few days to three weeks, whereas the Software-Design-Logo Project lasted four months. It was assumed that the length and complexity of the project would be an important factor in students' learning how to reflect on, revise, modify, or maintain their programs. The students in Software-Design-Logo had their minds on other issues besides "a program that works." They worked on their project while thinking about other people, about screen designs for *teaching,* about *interactivity* and *feedback*—much like professional software designers. In short, they were involved in a rich, meaningful, and complex task, working towards designing and programming a "real" product for "real" people.

4.2.2. The Evaluation Objectives and Questions

Many research questions could have been raised concerning the experimental treatment, since it involved so many variables, as well as a very integrative and complex pedagogical situation. However, for the purpose of this study, my objectives and questions for the experimental treatment's evaluation were narrowed down into two main sets of assessments: (a) an assessment of the experimental students' knowledge of basic fraction concepts; and (b) an assessment of the experimental students' knowledge of Logo programming concepts and skills. The experimental treatment interlaced the experimental students' learning of fractions and Logo with the designing and programming of instructional software. It was assumed that the treatment probably would change the experimental students' approaches and abilities in their learning of fractions and Logo, and that there would be a smaller change in those of the control students'. Therefore the research questions were divided into *two groups:* The first group explored the experimental students' learning and understanding of specific *fractions* concepts, and compared them with the control students' learning of fractions; the second explored the experimental students' learning and understanding of specific *Logo programming* skills, and compared them with the control students' learning of Logo. These questions had been designed to provide detailed documentation on the progress made by the experimental students in comparison with the individual control students. In other words, they did not attempt to document the individual learning processes and cognitive development of each child from the control classes in as much detail as for those of the experimental class.

The questions related to the experimental students' *knowledge of fractions* were the following: Would they be generally better at translating fractional representations? More specifically, what type of translation would they master more readily in relation to the students in the control classes (i.e., would the experimental students grow more proficient than the others at translating picture representation into symbols, words into pictures, symbols into words, pictures into pictures, etc?)? The theoretical framework for this last question on translations of fractional representations was mainly based on the work done by Behr, Lesh, Post, and Silver (1983), and by Lesh, Landau, and Hamilton (1983) for their NSF "Rational Number Concepts Project." Furthermore, would the experimental students relate to fractions in a more personal way, be better at talking about fractions, defining a fraction, and describing fractions in real-life situations? Would they be better at representing fractions by using real-life objects such as blocks, pegs, rods, or play dough? At manipulating these objects and answering questions while using them? At basic fractional operations, such as addition, subtraction, multiplication, or division? On the whole, would the students who learned fractions in a nonconventional way, and in a rare pedagogical situation, also get higher scores on the regular public school tests? More specifically, would the students who spent a lot of time "playing" with fractions at their own pace, and constructing their own representations of fractions, be able to pass the school's or the city's regular exams?

In order to compare the experimental students with the control students on their *learning of Logo programming,* I attempted to answer a number of questions. These questions first of all explored the differences between the experimental class and control class 1, since both classes spent the same amount of time programming every day and were both part of Project Headlight. Secondly, they explored the differences between the experimental class and control class 2—the latter using the computer much less frequently, as part of the school's conventional computer literacy program. The questions were the following: Would the experimental students use, know, and understand many programming commands and operations? Would they be better at understanding, implementing, debugging, and modifying someone else's programming code? At understanding and using the Logo REPEAT command? At understanding and using variables and inputs? Finally, would they be better at constructing codes for someone else's design or picture?

4.3. DATA COLLECTION AND ANALYSIS

As stated previously, my inquiry combined (a) an *educational intervention,* the design and implementation of The Instructional Software Design Project; and (b) a systematic *investigation* of that project. The investigation of the project integrated several research techniques: the creation of *individual case studies* about the processes of software design of the experimental students; and the *pre- and posttests* that compared all the experimental software designers with students who learned fractions and Logo according to different pedagogical methods.

A large amount of data was gathered during the course of the study. In the following chapters (Chapter II and III), the research questions will be answered in two ways: through describing in detail the step-by-step progress (the microgenetic processes) of one child from the experimental class (Chapter II); and through comparing the experimental class as a whole with the control classes (Chapter III).

I will describe my data-collection and analysis techniques in the context of each chapter (Chapter II and III). In general, qualitative and quantitative data were used for the case study, and for comparing the experimental students with the control students.

In neither chapter will I place an emphasis on microcausality, in other words, there will be no strong and direct correlations between an "X" aspect or variable of the treatment and an "X¹" aspect of the result. This is because the present study describes a rare pedagogical situation in which learning was considered to be a total activity; all the different kinds of learning were incorporated into each other, with emphasis on the contribution of each to all.

In Chapter II, entitled "Debbie's Case," this point will become clearer. The reader will see the profound interaction between all the different facets of Debbie's learning throughout the project and will also realize that Debbie's learning processes were often too complex for it to be possible to do more than speculate on a specific and discrete cause for each effect or outcome. In Chapter III, entitled "Results from Pre- and Posttests," I shall analyze the Logo and fractions results separately. This may create the impression of a microcausal-type investigation, but the reader must remember that it is quite artificial and was done strictly for clearness of presentation.

(Jacqueline Karaaslanian Photography)

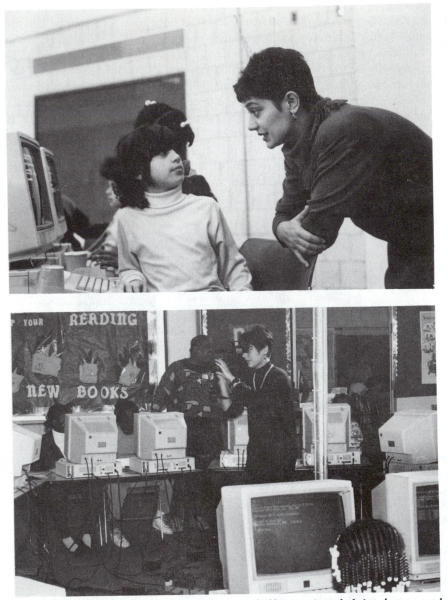

Data Collection through Structured and Unstructured Interviews, and through Ongoing Observations (Jacqueline Karaaslanian Photography)

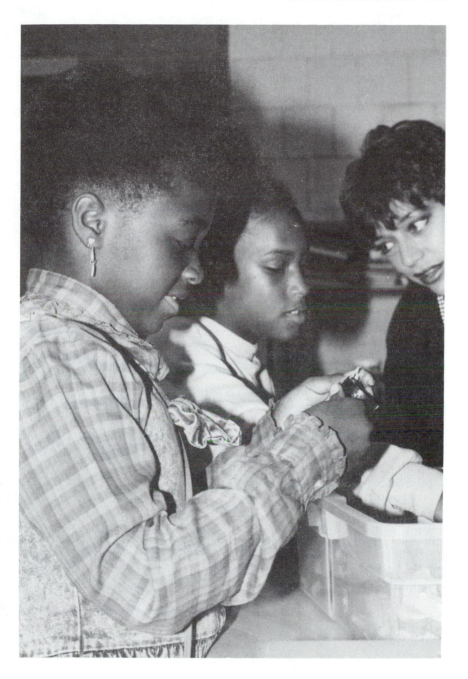

Chapter II
Debbie's Case

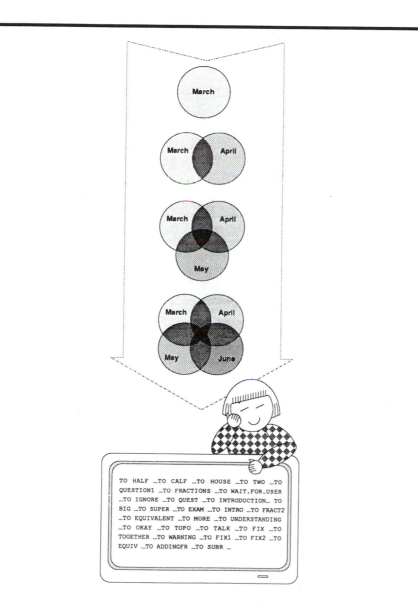

TO HALF ...TO CALF ...TO HOUSE ...TO TWO ...TO
QUESTION1 ...TO FRACTIONS ...TO WAIT.FOR.USER
...TO IGNORE ...TO QUEST ...TO INTRODUCTION... TO
BIG ...TO SUPER ...TO EXAM ...TO INTRO ...TO FRACT2
...TO EQUIVALENT ...TO MORE ...TO UNDERSTANDING
...TO OKAY ...TO TOPO ...TO TALK ...TO FIX ...TO
TOGETHER ...TO WARNING ...TO FIX1 ...TO FIX2 ...TO
EQUIV ...TO ADDINGFR ...TO SUBR ...

INTRODUCTION

The following case study describes the evolution of fractions and Logo knowledge in a 9-year-old girl I shall call "Debbie." The case will illustrate the advantages of the ISDP approach for an individual's learning. This approach was found powerful even in a domain that is known to be difficult and boring to many children: fractions. During ISDP, these "cold" and "depersonalized things" became personal and comprehendable to Debbie, one of the 17 inner-city fourth graders who participated in the project. Debbie was self-motivated throughout ISDP and created learning goals for herself in a domain that originally was a nonpreferred domain for her. However, throughout the project, and she found ways to be playful with fractions, she developed close relationship with them, and therefore turned them into personal entities—into fun things to know, learn, and understand.

WHO IS DEBBIE?

Debbie was an overweight and socially isolated girl who lived with her two working parents and a younger sister in a small apartment in Roxbury, an impoverished, black ghetto in Boston. She rarely participated in class and usually answered questions only when directly asked. She usually distanced herself from her peers, both in the classroom and in the school yard. Perhaps because of her excess weight, she never participated in schoolyard games and usually stood alone or, occasionally, chatted with one other girl. Debbie usually looked sleepy or bored in class. Physically, Debbie could be within inches of a school activity, but after observing her, I realized that, emotionally, she felt miles away. Her unhappiness was almost palpable, and her resentment made working with her difficult.

I had no initial plan to devote particular "research attention" to Debbie's involvement in the project, and even by the end of the study she was only one of several children I had accumulated notes on for in-depth case studies. Other children were more 'natural' candidates—more enthusiastic, more articulate, more skilled and successful in their software design and learning. But in analyzing the video data I had about her (see Harel, 1990b), together with my written notes, her Logo files and designer's notebook, I became more aware of the project's significance for her, and I grew to realize the many interesting developmental aspects in the evolution of her mathematical thinking about Logo and fractions that had occurred.

During the first 10 days, while Debbie's peers were getting started on the project, Debbie kept writing in her designer's notebook: *"Tomorrow I'll start my Fraction Project."* Unlike the other children, who eagerly said, *"Come see what I did yesterday!"* when I entered the classroom, Debbie did not let me see anything she accomplished and maintained a bristly silence. At first, she acted skeptical about her ability to handle the project. She complained, with a note of desperation, *"Do I really have to do this?"* *"What do you really want me to do?"* Her teacher told me this was Debbie's regular attitude. Debbie, she said, was *"a slow worker, who finds new ideas and assignments difficult to understand . . . an average student, with good writing skills but relatively low skills in math, definitely not the star of the class."* She also said Debbie had *"difficulties with some social aspects of classroom life."*

The best summary of "who Debbie is" is in fact provided by her own reflections in writing. On March 31, when she was well into the project, Debbie stopped working on her program; she left her Fractions Logo page, opened a new Logo page, and wrote two very personal poems. The same day she told me: *"Logo is good for many things, even for animated poems about myself."* In these poems Debbie confirmed my first impression that she was a depressed child. Originally, I felt very uncomfortable about presenting these two highly personal poems as part of my study. However, since they are worth more than a thousand of my own words about Debbie, I finally decided to quote them here.

She wrote her two poems using the following Logo procedures:

Poem No.1:

```
TO              NO
HT PR [This life is stupid to live in, nobody to love or care for you!
No one to drive you places and someone to see that you don't get hurt.
No one, no one to care or worry about you!]
HT SETC 1+RANDOM 14 REPEAT 20 [REPEAT 4 [RT 90 FD 30] RT 18]
END
```

Poem No.2:

```
TO              GROW
HT PR [Every day I grow and grow. In every way I see my self grow.
I grow to see other things, I grow to like, I grow to hate.
No matter what I see I grow!]
SETC 1+RANDOM 14 PD REPEAT 15 [REPEAT 360 [FD .2 RT 2] RT 20]
END
```

The structure of the two procedures is very similar. Each of them includes hiding the Turtle (HT), writing a statement about herself (PR [. . . . .]), then creating a simple animation. I interpret the first poem (or procedure) as Debbie's reflection on her anger about her "stupid" and lonely life (i.e., "This life is stupid to live in. . . No one to drive you places or someone to see that you don't get hurt. No one, no one to care about you!"). The animation in this procedure is a design of a circle of squares that appears in one color, and is selected randomly by the computer as one reads the poem. The second poem or procedure can be interpreted in two ways. First, as a child's reflection on growing (in age) in general. Secondly, and more specific to Debbie's problem, as a child's reflection on growing fat. The animation in the second poem, together with my knowledge of Debbie's awkward appearance, convince me that, in this second poem, Debbie was expressing her feelings about her excessive weight. The second animation is a circle that grows and grows and grows as one reads the poem on the screen. Because of her particular personality and the type of relationship we had established at the time, I felt that it was inappropriate to question Debbie about these two poem procedures.

In *The Second Self,* Sherry Turkle (1984, pp. 93–136) describes the case of Tanya, who, through her "world of words," established a strong relationship with the computer, and then, through the computer, established relationships with her peers and teachers (pp. 122–126). Like Debbie, Tanya felt comfortable with the computer when she used it for writing, for expressing something personal and painful. This, Turkle writes, was part of a process of "making things her own."

Turkle observed many children and adults using the computer as an "evocative object" that encouraged very deep self-reflections (Turkle, 1984; Turkle & Papert, 1990). Evocative objects, says Turkle, provoke a discourse in everyday life on topics that are usually more compartmentalized:

> The computer sits on many boarders; it is a formal system that can be taken up in a way that is not separate from the experience of the self. As such, it may evoke unconscious memories [feelings and emotions] of objects [or events] that lie for the child in the uncertain zone between self and not-self. . . Psychoanalytic theorists call these objects 'transitional' because they are thought to mediate between the child's closely bonded relationship with the mother and his or her capacity to develop relationships with other people who will be experienced as separate, autonomous beings. (Turkle, 1984, pp. 118–119)

Debbie also seemed to appropriate the computer—and the project—through self-expression. The fact that she could use the same object to comment on her life and feelings and to design instructional materials in mathematics seems to have strengthened her ties to mathematics, the project, and the people involved in the project.

The first evidence for Debbie's appropriation of the project occurred after the first 10 days of avoiding any overt work on the project. At that time, something seems to have 'clicked' for her. She became deeply engaged in her design and programming work and maintained this interest and involvement throughout, to the end. Why? What was the real source of her learning? I cannot isolate the direct contribution of particular aspects of the environment, but can share my intuitions and interpretations about which things contributed to this change (the reasons for this argument about the need for "holistic" style of data collection and interpretation are explained in greater detail in Harel & Papert, 1990). In the case of Debbie, four major conjectures presented themselves:

1. Debbie was involved in "learning through thinking about teaching." By designing instructional software, Debbie could experiment with social roles—particularly that of teacher or mentor to a younger child—that she was too shy to experiment with in ordinary human relations. She developed ideas about teaching and explaining which she applied, mainly through her program's instructional sentences, in a direct, sometimes stern manner. This greatly contrasted her usual passive and isolative stance.
2. Debbie seemed to have experienced genuine intellectual excitement with fractions. She appeared to develop personal relationships with fractions—an experience a regular math curriculum could not have offered to her. Well into the project, she commented that she was *"thinking about fractions all the time."* Her work and general improvement in math are further evidence of this.
3. During the project, Debbie began to emerge from her social cocoon. She came to be known for her good ideas and enjoyed feeling creative and successful. Other children wanted to see or play with her software, and gave her positive responses: *"I love it, Debbie!"* or *"This is fresh!"* Other students would also ask her to teach them how to do things: *"How did you ever make these colors change?"*
4. Debbie was involved in "total learning." With ISDP, we did not expect to transform Debbie's personality and social life. However, we did discover that the project helped Debbie make several important changes in her approach to learning. She worked on all fronts—emotional, social, and academic—during the project. She moved, in terms of objective pre- and posttest measures, from the low end of the medium-math level to well above the average high-math level, and joined a high-math level group the following year. Her accomplishments in Logo programming caused her to be "discovered" by her peers and teachers, and she often received positive comments about her work from them. After the completion of the project, her teacher remarked: *"I realized her rather sophisticated programming skills, her excellent ideas for teaching [fractional concepts], and her interesting representations. . . I never thought of Debbie as someone who was able to do all these wonderful things."*

In retrospect, Debbie's case is an interesting one. Yet, Debbie did not have the "ideal" personality for participating in a type of an experimental investigation that required a great deal of collaboration with the researcher and the continual sharing of ideas, thoughts, knowledge, designs, and programming problems. Interaction with her was sometimes difficult, and I often had to play games with her in order to elicit a meaningful response. Children like Debbie are often ignored by researchers in favor of children whose personalities and attitudes make them easier or more enjoyable to work with. I have chosen to devote this chapter to some parts of Debbie's case, not only because of its intrinsic interest and relevancy to the field, but because of the general importance of gathering data on children who are socially and academically at risk.

In addition, Debbie is an interesting case in the context of Piaget's theory of cognitive development—more specifically, his theory of the underlying patterns of thought during the different stages of cognitive development. In her processes of thinking, designing, programming, and learning, Debbie moved according to Piaget's progression scheme, both throughout the whole project and within each stage of her software design.

In her thinking and actions during the project, Debbie moved back and forth from being attentive to limited and static amounts of information, to considering several aspects of a situation simultaneously; she moved from concrete thought to more formal thought; she moved from rigid thinking that focused, for example, on one dimension of a programming problem, to more fluent and dynamic thinking related to several dimensions of her computer programs (we shall see this aspect through comparing her work during March, to the ways in which she later reorganized her software and programmed new superprocedures during June). She shifted from narrow and rigid actions to more flexible actions, so that she could grasp several aspects of a situation at once; and though she began by constructing very simple plans, designs, and screens, she later created more complex plans, designs, and screens, moving back and forth from simplicity to complexity. In general, Debbie learned to "break away," to free herself of rigidity, and acquired more flexibility within the project's length and breadth (across the board)—in her translating and combining representations of fractions, in her Logo programming techniques, in her planning and reflecting in the Designer's Notebook, and in her attitude towards the project as a whole.

Another theme that will be highlighted is related to the differences between the Vygotskian and Piagetian theories of learning. Debbie's learning suggests a combination of both. In other words, there were several situations in which Debbie learned from her peers or from the adults around her, imitated her friends' ideas and designs. She was also affected by my questions and interviews, and was strongly inspired by her culture. Nevertheless, side by side with those situations, she also spontaneously came up with her own ideas independent of her friends, or shifted from rigid to more flexible thought without the help of an adult. These two different aspects of learning (i.e., imitating as opposed to inventing, or being guided by an adult as opposed to being guided by her own intentions), created an interesting learning pattern that repeated itself in Debbie's work throughout the project. Vygotsky's perspective on the role of language in children's learning and thinking will also be emphasized throughout Debbie's case.

Finally, since Debbie is a strong case for Piaget's constructivist learning, for the importance of social-cultural learning, and for understanding the nature of learning in constructionist computer-rich environments—I see this case as a strong model for Papert's Constructionism.

THE DATA COLLECTED FOR THE CASE

Most of the data on Debbie's day-by-day microdevelopment were gathered in the same way as for the whole experimental class. They included the following:

Pre- and posttests and interviews. All children in Debbie's class, along with children in two control classes, were administered a battery of tests and were interviewed before and after the project (these are described in detail in Harel, 1988). Some of Debbie's results will be discussed in this case study, but since it is impossible here to give an adequate description of all the test instruments involved and their results, they will be described in an illustrative way (again, see Harel, 1988).

Process data. In preparing this case study, I had access to all of Debbie's LogoWriter programming files as well as to her writings and drawings in the designer's notebook. LogoWriter files include all Logo procedures saved each working day, and the designer's notebook includes written notes, designs, and hand-drawn plans. These had almost daily entries, covering the months of March, April, May, and June.

Video data. Debbie was videotaped several times during the period of ISDP—on several occasions when she was working at the computer, and at other times with her whole class in classroom discussions. These videotapes were an important component in my personal observations, since I was involved in many aspects of classroom and computer activities and was collecting information on several children (see Harel, 1990b).

Researcher's notes. In addition to all the above, I took notes on Debbie's progress and concerns on certain days, and occasionally conducted short interviews (in the form of informal conversations), particularly when something captured my interest, or when she asked me questions.

Information from the teacher. On several occasions I interviewed the teacher of the experimental class about Debbie. Most of our conversations were informal, taking place during lunch in the teacher's room, or in her classroom when her pupils were not present. Through these interviews, I gathered information about Debbie's background, ability, character, and progress. No specific format was used in these interviews. Most of our conversations were short and consisted in my asking the teacher questions such as: *"Tell me about Debbie,"* or *"What do you think about Debbie's last screen?"* or *"Why do you think Debbie was behaving this way yesterday?"* or *"Did you work with Debbie on using a* REPEAT *in her Half Fraction procedure?"* The teacher was interviewed again after reading the completed case (in Harel, 1988), and her comments are incorporated into this work and into the videotape I produced about Debbie (Harel, 1990b).

THE STRUCTURE OF DEBBIE'S CASE

Debbie's case, as a whole, is fascinating, very long, and quite complex (see Harel, 1988, pp. 76–244, 315–325, and 329–360). The exerpts of the case that are presented here include the information gathered on Debbie's processes during the month of March, and some parts from April, May, and June. The case is presented according to the *natural segmentations* of her own software design, construction, and modifications processes.

Often, Debbie was aware of these segmentations and made them explicit in her Designer's Notebook. For example: *"Today I'll finish my old fractions project. I'll start my new one about equivalent fractions."* Or *"I finished my House Scene. It works. I'll start my Scene about Thirds tomorrow."* However, as her program grew long and complex, her plans and reflections in the Designer's Notebook became complex as well. Because she attended to several aspects of her software simultaneously, her breaks, or segmentations, were not as obvious anymore. The following are Debbie's stage sequence in organizing and implementing her work.

March

1. GETTING STARTED WITH ONE-HALF (Segment Themes: half as prototypical fraction; representation of the half of the entire computer screen; vertical symmetry schema; "only the shaded, right side, is a fraction," thus, the undesignated left side is not a half, "it's nothing." During this phase, Debbie also switches to culturally general approach of drawing many polygons divided into parts; we see her aesthetic dissatisfaction with an overly busy screen, and her return to a 'home base' or an 'entry space'—i.e., working on halves only.)

2. MULTIPLE REPRESENTATIONS FOR HALVES: A FIRST STEP (Segment Themes: 'halves' are synonymous with 'fraction,' and 'fractions' are only on 'the right side of a vertically bisected object;' she still uses halves as her 'entry space;' overcomes vertical bisection/right-sided notion, and makes this a subject for her instructional software; includes a triangle— through collaborative learning; rhyming procedure names; language interest

as bridge into programming, but later she abandons for functional naming when she acquires feeling of safety and when complexity of her own work demands it; 'randomming' colors as instructional design consideration. . . Debbie gets social recognition as bonus; a model for project-based learning and children's revision of their own work.)

3. THE HOUSE SCENE: "FRACTIONS ARE EVERYWHERE" (or, THE SECOND STEP IN MULTIPLE REPRESENTATIONS FOR HALVES) (Segment Themes: integrating formal and real-world knowledge; pushing the limits: trying to mathematize a real-world scene into an equation, but gets units confused; thinking about fractions all the time; adding fractions assumes equal units—this is the deep structure beneath common denominator algorithm; using a piece of cultural knowledge in a personal way: PU-Home for chunking Logo code; understanding idiosyncratic and irelegant spaghetti code from the inside; evolution of Debbie's relationships to researcher; increasing fluency of understanding: showing one wheel as one-half of two wheels; high-level design considerations: March 30 entry—evolution of planning skills; emergence of modular design in Logo programming.)

4. TWO-THIRDS: "ONE OF THE FRACTIONS THAT TEACHERS USE MOST OFTEN AS EXAMPLES FOR TEACHING THEIR STUDENTS" (Segment Themes: picking up on an old plan; the FROG; playing with ideas; representing equivalence; seeing self as teacher and role playing; programming a quiz—increasing confidence.)

5. THE FIRST ATTEMPT TO CONNECT THE PARTS: CREATING A SUPERPROCEDURE (Themes: following internally generated and not externally imposed needs; discovering the 'wait-for-user trick'; reordering the part and interpretation; paradox: she explicitly assumes stance of designer, but her design criteria for abandoning chronological order indicate integration of knowledge and loss of original sensitivity.)

The month of March was Debbie's long initial period of investigating halves and their representations. Halves were the first fraction Debbie knew about. Unlike others in her class, Debbie worked exclusively with them for an entire month! We shall see how her understanding of halves and fractions in general evolved in the context of her development of software for teaching third graders about these concepts. Section 2.3., for example, describes Debbie's "House Scene," which marked a qualitative leap in her fluency of expression within the medium as well as in the understanding of the domain of fractions and the relation of symbolic expression to real-world objects. Section 2.4. shows Debbie breaking away from halves into a plan to teach about thirds.

The month of March was also Debbie's long initial period of investigating many "Logo programming tricks." During March, for example, she realized the need to create a procedure for the computer to choose randomly the colors of her graphics on the computer screen. She also found new ways to move the Turtle on the screen and became a fluent code generator. In Section 2.5., for example, we examine Debbie's first use of a superprocedure, which built on a self-directed move towards greater modularity throughout the month of March.

. . .

HIGHLIGHTS FROM DEBBIE'S PROCESSES DURING APRIL, MAY, & JUNE

April

6. CREATING THE SOFTWARE'S OPENING SCREENS: DEBBIE, RALLY, AND TERRY (Debbie as middle-out thinker; emphasis on computer as interactive device; relative sophistication in thinking about users; Debbie borrows graphical ideas from Rally; Debbie cuts her losses and quits programming Front-Intro—she returns to her own style of an introduction after experimenting with a Rally-styled one.)

7. DEBBIE'S FIRST SOFTWARE EVALUATION WITH BIBBY, A THIRD GRADER (Learning through teaching is not really the point, keeping an idealized learner in mind is—it's an active way to externalize and treat one's own conceptual difficulties; but session shows Debbie's expertise in shifting control back to herself a passive-aggressive personality.)

8. CREATING A NEW LOGO PAGE, "FRACT2": DEBBIE MAINTAINS STRONG RELATIONSHIPS BETWEEN NEW AND OLD KNOWLEDGE IN HER SOFTWARE AS WELL AS IN HER MIND (Growth of metalevel awareness of her project; acceptance of need for continual revision; emergence of a top-down method: fluency of styles (cf. earlier exclusive middle-out); combining new and old knowledge; Debbie struggles with GETPAGE and is sarcastic with computer; discourse on attitudes towards problem solving 'personified' as a computer.)

9. DESIGNING REPRESENTATIONS FOR EQUIVALENT FRACTIONS (works in parallel; uses Logo pages for some modularity; carries over early fixation on halves to understanding and representing many other fractions— this makes her feel confident about understanding any fractions; shows considerable excitement over concepts.)

May

9.1. IMPLEMENTING ONE REPRESENTATION FOR EQUIVALENT FRACTIONS (First mention of adding and subtracting fractions; note geometry knowledge, e.g., diving square into eighths, extensive use of Cartesian coordinates; modularizing her program using PU HOME; use of aesthetic judgment in picking colors.)

9.2.   ANOTHER SCREEN FOR EQUIVALENT FRACTIONS (Continues working on different things in parallel; apparently, great increase in programming skill, programming courses for kids put cart before horse—learning about modularity, efficiency, as rules instead of letting kids get some experience behind them—also, we note her processes of revision, of modularizing, of dealing at various levels of program organization.)

9.3.   THE "SESAME STREET" SCREEN: DEBBIE AND NAOMI (Imitation in learning, mindful vs. mindless imitation.)

10.   THE "ADDITION ASSIGNMENT" (Sensitivity to instructional design: she criticizes teacher's example and produces a better one; she reacts differently to a perceived assignment than to her own project—way in which children 'snapped to' and followed teacher's directions is evidence of fragility of new learning culture.)

11.   CREATING MORE EXAMS, "GOING OVERS," AND WORKING ON THE USER-FRIENDLINESS OF THE SOFTWARE

12.   THE SUBTRACTION SCENE

June

13.   FINISHING UP: AN OVERVIEW OF DEBBIE'S FINAL PIECE OF SOFTWARE (Welter of procedures, black humor of her warning letter, real modular approach in her combining of procedures.)
DEBBIE'S FINAL PIECE OF SOFTWARE INCLUDED THREE LOGO PAGES. WHEN PRINTED, IT IS ABOUT 15 PAGES LONG. IT IS PRESENTED AT THE END OF THE CASE.

Together, these sections reveal most of the existing information about Debbie's day-by-day processes of software design and her ways of learning fractions and Logo through that process. It is important to note that these segmentations and their sequences are *unique and specific to Debbie*. There are no two children in the experimental class with identical sections in terms of their actual number, content, or order. The segmentations of each of the 17 children's software-design processes revealed that these children generated, constructed, and followed different routes in their processes of software design and in their learning of Logo and fractions through the project.

Like the project itself, Debbie's case is presented in a process-oriented fashion—much like a documentary movie on movie making. I present Debbie's thoughts and actions in their context over a period of time, trying to capture Debbie's ways and sequences of working with fractions and programming, and showing how her work relates to the work of her peers. The reader first becomes familiar with Debbie's step-by-step process of creation, and later will be given possible interpretations of Debbie's actions and a view of her final product as a whole.

When Debbie started the project, she did not know how her final software would look, or what the parts of her final product would actually be. It would thus be misleading to present Debbie's software from the top (the final product's contents and objectives) to the bottom level (the product's actual elements), or from the whole to its components. To give an illustration of this, I do not start by describing her "Opening" and "Introduction" screens, which first appear when the software is running. These screens were created during April, almost two months after the project started, and after she had completed other screens. To take another example, she designed her screens about equivalent fractions in April, then left them aside, and implemented them in May. I describe these screens in their chronological order and in the *context* in which they were created. Their meaning and purpose are derived from their place in Debbie's process of creation, not just from their place in the final piece. I was more concerned with Debbie's processes and with the evolution of her knowledge and designing techniques than with the order of her screens in the final piece of software.

In other words, the following sections do not necessarily correspond with the structure of the screens in Debbie's final product; rather, with the sequence of Debbie's creation. These sections are conceptual and procedural in the way they describe her internal concepts and ongoing thoughts about fractions; her external conversations with the researcher and her peers; and her instructional designing or programming at a given time in the process. In this way, we can assess Debbie's microgenetic and conceptual development within the project through the evolution of her screen designs, through the complex interrelations between her software's parts, through her pedagogical considerations, and through her fractional representations.

MARCH

2.1. GETTING STARTED WITH ONE-HALF OF THE ENTIRE COMPUTER SCREEN

On March 10 and 12, Debbie drew two sketches representing halves in her Designer's Notebook (Figure 1). In our initial interview at the end of January, Debbie defined a fraction in the following way: *"A fraction is a half. Yeah. . . A half is a whole. A half is a fraction."* When she was asked to construct representations for any fraction using blocks, clay, rods, or pegs, she only built representations for halves. When shown illustrations of fractions on paper, she would touch the shaded part and say: *"This is a half, this is a fraction."* At one point, I pointed to the unshaded half and asked her:

Idit: *And what is this part?*
Debbie: *Uhm . . . this is nothing. Only the shaded part is a fraction, a half.*

For Debbie, apparently, fractions *are* halves. This is not so surprising. Papert (1980) has described pairing, a Bourbakian *groupment,* as the most primitive numbered grouping: children see twos everywhere—in male and female, in the body's bilateral symmetry, and so on. Splitting the pair is a simple reversal of this operation, and we might expect halving to be children's first and most fundamental notion of fractions. In fact, some writers have noted the special status of the "half" concept for young children in general (Kieren & Nelson, 1978; Behr et al., 1983; ETC, 1985). Others report that children's notion of a half is as a "special kind of a whole" and a "special kind of an operation" (see the Halving Operator, Smith, 1987; ETC, 1985); young children, they say, can partition quantities into halves quite accurately. All 51 children I interviewed at the start of my study chose to show a half of something (blocks, pegs, pictures) as their first "good example of a fraction," and 90 percent of the experimental children started their projects by representing halves or equivalents of halves in one way or another. Debbie worked with halves longer than the other children—for practically the entire first month of the project. In a more traditional school context, Debbie would not have been able to stay within a "halves microworld" she created for herself for so long, or to experiment so freely with ideas. But Debbie had created this microworld—and she seemed to know what she was doing. She

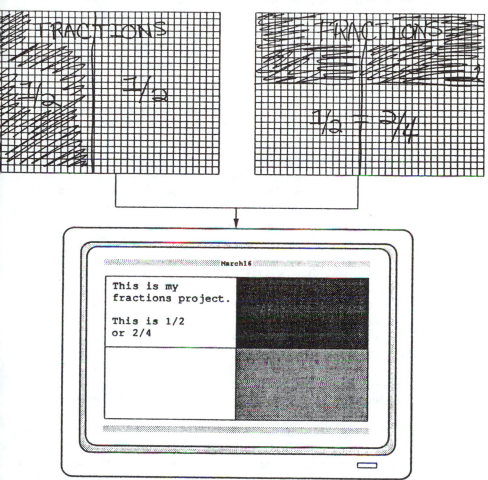

Figure 1.   Hand-drawn Sketches from March 10 and March 12 and their Implementation March 16.

used to it to explore fundamental ideas about fractions. By the time she moved on to other fractions, her understanding was already far advanced. The halves microworld served as an "entry space" for her, the kind of space children create when they encounter new and relatively unknown situations. This was a kind of conceptual home-base which Debbie needed time to consolidate.

At the beginning of the project, Debbie had an incomplete and unconventional notion of halves. One of her first comments to me about fractions, that *"only the shaded half is a fraction,"* suggests a different conception of fractions as an intellectual operation. Fractions are something you *"put on"* an object, according to Debbie. If you haven't put them there, she seems to say, they aren't there.

A look at Debbie's first sketch shows the whole screen symmetrically and vertically bisected, indicating that two halves make a whole. The second sketch shows that two-fourths make a half. She combined these ideas on March 16 and programmed her first screen. In her final piece of software, this screen would appear *after* the procedures OPENING AND INTRODUCTION, created 2 months later.

Shown in Figure 1 are the two hand-drawn sketches, followed by their final implemented computer screen. Note that Debbie has begun to break away from showing only the right side as the fraction in the hand-drawn sketches, while she retained this rigidity in her Logo programming implementation.

What was happening around Debbie during this time? While Debbie worked on her screen showing one-half, many of the other students began their projects by showing a simple collection of basic fractional representations on their computer screens. The most popular representations were of the half–fourth–eighth family, or the third–sixth–ninth–twelfth family, as represented by the three children's hand-drawn plans and designs in Figure 2.

Don's, Tania's, and Milton's plans represent the children's typical "getting-started" approach, which I call the *collection designs*. Many children started with the collection designs, by designing a screen divided into four or six parts. In each of the screen's parts they represented one fraction. Most of the fraction representations were done by dividing individual and familiar shapes (such as a circle, a square, a triangle, or a rectangle) into parts, some of these were shaded in. Another, more advanced representation (according to Lesh et al., 1983) was done by using a group of equal shapes, such as the group of eight small circles in Milton's design, where two of the circles were shaded in to show the fraction two-eighths.

As shown previously, Debbie did *not* begin with this approach of representing a collection of fractions on the screen. Rather, she began by representing one large half (using half of the computer screen). However, she saw the collection designs all around her in the Designer's Notebooks and on the computer screens of her peers. Judging from the next drawing in her Designer's Notebook, it seems that Debbie decided to adopt her classmates' idea of representing a collection of fractions. Figure 3 shows the designs that Debbie drew in her Designer's Notebook on March 11 and 19.

There are two interesting design considerations in these two hand-drawn pictures: (a) Debbie's process of *simplification of the design*. On March 11, Debbie planned first a busy screen on paper; then she "cleaned it up" on March 19, with the purpose of creating a design that would fit on the small screen of the IBM PCjr. As a designer, Debbie was aware of the "busy design" issue. My notes indicate that her reason for changing the design was *"I will never be able to*

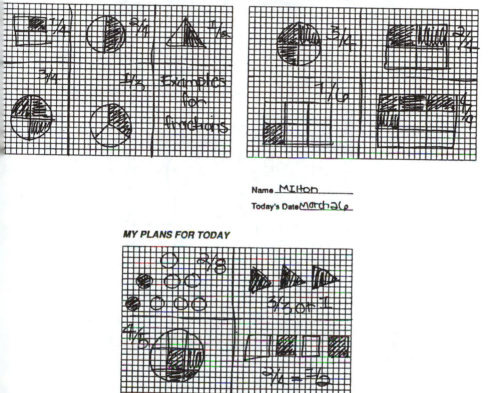

Figure 2.   Don's, Tania's, and Milton's Designs Represent the Typical "Getting Start-ed" Approach.

fit it all on one screen . . . too many things to see." The practical issue hidden in Debbie's reasoning was her difficulty (in terms of Logo) to create so many little representations on one screen. The other, more sophisticated, design issue was that even if she could fit all these representations on one screen, they would still be cluttered and visually confusing for her future user. Another design-related interest is (b) the *instructional sentence* that Debbie wrote at the top of her hand-drawn design of March 11: *"A fraction is when you divide something into equal parts or halves."* The rational-number "half" had a special identity in Debbie's mind even in this design (which shows fractions other than halves), as had been analyzed above.

126

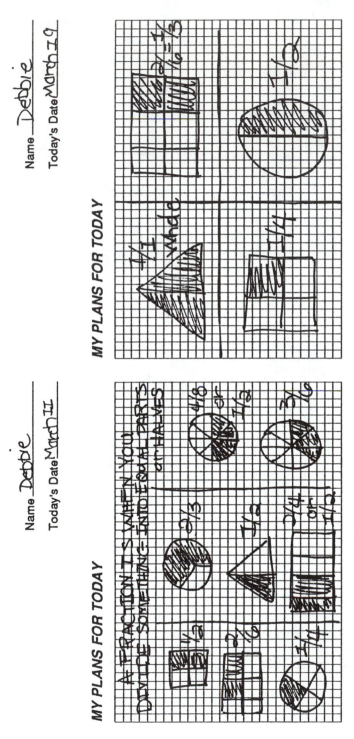

Figure 3. Debbie's Collection Designs from March 11 and March 19.

Debbie did not implement the two collection designs of March 11 and 19. Perhaps this is because she was so obsessed with working only with halves, and because she had so many ideas on how to teach about halves. Perhaps, at that time, she did not yet feel a need to move towards representing (or teaching about) other kinds of fractions. We will see later that, throughout the month of March, she continued to create different screens with a variety of representations for halves.

In a more traditional teaching context, Debbie would never have been allowed to dwell on halves for a whole month. But after seeing that she chose not to implement these two designs, I realized that Debbie needed more time before she was ready to move on and deal with other fractions. We shall see later that the fact that she spent so much time working with halves did not decrease her understanding of or her ability to work with other kinds of fractions or operations. In fact, she gave good answers in the posttests to questions involving other fractions or more complex operations than equivalences of halves. Debbie explored the properties of fractions by spending a lot of time with these halves— the fractions she felt most comfortable with.

2.2. MULTIPLE REPRESENTATIONS FOR HALVES: A FIRST STEP

On March 19 and 23, Debbie sketched plans for a screen showing multiple representations of fractions. As we see from the March 23 and 24 implementation, she relied on these ideas, although not literally, in the programming of the actual screen (Figure 4). Debbie is still concerned about showing that halves can be on the bottom and left as well as on the right.

A look at the procedure, which Debbie called CALF, shows how fast she was progressing in Logo programming. Compared to her first short and simple Logo procedure, which showed two quarters making up half of the screen, CALF is longer and more complex (see Section 2.11. in this chapter). Let us examine the nature of her work in more detail.

2.2.1. Rhyming Procedure Names

I asked Debbie why she had named this last procedure CALF, which creates four different shapes divided into halves. She said:

> Because they are . . . all showing different ways of halves. I already have a procedure HALF that does one large half or two-fourths on the screen. I couldn't name this one HALF too. I had to find another name. This name is cute, 'cause you read it in the same PAGE [these two procedures appear on the same Logo page one after the other]. First, TO HALF, and then, TO CALF. HALF, CALF. I like it like this. Because

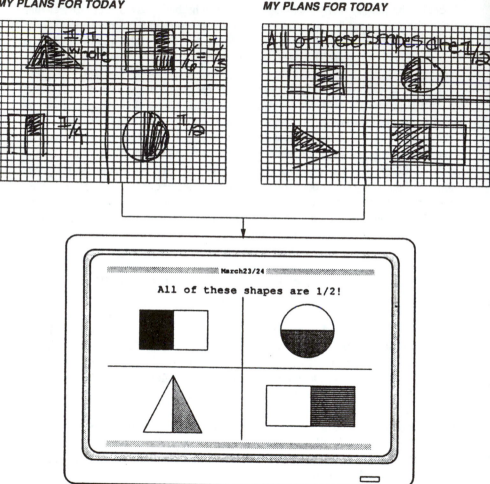

Figure 4.   Debbie's Collection Design from March 19 was Revised and Implemented on March 23 and Completed on March 24.

they are almost the same, but they're different. The names also are almost the same, but different.

Debbie realized that each procedure represented halves in a different way, so she decided that the procedure names should also correspond. Debbie liked writing poems, two of which we have already read in the introduction to this case. She wrote quite a few others that she would erase before the end of class.

She seemed to regard them as very personal, and I sometimes thought she saved
NO and GROW by accident. In any case, poetry writing was a personally meaningful activity for her. She seemed to have imported rhyming into this project as a
way of bridging an established interest with something new. When I asked her
about these procedure names, she smiled and seemed proud of her invention
(*"Read it! read it!"* she said). They seemed to carry a real affective charge.

One day in May (2 months after the CALF–HALF implementation), I asked her
why she no longer made procedure names rhyme. She said:

> Well, I started doing lots of other things for my fraction project. My program is
> very long now. I have to remember many procedures, and names, too. It's hard to
> find things if you don't remember their names, and what they do [according to their
> names].

Naming is a central concept in programming (Papert, 1980). "Good" programmers tend to write readable programs with meaningful variable or procedure
names, especially when the programs are long, so that debugging and revising
will be easier and remain under the control of the programmer (Carver, 1986;
Soloway, 1984). Through her process of composing a longer piece of software,
Debbie came to see the importance of naming things in a functional way so she
would be able to find where things were, and remember what they did. Shifting
from an idiosyncratic and personally meaningful naming strategy to a functional
one that is more generally understandable is indicative of intellectual growth.
Debbie no longer needed the bridge of poetry writing and was flexible enough to
adopt a new naming strategy. Neither Debbie's teacher nor I pressured her to
make this change. She made it on her own when she was ready and saw the need
herself.

2.2.2. "Randomming" Colors: Debbie Inspires Her Peers

During the course of the project, most new Logo knowledge first circulated
"through the grapevine." One child would learn something new and use it in his
or her program. Other children would see something new on that child's screen
and would want to do it themselves. The teacher often used the last five minutes
of the computer session to explain the new Logo material to all the children.

On most occasions, Debbie was not the first student to learn a new Logo skill,
use it in her program, or spread it around her class. But she was the first to use
the Logo operation RANDOM. (RANDOM is an operation that takes one input, a
positive integer. The output from RANDOM is a nonnegative integer that is lower
than its input. RANDOM 3, for example, selects one of three choices, and outputs
either 0, 1, or 2; RANDOM 5 selects one number out of 0, 1, 2, 3, or 4. One day in
March, after the CALF procedure had worked for several days, Debbie came to
me and asked,

Debbie: *How can I make it in different colors, so each time you get different colors?*
  Idit: *What do you think?*
Debbie: *Well, I think I can do it a lot of times with different colors. I can do procedures*
        CALF, CALF *1,* CALF *2. It's too much work. . . But, do you know how to do it?*

Children in Project Headlight knew they could get information on "Logo tricks" from MIT people, but we generally waited for a request or a more appropriate time to provide such information. Judging from her question, Debbie was ready to learn about RANDOM. Here, she was driven by an aesthetic approach to design, something we have already seen was important to her. I showed her the instruction, SETC 1+RANDOM 14. Each time this instruction is run, Logo selects one number out of 14, adds 1 to it (so that there will be no black or white selections), and outputs that number to the SETC command; this causes the corresponding color to appear on the screen (each number represents a color, and there are 15 colors available in the version of Logo the children were using). Although this is not a surefire way to get four different colors, it usually works and it adds an element of surprise. Debbie seemed to grasp this relatively complex instruction and incorporated it into her program. *"Now, they [her future users] can use my fraction project many times. They will not get bored. They will pay attention to what I am showing them!"* she said.

It wasn't long before Debbie's classmates saw this effect on her screen. They were also eager to use it, and it was shown to the class. Debbie thus gained some recognition as an innovator. For this shy and withdrawn girl, this was something new indeed.

2.2.3. Learning About Fractions and Logo Through Thinking About Teaching

The evolution of Debbie's CALF procedure demonstrates how two kinds of learning, individual concept development and social learning, were influenced by thinking about teaching others.

Fractions learning. The screen produced by the CALF procedure showed four geometric shapes divided into halves. All the designated parts were, in fact, halves; they were indicated by shading on either side, and the shaded halves were bisected not only vertically but also horizontally.

In designing the CALF screen, Debbie had overcome two earlier conceptions: (a) that shapes could only be vertically cut in half; and (b) that only the right side could be designated a half. She had also moved from thinking that the particular fractions a shape was divided into was exclusively determined by the *number* of parts, without necessary regard to their size.

Debbie's original notions were typical of many of her classmates, so that the unfolding of her own thinking may reveal some general developmental issues.

As part of the initial interviews, I had asked children to make a drawing

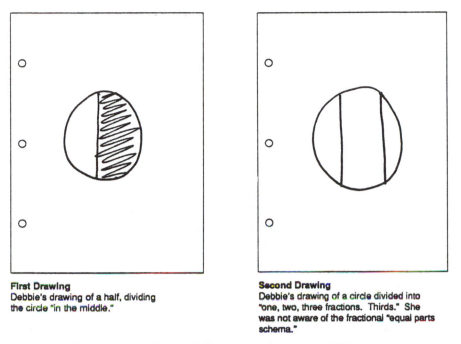

First Drawing
Debbie's drawing of a half, dividing
the circle "in the middle."

Second Drawing
Debbie's drawing of a circle divided into
"one, two, three fractions. Thirds." She
was not aware of the fractional "equal parts
schema."

Figure 5.   Drawings of Circles Divided into Halves and Thirds.

showing halves. Debbie drew a circle and divided it into two parts, saying as she drew: *"I divide it in the middle, right here. Here, this is a half, a fraction."* Immediately afterwards, I asked her to draw another fraction. She drew another circle and divided it into three parts, saying: *"I divide it here and here,"* and then, pointing and counting, *"One, two, three fractions. Threes. Uhm . . . thirds."* She drew and divided the second circle into three unequal parts (her two drawings are illustrated in Figure 5).

I then asked her to draw an example for one-third using a square. She first divided the square into halves. Then she divided the right half into two. She shaded in the top quarter and said, *"And this is a third."* Then, pointing and counting, she counted *"One, two, three, and one is shaded in. This is one-third"* (see Figure 6).

I showed Debbie a drawing of a square divided into halves with the right half shaded in. I asked her what the fraction in the picture was. As was previously indicated, she touched the shaded part and said, *"This is a half."* I asked her, *"And what is this other part?"* She said, *"This is nothing."* So I asked, *"This is nothing?"* *"Yes,"* she said, *"It's not a half. It's not a fraction"* (see Figure 7).

I then showed Debbie an identical square divided into two halves, but with the left side shaded in. I pointed to the shaded half and asked her, *"Is this a half?"* As she rotated the piece of paper to turn the square, she said, *"Not really.*

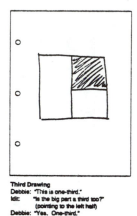

Figure 6.   Drawing of a Square
Divided into Thirds.

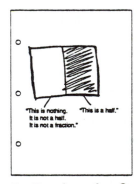

Figure 7.   Drawing of a Square
Divided into Halves, Right Side
Shaded In.

Uhm . . . yes. But you have to turn it kind of." Now with the shaded half on the right side again, she said, *"Yes. It's a half"* (see Figure 8).

Where does such an idea come from? In looking at the regular math curriculum's fractions worksheets, most illustrations shade the right side to indicate

Question: "Is this a half?"
Debbie: "Uhm... not really. But
          you have to turn it kind of."

Figure 8. Drawing of a Square Divided into Halves, Left Side Shaded In.

fractions (as in Figure 9). Education publishers' preference for such illustrations may reveal a genetic priority of such representations, or perhaps only a cultural predominance of things right-sided and a corresponding avoidance of things sinister.

Lesh, Landau, and Hamilton (1983, p. 310) have found that up to 7% of the children they tested from grades 4 to 8 have problems identifying a half with a slightly rotated circle (such as the one shown in Figure 10).

I also gave Debbie a picture of the rotated circle (as in Figure 10) and asked her which fraction it showed. She first turned her head, then rotated the paper to the right until the mid-line was perpendicular, and only then said, *"A half."*

Debbie's actions and thoughts in this situation suggest several interpretations. One is simply that her previous experiences with representations of halves were limited to representations of areas that were bisected vertically. But, thinking in terms of Piaget's perspective on children's preoperational rigidity, we might regard an inability to focus in a flexible way on two aspects of the situation (reorientation to primitive verticality and evaluation of symmetry) as characteris-

1/2   1/2

Figure 9. Typical textbooks' and School Worksheets' Representations of Fractions.

What is this fraction?

**Figure 10. A Slightly
Rotated Circle Divided
into Halves.**

tic of a stage in intellectual development. The literature on symmetry perception
and feature detection (e.g., Olson, 1975; Beiterman, 1986) provides another
interpretation, suggesting that children have a hard-wired, low-level, perceptual
symmetry detector. Olson found that young children develop right–left symmetry (which he calls low-level detection) much faster than the top–bottom symmetry. The vertical bisection of a square or circle might then, according to this
theory, be based on a primitive or intuitive concept of half. Recognizing other
representations might require translating them into this form or disabling the
intuitive concept. In Olson's terms, children might have to learn how not to use
the "vertical-only" symmetry detector, and to use other, more flexible symmetry
detectors.

Reviewing Debbie's design process in light of this thinking is interesting. Her
first computer screen represented her idea that a "fraction is the right-shaded side

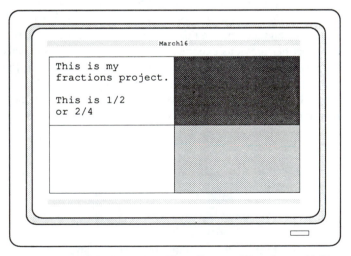

**Figure 11. Debbie's Very First Screen Showing a Half on
the Right Side.**

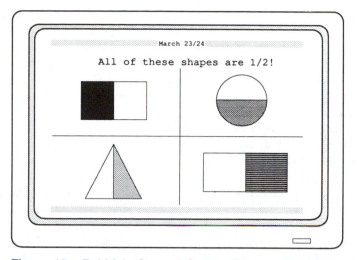

Figure 12. Debbie's Second Screen Showing the Halves on Different Sides of the Objects.

of a square" (see Figure 11).

However, in her second screen, made two weeks later on March 24, we see that the shaded halves were located on different sides—top, bottom, right, or left—of the four different shapes. She also wrote the following sentence at the top of the screen: ALL THESE SHAPES ARE $1/2$! (see Figure 12).

Through wanting to teach about halves, Debbie constructed her own representations for other children. Inspired by the short discussions we had in the classroom, she was probably involved in a process of thinking about "What is really difficult for me to understand that I can make easy for others." In ISDP, fourth-grade children were given the aim of designing instructional software for third graders, but very little time was actually spent with third graders. The project, then, was not really an example of learning-through-teaching in a real sense. Rather, the "learning self" was *externalized* onto an "idealized learner"—a learner who objectified the designer's learning self and recapitulated the designer's own learning processes.

This is precisely what happened with Debbie. Having just grappled with some basic ideas (what kind of thing a fraction is, where it can be shown), she had a new viewpoint ('you can put them anywhere') she wanted to communicate. She would make this viewpoint the subject of her designs and implementations.

Logo learning. Debbie's first procedure for the screen ALL THESE ARE $1/2$ was not skilled from a programming point of view. Debbie did program the square and circle using REPEAT, but she programmed a rectangle as REPEAT 4 [. . . .], only to discover that it should be REPEAT 2 [. . .]. At first she didn't know how to program a triangle at all. In her Designer's Notebook, Debbie, reporting the work of March 23, wrote: *"I had one problem. It was making a perfect triangle. Otherwise I had no problems. . . . I made one change because it messes up* [her procedure]. *So I did it over and over. Finally I asked Cassania* [a classmate] *and she helped me. She showed me how to do a perfect triangle. . . I finished that project* [i.e., the screen with the four shapes divided into halves]." In fact, Cassania had typed the code for the triangle directly into Debbie' program.

Eventually, Debbie added RANDOM for the colors, changed her rectangle procedure to REPEAT 2, and re-created the triangle using REPEAT instead of a string of commands. In part, she made changes to incorporate new knowledge, but she was guided by more than a programming esthetic. She was thinking about how to capture her users' attention. She told me that she was thinking about "how to make the CALF procedure less boring." Thus, she wanted to vary the colors on her screen so that her users would be more interested, and so *"they would learn better."* For Debbie, learning a new Logo skill was instrumental to implementing an instructional design.

This kind of revision occurred in dynamic interaction with the computer. Debbie did not think about the color issue while she was planning her screen in her Designer's Notebook. On paper, there were no colors or interactions with the colors, and her first implementation did not use colors either. But Debbie ran her fractions software every day, looked at her screens, and looked at her code. One day she added the colors, and in other revisions she would change the code for the triangle and rectangle.

Other Logo learning situations reported in the literature have documented the problems and difficulties young children have with programming in Logo (e.g., Pea & Kurland, 1984; Perkins & Martin, 1985; Heller, 1986). Most of the children in these studies wrote much smaller programs; when they were finished, and their programs were working, the programming process stopped. Debbie was in a process of constant revision and integration of material from various sources into her program. She wanted to make her project work, and needed Logo to make it work. Eventually, Debbie came to understand code she originally had not typed in herself and replaced it with more elegant code. This learning situation, as compared to those reported above, seems to have made Logo learning easy and natural. This is the state of Debbie's program by March 24.

```
TO HALF
SETC 9 FD 250          [cuts the screen horizontally]
PU HOME RT 90 SETC 1   [goes back home and changes the pen
                        color]
PD FD 320              [cuts the screen vertically]
PU SETPOS [40 45]      [goes to the center of the top-right
                        fourth]
LT 90 SETC 4 PD FILL   [fills it in red color]
```

```
PU SETPOS [40 -45]                [moves to the center of the bottom-
                                   right fourth]

PD SETC 3 PD FILL                 [fills it in pink color]
PR [This is my fraction project]

                                  [prints instructional sentence at the
                                   top of the computer screen]

PR [This is ½ or ²⁄₄]
PR []                             [skips a space]
PR [By Debbie]                    [prints her name]
END

TO CALF
HT SETC 1+RANDOM 14               [sets the pen color randomly]
PD FD 200                         [draws a vertical line across the
                                   screen]

PU HOME
RT 90
SETC 1+RANDOM 14                  [sets the pen color randomly]
PD FD 320                         [draws horizontal line across the
                                   screen]

PU HOME
PU SETPOS [30 50]                 [moves Turtle to position of circle]
SETC 12 PD
REPEAT 360 [FD.3 RT 1]            [draws a circle on the top right]
RT 90
PD FD 33                          [divides the circle in half]

PU SETPOS [45 40]
PD FILL                           [shades in the bottom half of the
                                   circle]

PD HOME
PR [ALL THESE FRACTIONS ARE ½.]
                                  [prints the instructional statement]
SETPOS [-60 50]                   [moves the Turtle to position of
                                   square]

SETC 1+RANDOM 14
PD REPEAT 4 [LT 90 FD 40]         [draws the square at the top left]
PU LT 90
FD 20
LT 90
PD FD 40                          [divides the square in half]
RT 90
FD 10
RT 90
PU FD 5 PD FILL                   [shades in the left half of the square]
PU HOME
SETC 1+RANDOM 14
```

```
SETPOS [35 -70]                          [moves Turtle to position of
                                          rectangle]
PD REPEAT 4 [FD 50 RT 90 FD 100 RT 90]
                                         [draws a rectangle at the bottom
                                          right]

RT 90 FD 50
LT 90
PD FD 49                                 [divides the rectangle in half]
PU RT 90
FD 25 RT 90
FD 10 PD FILL                            [shades in the right side of rectangle]
PU HOME
SETC 1+RANDOM 14
PU SETPOS [-105 -55]                     [moves the Turtle to position of
                                          triangle]

RT 45
PD FD 50                                 [creates a triangle]
RT 90
FD 52
RT 135
FD 73                                    [positions the Turtle for cutting the
                                          triangle into two equal parts]

REPEAT 2 [RT 90]
FD 36
LT 90
PD FD 35                                 [divides the triangle]
PU SETPOS [-55 -40]
PD FILL                                  [shades the half at the right side of
                                          the triangle]

END
```

2.3. THE HOUSE SCENE: "FRACTIONS ARE EVERYWHERE"

On March 23 Debbie wrote her plans in her Designer's Notebook (see Figure 13).

Debbie's hand-drawn plans for what she named the *House Scene* mark an important breakthrough for her in integrating real-world knowledge with formal, symbolic, mathematical thought. In addition, Her work on this project showed significant advances in planning and programming skills, in terms of organization of code and of separate parts of the larger project. But this was not all. Through the HOUSE Procedure, Debbie experienced a feeling of exhilaration in achieving something that became the object of admiration of her peers.

Today's Date *March 25, 1987*

MY PLANS FOR TODAY

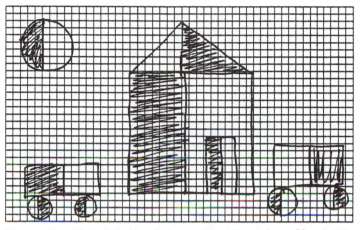

Figure 13.   Debbie's Hand-drawn Plan No. 1 from March 23.

Today's Date *March 23, 1987*

DESIGNS:

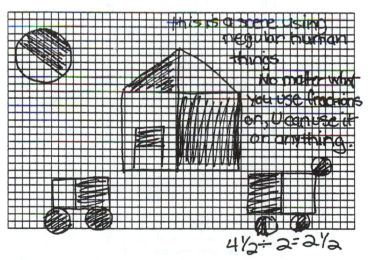

$$4\frac{1}{2} \div 2 = 2\frac{1}{2}$$

Figure 14.   Debbie's Hand-drawn Plan No. 2 from March 23.

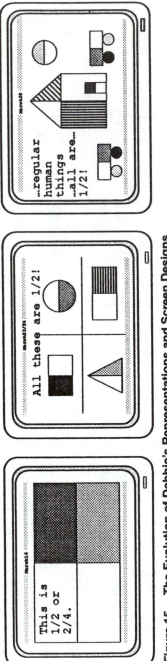

Figure 15. The Evolution of Debbie's Representations and Screen Designs.

140

2.3.1. Integrating Formal, School-Like, and Real-World Knowledge

For all the students in Debbie's class, fractions were primarily an entity of "school knowledge." When they were asked to give examples of fractions, only one girl described anything as basic as her mother cutting a cake into pieces. All the children began their software projects with school-like representations, showing geometric objects divided into fractional parts. Debbie had taken a crucial step with her HOUSE procedure towards integrating the formal, the school-like, and the everyday. I describe how she has accomplished to *transform her thinking* as a two-step process.

The first step was to shift away from showing fractions as parts of geometric objects only to using geometric objects to represent a 'human' scene—a sun, a house, and two wooden wagons. Debbie could not explain what motivated her to represent a *"regular human scene,"* but it represented a move away from a collection of geometric objects carrying a strictly mathematical message towards a scene lending itself to narrative description. This was also the time Debbie started saying that *"you can use fractions on anything."* For Debbie, the HOUSE procedure was the first overt attempt at weaving together of the school-like, the formal, and the everyday. Figure 15 traces this transformation.

I doubt that Debbie had ever been exposed to a real-life situation where all the real-life objects were divided into halves and a symbolic operation was attached to the situation. She was not imitating any of her peers, since she was the only one to come up with the idea of representing this particular real-life situation. For that reason, I do not interpret this moment of learning, or Debbie's thinking transformation, in a Vygotskian (1978) perspective. I suspect that Debbie did not produce this design by communicating with, or imitating an adult's action or idea; she did not internalize something from "the intellectual life around her" (Vygotsky, 1978, pp. 84–91). In this particular situation, she was not asked "leading questions," and was not in any kind of an "cognitive apprenticeship" (in the way described by J. S. Brown & Collins, 1985), or "reciprocal relations with a knowledgeable adult," professional software designer or fractions expert (in the way described by Palincsar & Brown, 1984).

My assumption here is that Debbie's ideas for constructing a representation of a house and her attempt to translate it into formal symbols appeared and were formed in her own mind. *I interpreted this as an example for a rather creative learning moment that happened in a child's own mind, independent of the people around her but perhaps dependent on the task and the materials she used.*

I have placed an emphasis on this issue because, during ISDP, Debbie did inspire other children, and on several other occasions was inspired by others. During the project, some kinds of learning were influenced by the culture—peers, teachers, MIT people, the nature of Logo, and the Designer's Notebooks; while other kinds of learning occurred due to the child's own mind, through his or her own constructing, thinking, representing and designing. During the course of this study, I tried, as much as possible, to identify (with the children) when they were inspired by their culture or when they came up with their own ideas. On most occasions it was difficult to tell which was which. Nevertheless, it seems to me that Debbie's House Scene example—her original design as well as her attempt to translate it into symbolic operation (whether or not it was implemented in the end)—can be seen as a model for a creative idea that resulted from one child's mind working independently of the environment, in a true Piagetian sense:

> Piaget has sometimes labeled his position *constructivism,* to capture the sense in which the child must make and remake the basic concepts and logical-thought forms that constitute his intelligence. Piaget prefers to say that the child is inventing rather than discovering his ideas. . . . The ideas in question do not preexist out there in the world, only awaiting their discovery by the child: each child must invent them for himself. By the same token, since the ideas have no a priori external existence, they cannot be discovered by a simple exposure [e.g., such as in imitation]; rather they must be constructed or invented by the child. Thus, Piaget's book dealing with the growth of the concepts of object, space, time, and causality . . . is not called *The Discovery of Reality,* but *The Construction of Reality in the Child.* (Gruber & Voneche, 1977, pp. xxxvi–xxxvii)

The second step moves back in another direction: it is the formalization of the everyday. Look at the illustration and equation Debbie wrote at the bottom of Figure 14.

When I saw Debbie writing this equation, I asked her what it was. She said, *"If you count all the halves in the picture you get [pause] four wholes and one half."* She counted the halves on the drawing as she answered my question. She put two fingers on the two wagons halves and said *"one,"* then put two fingers on the wheels of the right wagon and said *"two,"* then placed two fingers on the half-door and the half-house and said, *"three."* Continuing with her counting, she placed two fingers on the half-roof and the half-sun and said *"four;"* and finally put her pinkie on the half of the steering wheel of the wagon on the right and said *"and a half."* Our conversation continued:

Debbie: *Well, I don't think I'll use it. It's not really working.*
   Idit: *What's not really working?*
Debbie: *The wooden wagons work, the wheels work, but the sun and the roof together don't work. Not really.*
   Idit: *What do you mean?*
Debbie: *I don't know. I am not going to use it.*
   Idit: *Why do you divide it by 2 here?* [She wrote $4\frac{1}{2} \div 2 = 2\frac{1}{4}$.]
Debbie: *I don't know. I just tried to ask them questions* [by "them" she meant the users].
   Idit: *Try to use it.*

At that point, I did not want to distract her too much, realizing that she was eager to go to the computer to program her designs. Having worked exclusively with formal representations of fractions, Debbie had taken a bold step. She first moved back into the real world of human things and tried to "put halves on them," then moved into the world of mathematics and tried to symbolize her scene with an equation.

Again, I saw no evidence from other students' work that Debbie's idea of mathematizing the world, of representing her House Scene by use of an equation, was anything but *spontaneous*. It seems to have been an instance of constructivist, Piagetian learning. We see here, not a discovery of an idea well represented around her, but the reinvention or construction of one of the cleanest and most powerful forms of abstraction from the concrete: mathematical abstraction.

In the end, however, Debbie did not succeed in translating her House Scene into the symbolic representation of an equation. Perhaps after she counted all the half-objects in her picture, she realized that it worked for the wagons, meaning that the two halves on the different wagons were more or less equal in size and could therefore could be added into one whole. The two halves of the wheels of the right wagon were also equal and could therefore be added into one whole. However, the half of the door was not equal to the half of the house, nor was the half of the sun equal to the half of the roof. Debbie seemed to have realized this when she said that *"the wagons work, the wheels work, but the sun and the roof* together *do not work,"* meaning that their parts were not equal and could not be added into one whole. This was a very sophisticated perception of the properties of fractions, more specifically, the addition of fractions.

During the 40-minute postinterview in June, I assessed whether Debbie had indeed understood that adding fractions assumes adding equal parts, and whether or not she had understood the role of a common denominator. I brought out a box of Pattern Blocks (e.g., Harrison, 1972) and arranged two sets of the blocks on the table. One set consisted of two six-sided yellow shapes. The other set consisted of two four-sided red shapes. I told Debbie that I considered each set of blocks as a whole (see Figure 16). I asked Debbie:

Idit: *One child told me that I can take half of the yellow shape, and half of the red shape and write: $^1/_2 + ^1/_2 = 1$ . . . What do you think?*

Debbie: *No, you can't.*

Idit: *Why? This other child told me that it's true.*

Debbie: *[insisting] No. It's* wrong.

She took one-half of the yellow shape (one yellow block) and one-half of the red shape (one red block), put them together, and said *"They are not equal. You can't do that."* She then took two more red blocks from the box and attached them to my original set of red blocks, so that the two shapes (the red and the yellow) would be equal in size (2 yellows = 4 reds). Then she said: *"I'll do it like*

This is how the two yellow Pattern Blocks looked on the table. One whole composed of two yellow (six-sided) Pattern blocks.

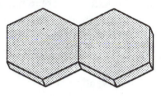

A second whole composed of two red (four-sided, trapezoidal) blocks.

Figure 16.   Pattern Blocks Problem.

this. Now they are equal." Debbie had in fact created the common denominator (2 yellows + 4 reds) in her process of adding the shapes. In doing so, she performed better than 90% of the control children, many of whom had performed better than she in the initial interview. What we see then, is that Debbie's self-directed project of exploration brought her up against a particularly tricky and fundamental principle of symbolic representation—that equal numerical symbols must correspond to equal parts of the object represented. Her attempt to represent her scene by means of an equation, though ultimately unsuccessful, nevertheless helped produce a solid sense of what adding fractions is all about. Unlike the traditional fractions curriculum, no stress was placed on finding the common denominator, part of the surface representation of fractions. Rather, by stressing explication of underlying representations, the project created a situation in which Debbie could fully assimilate the deep structure of adding only equal parts. This is a kind of indirect learning, which, as we shall see later, resulted in greater success with algorithmic manipulation than direct learning, focusing on the algorithms themselves.

2.3.2. Planning and Programming the House

The House Scene was Debbie's longest and most complex project to date. We shall examine her planning and programming processes in some detail to illustrate what was involved.

Debbie started planning this scene on March 23 and modified her plans on

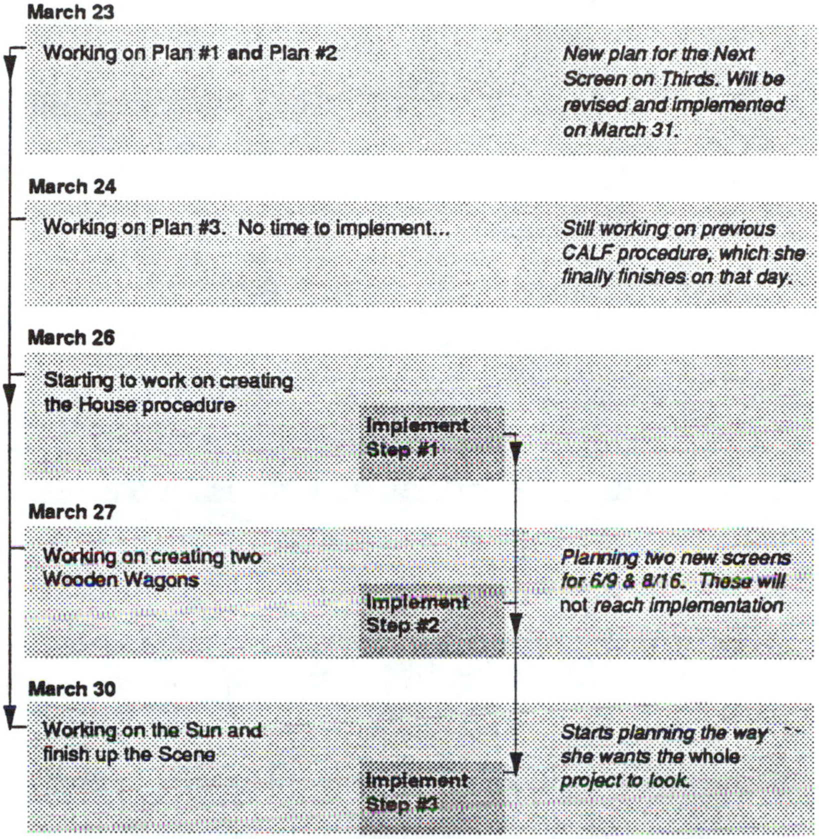

March 23

Working on Plan #1 and Plan #2

New plan for the Next Screen on Thirds. Will be revised and implemented on March 31.

March 24

Working on Plan #3. No time to implement...

Still working on previous CALF procedure, which she finally finishes on that day.

March 26

Starting to work on creating the House procedure

Implement Step #1

March 27

Working on creating two Wooden Wagons

Implement Step #2

Planning two new screens for 6/9 & 8/16. These will not reach implementation

March 30

Working on the Sun and finish up the Scene

Implement Step #3

Starts planning the way she wants the whole project to look.

Figure 17.   The Overall Structure of Debbie's Planning and Programming Work on the House.

March 24, even before trying to implement them on the computer. She began implementation on March 26, continued with implementation work on March 27 and 30, and finished the scene on March 30. The flowchart in Figure 17 shows how Debbie organized and completed her work on the House Scene.

Each box in the above diagram represents a phase in Debbie's complex process. In order to capture Debbie's evolution of thinking about the House Scene, replicas of Debbie's original drawings and written reflections from her Designer's Notebook are presented in detail. Her Logo programming code is presented when relevant, in order to show Debbie's ways of implementing her ideas and her programming processes.

The analysis of Debbie's instructional-designing and thinking transformations as shown in the two plans from March 23 (Figures 18 and 19) were already discussed. It is important to mention that on March 23 Debbie was still working

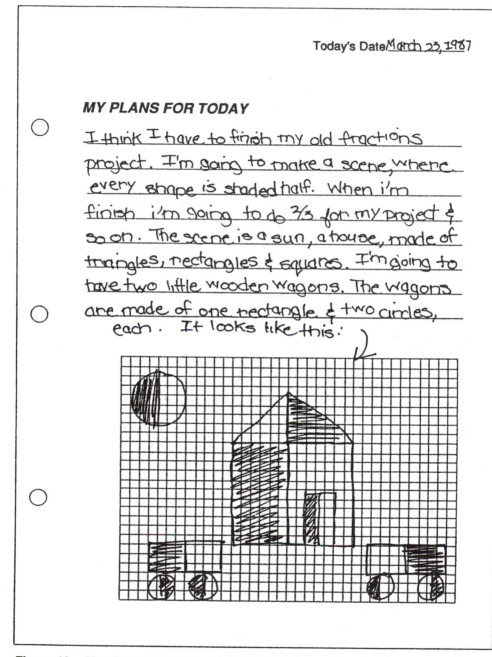

Today's Date March 23, 1987

MY PLANS FOR TODAY

I think I have to finish my old fractions project. I'm going to make a scene, where every shape is shaded half. When i'm finish i'm going to do ⅔ for my project & so on. The scene is a sun, a house, made of triangles, rectangles & squares. I'm going to have two little wooden wagons. The wagons are made of one rectangle & two circles, each. It looks like this:

Figure 18. March 23. Plan #1 from Debbie's Designer Notebook.

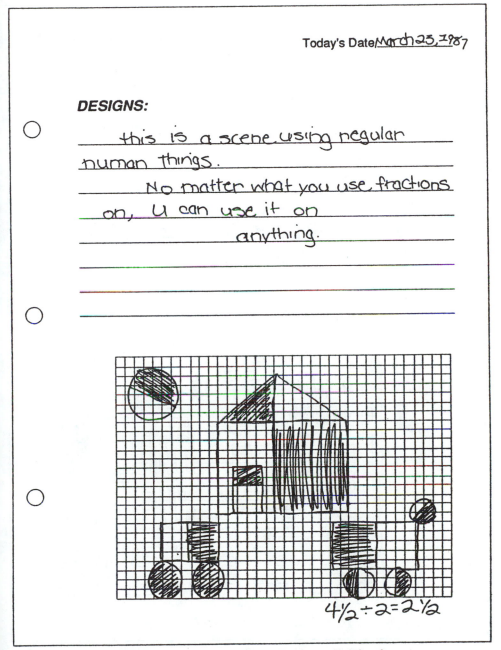

Today's Date March 23, 1987

DESIGNS:

    this is a scene using regular
human things.
        No matter what you use, fractions
on, U can use it on
            anything.

$$4\frac{1}{2} \div 2 = 2\frac{1}{2}$$

Figure 19.   March 23. Plan #2 from Debbie's Designer Notebook.

Today's Date March 24, 1987

MY PLANS FOR TODAY

TODAY I AM WORKING ON MY FRACTIONS
SCENE. IT IS ON THE TWO PAGES
BEFORE THIS ONE.

ANOTHER PICTURE IS BELOW, IT'S A
LITTLE BIT CHANGED.

I'm naming it HOUSE.

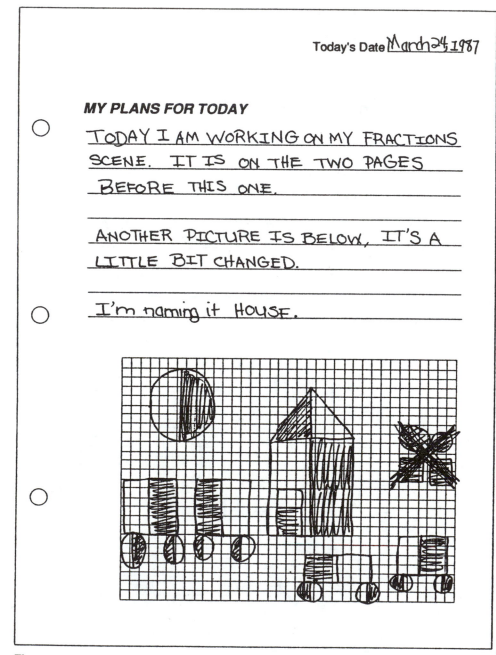

Figure 20.   March 24. Plan #3 from Debbie's Designer Notebook.

on her CALF procedure, and, on that day, she did not manage to start working on the HOUSE procedure.

Debbie was eager to start working on the House Scene on March 24. Before going to the computer, she created another design in her notebook: *"Another picture is below, it's a little bit changed"* (Figure 20).

I asked her why she had slightly modified it that day, and she answered: *"The more wagons I have, the more halves I can show."* She then paused for a second or two and continued: *"And the more halves I have, the . . . they can be on top of more sides."*

As stated in the previous sections, at that point in her instructional-design process, Debbie was very involved in showing children the idea that "the halves could be on any side of the shape" (one recalls the misconceptions she originally had in thinking that the half must be on the right side of the shape, and that the "empty" side was not a fraction). Debbie was in fact saying: The more wagons I create, the more representations of halves on the different sides of the wagons and wheels I will be able to show. She was probably thinking that these ideas would become much clearer to her users if she used as many examples as possible for the same phenomenon.

On that day, rather early in her process of planning, Debbie also stated in her notebook that she planned to name this scene *house*. She wrote: *"I am naming it HOUSE."*

Idit: *What will you name house?*
Debbie: *The procedure, of course.*
Idit: *Which procedure?*
Debbie: *The House Scene procedure.*
Idit: *Why house, and not wagons, or halves, or sun, or whatever?*
Debbie: *. . . 'Cause it's a scene about a house. And . . . [pause] the house is the biggest too.*

I asked Debbie these questions about her naming process for two reasons. First, I was interested in knowing whether or not she would give a name for each part of the whole picture (i.e., TO HOUSE, TO SUN, TO WAGON, etc.), and later create a superprocedure for all the objects shown in this scene. Secondly, I wondered why she had chosen a name that had no correspondence with the fractional representations it actually contained. One must remember that this was her third procedure in her project, and that she had named her previous procedures HALF and CALF, using a rhyming strategy and showing the purpose of the procedures (i.e., representing halves) by their names. However, Debbie's answers to my questions revealed that she had chosen to name her *entire* future procedure *house,* and was not yet planning to create sub-procedures for each of the objects or a super-procedure for the whole scene. She chose this name because it was for the House Scene, in which the house was the "biggest" and

Today's Date March 24, 1987

PROBLEMS I HAD TODAY

I had no problems today.
I had not accomplished to start my graphic
called "HOUSE,
The fraction scene.

***OVERALL, THE PROBLEMS I HAD TODAY ARE MAINLY RELATED TO (check in):

LOGO PROGRAMMING ✔ FRACTIONS   DESIGN
EXPLAINING OR TEACHING SOMETHING   OTHER

CHANGES I MADE TODAY AND WHY I MADE THESE CHANGES:

I made no changes either for the
same reason.

PLANS AND IDEAS FOR TOMORROW...

Figure 21.   March 24. Reflections Form.

most dominant object. In this way, by choosing this name, she emphasized the fact that she was actually designing a real-life, "regular human scene" of a house and its surroundings. In addition, her thoughts about naming demonstrated that, during the process of planning in writing, she was already thinking about the Logo's framework of programming, that is, about the implementation of her designs in a Logo procedure.

However, as on the previous day, March 23, Debbie was again involved in finishing her previous CALF procedure on March 24, and due to the computer-time constraints, she was again unable to start her House Scene. At the end of the computer time, after she had finally finished the CALF procedure, she went back to the classroom and wrote in her notebook (Figure 21):

In the Reflections forms in their Designer's Notebooks (i.e., the above "Problems I had Today" form), students would briefly describe whatever problems they had encountered that day. Whenever Debbie managed to solve her problems during the computer-time period, she would say, much like her peers, "I had no problems today." In general, the children reported their problems for one of two reasons: (a) when they got stuck with an unsolved problem at the *end* of a session; or (b) when they had a problem *during* a session that they could not solve by *themselves* and had to be helped by their teacher, myself, or their peers. This phenomenon—what children perceived as "problems" or defined as "problem solving"—requires further investigation. It seems to suggest that the children's own definitions and perceptions of these issues were slightly different from those of researchers involved in conducting studies about "children's problem solving."

Another interesting issue related to this particular Reflections form, and other similar ones, was Debbie's tendency to check "FRACTIONS" for the following item, in which the children were asked:

OVERALL, THE PROBLEMS I HAD TODAY ARE MAINLY RELATED TO (check in):
___ LOGO/X FRACTIONS/___ DESIGN/___ EXPLAINING OR TEACHING SOMETHING
___ OTHER: _____

It is important to note that all the other items on the Reflections forms were open ended. This was the only well-defined item, and had been designed by the researcher in order to capture the children's general feelings about what their problems related to, or what the main issues in each of the ISDP working sessions were. If they wished, they could check none of the options, check only one, check a few, or check all of the options. One day, I asked Debbie why she almost always checked "FRACTIONS" as her answer to this item. I was fascinated by her answer:

Debbie: *Because I don't have any other problems. My problems are in fractions.*
   Idit: *What do you mean?*
Debbie: *I don't have problems with Logo.*
   Idit: *Really*
Debbie: *I mean . . . [pause] I know how to solve it in Logo but not in fractions.*
   Idit: *Aha. . .*
Debbie: *I mean that . . . I have to learn about fractions. I still have to learn A LOT!*
   Idit: *And what about Logo, and designing your screens, and teaching third graders?*
Debbie: *Well . . . [pause]. . . It's not that I know it already, but* I can *think about it. I
        can. . . I usually know what to do. And with fractions it's much more trickier. I
        am thinking about fractions all the time. Besides, this is my Fractions
        Project. . . I do things about fractions. . . I do other things too. But I like
        explaining or teaching, there's no problem with that one. I have some problems
        with Logo, sometimes, but usually I can. . . Well, Naomi helped me once, and
        Don helped me once, and you helped me a few times. . . But I have [problems
        with] Logo* because *I've problems with fractions. [smiling] Do you
        understand?!*

I think I did understand . . . and I suggest here that Debbie's interesting
answer showed her general concept of the project as a whole.

   What did the Project really mean for her? For Debbie, it seems that the
project as a whole did indeed mean "fractions." It also meant teaching and
designing and programming and having fun, but above all, it meant "fractions."
My data indicate that Debbie was usually satisfied with her abilities in designing,
drawing, writing, and teaching. She also felt satisfied with her involvement with
Logo programming. She did not perceive her occasional need for help in Logo as
a problem. This may be a result of the culture and of people's general attitudes
towards Logo in Project Headlight. It also might be related to her notion that
having problems with Logo was an integral part of the "deal." On one occasion
she told me: *"There is no one here that doesn't have problems with Logo. No
one. You have bugs all the time but you fix them . . . to make your programs
work."*

   I find her thoughts about the relationships between the Logo and fractions
problems—that her ongoing difficulties with Logo related directly to (or were
caused by) those with fractions—very interesting. By stating her perceptions,
Debbie revealed her constant conflict (and her metacognitive awareness of that
conflict) of having many grandiose plans, and of wanting to design a complex
screen about fractions that could not be easily implemented in Logo (due to her
relatively limited skills in programming). This therefore caused difficulties in
Logo as well: *"But I have problems with Logo because I've problems with
fractions."*

   In addition, Debbie's motivations behind each of her screens usually were: her
thinking about her own problems with fractions, about what representation of
fractions she should create, and about how to teach third-grade children about

fractions. Moreover, in her regular math curriculum, Debbie was not very secure about her knowledge of fractions. She was not in the high-math group, and had not been able to pass any of the conventional math tests without making several mistakes, therefore getting average to low grades. She probably did not feel as satisfied about her fractions knowledge as she did about designing, teaching, or programming. (There were also no tests on designing, teaching, or programming.) All these reasons, taken together, probably explain why she only checked "fractions" in the Reflections Forms as her constant and main "problem" within the software design project.

March 26: Implementation Step 1. On March 26, Debbie finally managed to start implementing the House Scene. In her designer's notebook, she did not create any new plan, but referred her imaginary reader to her plans *"from the four previous pages"* of the notebook. In her plans of that day, March 26, she also summarized the changes she had made on March 24: *"I am making two extra wagons to it."* The following (Figure 22) is a replica of Debbie's Planning Form of March 26 from her Designer's Notebook.

Debbie started working on her House on March 26. She worked in the Logo direct-mode for a while, drawing the house and roof in different colors and sizes, placing them at different points on the computer screen. She then checked the list of commands accumulated in the Logo Command Center, deleted several lines, changed a few inputs for colors or sizes, and used the appropriate function keys for copying what she wanted to put in her procedure (i.e., with the Function 1 and the arrow keys she marked what she wanted to copy; with the Function 2 key she cut the marked command lines; she flipped the page and, with the Function 4 key, she pasted the lines into the Editor). She then created a procedure by adding a procedure name: TO HOUSE at the top of the list, and the word END to the bottom.

"Let's see . . ." she said to herself while flipping the page and typing HOUSE at the Command Center. The shapes looked rather disorganized on the screen, to say the least. Debbie spent a few seconds looking at the picture on the screen (probably analyzing it), and then entered the Logo Editor again. She used a rather sophisticated strategy for organizing her procedure and for detecting where the problems were: she deleted some interrelated FDs and BKs, and more important, she added PU HOME at the beginning of each "chunk." In other words, she divided the long procedure by typing PU HOME in six places: (a) at the beginning of the entire procedure, before the roof and the house outlines were drawn; (b) between drawing the house outline and drawing the line dividing the house into two halves; (c) between dividing the roof into halves and shading the left half of the roof in orange; (d) between shading the roof half in orange and drawing the door; (e) between dividing the door into two halves and shading of the top door half in red; and (f) at the end of the procedure. (Three other PU HOME were there already for moving the Turtle to desired spots on the screen. She did not change those.)

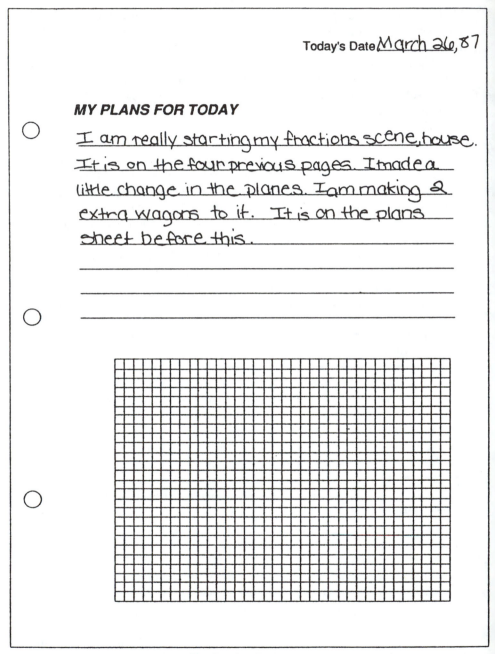

Today's Date March 26, 87

MY PLANS FOR TODAY

I am really starting my fractions scene, house. It is on the four previous pages. I made a little change in the planes. I am making 2 extra wagons to it. It is on the plans sheet before this.

Figure 22.   March 26. A New Plan for the Future.

The following is Debbie's procedure with my interpretations of the code (in brackets). I underlined the PU HOMEs Debbie added just before the end of that session to show the way she herself chunked her procedure into its meaningful units.

TO HOUSE   **[First Step. March 26]**
    <u>pu home</u>

setc 4   [sets the pen color to red]
pu setpos [-65 25]
                                [positions the Turtle at the top left corner of the house]
rt 45   [the angle needed to draw the left side of the roof]
pd fd 100   [draws the left side of the roof]
rt 90 fd 100   [turns right and draws the right side of the roof]
rt 135 fd 140 lt 90
                                [turns right and draws the bottom of the roof, which is also the top of1 the house]
setc 1   [changes pen color to blue]
fd 100   [draws the left side of the house]
setc 13   [changes the pen color to pink]
lt 90 fd 140   [turns left and draws the bottom line for the house]
lt 90 setc 10   [turns left and changes the pen color to green]
fd 100   [draws the right side of the house]
    <u>pu home</u>

pu setpos [10 0]
                                [moves the Turtle to one point on the middle line of the house]
setc 11   [changes pen color to light blue]
pu bk 75   [moves back to the bottom line of the house]
pd fd 100   [draws a line that divides the house into two halves, in light blue]
pu home pd fill   [fills the left half of the house in light blue]
pu setpos [10 25]
                                [moves to the middle of the top line of the house, or bottom of roof]
setc 12   [changes pen color to orange]
pd fd 68   [draws an orange-colored line that divides the roof into two halves]
    <u>pu home</u>

pu setpos [20 35]
                                [moves to the middle of the right half of the roof]
pd fill   [fills the right half of the roof in orange color]
    <u>pu home</u>

pu setpos [25 -75]
                                [moves to the bottom right of the house for creating the door]

```
setc 5              [changes the pen color to purple]
pd fd 60            [draws the left side of the door]
setc 9              [changes the pen color to blue]
rt  90 fd 30        [turns right and draws the top of the door]
rt  90
setc 4              [changes the pen color to red]
fd  60              [draws the right side of the door]
    pu home
pu setpos [25 -40]
                    [moves to approximately the middle of the door]
pu bk 3             [corrects Turtle position in the middle of the left
                    side of the door]
rt  90 pd fd 30     [turns right and draws a line that divides the door
                    into two halves]
pu setpos [36 -33]
                    [moves the Turtle to the middle of the top door
                    half]
pd fill             [fills the top door half in red]
    pu home
END
```

In fact, at the end of the computer time on March 26, I sat with Debbie and asker her what each of the lines in her Logo code meant. She observed how I wrote the code with her explanations on my piece of paper (she spoke slowly, as though aware that she was collaborating with me on my data collection). Her explanations were very precise and demonstrated her understanding of what the different commands in Logo were doing, as well as of what the relationships were between them. On this occasion, I also asked her whether there was another way to draw the house, the roof, and the door, other than drawing them line by line.

Debbie: *Yes. This is a rectangle (pointing at the house), a triangle (pointing at the roof), and another rectangle (pointing at the door). But I do it like this 'cause . . . you see . . . I changed the colors.*

Idit: *What do you mean?*

Debbie: *Each line is in a different color. It's nicer. Red line, green, pink, blue line [pointing at the different lines on the computer screen]. I could not use Repeats here and all of that, because of these colors.*

I find this an interesting point, because an outsider could have entered into this particular situation, read Debbie's HOUSE procedure, and said: "After all this time she invested in programming, this girl still does not know how to use REPEAT for creating simple rectangles or a triangle." Or "Look at her spaghetti code . . . with no subprocedures, etc." But having worked with Debbie, and knowing her previous procedures, I was aware that, by that time, she already

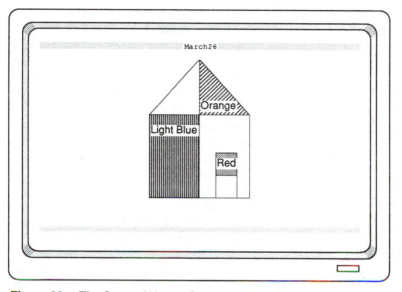

Figure 23.   The State of House Screen on March 26 (after Implementation Step 1).

knew how to use REPEAT and what using REPEAT meant in programming. Debbie *chose* not to use REPEAT in this design, because she wanted to program each line in a different color. Her answer to my question (my question did not include the words REPEAT or "subprocedures") also demonstrated that she clearly understood my question and its purpose, but that she *"could not use REPEATs here and all of that, because of these colors."*

At the end of computer time on March 26, Debbie's screen of the House Scene looked like Figure 23.

This screen was very colorful (and cannot easily be depicted in the limited black-and-white medium that is now used to describe it): the roof's outline was red; the line that divided the roof into two halves, and the roof's left half, were orange; the left side of the house was blue; the right side of the house was green; the bottom side of the house was pink; the top side of the house was red; the line that divided the house into two halves and the shaded half on its left were light blue; the left side of the door was purple; the top side of the door was blue; the right side of the door was red; and the line dividing the door into two halves and the top door half were also red.

What role did this process of playing with colors play in Debbie's learning? Debbie was really involved in a technical and mathematical project, and we can also recall that her teacher had originally described her as someone "not very interested in mathematics" and "quite low in math skills." However, in the context of this project she did not seem to perceive her work as personally irrelevant because of its mathematical and technical components. Observing her planning, designing, drawing, and implementations during the period of the House Scene might, in fact, make us think that Debbie was not involved in a math project at all, but rather in a visual arts project. The computer and Logo offered Debbie something she could not refuse: dealing with artistic goals, with drawing, with colors, and with combining colors. It is another example for a child's exercising mathematical skills by using the technology for artistic creation.

Turkle (1984), Weir (1986), and Papert (1986), among others, discuss these very issues quite often in asking how using a piece of advanced technology changes the child's relationship with things so technical or mathematical. Turkle, in her research, concentrated on describing cases of children who progressed quite deeply into programming but with artistic motivations. These findings seem to be relevant to Debbie's case as well.

Finally, at the end of the computer time on March 26, Debbie went to the classroom and wrote in her Designer's Notebook (Figure 24).

March 27: Implementation Step 2. In the March 27 entry, we can read that Debbie attempted to finish up her House Scene and start work on the two new screens shown on the grid below (Figure 25). She divided the grid in her Designer's Notebook into two parts. Each part represented one screen. The screen on the left was designed to show $^6/_9$, while the screen on the right was designed to show the equivalence of $^8/_{16} = ^1/_2$.

However, Debbie never managed to accomplish these two screens. When she logged into her computer, the first thing she did was run the procedure HOUSE she had created the day before. She smiled while looking at the computer screen. She ran the same procedure three more times while silently looking at her screen and mumbling something to herself, which I noticed as I was walking around the computers that day. I approached her and briefly asked her what her plans were for that day.

Debbie	*Did you see what I did yesterday?*
Idit:	*Of course. I was sitting next to you, for some of the time, remember?*
Debbie:	*Oh. . . Yea. . . But look. . .* [She pointed at her House picture on the screen].
Idit:	*I love it. Great job Debbie! And what do you think you'll do now?*
Debbie:	*Uhm. . . To change little things here and there and to finish it.*
Idit:	*Change what things?*
Debbie:	*[Instead of answering me, Debbie entered the Logo Page and deleted a few lines from her Logo code, and said] I don't need these now.*
Idit:	*Don't need what?*
Debbie:	*[long pause, deleting something . . . typing something else]. . . This.*

Debbie deleted most of the PU HOMEs she had added the day before. She also deleted the spaces and "shrank" the procedure "*so it would not take up too much*

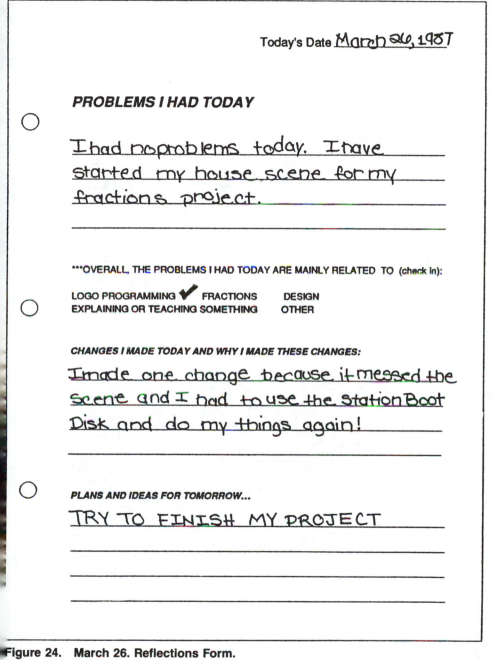

Today's Date March 26, 1987

PROBLEMS I HAD TODAY

I had no problems today. I have started my house scene for my fractions project.

***OVERALL, THE PROBLEMS I HAD TODAY ARE MAINLY RELATED TO (check in):

LOGO PROGRAMMING ✔ FRACTIONS   DESIGN
EXPLAINING OR TEACHING SOMETHING   OTHER

CHANGES I MADE TODAY AND WHY I MADE THESE CHANGES:

I made one change because it messed the scene and I had to use the station Boot Disk and do my things again!

PLANS AND IDEAS FOR TOMORROW...

TRY TO FINISH MY PROJECT

Figure 24.   March 26. Reflections Form.

Today's Date _March 27, 1987_

MY PLANS FOR TODAY

I will try to finish my fraction house.

I only need to finish the wagons and the sun.

If I have time. i'm going to start a new fractions project. I'll draw what it will look like below.

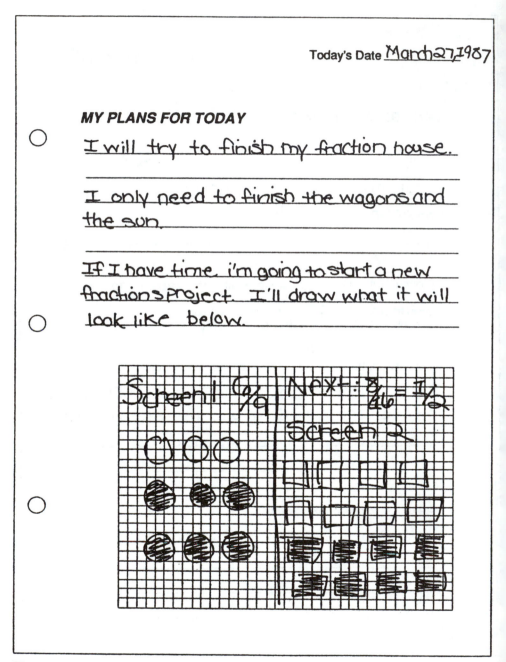

Figure 25.   March 27 Plan.

space on the Page." The following is the result of her modification of the house procedure on March 27:

TO HOUSE   [Second Step, March 27]
```
pu home setc 4 pu setpos [-65 25] rt 45 pd fd 100 rt 90 fd 100 rt
135 fd 140 lt 90
setc 1 fd 100 setc 13 lt 90 fd 140 lt 90 setc 10 fd 100
pu setpos [10 0] setc 11
pu bk 75 pd fd 100 pu home pd fill pu setpos [10 25] setc 12
pd fd 68
pu setpos [20 35] pd fill pu setpos [25 -75] setc 5 pd fd 60
setc 9 rt 90 fd 30
rt 90 setc 4 fd 60 pu setpos [25 -40] pu bk 3 rt 90 pd fd 30 pu
setpos [36 -33] pd fill
pu home
```
END

After doing the above, Debbie typed "house" in the Command Center and was satisfied to see that her changes did not ruin the procedure, and that the executed picture remained the same. In direct mode she started programming one of the wooden wagons at the bottom left of the computer screen. Her finalized wagon was programmed in the following code:

```
pu setpos [-150 -40]   [moves the Turtle to the bottom-left screen]
pd repeat 2 [fd 30 rt 90 fd 60 rt 90]
                        [draws a rectangle, the body of the wagon]
pu home pu setpose [-155 -50]
                        [moves the Turtle to the place of left wheel]
setc 1+random 14     [random selection for the wheel's color]
pd repeat 360 [fd .2 rt 1]
                        [draws the left wheel]
pu home pu setpos [-120 -40]
                        [moves the Turtle to the middle of the wagon]
setc 4 pd fd 30 pu rt 90
fd 20 rt 90 fd 10 pd fill
                        [draws a red line that cuts the wagon into two
                        halves, and moves the Turtle to shade in the right
                        half]
pu home
pu setpos [-145 -50] pd fill
                        [moves the Turtle into left Wheel, shades it]
pu home
setc1+random14
pu setpos [-90 -50]    [moves the Turtle to right side of the wagon]
pd repeat 360 [fd .2 lt 1]
                        [draws right wheel in a randomly-selected color]
```

setc 4 lt 90 pu fd 10 pd fill pu home
                    [shades in red the whole right wheel]

We can see that Debbie decided to shade in the wheels completely, each in a different color, instead of shading only half of each. In regard to her shading of the wheels, she said: *"It's easier* [in terms of programming]. *They are each* [each wheel] *shaded in a different color, so it's like a half too."* In other words, due to programming constraints, Debbie decided to change her original plans (of shading a half of each wheel) and decided, instead, to shade each wheel in a different color. In this way, she considered the two wheels together to be a whole, so that each whole wheel, being in a different color, became the half of the whole.

After working on this for a while, and after finalizing all the SETPOSitions, REPEATS, SETColors, the sizes of the wagon and its wheels, Debbie tried her procedure line by line several times. Originally, she had written REPEAT 4 [FD 30 RT 90 FD 60 RT 90] as her commands for the rectangle that represented the body of the wagon. This is a typical mistake among young programmers, who often transfer their knowledge of how to make a square—REPEAT 4 [FD 30 RT 90]— into their programming of a rectangle.

I do not think that Debbie shared this misconception but was probably just careless in typing the commands. Also, her previous procedures and her Logo Post-Tests indicated that she understood that concept well. However, after the teacher commented on the fact that *"REPEAT 2 would be a more accurate way of doing that,"* Debbie said, *"I know. . . I know"* and quickly changed the rectangle commands into REPEAT 2 [FD 30 RT 90 FD 60 RT 90]. We can also see how Debbie used SETPOSitions for almost all of the positionings of the Turtle on the screen. This time, she used the PU HOME strategy to place the Turtle at the center of the screen before each SETPOS, which helped her think about and figure out the different x and y coordinates. In addition, she was accurate in her circles commands, which she could draw both clockwise and counterclockwise.

Finally, she copied the lines of code from the Command Center, using the appropriate function keys, and pasted them in her HOUSE procedure:

TO HOUSE [Third Step, March 27]
```
pu home setc 4 pu setpos [-65 25] rt 45 pd fd 100 rt 90 fd 100
rt  135 fd 140 lt 90
setc 1 fd 100 setc 13 lt 90 fd 140 lt 90 setc 10 fd 100
pu setpos [10 0] setc 11
pu bk 75 pd fd 100 pu home pd fill pu setpos [10 25]
setc 12 pd fd 68
pu setpos [20 35] pd fill pu setpos [25 -75] setc 5 pd fd 60 setc 9
rt  90 fd 30
rt  90 setc 4 fd 60 pu setpos [25 -40] pu bk 3 rt 90 pd fd 30
pu setpos [36 -33] pd fill
pu home pu setpos [-150 -40] pd repeat 2 [fd 30 rt 90 fd 60 rt 90]
```

```
pu home
pu setpose [-155 -50] setc 1+ random 14 pd repeat 360 [fd .2 rt 1]
pu home pu setpos [-120 -40] setc 4 pd fd 30 pu rt 90 fd 20 rt 90
fd 10 pd fill
pu home pu setpos [-145 -50] pd fill pu home setc 1 +random 14 pu
setpos [-90 -50]
pd repeat 360 [fd .2 lt 1] setc 4 lt 90 pu fd 10 pd fill pu home
END
```

She ran the procedure to see if it worked, and it did. The computer time was over. That day, Debbie wrote in her Designer's Notebook (Figure 26).

Debbie did not report on changing her original plans about the representations of halves using the wagon wheels (i.e., shading the whole wheel instead of a half of each wheel). Instead, she wrote: *"I made no changes except try to finish the House Scene."*

The next screen (Figure 27) represents how Debbie's House Scene looked at the end of the computer time on March 27.

March 30: Implementation Step #3. On March 30, Debbie was planning to finish the House Scene. She also wrote about her attempts to start planning the way she wanted the project to look (Figure 28):

> Idit: *Which project, Debbie?*
> Debbie: *My Fractions Project.*
> Idit: *And what do you mean by planning the way you want it to look?*
> Debbie: *I have three things now. HALF, CALF, and HOUSE. I have to check how they look together.*

Because she was very eager to finish the House Scene, I did not want to bother her anymore. She started to work on the second wagon while I was talking to her. However, this was the first time Debbie had ever mentioned anything about planning how the project would look as a whole, and how her screens might look together In fact, she dealt with this issue at the end of the following day's computer-time period, on March 31. She then realized the need to make decisions about the order of her procedures (she had five by then) and finally created a superprocedure.

On March 30 Debbie also wrote: *"If I have time, I will use some of my notes."* By this I think she meant to use her notes from March 23, 24, and 27, which were related to the designs she planned to accomplish *after* the House Scene was completed. We can see that Debbie intended and finally did make full use of her designer's notebook. She planned new designs while still involved in the implementation of old ones, and referred to previous plans and drawings several times during the process. She enjoyed planning screens in advance and did not seem to perceive this as a waste of time. On the contrary, she planned screens because she

Today's Date <u>March 27, 1987</u>

PROBLEMS I HAD TODAY

<u>I had no problems today.</u>

***OVERALL, THE PROBLEMS I HAD TODAY ARE MAINLY RELATED TO (check in):**

LOGO PROGRAMMING ✔ FRACTIONS   DESIGN
EXPLAINING OR TEACHING SOMETHING   OTHER

CHANGES I MADE TODAY AND WHY I MADE THESE CHANGES:

<u>I made no changes except try to</u>
<u>finish the House scene.</u>

PLANS AND IDEAS FOR TOMORROW...

<u>I want to finish my house fraction</u>
<u>scene.</u>

Figure 26.   March 27. Reflections Form.

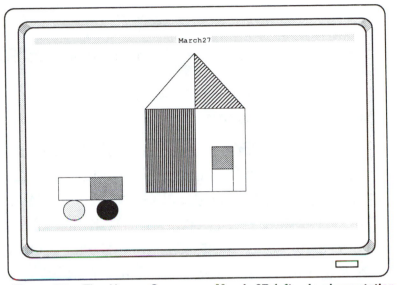

Figure 27.   The House Screen on March 27 (after Implementation Step 2).

thought she would eventually go back to her notes when the time came to implement them.

While working at the computer, Debbie programmed another wooden wagon in a very similar way to that of her first wooden wagon, of March 27. She also succeeded in programming the sun and in adding an instructional sentence at the top of her screen.

By the end of March 31, Debbie's House procedure was the following (with my interpretations in brackets):

TO HOUSE [Third and Final Step, March 30]
 [THE HOUSE, THE DOOR, AND THE ROOF:]
pu home setc 4 pu setpos [-65 25] rt 45 pd fd 100 rt 90 fd 100
rt 135 fd 140
lt 90 setc 1 fd 100 setc 13 lt 90 fd 140 lt 90 setc 10 fd 100
pu setpos [10 0] setc 11
pu bk 75 pd fd 100 pu home pd fill pu setpos [10 25] setc 12
pd fd 68
pu setpos [20 35] pd fill pu setpos [25 -75] setc 5 pd fd 60 setc 9
rt 90 fd 30
rt 90 setc 4 fd 60 pu setpos [25 -40] pu bk 3 rt 90 pd fd 30
pu setpos [36 -33] pd fill
 [THE LEFT WOODEN WAGON:]
pu home pu setpos [-150 -40] pd repeat 2 [fd 30 rt 90 fd 60 rt 90]
pu home

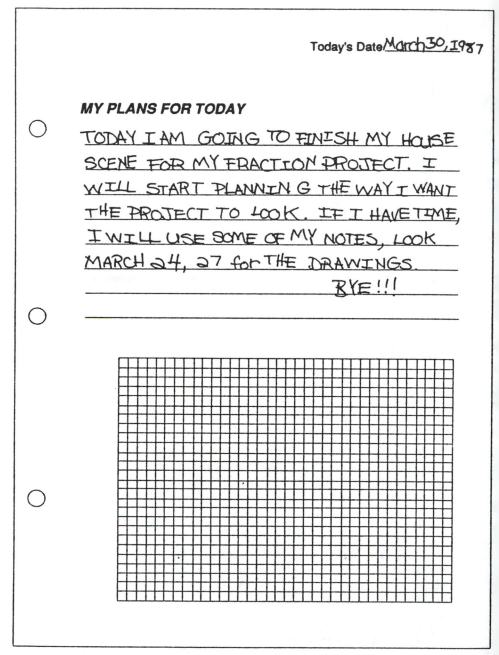

Today's Date _March 30, 1987_

MY PLANS FOR TODAY

TODAY I AM GOING TO FINISH MY HOUSE SCENE FOR MY FRACTION PROJECT. I WILL START PLANNING THE WAY I WANT THE PROJECT TO LOOK. IF I HAVE TIME, I WILL USE SOME OF MY NOTES, LOOK MARCH 24, 27 for THE DRAWINGS.
                                    BYE!!!

Figure 28.   March 30. Plan.

```
pu setpose [-155 -50] setc 1+ random 14 pd repeat 360 [fd .2 rt 1]
pu home
pu setpos [-120 -40] setc 4 pd fd 30 pu rt 90 fd 20 rt 90 fd 10
pd fill
pu home pu setpos [-145 -50] pd fill pu home setc 1 +random 14
pu setpos [-90 -50] pd repeat 360 [fd .2 lt 1] setc 4 lt 90
pu fd 10 pd fill
```

[THE RIGHT WOODEN WAGON:]
```
pu home pu setpos [85 -45] pd repeat 2 [fd 30 rt 90 fd 60 rt 90]
rt  90 fd 30 lt 90 fd 30 pu lt 135 fd 15 pd fill pu home
setc 1+random 14 pu setpos [80 -55] pd repeat 360 [fd .2 rt 1]
setc 4 pu rt 90 fd 10
pd fill pu home pu setpos [155 -55] pd repeat 360 [fd .2 rt 1]
setc 4 lt 90 pu fd 10 pd fill
```

[THE SUN:]
```
pu home pu setpos [95 65] setc 14
pd repeat 360 [fd .3 rt 1] rt 90 pd fd 35 pu home
pu setpos [115 75] pd fill
```

[THE INSTRUCTIONAL SENTENCE:]
```
pr [This is a house. Almost every shape is ½! I am trying to say, that you
use fractions, almost every day of your life!]
```
END

On March 30, at the end of the computer time, Debbie returned to her classroom and wrote in her notebook (Figure 29).

Debbie wrote that she had finished the House Scene but had "not accomplished all of it." I think she was referring to her plans of March 24 and 27 to create four wagons in the scene. Apparently Debbie was aware of her misimplementation of part of her original plan (i.e., having decided not to create four wagons, only two: one on the right side of the house, the other on the left). I never asked her why she had made that decision. I assume it was because she really wanted to finish the House Scene in order to go on with the rest of the Project and start working on new screens.

Debbie also wrote (in the above Reflections form): *"I made no changes but* I did three or four more procedures" [emphasis added]. What did she mean by this?

One possible interpretation is that she did not understand the meaning of the word *procedure,* or that she misused it in her writing. However, knowing Debbie's knowledge of programming and her previous uses of procedures and subprocedures, I suggest interpreting her words in another way. I believe that, although she programmed the whole scene in one long procedure that she named *house,* she really viewed each of its parts as a separate unit. In other words, on that day she added the right wagon procedure (one part), the sun procedure (another part), and the instructional sentence procedure (a third part). To my mind, Debbie's written sentence above (i.e., *"I did three or four more pro-*

Today's Date March 30, 1987

PROBLEMS I HAD TODAY

I had no problems today. I have accomplished everything I planned today, except finish ALL of it,

Of course I couldn't!

***OVERALL, THE PROBLEMS I HAD TODAY ARE MAINLY RELATED TO (check in):

LOGO PROGRAMMING   FRACTIONS   DESIGN
EXPLAINING OR TEACHING SOMETHING   OTHER

CHANGES I MADE TODAY AND WHY I MADE THESE CHANGES:

I had no   I made no changes but I did three or four more procedures.

PLANS AND IDEAS FOR TOMORROW...

I WILL DO MORE FRACTIONS PROJECTS!!!

BYE!!!

Figure 29.   March 30. Reflections Form.

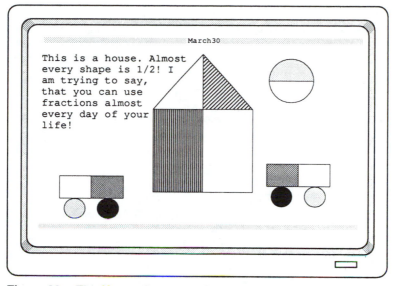

Figure 30.   The House Screen is Completed.

cedures") represents her *modular way of thinking*. She did not actually use subprocedures for each of the objects in the House Scene, but she definitely thought of each object as a separate part or, in her words, a procedure.

The final product was different than Debbie's original plans in several ways (the size, number, and colors of the wagons; the location of the sun; the instructional statement on the screen; etc.). For example, on March 23 she planned to print on the screen: *"This is a scene using regular human things. No matter what you use fractions on, you can use it on anything."* However, in the final version of the House Scene of March 30, she decided instead to write: *"This is a house. Almost every shape is ¹/₂! I am trying to say that you use fractions, almost every day of your life!"* I perceive the two versions of the instructional sentence as very similar in terms of their overall instructional message.

Debbie managed to run the finalized HOUSE procedure twice before the computer time was over. She insisted that her teacher and Naomi, who sat next to her, look at it. Her teacher was very impressed and asked Debbie to print the screen (create a hard copy) so they could hang it on the class Logo-Ideas board. Debbie also asked her friend Cassania to look at the House Scene. Cassania walked over to Debbie's computer with two other children from the class, a boy and a girl. They were all impressed, crying, "Debbie this is cool!" "Debbie this is the freshest!" "Neat, Debbie, neat!" At the end of the computer time on March 30, Debbie's House Scene was completed (see Figure 30).

In summary, we note a significant growth in Debbie's planning and programming skills during this phase. She was able to think about past, current, and

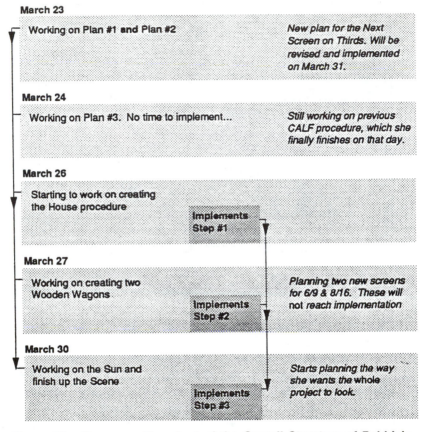

Figure 31.   Summary Flowchart of the Overall Structure of Debbie's Planning and Programming Work on the House Scene.

future projects simultaneously, and to use her Designer's Notebook to keep her on track. At the same time, she was flexible enough to change her plans so that she could keep to a schedule and reduce her workload. As a summary, let us examine again the general structure of her complex processes of designing and constructing this screen. It is seen as a flowchart in Figure 31.

In addition, we saw that Debbie's approach to debugging was basically a positive one. She seemed confident that she could develop whatever Logo skills she needed to carry out her ideas. In fact, her programming shows greater complexity, which she managed through a personal but successful method of chunking, which she eventually eliminated to save space on the Logo page. Clearly, implementing personal goals—like painting the House Scene in an eye-catching way—overrode any programmer's aesthetic she might have had about efficient use of REPEATs in programming geometric shapes. But we see that she made a choice, and the choice was not determined by ignorance. Her colorful screen was quite the hit with her fellow students, a reaction that must have buoyed her increasing confidence.

2.4. TWO-THIRDS: "ONE OF THE FRACTIONS TEACHERS USE MOST OFTEN AS EXAMPLES FOR TEACHING THEIR STUDENTS"

Debbie's goal after finishing her House Scene was to create a representation for two-thirds, something she had decided to do while in the planning stage of the House Scene. In her March 23 notes she wrote: *"I think I have to finish my old fractions project [the third screen she had created, with the four shapes divided into halves, see Section 3 above]. I am going to make a scene where every shape is shaded half. When I'm finish I'm going to do $2/3$ for my project & so on."* On March 31, when she finally finished the House Scene, she decided to take a short break to write poetry and then work on representing thirds. The plan from her Designer's Notebook is shown in Figure 32.

Debbie's said on her design (in Figure 32), which she playfully called "A FRACTIONAL FROG," that she had not planned to draw a frog, but that it looked like one after she finished drawing it, so she gave it this name. In the design, she emphasized the idea of shading the different sides of the halves or thirds, showing that, in her words, *"it doesn't matter which side of the shape is shaded in— all the parts, whether they are shaded or not, can be fractions."*

Debbie thought of this design as being divided into three parts. The first, the "frog's ears," is made up of the two top circles divided into thirds—the right circle showing $1/3$, the left circle $2/3$. The second part, the "frog's eyes," is the two middle circles showing halves. The left half of the right eye, and the right half of the left eye, are shaded. The third part, which she called "the frog's necklace," is composed of six small circles and shows that $3/6 = 1/2$.

The ears and eyes are still in the mode of "showing fractions," or thirds and halves, respectively. The necklace shows how to use sixths to make the transition between thirds and halves. While this is not explicit in the drawing, an interview with her that day made her intention clear:

Idit: *Why did you put all these things in one design?*
Debbie: *Because sixths can be thirds . . . and sixths can be halves. . .*
Idit: *What do you mean?*
Debbie: *You can put two sixths on one third.*
Idit: *Why did you choose not to show that here?*
Debbie: *. . . 'cause I wanted to show something else here. That you can put three-sixths on top of one-half too. Everybody knows that $2/6 = 1/3$.*

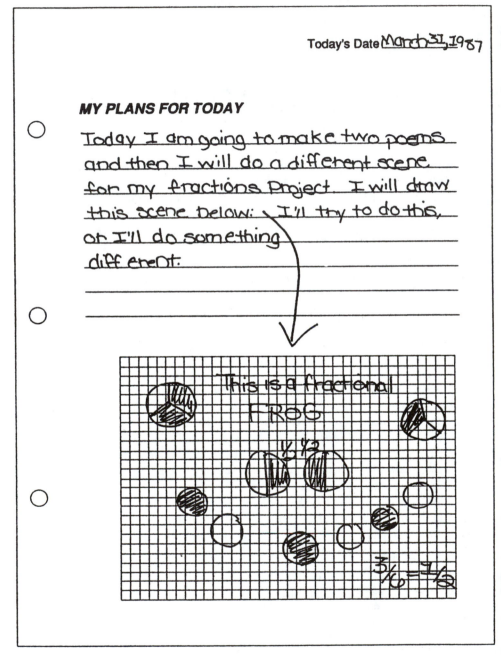

Today's Date March 31, 1987

MY PLANS FOR TODAY

Today I am going to make two poems and then I will do a different scene for my fractions project. I will draw this scene below: I'll try to do this, or I'll do something different.

This is a fractional
FROG

1/3 1/3

3/6 = 1/2

Figure 32.   March 31. Plan.

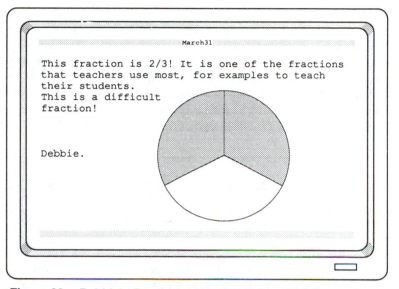

Figure 33. Debbie's Screen for Teaching about Thirds.

I assume that Debbie had decided not to show, in this particular design, that $2/6$ = $1/3$, since *"everybody knows that"* (in other words, *she* knew it). By that time, she understood the equivalence between thirds and sixths, easily responding to the questions I asked her about this equivalence.

Debbie never implemented the Fractional Frog design. Instead, she implemented only one part of this design, the frog's right ear. She programmed one big circle divided into thirds and shaded two of those thirds (see Figure 33).

The instructional sentence Debbie wrote on that screen suggests her awareness of three things: (a) thirds are generally more difficult fractions than halves; (b) since thirds are difficult, teachers use them most often as examples to teach their students; and (c) now that she herself is teaching, she is using thirds like all other teachers.

Debbie seemed to be enjoying this role playing. She not only wanted to present difficult material, but she also wanted to test it. The structure of ISDP facilitated this direct empowerment. On the one hand, the children's activities were not graded, but, on the other hand, they were encouraged to teach and test others. Thus, they were able, if only in a small way, to shift status roles. Like their teacher, their learning was not subject to graded testing (the children were clear that pre- and posttesting was not for purposes of grading), although they had been empowered to teach and test as they liked. By doing so, they demystified the teacher's role and made their own role as students more comfortable. Debbie's particular decisions revealed something else about the principle of learning-through-teaching. While she was still "externalizing the learning self," (as we discussed in Section 2.2) she began to assimilate some knowledge (e.g., that $1/3 = 2/6$) to the point where she claimed that "everybody knows that." In order for her to retain sensitivity about what is easy or difficult, it seems that the gap between her own learning and her instructional design was very small. In other words, more than the learning self was being externalized; she had begun to construct a personality as a teacher or a sophisticated cognizer. Learning involves more than construction of a path into a given area of knowledge; it also involves assimilation of that knowledge into larger intellectual structures where the details of the learning path are forgotten.

2.4.1. The Programming Ideas Behind Logo Quizzing Procedures

On March 27, in response to the students' needs and requests, we conducted a 10-minute discussion on creating interactive screens or quizzing procedures. In this session, the teacher showed the children how to create a procedure that asked the user a multiple-choice question, took the user's input or answer, and gave the user appropriate feedback for a right or wrong answer. Students suggested different approaches, expressing their ideas and feelings about what they considered appropriate ways for asking questions—giving hints, providing the user with an option to "try again," "allowing" the computer to give the right answer, and so on.

During those ten minutes, the children were learning and discussing two concepts simultaneously: (a) Logo programming concepts, such as how to use conditionals, and conditionals evaluation (i.e., the Logo possibility to choose between two expressions to evaluate), how to use IFELSE as an operation, how to create a space in the computer memory for variables (i.e., for accepting the user's input), how to use READLIST or READCHAR, how to use recursion, and how to format all the above in Logo (i.e., where and why to use brackets, parentheses, quotation marks, or colons); and (b) instructional design concepts, such as how to ask questions, what pictures to use if any, what explanations or hints to include, what feedback to give, how to make their programs "user friendly," and so on.

Let us focus for a moment on the Logo programming (list processing) concepts included in a basic "testing procedure." In general, when IFELSE is used as an operation, it requires three inputs. The first input must include an expression that evaluates the input as either true or false; the second and third inputs must be lists containing Logo expressions, instructions, and commands. If the first input's value is true, then the output of IFELSE is a result of evaluating the second input; if the first input's value is false, then the output of IFELSE is a result of evaluating the third input. As an example, let us follow this simple procedure, called QUIZ:

```
TO QUIZ
PR [2∨3 + 2∨6 = ? Please choose one answer: 3∨6, 4∨9, 1,
         4∨18]
```
> [Logo prints the above multiple-choice question on the screen.]

```
NAME READLIST "USER.ANS
```
> [The user types an answer which Logo "reads" and saves in a special memory slot called USER.ANS. The programmer has specified the slot's name.]

```
IFELSE (:USER.ANS=[1])
```
> [Logo compares the value of USER.ANS with 1, if the user's answer is "1"; then Logo executes the second input which is the next line of code.]

```
[PR [That's right! Great job! 2∨3 + 2∨6 = 6∨6 = 3∨3 = 1]]
```
> [This is what Logo prints (or does) if the value of USER.ANS = 1 is TRUE]

```
[PR [Well, I guess you must try that one again. Think about how many
sixths equals 2∨3, or how many thirds equals 2∨6. . . Try again. . .] CT
QUIZ]
```
> [This is what Logo executes as the feedback, if the value of USER.ANS = 1 is FALSE; it prints a statement, clears the text on the screen, and calls the procedure QUIZ again.]

```
END
```

In this model procedure, Logo first printed a question, then "read" the user's input, saved it, and later evaluated the user's answer; if the user's answer was, for example, "1," Logo printed on the screen the feedback for the "true" value (that is: THAT'S RIGHT! GREAT JOB!). However, if the user's answer was something other than 1, then Logo printed the second feedback, cleared the text on the screen (CT) and called up the procedure again (QUIZ).

This short procedure, in fact, includes within it several complex programming concepts including the idea of *recursion*. A *recursive procedure* is a procedure that calls itself a subprocedure. In general, "Recursion is an idea that is very simple once you understand it, but which many people have trouble learning about" (Harvey, 1985, p. 70; see also Kurland & Pea, 1983). There are several different ways to approach recursion (e.g., Harvey 1985, pp. 54–120, 142–160). In the above procedure, for example, I included the recursive call as the last instruction. This is called a *tail recursion*. There is a lot to say about the meaning of tail recursion and other, more complex types of recursion. Several researchers have studied children's and adults' misconceptions and understanding of the different types of recursion; however, it is beyond the scope of this section to review the typical problems children and adults had with the idea of recursion and with recursive procedures. Debbie did not demonstrate any misconceptions regarding tail recursion (the only type of recursion she knew and used). In fact, we will see later that she used it quite often in her Project.

2.4.2. Processes of Programming the Representation for Two-Thirds

Debbie's code for the large circle divided into two-thirds was as follows:

```
TO TWO
PU HOME
SETC 1+RANDOM 14          [The computer randomly selects a pen
                          color.]
PD REPEAT 360 [FD 1 RT 1] [Creates a big circle.]
PU SETPOS [60 5]          [Positions the turtle in the middle of the
                          circle.]
SETC 1+RANDOM 14
PD FD 53                  [Draws lines for dividing the circle into
                          thirds.]
PU BK 53
RT 135 PD FD 57
PU BK 57 RT 90
PD FD 62
PU BK 62
RT 45
PU FD 20
SETC 1+RANDOM 14
PD FILL                  [Shades in one third.]
PU BK 40
PD FILL                  [Shades in the second third.]
PU HOME
WAIT 100 PR [THIS FRACTION IS 2∨3 ! IT IS ONE OF THE FRACTIONS
TEACHERS USE MOST FOR EXAMPLES TO TEACH THEIR STUDENTS.]
                          [Prints the instructional statement.]
                          [Prints the instructional statement.]
END
```

This was Debbie's first step in programming her representation of two-thirds. On March 31, it took her 25 minutes to write this procedure, try it, and fix it. She then decided to create her testing procedure, which she called QUESTION1. Using her notes from the classroom discussion of March 27, and with my help, she flipped into the Logo editor and wrote:

```
TO QUESTION1
PR [IS THIS FRACTION, 1∨2, 3∨4, 2∨3, OR 1∨26 ?]
NAME READLIST "ANSWER
IFELSE (ANSWER = [2∨3])
[PR[GREAT!!]] [PR[PLEASE TRY AGAIN] CT WAIT 30 QUESTION 1]
END
```

This procedure prints a question at the top of the screen, asking the user: IS THIS FRACTION $^1/_2$, $^3/_4$, $^2/_3$, OR $^1/_{26}$? The user types in an answer. Logo then reads the user's input (i.e., the answer), and saves it in a memory slot, which Debbie named ANSWER. If the user's answer is "$^2/_3$," Logo prints GREAT! and the procedure is over (or done). If the user's answer is different from $^2/_3$, Logo prints PLEASE TRY AGAIN, remains within the same procedure, but calls it again (i.e., reprints the question). Debbie meant to attach this procedure to her TWO procedure, as described in the following paragraphs.

As soon as Debbie finished typing the QUESTION1 procedure (with my help), and before she even executed it, she entered another line of code to the TWO procedure completely on her own (the videotape shows I was not sitting next to her). This line appears in boldface below:

```
TO TWO
    .
    .
    .
                            [See above, she did not change anything
                            here.]
WAIT 100 PR [THIS FRACTION IS 2\3!
IT IS THE FRACTION TEACHERS USE MOST,
FOR EXAMPLES TO TEACH THEIR STUDENTS.]
WAIT 150
CT QUESTION1                 [She added a WAIT 150, left the picture on,
                            cleared text, and called her testing procedure
                            QUESTION1.]

END
```

Only after she had completed her changes in the TWO procedure did Debbie execute her modified procedure. She called me to come watch it. She was thrilled to find that it worked the way she wanted. She evaluated it by asking Naomi, who was sitting beside her, to try it. It worked for Naomi, too.

2.5. THE FIRST ATTEMPT TO CONNECT THE PARTS: CREATING A SUPERPROCEDURE

Towards the end of the computer time on March 31, Debbie left her poems aside and went back to work on her project. Debbie now had five separate procedures in her Project. The order in which she created them was the following:

1. HALF, designed and programmed on March 9, 10, and 11, and completed on March 16.
2. CALF, designed on March 19 revised on March 23, and completed on March 24.
3. HOUSE, designed and worked on from March 23 to March 30.
4. TWO, designed and programmed on March 31.
5. QUESTION1, also completed on March 31.

In order to execute and check how all the procedures looked together, Debbie had to type one procedure name after the other into the Command Center. She did not yet have any superprocedure that called for all the procedures to appear one after the other. By March 31, Debbie's project started to be, in her words, "really long." It was the first day her project became really meaningful to her as an entity and, as we shall see, it was the first time she decided to use a subprocedure.

Researchers in other studies (e.g., Pea & Kurland, 1983; Heller, 1986; Carver, 1986; Perkins & Martin, 1985; and others) have reported on children's writing nonmodular codes (i.e., the spaghetti-code phenomenon). They found that children did not understand the meaning or purpose of a superprocedure and rarely used superprocedures or subprocedures in their programs unless they were explicitly instructed to do so, as in Carver's (1987) study.

Although Debbie had made some steps towards modularity in her use of PU HOME to divide up her House Scene, she did not use super- or subprocedures until one full month into the project. Her experience, as well as the experiences of other children in the study, throws a different light on research about children's understanding of modularity. That is, children with minimal exposure to Logo, or with minimal explicit instruction in it, do not show much learning, understanding, or knowledge of how to use superprocedures and subprocedures. But children involved in an extensive and intensive programming project will often come to see the need for these on their own.

All the children in ISDP, much like Debbie, eventually created superprocedures and subprocedures. Debbie created five subparts before she decided to create a superprocedure. She first created and thought of each screen or representation as an independent part, with a specific name and role. Only after several procedures worked did she realize that she had "enough parts" to bring them together into a whole—her superprocedure.

When I saw her doing this, I asked her why she had created a superprocedure at all, and why she had chosen to do so at that particular time. She said: *"Now I have enough things [parts] to put together, HALF, CALF, TWO, QUESTION1, and HOUSE. I am tired of typing these [procedure-names] all the time."*

Here we have two very good reasons for creating a superprocedure: (a) conceptual issues—*"I have enough things to put together"* into a whole, or in other words, enough things she could consider a whole; and (b) practical issues—*"I'm tired of typing"* these procedure names over and over again. Thus, she has learned about the purpose and meaning of a superprocedure through experience.

Debbie worked on her superprocedure in three steps. Connecting the parts was not an easy job for her. I observed how long it took her to work out the problem of how and in what order to connect the parts. First, she wrote in the Logo editor the following superprocedure:

```
TO FRACTIONS [the first step]
HALF
CG CT CC
CALF
CG CT CC
TWO        [Includes QUESTION1]
CG CT CC
HOUSE
CG CT CC
END
```

2.5.1. Changing the order of the parts. Although Debbie created the procedure TWO after the procedure HOUSE, she decided to put TWO before HOUSE in her superprocedure. I asked her why. Debbie answered: *"Because it's* [the procedure TWO] *easier than the House Scene* [the procedure HOUSE], *and also the House Scene is nicer."* She considered the two-thirds representation to be less complex, and not as nice as the House Scene. We may not agree with Debbie's assessment of complexity. Certainly, the House Scene was more complex to program and involved much more complex reflection (integrating real-world and formal thinking and trying to translate the scene into an equation), but in the end the scene did not really convey this complexity. Nevertheless, we see that Debbie is applying aesthetic and pedagogical criteria in deciding how to order her presentation; she did not just present them chronologically in the order of creation.

2.5.2. Connecting the Subparts while Thinking about the Target Users

When Debbie executed the FRACTIONS superprocedure for the first time, the different screens were switching too quickly from one to the other. This happened because of the CC (Clear the Command Center), CG (Clear the Graphics), and CT (Clear the Text) commands she wrote after each of the procedures. In order to solve this problem, she first tried to eliminate the CC CT CG lines, but this did not work. "Oh! No!" she cried. The screens were drawn one on top of the other, and the turtle was not at HOME position at the beginning of each procedure, which resulted in chaos. Her second step towards a solution was to add a series of WAIT commands after each procedure, before the CC CG CT line.

```
TO FRACTIONS [the second step, adding WAIT 150 between the picture
and its clearing]
HALF WAIT 150
CG CT CC
CALF WAIT 150
CG CT CC
TWO  WAIT 150
CG CT CC
HOUSE WAIT 400
END
```

Other children in the class had similar problems connecting the subparts into a whole. Debbie solved this problem by adding WAIT between screens before clearing them, as is shown in the Logo code above.

A few days before, another child, named Don, had asked me how to write a program that instructed the user to *"press any key to go on."* He told me that *"The same WAIT 100 is not good for all the children,"* meaning, that it might be too slow for some children or too fast for others. Don wanted to give more control to the users, allowing them to advance in his program at their own pace. He told me that he had seen *"that trick in one of Harry's programs."* (referring to a member of the MIT research and support staff). It was not clear to me what Don meant, and I asked Harry about it. As a result, on March 31, Harry came into the classroom, where the children, their teacher, and I were gathered; he stayed for 10 minutes, and showed the children how to create a procedure that presented something on the computer screen and that instructed the user to press any key to proceed to the next screen.

At the end of the day, after Harry's demonstration, Debbie rushed to her computer and added the new procedure to her project. All the children had learned about WAIT.FOR.USER, but Debbie was one of the first children to implement it. It seems to have fit in well with her instructional design thinking.

2.5.3. A Summary of Debbie's Activities on March 31

Debbie accomplished a great deal on March 31. Her processes of design and programming on that day demonstrate both a clear case for "cultural learning" (e.g., Vygotskian perspective) and for "individualist constructivist learning" (e.g., Piagetian perspective). In other words, we can see how her own innovative activities (e.g., her creating a screen for thirds, as well as the instructional sentence, or her connecting the five procedures in a superprocedure) were interlaced and influenced by what was happening within her culture at that time (e.g., her learning about the list processing and quizzing procedures in Logo, or about the WAIT.FOR.USER trick). Figure 34 attempts to capture the sequences and complexity of Debbie's activities on March 31, as well as the history of her planning and designing, the various kinds of learning, and the implementation phases.

March 23

..."When I'm finish I'm going to do 2/3 for my Project..."

March 30

..."I will start planning the way I want the Project to look..."

March 31

When Debbie finished her "House Scene" she remembered her general plan to do something on thirds. She decides to create a design for this plan in her Notebook.

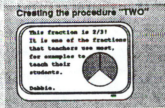

Debbie implements only a small part of her original design.

Creating the procedure "TWO"

This fraction is 2/3! It is one of the fractions that teachers use most, for examples to teach their students.

Debbie.

While she implements TWO Debbie composes an "Instructional Sentence" which captures the instructional purpose of her screen.

Debbie generates a new plan while she works on her screen for thirds. She decides to use the picture in a "testing procedure" which she creates and calls QUESTION 1.

When Debbie finishes her procedures TWO and QUESTION1, she remembers her plan to think on the "way I want the project to look." She has five separate parts: HALF, CALF, HOUSE, TWO, and QUESTION1, which she decides to connect together in a super-procedure.

Debbie learns about the Wait.For.User "trick." She implements it right away in her super-procedure.

At the end of March 31, Debbie creates this super-procedure. She places TWO before HOUSE, because "TWO is easier than HOUSE, and HOUSE is nicer than TWO."

```
TO FRACTIONS
HALF Wait.For.User CG CT CC
CALF Wait.For.User CG CT CC
TWO Wait.For.User CG CT CC
HOUSE Wait.For.User CG CT CC
END
```

Figure 34.   A flowchart tracing Debbie's activities on March 31.

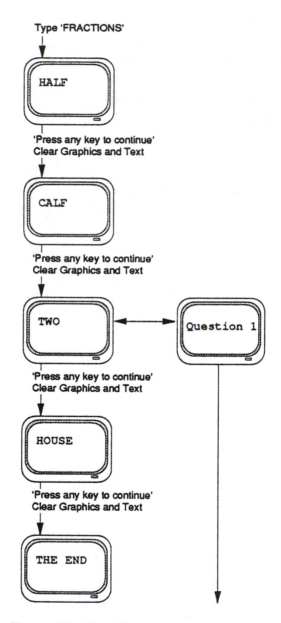

Figure 35. The Structure of Debbie's Software by the End of March 31.

At the end of the day (March 31) Debbie's program was as modular as follows:

```
TO FRACTIONS [the third step, adding the WAIT. FOR.USER subprocedure]
HALF   WAIT. FOR.USER
CG CT CC
CALF   WAIT. FOR.USER
CG CT CC
TWO    WAIT. FOR.USER
CG CT CC
HOUSE   WAIT. FOR.USER
CG CT CC
END

TO WAIT. FOR.USER
TYPE [PRESS ANY KEY TO GO ON]
IGNORE READCHAR
END

TO IGNORE :KEY
END
```

Figure 35 sketches the structure and flow of Debbie's program at this point, at the end of Debbie's first month of working on her software.

APRIL

2.6. CREATING THE SOFTWARE'S OPENING SCREENS:
QUEST, FRONT, AND INTRODUCTION

So far we have seen how, throughout the month of March, Debbie created five different screens: the first HALF screen—a large square filling the whole screen, with one big half (composed of two-fourths) shaded in on the right side of it—representing $1/2 = 2/4$; the geometrical CALF screen—four different shapes, a rectangle, a square, a circle, and a triangle, each divided into halves—teaching that "All these shapes are $1/2$!"; the thematic HOUSE screen—a house, its roof, and its door, each divided into halves, two wagons and their wheels divided into halves, and a sun divided into halves—teaching that "fractions are all around you" and that "you can use fractions almost every day of your life"; the TWO screen—one bit circle divided into thirds, with two of the thirds shaded in—explaining that thirds are difficult fractions "that teachers use most, for examples to teach their students"; and the QUESTION1 screen—which used the latter two-thirds representation and asked the user which fraction was represented in the picture—teaching the user how to translate a pictorial representation of thirds into a symbolic representation of thirds. On March 31, Debbie connected her screens and created a superprocedure which she named FRACTIONS. This super-procedure enabled a software user to type the word "FRACTIONS" in the Logo Command Center and run the software.

At this point, Debbie realized the need for an opening screen. Debbie's various steps in planning, designing, implementing, and modifying the introduction to her software are presented in the following subsections. To summarize briefly, Debbie, on April 1, constructed her procedure QUEST as her original opening screen. Her instructional design approach is presented in the context of those of her peers'. Influenced by her peers, Debbie, on April 6, designed another introductory screen in her Notebook, which she called FRONT. During its implementation phase Debbie decided not to finish this particular design; instead, she went back to her QUEST procedure and modified it. In addition, at the end of the computer time on April 6, she created yet another procedure for her introduction, which she named INTRODUCTION.

In Section 2.6.1., I describe Debbie's implementation of QUEST and analyze how it relates to what two other children created for their opening screens. In

Section 2.6.2., I describe Debbie's design of the FRONT, which was strongly influenced by one of her peers' designs for the opening screen; in this Section, I also explain Debbie's decision not to finish this particular design. In Section 2.6.3., I describe Debbie's new INTRODUCTION procedure and show how she went back to her procedure QUEST and modified it.

2.6.1. QUEST: Designing and Implementing the First Procedure for the Software's Opening Screen

On April 1, Debbie suddenly decided to design and implement her opening screen. Although she had previously generated ideas in advance for "new" forthcoming screens while still working on an "old" screen, we had never seen her try to create an opening screen. April 1 was the first time Debbie wrote anything in her Designer's Notebook about creating an introduction: *"Today I am going to work on my INTRODUCTION, IN FRACTIONS. Then I'm going to do another graphic for it. P.S., There's a bug on your head! April Fool. . ."*

It was Debbie, completely on her own, who decided to create the opening screen at that particular time (rather than earlier). She also decided where to place it in the context of her process of software design. By then, however, many other students had already designed and implemented an introduction or an opening screen earlier on in their process of software design; the idea of creating an opening screen therefore existed in the classroom long before Debbie decided to create one, and probably influenced her decisions about it.

A brief example of one approach to the design of an opening screen will be taken from the software of *Terry*, a tall, cheerful boy with blond hair and large blue eyes, who was in the high-math group. Terry was popular among his peers and teachers, who considered him to be one of the brightest pupils in the class. Very early in his processes of software design, Terry created an opening to his software which was composed of two colorful screens: the first read: FRACTIONS BY TERRY WILLARD, in which each letter was painted in a different color, his name was labeled in yellow, and the background was painted in blue; the second screen for his opening was a *menu*, or a *table of contents*, for his software as a whole, in which he labeled the words in yellow over a red background. Both screens are shown below (Figure 36).

As another example, let us briefly follow another girl, *Rally*, who, during the computer sessions, sat only two seats away from Debbie. Rally was a black girl from the high-level math group, known by her peers and teachers to be very sociable and successful in everything, including writing, drawing, Logo, and mathematics. In general, Rally, a 'top-down' thinker much like Terry, also followed a different route from Debbie's in her processes of software design—she had different ideas about fractions and teaching, and used quite a different style in implementing these ideas.

Rally planned to create an opening screen as early as the second week into the

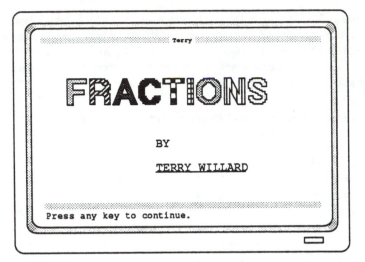

Figure 36. Terry's Opening Screen as of March 19.

project. Already on March 10, in one of her first plans in the designer's note-book, Rally wrote: *"I will start on my fractions project. I will draw different fractions and tell what fractions they are. I selected this because it seems very easy. I want to teach them different fractions. I might make opening page, Welcome To Fractions."*

However, although Rally worked on another screen (about fourths) for the following 10 days, she constantly mentioned and drew plans for an opening page in her Designer's Notebook. For example, on March 12 she wrote that her plans for that day were to *"make questions for the kids about fractions, see the design on the next page. [I will] try to make an opening page that will say Welcome To Fractions [and she drew the opening screen on a special grid in her Notebook]."* On March 19 she wrote: *"Today I will definitely make the opening page . . . [and drew it again]."*

On March 23 Rally wrote: *"My plans for today are to do my opening page and if I have time, I will make stars around it."* She drew it again with the stars. On March 26 she wrote: *"I will finish making designs around my opening page. I will also make shapes that look like fractions and stamp them around it."*

At the end of the computer time on March 26, Rally finally wrote in the Reflections form in her notebook: *"I finished everything!!! I had no problems."*

By that time (March 26) Rally's first instructional screen showed four squares of the same size, placed evenly on the screen from right to left; and in each of them she shaded one-fourth, two-fourths, three-fourths, and four-fourths, respectively. In addition to that screen, she also had an opening screen which read: WELCOME TO FRACTIONS! It had originally been designed in many colors, and was implemented accordingly with many little stars and small representations of fourths spread all over the screen. In short, Rally was involved for a long time in thinking about, and implementing her detailed opening screen. She programmed it using the Logo Writer Shapes Page to create a shape for each character, the stars, or the little fraction representations, and then she used the Logo regular command for placing the shapes and connecting them on the computer screen. Rally presented her software users with this opening screen (Figure 37).

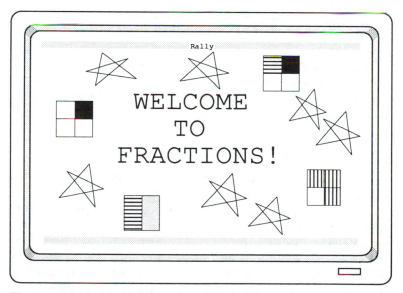

Figure 37.   Rally's Opening Screen as of March 26.

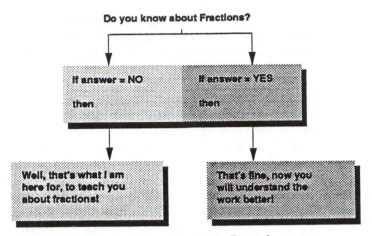

Figure 38.   The Structure of Debbie's Procedure QUEST.

In a completely different style, Debbie, in her opening screen, used white plain text over a black background, and asked her users a question using the following Logo procedure:

TO QUEST
PR [Do you know how to do fractions?]
name readlist "answer
ifelse :answer = [no] pr [Well, that's what I'm here for, to teach
you about fractions!]]
[pr [That's fine. Now you will understand this work better!]]
END

The structure of Debbie's procedure QUEST is depicted in Figure 38.

Three differences between Rally's and Debbie's approaches to instructional software design can be interpreted from the preceding information (Terry's instructional design approach and implementation style will be considered equivalent to Rally's in this case).

1. First, *Rally,* who seemed to be constantly thinking in a *top-down style* felt a need, first of all, to plan the opening screen for her program; whereas *Debbie,* who was probably more of a *middle-out thinker,* did not feel the need to do this until she had a finished entity to create an opening screen for. (Other examples for the top-down, middle-out, and bottom-up styles of thinking can be found in Turkle, 1984; Papert, 1980; and Weir, 1986).

2. The second difference between Rally's and Debbie's approaches for designing their opening screens shows two uses of the computer as an instructional medium. Debbie's opening screen took advantage of the computer's interac-

tive capabilities and was designed as a question, much like a teacher's opening of a lesson in a classroom (i.e., "Do you know about fractions?"); Rally's opening screen, on the other hand, was more like the opening page of a book about fractions, or a cheerful first screen in a movie about fractions (i.e., "Welcome To Fractions!"). Both screens were instructionally designed to motivate the user, each in a different way: the user in Rally's scenario was presented with a very colorful, attractive, and inviting first screen; the user in Debbie's scenario was presented with a rather plain, text-only screen, but was also required to be immediately active and reflective in his process of learning.

3.   The third difference of the opening screens was their presentation of the purpose of each software. Rally's screen invited the user into the "world of fractions," giving the impression that fractions were entities one could visit. In Debbie's opening screen, if the user typed NO, [i.e., I do not know about fractions], the program (which represented Debbie's voice) answered: WELL, THAT'S WHAT I'M HERE FOR, TO TEACH YOU FRACTIONS! (i.e., the purpose of Debbie's program was to teach fractions). If the user typed YES [i.e., I do know about fractions], Debbie's program answered: THAT'S FINE. NOW YOU WILL UNDERSTAND THIS WORK BETTER! (i.e., the knowledgeable user would understand Debbie's work better). In addition, Rally was inviting everybody in the same way, whereas Debbie was considering two types of users: the ones who did not know about fractions, and the ones who already knew about fractions. At the end of the computer time on April 1, Debbie's superprocedure looked like this:

TO FRACTIONS
QUEST   **[i.e., the new addition to the program]**
WAIT. FOR.USER   CG CT CC
HALF
WAIT. FOR.USER   CG CT CC
CALF
WAIT. FOR.USER   CG CT CC
TWO
WAIT. FOR.USER   CG CT CC
HOUSE
WAIT. FOR.USER   CG CT CC
END

2.6.2. FRONT-INTRO: Designing Another Opening Screen

During the computer time on April 2, the day after Debbie finished her QUEST Procedure, she worked with a third grader. This first evaluation session is described in Section 2.7. However, we will side-step it for a moment, since a few days later, on April 6, Debbie began thinking again about her introduction. She was probably not fully satisfied with her introductory screen QUEST, and because she was strongly influenced by her peers' work, and especially by Rally's opening page (which was described in Section 2.6.1), Debbie added a new design in her Designer's Notebook, which she called the FRONT-INTRODUCTION (i.e., something that would appear in front of the existing introduction QUEST). Debbie's plans from April 6 are shown in Figure 39.

Debbie called this design the FRONT-INTRO. She meant to put it in front of the introduction she had already created, named QUEST. One interesting aspect of Debbie's plan above is the fact that she drew representations for the equivalence of $1/2$ and $2/4$ (i.e., the representations that *she* circled in her Plan Form for April 6). It seems as though, by that time, she still strongly believed that this particular equivalence between halves and fourths was very basic to one's knowledge about fractions. One recalls that she had designed her very first screen (i.e., in Section 2.1.) to teach that $1/2 = 2/4$; now she decided to include this fractional equivalence in her introduction as well. In that plan, she also repeated her representations of halves or two-fourths on the right side of each shape.

Did she think that these types of representations (on the right side of each shape) would be more appropriate for beginners in fractions? Had she herself not fully overcome this misconception (i.e., that a half must always be on the right side of the shape)?

These questions require further investigation. I believe that, in general, the children's drawings in their Designer's Notebooks did represent their spontaneous and nonreflective thoughts about fractional representations; and that the children's reflections about their drawings usually occurred during the programming implementation phases or after the computer-time was over. (In addition, there is one part of this design that I do not understand. I have no idea why Debbie wrote those numbers at the bottom of her design grid. For unknown reasons, Debbie designed three lines at the bottom of her grid that were composed of question marks, messy curved lines, and many numbers.)

During computer-time Debbie started working on her plan for the new introduction. In her Logo file she added the following code:

TO FRONT
[She left it empty. It represents Debbie's creation of a plan during the implementation phase]
END

TO V
```
pu setpos [-85 55]
rt 135
setc 1+random 14 pd fd 20
lt 100
```

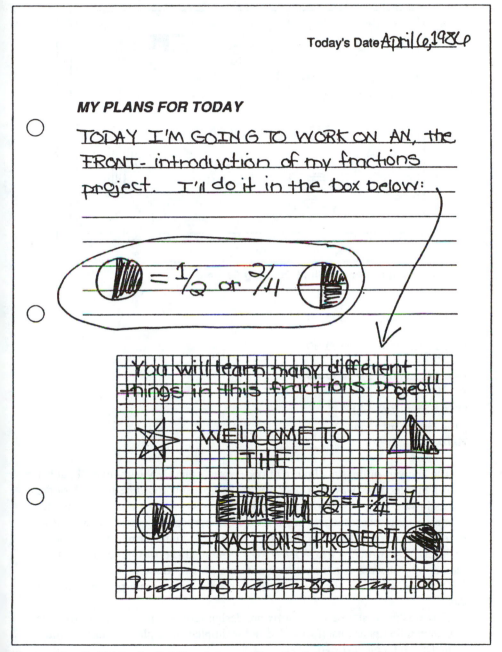

Figure 39.   Debbie's April 6 Hand-drawn Plan for the Opening Screen.

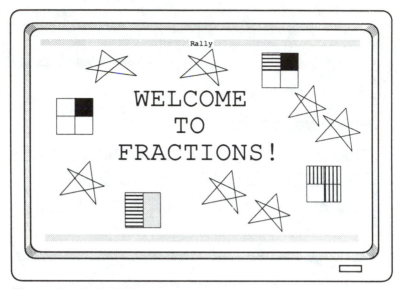

Figure 40.   Rally's Final Opening Screen.

```
setc 1+random 14 pd fd 19
rt  100
setc 1+random 14 pd fd 20
rt  100
setc 1+random 14 pd fd 20
rt  100
setc 1+random 14 pd fd 19
```

[She left it unfinished]
END

The analysis of this small piece of code reveals that Debbie thought about her FRONT in a modular way. Her plan was to create a subprocedure for each of the letters in W-E-L-C-O-M-E T-O T-H-E F-R-A-C-T-I-O-N-S P-R-O-J-E-C-T! and to later connect all the subprocedures together in a superprocedure named FRONT. However, at the end of that session she wrote in the Reflections form in her Notebook: *"I WILL NOT MAKE A FRONT-INTRO."* Although she was quite aware of the reason why she did not intend to make this screen, Debbie checked "LOGO PROGRAMMING" in the above Reflection form as her main problem for that day.

This was the first time in her software design process that Debbie, *during* the implementation phase itself, decided not to implement a plan because of some technical problems in Logo.

We have seen that Debbie had previously designed screens that she never

Today's Date _April 6, 1987_

PROBLEMS I HAD TODAY

I HAD A FEW PROBLEMS. MY "W"
I WAS NOT ABLE TO MAKE
ANS WILL NOT MAKE A FRONT-INTRO

***OVERALL, THE PROBLEMS I HAD TODAY ARE MAINLY RELATED TO (check in):

✔ LOGO PROGRAMMING   FRACTIONS   DESIGN
EXPLAINING OR TEACHING SOMETHING   OTHER

CHANGES I MADE TODAY AND WHY I MADE THESE CHANGES:

I MADE NO CHANGES

PLANS AND IDEAS FOR TOMORROW...

NONE

Figure 41.   Debbie's April 6 Reflections Form.

actually implemented, but we never saw her starting to implement something and then stopping it in the middle. Moreover, the problems she had, according to her, were related to Logo programming; but I perceive her problems as related mainly to her impatience, rather than to her lack of knowledge or skills in Logo. I never actually discussed with Debbie why she had first decided to plan FRONT-INTRO, or why she decided to stop and eliminate it in the middle of the implementation phase. It seems, however, according to what she wrote, that she had problems crating the letter *W*. She probably spent a long time trying to figure out how to make the *W* look like a real "*W*". However, when her attempts were unsuccessful, she decided not to implement that screen at all. It was not a programming problem per se, but rather a problem in constructing the shape of a letter. The *W* was difficult to implement in Logo due to its diagonal lines and internal angles, and Debbie saw it as an obstacle. She did not like the way it looked on the screen: *"When I try it, it doesn't look like a real W,"* she said, *"it looks crooked."*

Debbie's peers used the Logo Shapes page and the Logo Labeling capabilities to print words or characters in their opening screens; but Debbie, for an unknown reason, did not use the Shapes page. Her work with the *W* during that session definitely exhausted her patience. However, I assume there were other reasons why Debbie decided not to continue implementing this plan. First, I suspect it was because this particular design was not really her own idea. It was too similar to Rally's opening page, and perhaps Debbie did not feel happy about this. Also, it was a rather time-consuming screen to implement. In order to finish it, Debbie needed to work for a long time on constructing each of the characters, one by one. This construction required very precise work and a great deal of attention to details. It seemed to me that Debbie, unlike Rally, did not enjoy this type of work. If one recalls, Rally had worked on her very similar opening screen using the Logo Shapes page, for 10 days. Rally enjoyed the construction of each character or shape; and the opening screen, in principle, was very important to her (in the same way it was important to Terry, whose screen is described above). Debbie, however, probably had less tolerance for work of this kind and was not ready to deal with this type of very detailed and precise work. Her struggling with the *W* was enough of an experience to reveal to her that she was not ready to continue or invest many days in this activity.

2.6.3. The New Introduction

During the last 15 minutes of the computer-time on April 6, Debbie cancelled her plans for the construction of the FRONT-INTRO, and instead she created and added a new introduction:

TO INTRODUCTION
pr [Hello, my name is Debbie. I am going to teach you how to do fractions. The first thing that I am going to teach you is the half of the screen. The scene is a half or two fourths.]
END

She then entered her superprocedure and replaced the QUEST procedure with the new INTRODUCTION procedure, so that her super-procedure FRACTIONS looked like the following:

TO FRACTIONS
INTRODUCTION
[This had been QUEST's position before Debbie *replaced* it with
INTRODUCTION]
WAIT. FOR.USER CG CT CC
HALF
WAIT. FOR.USER CG CT CC
CALF
WAIT. FOR.USER CG CT CC
TWO
WAIT. FOR.USER CG CT CC
HOUSE
WAIT. FOR.USER CG CT CC
END

She ran her revised superprocedure twice, and reentered the Editor. She then added graphics for her procedure QUEST. The Logo code is presented below followed by a picture of the computer screen (Figure 42).

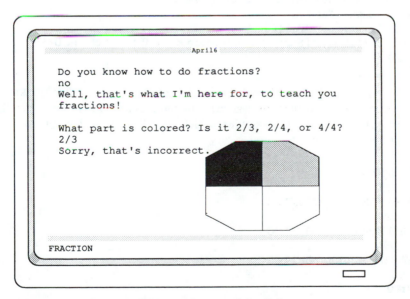

Figure 42. The Procedure QUEST as of April 6.

```
TO QUEST
pr [Do you know how to do fractions?]
name readlist "answer
ifelse (:answer = [no])
[pr [Well, that's what I'm here for to teach you fractions!]]
[pr [That's fine. Now you will understand this work better!]]
```

[This was, up to this point, Debbie's original QUEST procedure; from here on the graphics and interactivity are new:]

```
pu home pd repeat 8 [setc 1 +random 14 rt 45 fd 50]
pu bk 25
rt 90
pd fd 120
bk 60
lt 90
pu bk 60
pd fd 121
bk 70
rt 45
pu fd 20
setc 1+ random 14
pd fill
pu home
rt 90
pu fd 20
setc 1+random 14
pd fill
pr [What part is colored? Is it 2V3, 2V4, or 4V4 ?]
name readlist "answer
ifelse (:answer = [2V4])
[pr [GREAT!]] [pr [Sorry, that's incorrect.] wait 50 cg ct cc QUEST]
END
```

As we saw previously, Debbie decided to replace her procedure QUEST with the procedure INTRODUCTION (in her superprocedure FRACTIONS). After this, Debbie created a new superprocedure which she called BIG, and put QUEST within it, at the top of procedure BIG:

```
TO BIG
QUEST
WAIT.FOR.USER  CG CT CC
HALF
WAIT.FOR.USER  CG CT CC
HOUSE
WAIT.FOR.USER  CG CT CC
TWO
END
```

I asked Debbie,

Idit: *What is this procedure, Debbie?*
Debbie: *A different one for my fractions project.*
Idit: *How is it different?*
Debbie: *I put* QUEST, *not the* INTRODUCTION. *I put* HOUSE *before* TWO, *I didn't use* CALF.
Idit: *Why?*
Debbie: *Because.*
Idit: *Aha. . . .* [I started to move away]
Debbie: *O.K. . . O.K. . . 'Cause now I have two of them. Which one you want to see?*
Idit: *So you created two of them. . .*
Debbie: *Yes. Two different fractions Projects! Which one you want to see?*

I asked to see both, when she showed to me Debbie seemed to enjoy the fact that she now has two slightly different fractions projects. The two super-procedures (BIG and FRACTIONS) had some parts in common, and some parts that were different or connected in different sequences. I interpret Debbie's act of creating (and enjoying) her two superprocedures as an experiencing of the pur-pose and idea of *modularity*—one of the central ideas in programming (e.g., Papert, 1980).

Debbie wrote a modular program in which each piece could be understood and used separately. Each of Debbie's procedures could be read and executed in isolation, on its own. Debbie probably realized during this particular session that she could connect her parts in many different ways. She was very proud when she asked me: *"Which one you want to see?"* For the first time, she had discov-ered the trick of using similar elements for making two fractions projects.

To summarize, the structure of Debbie's processes of designing, redesigning, implementing, and modifying her introduction screens on April 1 and 6, and the way her actions related to or were influenced by her peers' actions, are shown in Figure 43. (This is not a final diagram for Debbie's processes of creating an introduction to her software. She would return to the problem of the introduction during April, May, and again in June, and add other parts to it. These additions to the introduction will be described in later sections.)

2.7. DEBBIE'S FIRST SOFTWARE EVALUATION

On April 2, the teacher of the experimental class, another third-grade teacher, and I spontaneously organized a collaborative computer session for one third-grade and the experimental fourth-grade class. The purpose of this session was to give the experimental students a chance to evaluate the effectiveness and appeal of their software with third graders (their target users). The third-grade teacher was also interested in this collaboration for the purpose of having the fourth

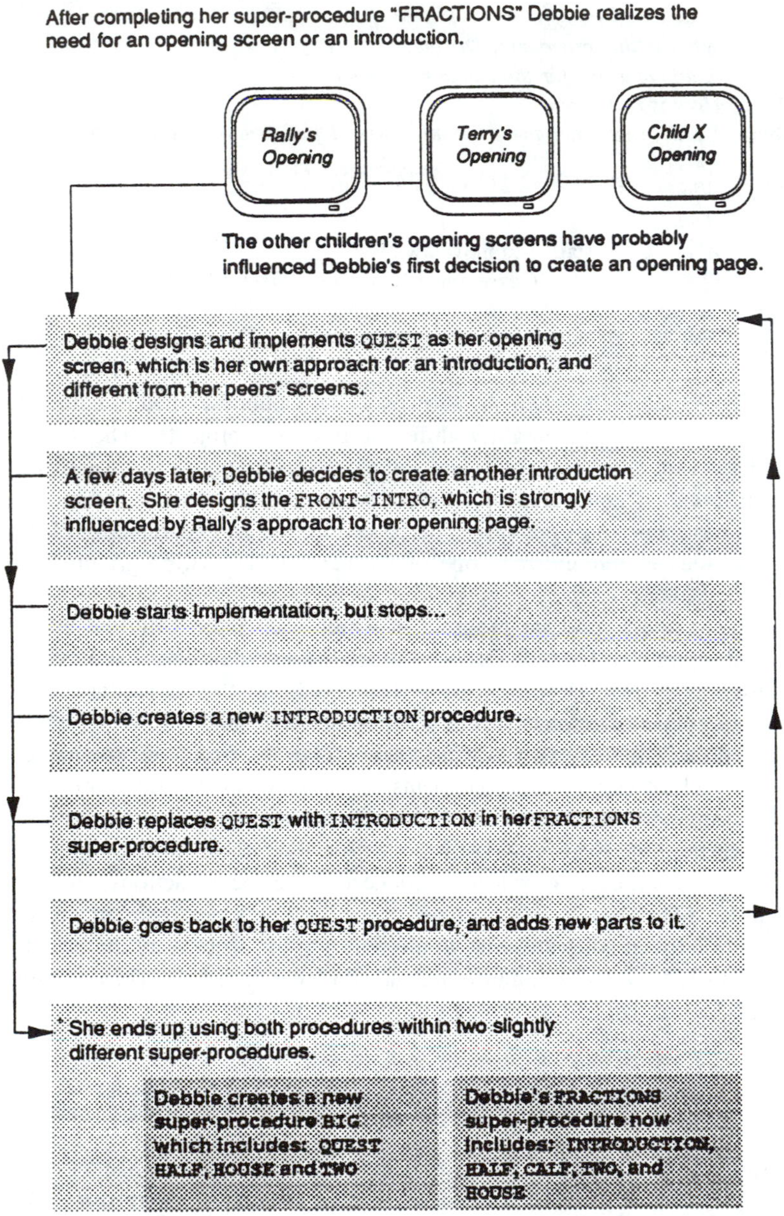
After completing her super-procedure "FRACTIONS" Debbie realizes the need for an opening screen or an introduction.
Rally's Opening
Terry's Opening
Child X Opening
The other children's opening screens have probably influenced Debbie's first decision to create an opening page.
Debbie designs and implements QUEST as her opening screen, which is her own approach for an introduction, and different from her peers' screens.
A few days later, Debbie decides to create another introduction screen. She designs the FRONT-INTRO, which is strongly influenced by Rally's approach to her opening page.
Debbie starts implementation, but stops...
Debbie creates a new INTRODUCTION procedure.
Debbie replaces QUEST with INTRODUCTION in herFRACTIONS super-procedure.
Debbie goes back to her QUEST procedure, and adds new parts to it.
She ends up using both procedures within two slightly different super-procedures.
Debbie creates a new super-procedure BIG which includes: QUEST HALF, HOUSE and TWO
Debbie's FRACTIONS super-procedure now includes: INTRODUCTION, HALF, CALF, TWO, and HOUSE

Figure 43. Debbie's Processes of Designing, Redesigning, Implementing, and Modifying her Introductory Screens on April 1 and 6.

graders help her pupils with their programming projects. The teachers assigned one third-grade child to each fourth-grade child according to gender and level. Their decisions were also based on which children would most enjoy working together and would work best together. This session was divided into two units: during the first unit, each of the third-graders was asked to use his or her fourth-grade partner's Fractions software and to offer comments about it. This Evaluation Session lasted 30 minutes. In the second unit, the roles switched, and each fourth grader worked with his or her third-grade partner on the latter's project; if they preferred, they could work on any other collaborative project. We did not tell the children what to do, what to ask each other, or how to work together. This may be one of the reasons why this spontaneous session was not very successful in terms of the fourth-grade children's understanding of what the evaluation meant. Many of them treated it more like a demonstration session, and only a few used this session to teach about fractions or to evaluate the clarity or appeal of their representations and screens.

Decentering was a difficult task for many of the experimental children. They could think about their users while designing their software, but many of them were not ready to consider their users' comments, or seek criticism on the quality and contents of their fractions programs. Beyond that, it was still interesting to walk around and see the different ways these children interacted with each other and worked together. The teachers, their pupils, and I felt that this was the beginning of something positive that should happen more often in the school, and that all sides gained something from working together. It was a difficult session to organize logistically, so only three other similar sessions were conducted during the months of April and May. It is beyond the scope of this chapter to describe what went on during these collaborative sessions, or what the different children, fourth or third graders, gained from it.

Nevertheless, let us briefly look at what Debbie accomplished in that first collaborative session on April 2. That day, in her Designer's Notebook, Debbie wrote (Figure 44).

During the April 2 session, Debbie showed her Fractions program to Bibby, the third-grade girl who was working with her. They were rather silent during most of the session, probably because it was the first one of its kind for them; they could not yet define the rituals of this specific interaction and were not sure who was supposed to assume what role. Debbie's partner, Bibby, was fascinated with Debbie's software, and her face was quite serious while she watched the software, start to finish. She read the text on the screen word by word, and pressed the keys when she wanted to continue. When it was over, she looked at Debbie and said:

Bibby: *This is nice. Can you do this again?*
Debbie: *You can type the word fractions yourself* [i.e., fractions is the name of the super-procedure]

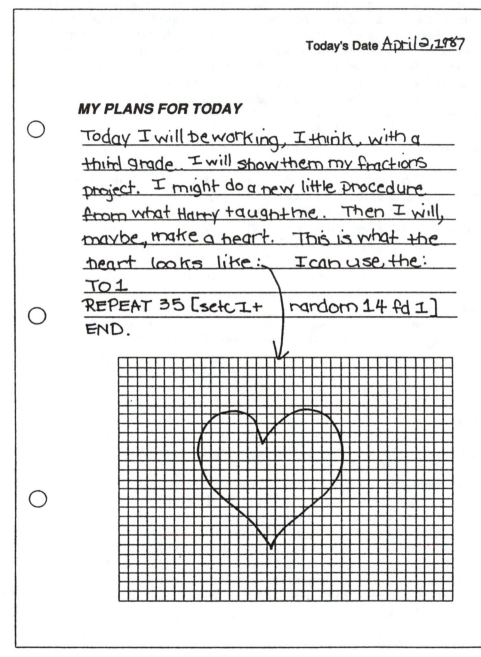

Today's Date April 2, 1987

MY PLANS FOR TODAY

Today I will be working, I think, with a
third grade. I will show them my fractions
project. I might do a new little procedure
from what Harry taught me. Then I will,
maybe, make a heart. This is what the
heart looks like: I can use, the:
TO 1
REPEAT 35 [setc 1+   random 14 fd 1]
END.

Figure 44.   April 2. Plan.

Bibby: *Oh . . .* [and she types it slowly in the Logo Command Center]

Debbie: *That's it. Press enter.*

Bibby [*Asking after reading the opening screen*]: *What will happen if I say, Yes?* [to the question "Do you know about fractions"]

Debbie: *Do you really know about fractions already?*

Bibby: *Sort of. . . We started something. . .*

Debbie: *O.K. then. . .* [Bibby gets an approval to type "Yes," and so she does]

Bibby [*reads the answer on the computer screen: "That's fine. Now you will understand this work better." She smiles for the first time, and continues watching screen after screen executed before her eyes*]: *This is a long program. Really long. How did you do that?*

Debbie [*probably perceives this comment as a compliment, and answers*]: *. . . Thanks.*

Bibby: *Can you show me how you did it?*

Debbie: *Sure.* [Debbie flips into the Editor page and runs the cursor down the screen, reading the names of each of her procedures] *Quest. . . . Half. . . . . this is Calf. . . . . this is House. . . . this is Two. . . . this is, Question1. . . . and this is Fractions. This is Wait.for.user and Ignore. Fractions is the whole thing together. It's my superprocedure.*

Bibby: *Oh. . .*

Debbie [*sensing that Bibby is puzzled*]: *Do you know what's a superprocedure?*

Bibby: *No.*

Debbie: *It's a procedure, that* [pause] *you can put in it many other procedures, together.*

Bibby: *Aha. . .*

Debbie [*places the cursor within the superprocedure and "walks" Bibby through it*]: *This is the opening, Quest. This is the first procedure, Half. Then I put Wait.for.user, to ask you type any key to continue, remember?* [doesn't wait for an answer], *then CG CC CT.*

Bibby: *I know. . . Clear the screen. . . Clear the words. . .*

Debbie: *Exactly.* [She continues] *Then the same thing with Calf. Then the same with Two, the same with House, and this is it. The end.* [pause] *But I'm going to add many new graphics to it.*

Bibby: *Can you teach me how to do it?*

Debbie [*does not really answer that question. Instead, she opens her designer's notebook and shows Bibby her design of the heart, which was on her Plans Form of April 2*]: *Do you want to do something like this?* [Points at her drawing of the heart in the Designer's Notebook]

In the background the two teachers were announcing that it was time to switch roles, and the fourth graders should now help the third graders with their programs. Debbie asked her teacher if she and Bibby could program the heart she had planned instead. The teacher approved, and they started to work on it. Bibby then said: *"Yeah . . . let's work on the heart. I like it."*

Bibby and Debbie were both sitting at their own computers, writing the Logo commands simultaneously. Debbie was in fact leading the session, speaking in a louder voice and saying what they should type, while Bibby mumbled and echoed Debbie's words, while typing them into the computer; it was though Debbie were playing the soprano, and Bibby the alto. After every three characters of code, Debbie would look at Bibby's computer to check whether she had mistyped anything. At the end of the computer session, both Bibby and Debbie had an identical procedure named HEART in their Logo files. They ran it simultaneously, twice. When the third graders went back to their classroom, I approached Debbie and asked her,

Idit:	*How did it go?*
Debbie:	*O.K.* [it was a very lengthy O.K., in a somewhat disappointed tone of voice]
Idit:	*What did she tell you about your fractions project?*
Debbie:	*I think she really liked it.* [cheering up]
Idit:	*Great.*
[pause]	
Idit:	*Did she tell you to change anything now after you saw her using it?*
Debbie:	*No.*
Idit:	*Do you feel you should change anything now after you saw her using it?*
Debbie:	*No.*
Idit:	*O.K., I guess that it's perfect then.*
Debbie:	*Yes.* [pause] *I even showed her the program. I showed her the super-procedure.*
Idit:	*Aha. And what did she think?*
Debbie:	*That it was really long.*
Idit:	*So?*
Debbie:	*I guess they* [the third graders] *are not used to such long programs.*
Idit:	*Does long mean good or bad or. . . .*
Debbie:	*Good, I guess. 'Cause it has many different things. She also liked my House.*

We can see that Debbie was not seriously inspired by this session and did not actually use it for a systematic checking or testing of the different parts of her program.

In general, this first session showed me that evaluation is a rather sophisticated skill. It seemed, however, that some children intuitively understood it while other did not. This skill is not often exercised, if it is exercised at all, in educational practice. I did notice several children asking the third graders evaluative questions related to the software's appealing characteristics such as: "Is it nice?" "Is it clear?" "Boring!?" "Did you like it?" etc. Also, three of the children actually conducted mini teaching sessions with their third-grade partners and supplemented their demonstrations with explanations about fractions (i.e., "did you know that $3/6$ equals $1/2$?" or "Count, one, two, three. Out of, one, two, three, four, five. This is three-fifths"). Some children even explained to their third-grade partners why they had designed a screen in a specific way, or what they had wanted to teach (i.e., "This screen teaches you about equivalence of fractions" or "this screen teaches you about fourths. It's tricky"). But, as far as I know, Debbie did not implement any of these evaluation strategies. She did not seek information about her product, how it worked for Bibby, what Bibby did or did not understand, and so on. She just sat there and watched passively, while Bibby looked at the execution of Debbie's program. Bibby did give Debbie a feedback: "This is nice. Can you do it again?" In fact, Bibby showed interest in learning "how to do it," but Debbie was more interested in programming the Heart.

On the whole, Debbie gave her third-grade partner a simple demo. And if she taught her anything at all, it was about programming and not about fractions. She walked Bibby through her superprocedure and explained to her what a super-procedure was and what its role was in her software. Unlike many of her peers, Debbie also seemed a bit nervous, perhaps because she was socially insecure in general, or because she feared criticism of some sort. It is reasonable to assume that she was afraid Bibby would not like her screens and representations—or would not find them difficult to program. After all, Debbie had invested a lot of time and thought working on them.

The ideas behind this evaluation session, its role in the children's learning, and the different strategies that were used by the fourth- and third-grade children during that session require further investigations. In general, I think that a girl like Debbie needs to undergo more of these sessions in order to learn how to collaborate with younger children, how not to fear their potential criticism, and how to make positive use of such interactions with younger users. By doing so, Debbie could acquire new information that might inspire her own designing, programming, and modifications. In addition, the way Debbie handled the programming of the Heart shows that she did not really collaborate, but rather told Bibby exactly what to do and how to do it. I am not sure whether Debbie was aware of her own fears of criticism; but she was clever enough to shift the control from the evaluator (Bibby) to herself. Then she, who had originally planned and knew how to do the Heart, made Bibby follow her orders. Furthermore, Debbie was probably the kind of girl who needed time to learn to enjoy social interaction. Debbie also showed anxiety and lack of interest in her relationship with me when the project first started. It took me a long time to understand how to work with her, and what type of interaction or collaboration she would accept. She never allowed me to suggest anything to her that was not already an idea of her own. The few times I did make a suggestion, she became very reserved, negative, and silent, unlike the other children I had worked with, who grew animated and inspired by the same comment. Finally, it might have been a good idea to conduct a short Focus Session before the Evaluation started, in order to clarify, with the children/software-designers, what software evaluation meant, and suggest which kinds of evaluation questions asked by the fourth graders might prove useful and productive.

2.8. CREATING A NEW LOGO PAGE FRACT2: DEBBIE MAINTAINS DYNAMIC RELATIONSHIPS BETWEEN *NEW* KNOWLEDGE AND *OLD* IN HER SOFTWARE AND IN HER MIND

The relationship between new knowledge and old is an important aspect of this study as a whole. But it is highlighted here because Debbie's plans, processes, and reflections on April 7, and during the following weeks, were very rich in information about this particular issue. We saw that, during the month of March (i.e., Sections 2.1. to 2.5.), almost all of Debbie's plans and designs corresponded, more or less, with her implementations. Even though she designed several screens that never reached implementation, or designed screens in advance and implemented them in later days, we could still follow her thinking in a somewhat organized fashion. During March, when all of her work was included in one Logo Page, it was simpler (for me as well as for Debbie) to analyze which were the new parts she added each day, and which parts she changed, eliminated, or left unchanged.

However, the day Debbie's program began to grow beyond one Logo Page and became more complex was also the day Debbie's thinking started to be more complex and much more dynamic and concurrent. Moreover, she began to grow relatively more involved in the programming aspect of her software, rather than principally in the learning of fractional concepts or in the designing of fractional representations. She became much more involved in moving procedures from one Logo Page to another, creating new superprocedures and discovering new combinations of subprocedures within those superprocedures. She concentrated more on the user's interaction with her software, and added short introductions and instructional sentences here and there. She was also very involved in finding ways to connect the different Logo Pages (i.e., during April she worked between three pages: FRACTION, FRACT1, and FRACT2). On the whole, during the month of April Debbie solved many technical problems relating to which procedures belonged on which page, although she was occasionally confused and once gave the same name to two different procedures.

In the previous sections I often analyzed Debbie's learning of fractional concepts and especially her thinking through the concept of halves. However, in the following sections, I emphasize her learning of Logo. Section 2.8.1. describes how Debbie planned to connect or integrate her new knowledge with the old, and the ways she wrote about it in her Designer's Notebook; Section 2.8.2. describes which connections between pieces of knowledge Debbie actually discovered while working with the computer. In other words, Section 2.8.2. emphasizes the relationships between Debbie's plans and their reality in implementation.

2.8.1. April 7: Debbie's Plans

This is what Debbie wrote in the designer's notebook on April 7: *"Today I will do something else. I can't fit any more work on my fractions page. So I'm gonna do a new page called 'Fract2.' I'll do equivalent fractions on Fract2. I might do some more poems. If I have time I'll add much more stuff on other page, that I've learned."* This particular plan contains many interesting issues that need to be carefully highlighted and interpreted in relation to the dynamic relationships between new and old pieces of knowledge. Here is how I interpret Debbie's plan:

1. Today I will do *something else*. In other words, I have finished everything I wanted to do so far, and all the things I'll do from now on are new and different (i.e., "something else").
2. I can't fit any more work on my existing Logo Page named FRACTION. Therefore, I'll start a *new page* which I am planning to name FRACT2.
3. On the *new* FRACT2 page I'll create representations of *equivalent fractions* (for sure).
4. On the *new* FRACT2 page I'll do some more *poems* (maybe).
5. If I have time, I'll *add much more* stuff on the *old* page (named FRACTION).
6. The new things that I'll add to the *old* page are things that *I've recently learned*.

The "doing something else," the first point above, could refer to all the points that are listed under it: new page, called Fract2; new representations for equivalent fractions; new poems; and new procedures in the old page.

On April 7, Debbie really wanted to start "something else." She also wanted to create a new page, FRACT2. On FRACT2 she planned to do something new. I assume she also meant "something else" in terms of fractional representations, since she wrote about her plans to *"do equivalent fractions on Fract2."* However, Debbie also planned to *"add much more stuff on the other page,"* using the new knowledge that she had recently acquired.

The fact that Debbie was considering starting something new no longer meant that she was completely done with the Page she had previously been working on. On the contrary, her writing reflected her awareness of the need to go back to the existing procedures that were already working, and to maintain them, modify them, and add new parts to them, using new knowledge she had just learned. She was aware of learning new things and was interested in applying them even to existing procedures that already worked well. We can see that ISDP indeed involved Debbie in complex maintaining processes, and in going back and forth between the old material and the new: She was willing to update the old, revise it, and connect it with the new material she was now learning.

In fact, Debbie's plan on April 7 is quite complex and represents her broad treatment of and interest in her Fractions project as a whole: The fact that she was planning to start a new page does not mean that she should put aside the old page; on the contrary, she was planning to continue to modify the old page as well. The fact that she was planning to start a new representation for equivalent fractions does not mean that she was going to leave aside her previous representations; instead, she would continue working on her old representations and add things to them, since she had recently learned new things that could be applied to the old representations or to their procedures. Her desire to write poems is also reflected in this plan—the fact that she was involved in the Fractions project did not prevent her from taking short breaks or doing other things when she felt like it.

2.8.2. April 7: Debbie's Implementation

Debbie's plans and their interpretation have already be presented. Let us enter reality, and analyze which plans Debbie actually accomplished, which she wanted to work on, and why.

Towards the end of the computer session on April 6, Debbie had a difficult time trying to add or change things in her FRACTION Logo page. The page was full.

In general, there is a space for 4,096 bites on each Logo page (on both of its sides together). In her program, Debbie had an average of 20 characters per line; and by April 6, the computer "complained" that there was no more space on her FRACTION page, since she had approximately 150 lines of code in her software. Therefore, when she ran her software, the name and format of the page took 609 bites, the procedures on its Editor side took close to 3,000 bites, and the pictures and text on the executed screen (the flip side) probably took all the remaining 385 bites of the memory space available per Page. Because of this problem, her screens "froze," and many times the cursor got stuck—the computer could not work beyond 4,096 bites per Page. Debbie realized that the page was full, and that she, in her own words, could not "*fit any more work on her Fractions page.*" She consulted with her friends and learned that many of them had, in similar cases, started a new page.

We have also seen that on April 7 Debbie wrote about her plan to "*do a new page called Fract2.*" In FRACT2, she planned to start new procedures for representing equivalent fractions. From then on we continuously read about her many plans and designs for representing equivalent fractions. However, analyzing her Logo online files reveals that she did not actually accomplish much of this during the month of April. Rather, she worked on other parts of her software in April, and only started implementing and modifying the screens on equivalent fractions at the beginning of May. Debbie did create a new Logo page on April 7, but did not start programming her procedure for equivalent fractions. Instead, she typed in her FRACT2 page the following:

```
TO EXAM
END

TO INTRODUCTION
END

TO QUEST
END

TO BIG
END

TO TOPO
END

TO INTRODUCTION
END

TO WAIT. FOR.USER
END

TO IGNORE :KEY
END

TO SUPER
END
```

We can see that Debbie first typed nine procedure names, which she was planning to include on her new Page FRACT2. Five of those existed already in her old Page (i.e., INTRODUCTION,QUEST,BIG,WAIT.FOR.USER, and IGNORE), while the other four were mentioned here for the first time as new procedure names that would probably lead to new parts she was planning to create that day.

In that act alone, we can see that Debbie was thinking about, and relating, the old parts with the new. She then went back to her old FRACTION page and, using the appropriate function keys and arrows, copied her five existing procedures, one by one, transferring them to her new Logo page FRACT2. This second step resulted in the following code on the new FRACT2 page:

TO EXAM   [does not exist yet]
END

TO INTRODUCTION
                [this procedure exists; it was created on April 6]
pr [Hello, my name is Debbie. I am going to teach you how to do fractions.
The first thing I'm going to teach you is the half of the screen.
The scene is a half or two fourths.]
END

TO QUEST   [one part of this procedure was created on April 1, and the other, on April 6]

pr [Do you know how to do fractions?]
name readlist "answer
ifelse (:answer =[no]) [pr [Well, that's what I am here for, to teach you
fractions!]]
[pr [That's fine. Now you will understand this work better!]]
pu home pu repeat 8 [setc 1+random 14 rt 45 fd 50]
pu bk 25 rt 90 pd fd 120 bk 60 lt 90 pu bk 60 pd fd 121
bk 70 rt 45 pu fd 20 setc 1+random 14 pd fill
pu home rt 90 pu fd 20 setc 1+random 14 pd fill
ct pr [what part is colored? Is it 2V3, 2V4, or 4V4?]
name readlist "answer
ifelse (:answer = [2V4]) [pr [GREAT!]] [pr [Sorry, that's incorrect]
ct cg QUEST]
END

TO BIG   [this super-procedure was created on April 6]
QUEST
WAIT. FOR.USER   CG CC CT
HALF
WAIT. FOR.USER   CG CT CC
HOUSE
WAIT. FOR.USER   CG CT CC
TWO
END

TO TOPO   [does not exist yet]
END

TO INTRODUCTION [probably a new one, does not exist yet]
END

TO WAIT. FOR.USER[this procedure was created on March 31]
type [PRESS ANY KEY TO CONTINUE]
IGNORE readchar
END

TO IGNORE :key   [was created on March 31]
END

TO SUPER   [does not exist yet]
END

(I know little about Debbie's rationale in choosing these particular procedures
from the old FRACTION page, or in choosing these particular names for her new
procedures.)

The third thing Debbie worked on after accomplishing the above was her new
procedure SUPER. She created SUPER because she needed one procedure within
page FRACT2 that would call the old page FRACTION. So she typed:

TO SUPER
GETPAGE "FRACTION
WAIT.FOR.USER
END

During her process of creating another Logo page for her Fractions Project, Debbie, like the other children in her class, had to learn two new Logo instructions: GETPAGE and GETTOOLS. It is important to understand the difference between those two instructions, because Debbie had certain misconceptions regarding them that needed to be overcome.

When Debbie typed GETPAGE "FRACTION while still in the FRACT2 page, Logo automatically had to move from FRACT2 to the other page, FRACTION. Debbie forgot to tell Logo what to do after it moved to FRACTION, or what procedures to execute. Instead, she should have typed:

TO SUPER
GETPAGE "FRACTION
FRACTIONS   [this is what she should have typed, i.e., the name of the
             super-procedure on her FRACTION Page]
END

When Logo moved from FRACT2 it forgot everything about it, including the name of the procedure that had instructed it to move (i.e., SUPER in this case). But Debbie also had the possibility of typing GETTOOLS "FRACTION while on the FRACT2 page. GETTOOLS "FRACTION would have given Logo access to any procedure that was on the FRACTION page. This would have been a better solution for Debbie: to use her procedure BIG, which included HALF, CALF, HOUSE, and TWO, four procedures that existed only on her old FRACTION page.

Debbie struggled with this problem of GETTOOLS and GETPAGE during the rest of the project. She got confused about which page should call which procedure, and which page should include which tools or procedures. In a way, both GETTOOLS and GETPAGE possess qualities of modularity, requiring the construction of relationships between whole pages as well as between the pages' individual components. These connections between pages become a higher level superstructure of the procedures themselves and of their interrelations with the different superprocedures. A great deal of expertise and experience are needed to fully understand this problem.

Debbie's program of April 7 was a turning point in that regard: It was the first time she was dealing with this problem of pages relations and interrelations. My observations and a brief analysis of the other children's programs revealed that many children struggled with the same problem. I also knew that the children who had dealt with the problem earlier in the project learned to master it, having devoted sufficient time to constructing and manipulating these interrelations between the various pages of their Fractions programs. As we continue to follow Debbie's processes in the following days, we will see that she continued to try to solve this problem and managed to work it out for herself.

The next thing Debbie did on April 7 was to write the new procedure INTRODUCTION. It was the first time I had ever seen Debbie use the same procedure name on the same page and within the same program. Here is what she typed:

TO INTRODUCTION
pr [Hello, again! Haven't you learned enough?]
name readlist "answer
[pr [I guess you want to learn more!]]
wait 50 ct
END

Seeing this procedure in her program, I asked her,

Idit:	*Debbie, what is this procedure?*
Debbie:	*It's another one.*
Idit:	*Another what?*
Debbie:	*Another introduction for the second time.*
Idit:	*What do you mean?*
Debbie:	*I will use it in here*

[she talks as she moves the cursor up to TO TOPO, and types]
TO TOPO
BIG WAIT 90 CT
INTRODUCTION
END

Debbie:	*That's what it's for.*
Idit:	*Aha. . . Are you planning to try it out now?*
Debbie:	*Yes.*

Debbie flipped the page and tried to run her procedure TOPO, which of course did not work. This was because Debbie was still working within her FRACT2 page. The procedure BIG was included within it, and its first subprocedure QUEST was also included, though the rest of the subprocedures in BIG were not. So Logo, after executing QUEST, gave her a message about not knowing how to do HALF. Debbie was puzzled for a long time after this. I decided not to let her think about for a while before I helped her. I stepped away and watched another child's program. It was the end of the computer session, and Debbie had to wait, until the next day before she realized that it was not a good idea to use the same procedure name for two different procedures (i.e., the two INTRODUCTION procedures).

In the Reflections form of April 7 Debbie wrote (Figure 45).

In this form, Debbie only reported on one problem she had initially had with

Today's Date April 7, 1987

PROBLEMS I HAD TODAY

I had one problem. When I tryed to go on the other side of the page. But it kept saying "MISSING A" I guess...

***OVERALL, THE PROBLEMS I HAD TODAY ARE MAINLY RELATED TO** (check in):

LOGO PROGRAMMING ✔ FRACTIONS   DESIGN
EXPLAINING OR TEACHING SOMETHING   OTHER

CHANGES I MADE TODAY AND WHY I MADE THESE CHANGES:

I made no changes today, thank you for being cooperative...

PLANS AND IDEAS FOR TOMORROW...

NONE

Figure 45.   April 7. Reflections Form.

one of the brackets in her new INTRODUCTION procedure (i.e., "MISSING A "]" IN INTRODUCTION"). I do not know why she did not report on the problem she encountered while running her procedure TOPO, which included BIG and INTRODUCTION.

Strangely enough, although she did make some changes in her program on April 7, on her form she wrote *"I made no changes today."* But she also added: *"Thank you for being so co-operative. . ."*

What did she mean by *"Thank you for being so co-operative. . ."*? Who was she referring to? Was she talking about the computer's being cooperative, or was she being sarcastic and really commenting on the fact that the computer had not been cooperative during that session? Perhaps she was talking to her Designer's Notebook, which was always cooperative and never gave her any trouble. Or perhaps she was referring to my being cooperative or, on the contrary, if she was being sarcastic, not cooperative at all. Her reasons for writing this sentence remain unknown to me. I invite the reader's interpretation of this mystery.

In summary, one of the important aspects of ISDP as a whole was its ability to offer Debbie a learning environment that, by its nature, forced her to combine new Logo knowledge and skills with old. In fact, this is one of the qualities of the processes of programming in general (e.g., Papert, 1980, 1986). By analyzing Debbie's software construction processes, we have seen how she discovered that there were many ways to program the same thing. We have also seen how as she learned a new skill, she reprogrammed an old screen or modified her old procedures using the new skills she had learned (for example, Debbie reprogrammed her CALF procedure after learning how to use 1+RANDOM 14 for randomming the colors of the shapes); she also learned to connect old procedures with new (for example, Debbie connected HALF with CALF, and later connected both with HOUSE, and then with TWO, and a month later with QUEST). Debbie also used the same parts or procedures in several superprocedures (for example, having created two superprocedures BIG and FRACTIONS, she discovered in the following weeks additional ways to combine the old parts with new parts for different purposes, creating even more superprocedures).

In the more conventional learning situations in her school life, Debbie would usually learn something for some time, and later put it aside (when the assignments were completed or when the related tests were over). She would then start learning something else, put it aside; learn another new thing, put it aside; and so on. Most of the time, Debbie's individual pieces of knowledge would remain unrelated to one another, never to be properly integrated in her mind or in her learning experiences. If we believe that Debbie's knowledge and learning abilities were a result of the conditions in which she was being educated, it seems that these routines must have been an obstacle and a negative influence on her style of thinking, her capacity for knowledge, and her attitude towards her own knowledge and thoughts in general. I think that one risk of Debbie's usual school learning conditions was that knowledge of different subjects becoming fragile, local, limited, and neither fluent, flexible, connected, nor integrated (e.g., this is what diSessa, 1985, calls "knowledge in pieces," Perkins (1985) calls "fragile knowledge," or what Gestalt psychologists in the 1940s described as "rigidity vs. flexibility in knowing and learning").

However, in this long, integrative, and complex project, Debbie could not separate her knowledge about fractions from her knowledge of Logo; nor could she put aside her old knowledge of those subjects. In order to make sense of the software as a whole during the four-month period of the project, Debbie needed to learn to connect the old pieces of knowledge with the new, or to modify the old parts of her program by using her new knowledge. Several examples of this new ability have already been given, and more will be presented; for in April, May, and June, Debbie, having learned many new things along the way, went back to the procedures and representations she had programmed in March, revised them, or simply reused them in new contexts.

2.9. DESIGNING AND REPRESENTING EQUIVALENT FRACTIONS OF HALVES

In her Designer's Notebook, Debbie drew many designs for her new screens about equivalent fractions. However, *only two* were actually implemented by her (during the first 3 weeks of May). Debbie managed to fully complete one screen, and told me that she had created this screen for *"Teaching that six-twelfths equal one-half, two-fourths equal one-half, four-eighths equal one-half, and ten-twentieths equal one-half."* I shall describe her processes of designing and implementing this screen in Section 2.9.1. However, the second screen about equivalent fractions, which she started to work on during the third week of May, was never completed. I shall briefly describe that second incomplete screen in Section 2.9.2, and give the reasons why she did not complete it. Then, in section 2.9.3, I shall analyze in detail one of Debbie's equivalent fractions designs, the one from April 14, comparing it with another student's design. This particular design is interesting from the point of view of imitation and cultural learning.

2.9.1. Equivalent Fractions: Screen No. 1

As previously stated, as early as April 7, Debbie announced for the first time her plan to create a screen for equivalent fractions: *"Today I will do something else. I can't fit any more work on my "fractions page. So I'm gonna do a new page called Fract2." I'll do equivalent fractions on 'Fract2.' I might do some more poems. If I have time I'll add much more stuff on other page, that I've learned"* (emphasis added). Throughout the months of April and May, Debbie wrote, planned, designed, replanned, and redesigned in her Notebook a series of screens for equivalent fractions, which she meant to implement in FRAC2, her new Logo page.

I shall now briefly review several of the written plans and hand-drawn designs created by Debbie from April 7 through May, which pertain to her work on equivalent fractions. The reader should realize that, during these months Debbie was also working, in parallel, on many other screens and procedures. Some of this parallel work is reflected in her written plans: In almost all of her written plans, Debbie wrote about two or three things she was planning to accomplish on the same day. It is very difficult to describe her parallel thinking and programming processes, or her simultaneous accomplishments in this linear medium of writing. The more complex and large Debbie's project grew, the more complex her actions and thoughts became. As a result, it became quite difficult to describe and analyze in detail her phases and processes during these months.

In Figure 46 we can see that Debbie represented for the first time a representation of the fraction "tenths." She used a group of discrete geometric objects (squares for the tenths, and circles for the sixths). I remember passing by her desk in the classroom. I stopped when I saw her drawing this. She looked at me and said:

Debbie: *Equivalent fractions.* [she smiled]
Idit: *Yes. I see.*
Debbie: *I'm going to show all the fractions in the world like this.* [she said in a proud voice]
Idit: *All the fractions in the world?!*
Debbie: *Well not all of them, but many. All the halves.*
Idit: *All the halves? What do you mean?*
Debbie: *You know. Sixths, three-sixths. Fourths, two-fourths. Eighths, four-eighths. Tenths, five-tenths. Sixteenths, eight-sixteenths. Eighteenths, nine-eighteenths. Twentieths, ten-twentieths. All of those at least.*
Idit: *It sounds like a lot of work, Debbie! Good luck!*
Debbie: *Then, I'm gonna teach each one alone on the screen, and then, all of them together, to show all of them, and that they all equal one-half!*

There is no doubt that Debbie had a very strong concept of equivalences of halves. In her answer to my question, as described above, she demonstrated great ease at verbalizing and moving within the half equivalence class, and she included many fractions of this class in her statements (i.e., fourths, sixths, eighths, tenths, twelveths, sixteenths, eighteenths, and twentieths). She was also able to freely divide these fractions into halves. Furthermore, she had an interesting idea on how to teach the concept of equivalences of halves: by showing her users multiple examples, first one by one, and then all together on the same screen. I think Debbie's initial attempt to represent "*all the fractions in the world like this*" is very interesting: It shows that she felt more secure about fractions in general. She was no longer intimidated by them. She spoke with great assurance

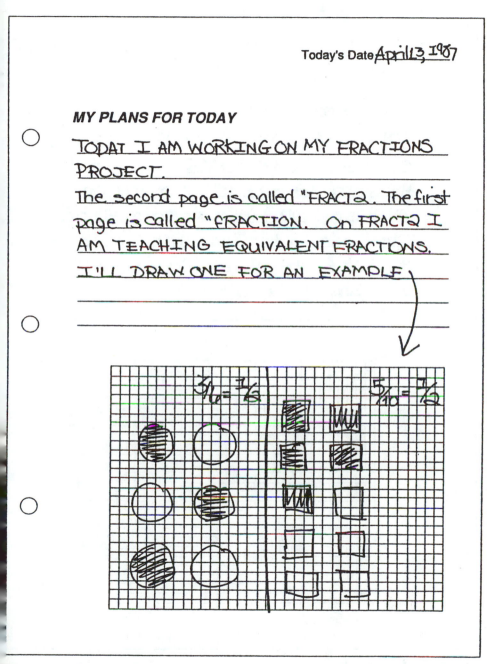

Today's Date April 13, 1987

MY PLANS FOR TODAY

TODAT I AM WORKING ON MY FRACTIONS
PROJECT.

The second page is called "FRACT2. The first
page is called "FRACTION. On FRACT2 I
AM TEACHING EQUIVALENT FRACTIONS.
I'LL DRAW ONE FOR AN EXAMPLE.

Figure 46.   April 13. Plan.

Today's Date <u>April 14, 1987</u>

MY PLANS FOR TODAY

<u>TODAY I AM GOING TO DO EXACTLY. LOOK</u>
<u>ON PREVIOUS PLANS PAGE. I'm going to do</u>
<u>this graphic for my fractions project, on Fract 2,</u>
<u>which is equivalent fractions and a little more.</u>
<u>I am going to try to do what I wanted for</u>
<u>the rest of the week. Another graphic</u>
<u>I'm going to try to do is:</u>

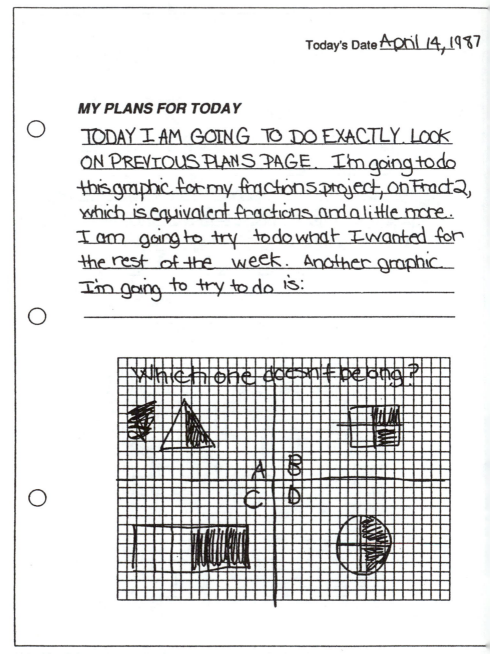

Figure 47.   April 14. Plan.

and gave the impression that she was in control. In the following plans and drawings we will see that Debbie did indeed make serious attempts to represent as many equivalences of halves as possible. A day later, on April 14th, Debbie generated a new plan for representing equivalent fractions (Figure 47). This particular plan will be discussed in detail later, in Section 2.9.3.

We shall now progress with Debbie to the month of May, during which she continued to work on her designs and screens for equivalent fractions, and in parallel, on several other screens and programming problems.

MAY

DEBBIE'S MULTIFACETED WORK ON REPRESENTING
EQUIVALENT FRACTIONS CONTINUES

At the first week of May, after coming back from the school's Easter Vacation, Debbie continued her work on representing equivalent fractions. She generated two new plans on May 4 (Figure 48) and wrote in her Designer's Notebook on May 5th: *"Today,* no matter what, *I'm working on equivalent fractions. But before that I'm going to do the test for what a fraction is. Look on previous 'my plans for today' sheets for the equivalent fractions graphics. Bye!!!"*

Debbie did begin to implement her Equivalent Fractions screen on May 5. Here is what she succeeded in programming on the computer for equivalent fractions (Figure 49).

On May 11, Debbie wrote in her Notebook: *"Today I am going to do equivalent fractions from my disk. The next one I'll do is adding and subtracting in one or on one page. I'm going to use what I learned today in it. !!!!!!!Bye!!!!!!!"*

She then continued to implement the above screen from May 5 (Figure 49). But in her plan, we can see that in parallel to her thinking about representations for equivalent fractions, she generated a new plan for representing addition and subtraction of fractions. However, Figure 50 shows what she actually succeeded in programming on May 11.

On May 18 Debbie wrote: *"Today I am going to work* a whole lot more *on equivalent fractions. But I'm also going to make the exam. In other words, the test. I'm finishing the addition assignment first. See you soon!"* (No hand-drawn design was created that day). Figure 51 shows what Debbie accomplished on the computer on May 18.

On May 20 Debbie wrote: *"Today I'm going to do what I can, for the rest of my equivalent fractions project. Then, if there's time left I'm going to explain what I did in the addition of fractions assignment. !!!!Bye!!!!"* (Again, no hand-drawn design was created that day.)

However, on May 20, Debbie did not add anything to her Equivalent Fractions procedure. Instead, she worked on her Addition scene, which will be described later.

On May 20 she wrote: *"Today I'm working on my equivalent fractions project.*

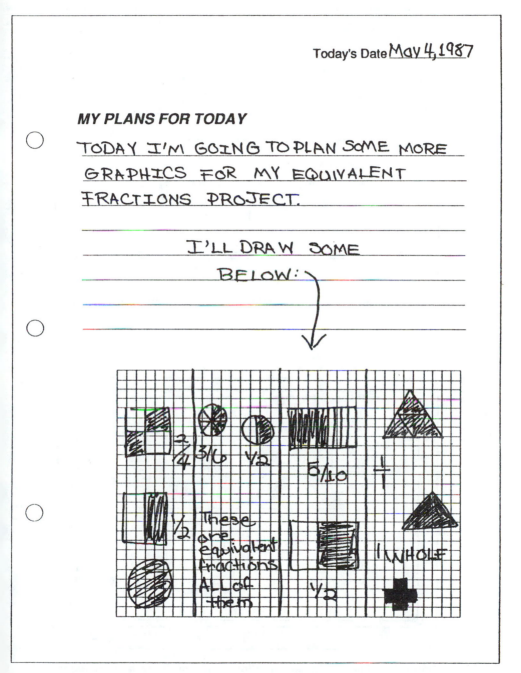

Figure 48.   May 4. Plan.

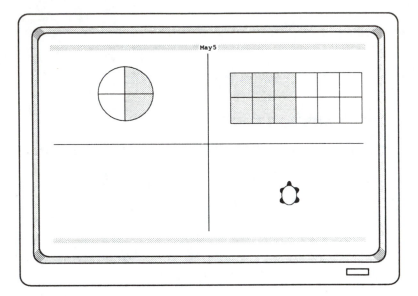

Figure 49.   May 5. Implementation Step 1 of Equivalent Fractions Screen.

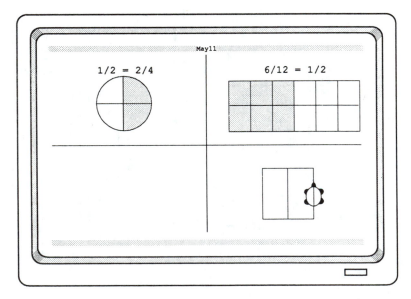

Figure 50.   May 11. Implementation Step 2 of Equivalent Fractions Screen.

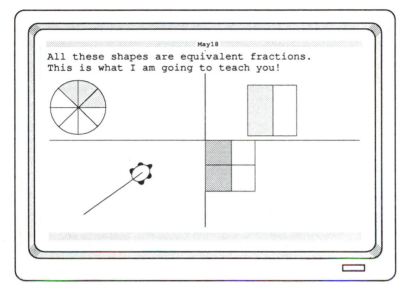

All these shapes are equivalent fractions.
This is what I am going to teach you!

Figure 51. May 18. Implementation Step 3 of Equivalent Fractions Screen.

I'll fix it and finish it, if I can!!! *I'm gonna also finish adding fractions. !!Bye!!*"

Finally, on May 22, Debbie finished her procedure for representing equivalent fractions. Her final screen is represented in Figure 52.

Debbie's Reflection form indicates that she was very happy and satisfied with her completion of this screen. On May 22 she wrote in her Designer's Notebook: *"Today I had not one lousy problem! I'm glad too!!! I finished one equivalent fractions, but not the other that I planned."*

We can see that Debbie has in mind another screen for equivalent fractions (i.e., "But not the other one that I planned"). She will implement it in the next few days.

The following is Debbie's procedure EQUIV for the representation of equivalent fractions.

TO EQUIV

PU HOME SETC 13	[changes pen color to purple]
PD FD 190 PU HOME	[cuts the screen in the middle, vertically]
RT 90 PD FD 320	[cuts the screen in the middle, horizontally]
PU SETPOS [20 10] SETC 1 PD	[positions the Turtle in the top right of the screen]

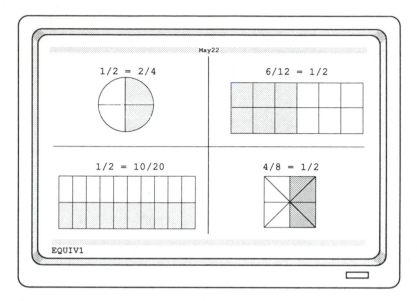

Figure 52. May 22. Implementation Step 4 of Equivalent Fractions Screen.

REPEAT 2 [FD 60 RT 90 FD 120 RT 90]	[draws a purple rectangle in the top right]
LT 90 BK 20 RT 90 FD 60	[cutting the rectangle vertically into six equal parts]
RT 90 FD 20 RT 90 FD 60 LT 90 FD 20 LT 90 FD 60 RT 90 FD 20 RT 90 FD 60 LT 90 FD 20 LT 90 FD 60 RT 90 FD 20	
RT 90 PU FD 30 RT 90 PD FD 120	[cuts the rectangle horizontally, in the middle, which creates twelve-twelfths]
PU HOME PU SETPOS [30 30] SETC 9 PD FILL	[shades in blue one-twelfth]
REPEAT 2 [PU FD 20 PD FILL RT 90 PU FD 20 PD FILL]	[shades in four more twelfths; five are shaded now]
PU RT 90 FD 20 PD FILL PU HOME PU SETPOS [15 80]	[shades the sixth twelfth in blue]
LABEL [6∨12 = 1∨2]	[prints 6/12=1/2 in yellow over the rectangle]
PU HOME	[finishes the representation for *sixth-twelfths equals one-half*]
PU SETPOS [-60 50] SETC 3	[positions the Turtle in the top left of the screen]
PD REPEAT 36 [FD 7 LT 10]	[draws a turquoise circle in the top left of the screen]

LT 90 FD 80	[cuts the circle horizontally in its middle]
BK 40 RT 90 FD 43 BK 80	[goes back the length of the circle's radius, turns right ninety degrees and cuts the circle vertically in its middle. The circle is now divided into fourths]
PU HOME	
SETC 11	[changes the pencolor to light blue]
PU SETPOS [-75 65]	[positions the Turtle at top right fourth of the circle]
PU BK 10 PD FILL	[shades one-fourth of the circle in light blue]
PU BK 20 PD FILL	[shades the circle's bottom-right fourth in light blue]
PU HOME	
PU SETPOS [-65 80]	[positions the Turtle over the circle]
LABEL [1∨2=2∨4]	
PU HOME	[prints the equivalence *one-half equals two-fourths*]
SETC 4 PU SETPOS [25 -80]	[changes pen color to red, positions Turtle in the bottom right of the screen]
PD REPEAT 4 [FD 50 RT 90]	[draws a red square]
FD 25 RT 90	
FD 50 BK 25 LT 90 FD 25 BK 50 FD 25	[cuts the circle horizontally, then vertically]
RT 45 FD 32 BK 64 FD 32 LT 90 FD 32	[cuts the circle diagonally twice, creates eights]
BK 64	
PU HOME	
SETC 12 PU SETPOS [60 -35] PD FILL	[changes pen color to orange, fills in one-eighth]
PU BK 5 RT 90 PU FD 10 PD FILL	[shades two more eighths in orange]
RT 90 PU FD 30 PD FILL	[shades the fourth eighth in orange]
PU HOME	
PU SETPOS [45 -15]	
LABEL [4∨8=1∨2]	[prints the equivalence, *four-eighths equal one-half*]
PU HOME	
SETC 2 PU SETPOS [-140 -85]	[changes pen color to green, positions Turtle the bottom left of the screen]
PD REPEAT 2 [FD 60 RT 90 FD 120 RT 90]	
	[draws a green rectangle]
PD REPEAT 10 [SETH 90 FD 12 LT 90 PD FD 60 BK 60]	
	[cuts it vertically into ten-tenths]
FD 30 LT 90 FD 120	[cuts the rectangle horizontally, which creates twenty-twentieths]

```
PU HOME
SETC 10 PU SETPOS [-135 -40]              [changes pen color to light green,
                                          positions Turtle in the bottom left
                                          twentieth of the rectangle]

PD FILL PU RT 90 FD 10 PD FILL            [shades in light green one twentieth
                                          after another]

PU FD 15 PD FILL PU FD 10 PD FILL
PU FD 10 PD FILL PU FD 15 PD FILL
PU FD 10 PD FILL PU FD 10 PD FILL
PU FD 12 PD FILL PU FD 15 PD FILL         [finishes shading ten-twentieths in
                                          light green]

PU HOME
SETPOS [-105 -15] LABEL [10∨20 =1∨2]
                                          [prints the equivalence, ten-twentieths
                                          equals one-half]
END
```

Debbie's EQUIV procedure is very readable, and is efficiently and beautifully organized. She uses the PU HOME to break between each component within a given representation (e.g., separating the drawing of the outline of the rectangle and the cutting of it into sixths); and she also uses PU HOME between each of her representations, separating them from each other. She uses SETPOS freely. In fact, this particular screen division (into four parts) was often used in her software. Debbie found this method convenient for showing multiple representations on one screen; but it also enhanced her knowledge of the Cartesian coordinate system. I asked her about it:

Idit: *How does it work with the pluses and minuses in the different SETPOS?*
[Even though my question was not phrased very clearly, Debbie understood exactly what I meant]
Debbie: *[she pointed on the screen, moving her finger on the screen's four fourths counter-clock-wise, and answered very quickly] plus and plus, plus and minus, minus and minus, minus and plus.*

In the EQUIV procedure Debbie also properly used REPEATs for the rectangles, the square, and the circle; furthermore, her solution for cutting the rectangle representing ten-twentieths was very elegant (e.g., REPEAT 10 [SETH 90 FD 12 LT 90 PD FD 60 BK 60]). I asked her why she had not used this set of commands for the top rectangle representing six-twelfths. She told me the following:

Debbie: *I did it [the rectangle which represents twelfths] a long time ago and I didn't think about it then, about how to do it like this. I only found out about it today.*
Idit: *How did you find it?*
Debbie   *I tried and tried and tried until I found out about it.*
Idit: *Just like that*
Debbie: *Yea.*

Idit: *But how??*

Debbie: *I had to do it here, because there are many lines to divide it to [i.e., to divide the rectangle into twenty parts] so it shouldn't take too long to write it this way.*

Debbie's answer indicates that she had discovered this elegant code (for dividing the rectangle into twentieths) by trial and error (i.e., "*I tried and tried and tried*") because she wanted to avoid writing a long and repetitive piece of code. This line of code, as well as her procedure EQUIV as a whole, shows, to my mind, a great jump in Debbie's knowledge of programming.

In addition, Debbie's use of colors is interesting. She matched the colors of the geometric shapes' outlines with the colors of their shaded-in parts: she painted the outline of the square that represents four-eights in red, and its shaded-in parts in orange (which on the screen looks like light red); she painted the rectangle that represents six-twelfths in purple, and its shaded-in parts in bluish- purple; and she painted the outline of the rectangle representing ten-twentieths is dark green, and its shaded parts light green; finally, she painted the circle representing two-fourths in torquoise, and its shaded-in parts in light blue. In other words she did not pick the colors randomly, but she used her aesthetic judgment to decide which colors to use and what sets of colors to use together for one shape.

2.9.2. Equivalent Fractions: Screen Number 2

Apparently Debbie considered her representing of equivalent fractions as a mini-project within the whole project. In what she called the "*Equivalent Fractions Project,*" she wanted to show as many representations as possible for equivalences of halves. Her conversation with me on April 13, her Reflections form of May 22, and her Plans form of May 26 (Figure 53) indicate this clearly. However, the school year was almost over, and Debbie was not able to accomplish her grandiose plans. During the last 3 weeks of the project, she was very concerned with other issues of optimization, reorganization, interactivity, and the presentation of her final piece of software.

In the following, I shall briefly present the other screen for equivalent fractions that Debbie designed on May 26 and 27 (Figures 53 and 54) which were partly implemented. This screen never became part of her final software. because she did not manage to finish it.

The following is Debbie's incomplete Logo code for her second screen on equivalent fractions with my interpretations in brackets:

TO EQUIV2

SETC 11 PD FD 200 PU HOME	[divides the screen vertically in light blue]
RT 90 SETC 10 PD FD 320 PU HOME	[divides the screen horizontally in light green]
SETC 4 PU SETPOS [15 55]	[changes the color to red, positions

Today's Date May 26, 1987

MY PLANS FOR TODAY

TODAY I AM GOING TO FINISH MY
FRACTIONS PROJECT ON EQUIVALENT
'THE FINALS!' I'LL PUT THREE
EXAMPLES OF WHAT MY GRAPHICS
ARE.

!!!!! BYE!!!!!

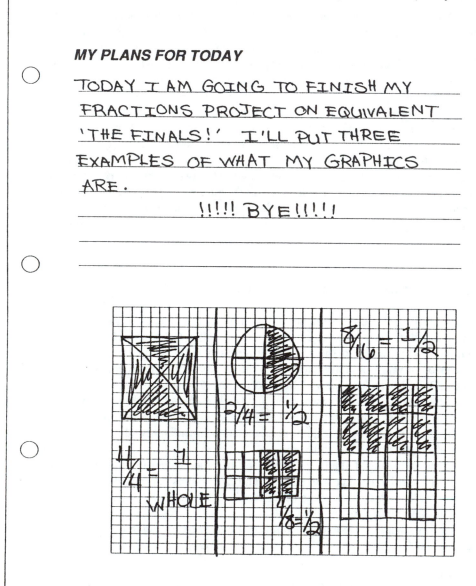

Figure 53.   May 26. Plan.

Today's Date May 27, 1987

MY PLANS FOR TODAY

TODAY I'M GONNA TRY, TRY, TRY TO
FINISH MY FRACTIONS PROJECT ON
EQUIVALENT I TRIED YESTERDAY
BUT I WAS NOT ABLE TO.

HERE IS ANOTHER GRAPHIC FOR
IT.

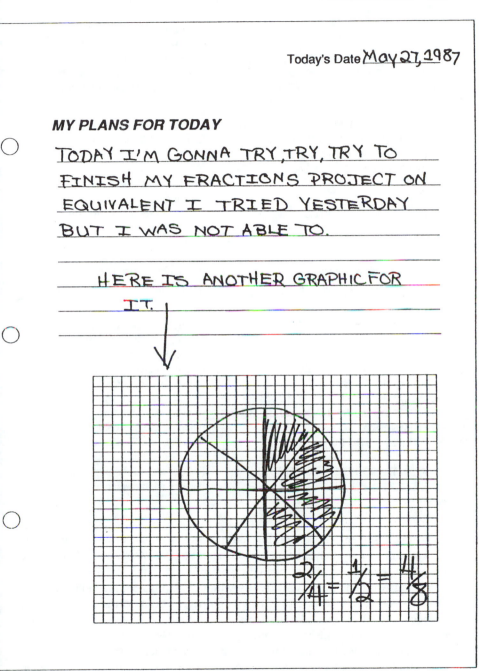

$$\frac{2}{4} = \frac{1}{2} = \frac{4}{8}$$

Figure 54.   May 27. Plan.

PD REPEAT 4 [RT 90 FD 50] — [the Turtle in the top right of the screen]

PD REPEAT 4 [RT 90 FD 50] [draws a red square]
RT 90 FD 25 RT 90 FD 50 BK 25 [divides the square into two halves]
PU RT 90 FD 10 SETC 12 PD FILL [shades the left half in orange]
PU HOME

SETC 12 PD REPEAT 4 [RT 90 FD 50] [draws an orange square]
PU RT 90 FD 25 RT 90 PD FD 50 [divides it into fourths]
PU BK 25 LT 90 PD FD 25 BK 50
PU SETC 4 LT 90 FD 14.1/2 RT 90
PU FD 5 PD FILL [shades in red the top-left fourth of the square]

PU RT 90 FD 15 PD FILL [shades in red the bottom-left fourth of the square]

PU HOME

PR [ALL THESE SHAPES ARE EQUIVALENT FRACTIONS. THIS IS WHAT I
AM GOING TO TEACH YOU!] [prints the instructional statement]
PU HOME

SETC 5 PU SETPOS [-155 35] [changes the pen color into light purple, positions the Turtle at the top left of the screen]

PD REPEAT 180 [FD 1 RT 2] [draws a purple circle]
PU RT 90 PD FD 56 [divides the circle into halves]
BK 28 LT 90 FD 28 BK 56 FD 28 RT 45 [divides the circle into fourths]
FD 28 BK 56 FD 28 LT 90 FD 28 BK 56 [divides the circle into eights]
PU HOME SETC 13 [changes the pen color to pink]
PU SETPOS [-120 50] [positions the Turtle in one of the circle's eights]

PD FILL RT 90 PU FD 10 PD FILL [shades two of the eights in pink]
PU BK 20 PD FILL [shades another eighth in pink]
END

Debbie's screen was left unfinished at the end of the Project (Figure 55).

According to my conversation with Debbie, this is how she wanted this screen to look at the end, when finished (Figure 56).

During April and May, concurrently with her "Equivalent Fractions Project," Debbie continued to work on her two Logo pages, FRACTION and FRACT2. She connected and disconnected procedures from one another, created and eliminated procedures from her superprocedures, and so on. Debbie began to grow relatively more involved in the programming aspect of her software. She became much more involved in moving procedures from one Logo page to another, creating new superprocedures, and discovering new combinations of sub-procedures within those superprocedures. She concentrated much more on the

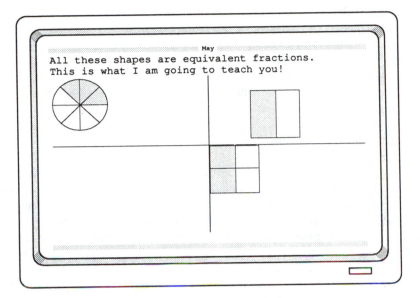

Figure 55.   The Unfinished EQUIV2 Procedure.

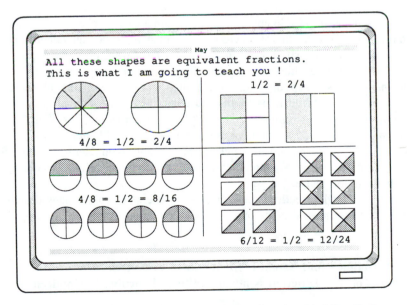

Figure 56.   The Way Debbie Wanted EQUIV2 to Look at the End.

user's interaction with her software and added short introductions and instructional sentences here and there. She was also very involved in finding ways to connect the different Logo pages. Her processes of doing this, although incredibly interesting and complex, are beyond the scope of this book.

On April 13, for example, Debbie deleted some procedures from her FRACT2 page, and decided to leave only the following: INTRODUCTION2.WAIT.FOR.USER and IGNORE,EQUIV,MORE, and UNDERSTANDING. On her other FRACTION page she included: HALF,CALF,HOUSE,WAIT.FOR.USER, and IGNORE. She also had her superprocedure, FRACTIONS, which included: HALF,CALF,TWO,HOUSE,EXAM, QUESTION1, and QUEST.

Later in the month of April Debbie created another superprocedure, which she named OKAY.OKAY became a component in the procedure EXAM; and EXAM asked the user whether or not he or she remembered what he or she had learned about fractions so far. If the user answered that he or she remembered nothing, OKAY made it possible for him or her to go over the materials learned (Debbie chose to go over four procedures, in the following order: HOUSE,HALF,CALF, and TWO). If the user answered that he or she did remember everything he or she had learned, the procedure SUPER was called to provide additional new information. Debbie connected this to GETTOOLS FRACT2,INTRODUCTION,EQUIV,MORE, and UNDERSTANDING. While she was working on the various exams, testing questions, and quizzes, Debbie used many of her existing procedures, reorganized them in different orders and sets, and added little pieces of code where she felt they were needed.

In general, during April and May, there were many discrepancies between Debbie's plans in her Notebook and their implementation (or nonimplementation) at the computer; that is, she constantly planned to do equivalent fractions, but every day, after she logged-in and ran her software on her computer, she decided to do other things related to fitting and connecting her pieces of code together. Still, she kept drawing and planning many screens for equivalent fractions, but in her Reflections Forms she constantly and accurately reported: "*I didn't accomplish starting my equivalent fractions on fract2,*" or "*I added more procedures,*" or "*I added more things to my pages,*" or "*I changed the order of my screens,*" or "*I made a new superprocedure,*" and so on. Her Reflections form from April 13 (Figure 57) offers a typical example of her reflections during this implementation phase:

In the following section I shall emphasize one of Debbie's many designs for equivalent fractions: it is the one she designed on April 14, the "*Sesame Street Screen.*"

2.9.3. Debbie's and Naomi's "Sesame Street Screens:" An Analysis of Two Different Kinds of Cultural Learning in Children

In tracing the origin of children's screen designs, I often found interesting phenomena. I shall discuss one of those here. But let us step back for a moment

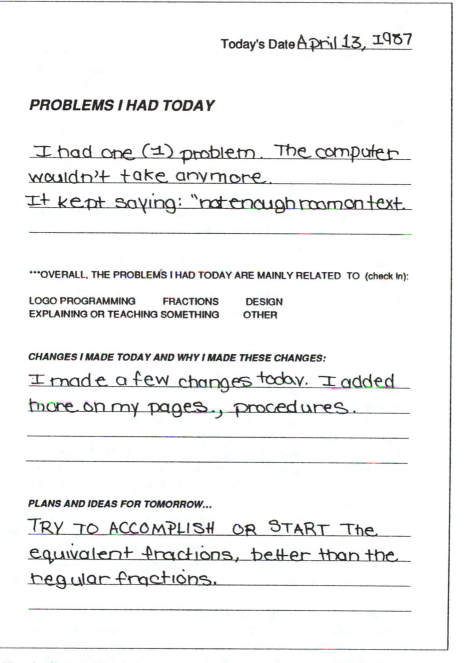

Today's Date April 13, 1987

PROBLEMS I HAD TODAY

I had one (1) problem. The computer wouldn't take anymore.
It kept saying: "not enough room on text.

***OVERALL, THE PROBLEMS I HAD TODAY ARE MAINLY RELATED TO (check In):

LOGO PROGRAMMING   FRACTIONS   DESIGN
EXPLAINING OR TEACHING SOMETHING   OTHER

CHANGES I MADE TODAY AND WHY I MADE THESE CHANGES:

I made a few changes today. I added more on my pages., procedures.

PLANS AND IDEAS FOR TOMORROW...

TRY TO ACCOMPLISH OR START The equivalent fractions, better than the regular fractions.

Figure 57.   April 13. Reflections Form.

and recall how, on April 14, Debbie wrote and drew the following in her Designer's Notebook (Figure 58).

Although Debbie never implemented this particular design in Logo, I chose to analyze it here in detail because it provides us with an interesting comparison of the different qualities of imitation or cultural learning in two children.

Obviously, it is not possible to find which one of these four representations (in Figure 58) that Debbie drew in her notebook "does not belong," since, in fact they all represent halves!

In the following subsections I shall clarify the 'cultural origins' of Debbie's design. For that purpose, I will briefly describe the way Naomi, another girl from the experimental class, created a similar design by imitating "Sesame Street's" famous scenario, "Which of these four belong together, and which one of these does not belong."

I will then show how Debbie imitated this idea from Naomi's software, and the ways in which she transferred it without fully understanding (a) the general structure of this scene from "Sesame Street," and (b) the fractional or instructional concepts that were embodied in her friend's screen.

From analyzing the two girls' processes and products of imitation, I conclude that two qualitatively different imitations were found. Through this comparison I offer a reexamination of Vygotsky's beliefs about the role of imitation in learning, as well as a reevaluation of his use of the word *imitation,* in terms of these two girls' processes and products.

Naomi's screen. One girl from experimental class, Naomi, who was sitting next to Debbie during most computer sessions, had worked during the second week of April on a very original and creative screen which she had called the "Sesame Street Screen."

One of the instructional goals of the well-known "Sesame Street" television series (which is produced by Children's Television Workshop) is to teach children about classification, sorting, and grouping (Lesser, 1974). One treatment of this goal is to show children four objects, three of which have an attribute in common; the child is required to sort out the one "inappropriate" object out of the four presented, on the basis of: *size* (i.e., height, length, etc.); *form* (i.e., circular, square, triangular, etc.); *function* (i.e., to ride in, to eat, to read, etc.); or *class* (i.e., vehicles, animals, etc.). These scenes are designed so that children will be able to observe and examine the properties of the four given objects, verbalize their reasons for grouping three objects together, say why they belong together, and therefore discover "which one does not belong" (e.g., Lesser, 1974, p. 67).

Naomi, on her own, spontaneously came up with the idea of imitating this popular "Sesame Street" scene that shows four different objects on the TV screen. She successfully managed to appropriate it, use it in her teaching about fractional representations, and implement it in Logo. On April 10, Naomi finished her screen (see Figure 59).

The minute Naomi announced "*I am done! It works!*" many of her friends (and

Today's Date April 14, 1987

MY PLANS FOR TODAY

TODAY I AM GOING TO DO EXACTLY. LOOK
ON PREVIOUS PLANS PAGE. I'm going to do
this graphic for my fractions Project, on Frac12,
which is equivalent fractions and a little more.
I am going to try to do what I wanted for
the rest of the week. Another graphic
I'm going to try to do is:

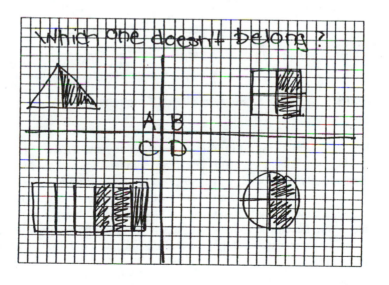

Figure 58.   April 14. Plan.

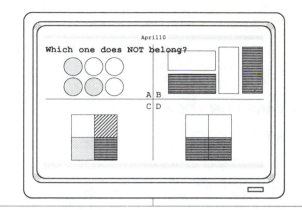

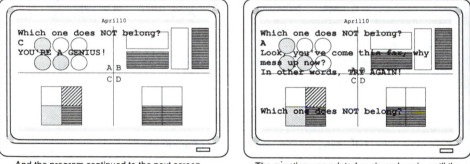

If the user typed C, the computer answered...

If the user typed A, B, or D, the computer answered...

And the program continued to the next screen...

The question was printed again and again, until the user found the right answer. Then, the program continued to the next screen...

Figure 59.   Naomi's "Sesame Street"/Fractions Screen.

Debbie among them) sat in front of her computer and tried it out. Naomi, unlike Debbie, was a very cheerful, talkative, enthusiastic, and successful child both academically and socially. She was also always willing to explain *anything* she did in a very detailed and articulate fashion. On April 10, I approached her, as the other children were doing, and said to her: "What a wonderful idea, Naomi!" and before I even had a chance to ask her anything, Naomi provided me with the following explanation of her screen design, which I find quite unique and delightful:

> This is my Sesame Street Screen. [Long pause, she watches how one of her friends uses it. Then she looks at me:] It is tricky you know. I designed it so option A will *really really* trick them. Because, B, C, and D, are showing fourths [pointing on B, D, and C on the screen]: here, there are two-fourths in a group of four rectangles; here, two-fourths in the square; and here, three-fourths in another square. And, these [representations B, C, and D] are all showing pictures of squares and rec-

tangles, so you'll think: That's it! I found it! [pointing at A with her left hand and at B, D, and C with three fingers of her right hand] These [B, D, and C] go together!' Confusing, Ha?! But Option A is showing six circles. Three-sixths are shaded in. So that you'll think right away that A doesn't belong [she imitated the voice of a younger child]:' What are these *circles* and *sixths* doing here . . .' [she laughs] So you'll think, 'they definitely do not belong here!' But, if you look very carefully [she now speaks in a teacher's voice], you can see that A, B, and D are showing *halves,* and that C is the one that doesn't belong, 'cause it's showing three-fourths! And that's it!

Naomi's detailed explanation speak for itself. She was aware of the major strategies the "Sesame Street" instructional designers used in their scenes on TV; and she was also aware of their "tricking techniques." Naomi was able to analyze and break apart the underlying instructional concepts of this scene, and to later reconstruct it to suit her own purposes and instructional goals. She was also seriously considering her target users, what they might think, say, or do, as they solved the puzzle she had given them, and so on. (In fact, even before April 10, while she was still planning that screen and during its implementation phases, Naomi provided me with several quite similar, but not as detailed explanations for it. I shall also note here that throughout the project, Naomi came up with many creative and unique screen designs, which should be analyzed and will be described in detail in my forthcoming case about her.)

Debbie's design. At first, I was not aware of Debbie's design of April 14, since she had decided not to implement it in Logo. I discovered it in her Note-book about 3 weeks after she had designed it; only then did I realize how much Naomi's "Sesame Street Screen" had influenced Debbie. Although Debbie, in her design of April 14, attempted to imitate the "Sesame Street" scenario, we shall now examine how much less sophisticated she was in her imitation and in her understanding of the "Sesame Street" instructional design techniques than was Naomi. For that purpose, let us examine *Debbie's* design once again (Figure 60).

Debbie, to use Naomi's words, did not "trick her users" at all. She created four simple representations, each one of them, in fact, representing halves: Option A represented a half of a triangle; B, a half of a square; C, a half of a rectangle; and D, a half of a circle. One needs to recall here that Naomi also focused on halves as the common attribute among the three representations that 'went together,' but that, in Naomi's screen, the representation that "did not belong" was the one of three-fourths of a square.

One also needs to recall that Naomi "tricked her users" by showing them three-sixths in option A, which in fact possessed the common attribute (three-sixths equal one-half). She managed to "trick" Debbie quite successfully. Debbie imitated that "trick of sixths" in her representation of three-sixths (in the rec-tangle at the bottom-left), but she considered it to be the item that "didn't belong," it being "three-sixths and not a half."

One day in May, I took Debbie out of the classroom. We sat together in the

Today's Date April 14

MY PLANS FOR TODAY

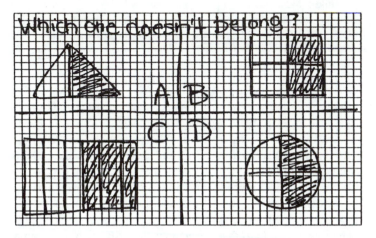

Figure 60.   Debbie's Hand-drawn "Sesame Street" Design.

Headlight teachers' room and went through her Notebook. Among other things, we talked about that particular design. Our short conversation about this design is reported below, with my own comments in brackets:

Idit: *So which one doesn't belong, Debbie?*
Debbie: *Can't you tell?!*
Idit: *Uhm . . .*
Debbie: *It is like Naomi's. You know*
          [Note that Debbie did not say, "it's like in "Sesame Street," rather, "it's like Naomi's"; in other words, she perceived herself as imitating Naomi's idea. She knew that I "understood" Naomi's screen, because she had seen us talking about it. She therefore referred me to Naomi's screen, and expected me to figure out her own design since it resembled Naomi's]
Idit: *Oh. . . Yea. . . Now I remember, Naomi also made something like this.*
Debbie: *I did not have enough time to do it on the computer, I made other things instead.*
          [She puts her hand on her Designer's Notebook, attempting to turn that page and put an end to our conversation on that particular design].
Idit: *Yes, I know that you created many other things.*
Debbie: *I like it though.*
Idit: *You like what?*
Debbie: *This design*
          [she points to her plan of April 14]
Idit: *What do like about it?*

Debbie: *Do you know "Sesame Street"? It's like a quiz. They [on TV] always show you four different things and you have to guess which one doesn't belong.*
          [Now she relates it to "Sesame Street" for the first time. She seems to generally understand the "Sesame Street" scenario; she also quietly mumbles the famous song from that scene on the TV show].

Idit: *So. . . Which on [doesn't belong]?*

Debbie: *Don't you know about fractions??*

Idit: *Well. . . What do I have to know in order to solve it?*

Debbie: *You know . . .*

Idit: *Please tell me, help me*
          [I say this in a pleading voice, and we both smile]

Debbie: *C doesn't belong of course.*

Idit: *Oh! I see. . . But, why?*

Debbie: *Because.*

Idit: *What do you mean?*

Debbie: *C is three-sixths, so it doesn't belong.*

Idit: *Oh. . . What I thought was different. It's really strange. I thought that C shows one-half, and A, B, and D, are also showing one-half. That's why I couldn't solve it!*

Debbie: *Yea . . that's true . . .*
          [Long pause, she examines her design once again; she puts her finger on the picture, then looks towards the ceiling, and says]

Debbie: *Yea . . that's true too. But C is three-sixths.*
          [I see this as a sign of her rigidity]

Idit: *And three-sixths do not belong . . . I see.*

Debbie: *Naomi's screen is better, I guess.*
          [She begins to feel insecure, but at the same time begins to break away from her rigidity].

Idit: *What do you mean by 'better'? Why?*

Debbie: *I don't know . . .*
          [A very long pause. She seems a bit puzzled, as though unable to figure out why I am bothering her with this particular design, or wondering whether she has done something "wrong." Perhaps she is trying to recall "Sesame Street" scenes of this kind, or what Naomi did on her screen, and how she herself could have made her screen "better"]

Idit: *What are you thinking about?*
          [No answer. I know that Debbie rarely answers questions of this kind, so I wait a few seconds, see that she is not going to answer, and continue:]

Idit: *That's it. Now I got it! C doesn't belong because it shows three-sixths!*
          [I am trying to make her feel better and more secure . . .]

Debbie: *Or, nothing doesn't belong because they all show one-half!*
          [She gives me a shy smile. She says "OR," meaning that she is only partially willing to play my game, and become only a tiny bit more flexible]
          [she pauses, looks towards the ceiling,]   . . Or . . .
Or . . . I should change it . . . Uhm . . . I'll change the rectangle to fifths. To three-fifths. Now it really doesn't belong here.
          [i.e., "Hey researcher, now I know what you were looking for!"]

Idit: *You'll change it? . . . Why change!?*

Debbie: *Because A, B, and D show halves, and C doesn't. It shows fifths. If I change it,*
         I mean here,

[She emphasizes the word "if." She then points to the rectangle. There is a
pencil near her hand, but she does not use it. She does not actually change
her original design. Apparently, the progress from thought to action is quite
difficult for her in this context].

Idit: *Are you planning to change it? Are you planning to create it on the computer*
         one day?

Debbie: *No.* [A very loud "NO". . . Pause].

See . . . I drew it long time ago. . . Now I am making another scene. I don't think I
should use this one at all.

[pause]

Naomi already finished it. I am making another thing instead.

"Long distance" and "short distance" types of imitation. Several issues need
to be discussed in this context. Comparing Naomi's and Debbie's imitation
processes, their designs, and the quality of their explanations of the designs
reveals interesting differences in their intellectual levels in general, and between
their levels of understanding of the "Sesame Street" instructional design approach in particular.

Naomi initiated the idea of imitating "Sesame Street" and constructed a comprehensive design for it completely on her own, without the assistance of others,
without demonstrations, and without a need for leading questions on my part.
Debbie, on the other hand, imitated "Sesame Street" (via Naomi's demonstration), but, in order to fully understand the concepts that were involved in that
design, she needed my assistance and required many leading questions in order
to grasp the underlying structure of the concepts involved (i.e., of instructional
design and fractional representations). According to Vygotsky (1978), imitation
is an important factor in children's learning:

> A full understanding of the concept of the zone of proximal development must
> result in re-evaluation of the role of imitation in learning. An unshakable tenet of
> classical psychology is that only independent activity of children, not their imita-
> tive activity, indicates their level of mental development. . . . But recently psy-
> chologists have shown that a person can imitate only that which is within her
> developmental level. (pp. 87–88)

To my mind, Vygotsky's belief that "a child can imitate only that which is
within his developmental level" does not provide a sufficient explanation of the
real differences between Debbie and Naomi in this particular context.

We have examined how the two girls were able to imitate "Sesame Street":
can we then say that they (a) imitated it in the same way? (b) were both on the
same cognitive-developmental level? (i.e., because both could imitate only what
was within their developmental level). I do not think so, for we also saw that one
of the girls (Debbie) was indeed imitating an idea in the Vygotskian sense,
whereas the other girl (Naomi), strange as it may sound, was imitating an idea in

a strong constructivist fashion. Naomi's processes and product of imitation were proven to be more systematic and comprehensive, whereas the Debbie's were more superficial, limited, and incomplete.

I find Piaget's famous constructivist argument—that each time one prematurely shows children something they could have discovered themselves, the children are kept from inventing it, and consequently, from understanding it deeply and completely—to be very relevant here—not in a teacher–student framework, but rather in a student–student framework. My assumption is that both girls were equally familiar with the "Sesame Street" scenario (Debbie explained it very well during our conversation in the teacher's room); however, Naomi, in this case, prevented Debbie from "discovering this idea for herself," to use Piaget's argument, and from understanding it completely. Debbie's imitation was therefore not as powerful or deep as Naomi's imitation of the same ideas.

In other words, Naomi discovered that she could borrow the "Sesame Street" classification scenario for her own instructional purposes. The "Sesame Street" scene existed in her culture—although not directly in her school culture—and she did indeed imitate it, but it was a "long distance" imitation. Naomi's thoughts, actions, and explanations should be perceived and interpreted as processes of reinvention. *She* was the one who discovered the "Sesame Street" scene's relevance, its underlying structure, and its "tricking" techniques (no one had ever told her about this), and *she* retrofitted the concepts involved in these scenes for her own software in a systematic way and with a deep understanding of them. Moreover, she invented *her own methods* for using this instructional strategy in the context of her software about fractions. (Was it a higher level imitation? I believe that it was a question of qualitative difference, and not just a difference in level.) In short, although Naomi did indeed imitate "Sesame Street," I still believe that she was involved in invention.

Debbie, on the other hand, was involved in "short distance" imitation. Debbie did not discover the idea of borrowing the "Sesame Street" classification scene for her project; she was not involved in a high-level reflection or paying attention to the characteristics of the "Sesame Street" scene and its "tricking techniques," she did not consider how they might fit into her software in the way Naomi's had. Instead, she liked Naomi's idea when she saw it on her computer; she was familiar with the idea and was generally able to understand it; then, with minimal reflection and without a deep understanding of it, she designed an almost identical screen. But, in fact, Debbie was rather confused about how to use it "properly" for the purpose of teaching about fractions and their representations.

To summarize, I see these two situations of "long-distance" and "short-distance" imitations as resulting in two different qualities of thinking: one was "mindful" and insightful, the other, "mindless" and superficial (to borrow from Salomon's terminology, 1979, 1986). These became two kinds of cultural learnings: Naomi was strongly influenced by the "Sesame Street" culture, but I believe that, since she had discovered it on her own and borrowed it from a long distance, she eventually pursued a higher level and richer route in her cultural learning than Debbie did. Whereas Debbie was only influenced 'second hand' by the "Sesame Street" culture: it was, in fact, Naomi's innovative approach that influenced Debbie's designs on April 14. Perhaps because of its being "second hand" (i.e., not Debbie's own idea) and a "short distance" imitation, Debbie was not as mindful as Naomi when she imitated it, nor motivated to invest time and thought in reconstructing and implementing this idea.

However, I do believe that Debbie gained something from imitating Naomi's approach, even though she did not expand on it. I also believe that she gained something from her discussion with me. This is why I have interpreted Debbie's imitation activities as "learning," and furthermore, of a "cultural kind."

Two girls—two styles of thinking and expression. This episode also provides information for another comparison: a comparison between the two girls' different styles of thinking and expression. I consider Naomi as someone with very high metacognitive and verbal (or communication) abilities, and Debbie as someone with much lower abilities of this kind (i.e., one needs only to compare Naomi's holistic and systematic explanations with Debbie's short and rigid answers in the two conversations reported above).

All I needed to do was to approach Naomi, and with minimal or no prompting I was provided with very articulate, detailed, and sophisticated explanations about anything I wanted to know, whereas with Debbie, it took many efforts on my part to make her explain and reflect on something. I needed to constantly play games with Debbie and maneuver around her frequent negative responses such as *"I don't know,"* *"Uhm. . . Because,"* or, *"You, know."*

Some people might say that Debbie is the type of child who requires a greater experience of adult–child scaffolding, whereas Naomi does not. But through working with Debbie, I came to suspect that she did not enjoy scaffolding (and one should also differentiate here between *scaffolding* and *paying attention;* Debbie very much appreciated the latter). Most of the time I realized that she wanted to be left alone and not be asked to explain too many things; and that she preferred, if she were to discuss anything, to discuss *her own* ideas and inventions (as opposed to the researcher's ideas and concerns), when *she* felt like it (rather than when the researcher found it appropriate).

Debbie was allowed to discuss things as she wished in the context of ISDP. She was able to invest a great deal of time on her own thoughts and inventions. She thought about teaching *other* children. I believe that these are the reasons why Debbie grew to develop more reflective skills, refined her ability to explain things, opened up, and became relatively more sociable and communicative (and not necessarily and solely because of the researcher's interventions).

To summarize, the flowchart in Figure 61 captures Debbie's stage sequences in working on her Equivalent Fractions Project. The diagram is limited in its ability to capture all of Debbie's activities during this phase (April and May); it does, however, attempt to represent the long period of time in which Debbie was involved in designing, representing, redesigning, and programming Equivalent

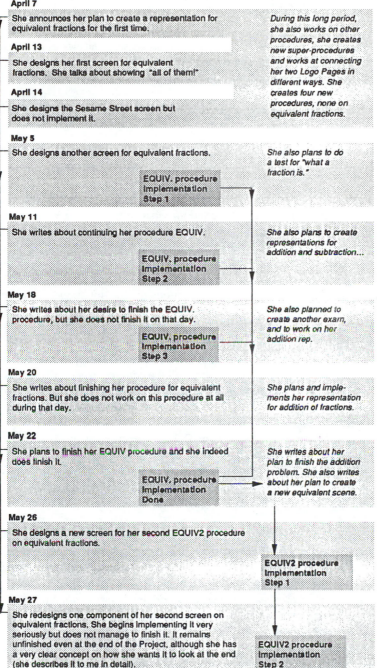

April 7

She announces her plan to create a representation for equivalent fractions for the first time.

During this long period, she also works on other procedures, she creates new super-procedures and works at connecting her two Logo Pages in different ways. She creates four new procedures, none on equivalent fractions.

April 13

She designs her first screen for equivalent fractions. She talks about showing "all of them!"

April 14

She designs the Sesame Street screen but does not implement it.

May 5

She designs another screen for equivalent fractions.

She also plans to do a test for "what a fraction is."

EQUIV. procedure
Implementation
Step 1

May 11

She writes about continuing her procedure EQUIV.

She also plans to create representations for addition and subtraction...

EQUIV. procedure
Implementation
Step 2

May 18

She writes about her desire to finish the EQUIV. procedure, but she does not finish it on that day.

She also planned to create another exam, and to work on her addition rep.

EQUIV. procedure
Implementation
Step 3

May 20

She writes about finishing her procedure for equivalent fractions. But she does not work on this procedure at all during that day.

She plans and implements her representation for addition of fractions.

May 22

She plans to finish her EQUIV procedure and she indeed does finish it.

She writes about her plan to finish the addition problem. She also writes about her plan to create a new equivalent scene.

EQUIV. procedure
Implementation
Done

May 26

She designs a new screen for her second EQUIV2 procedure on equivalent fractions.

EQUIV2 procedure
Implementation
Step 1

May 27

She redesigns one component of her second screen on equivalent fractions. She begins implementing it very seriously but does not manage to finish it. It remains unfinished even at the end of the Project, although she has a very clear concept on how she wants it to look at the end (she describes it to me in detail).

EQUIV2 procedure
Implementation
Step 2

Figure 61. Debbie's Processes of Designing, Representing, Redesigning, and Programming the Screens about Equivalent Fractions During April and May.

241

Fractions of halves; the complexity of her processes; and her parallel thinking about implementing several plans and screens during each computer session.

2.10. THE ADDITION SCREEN ASSIGNMENT

On May 14 the teacher of the experimental class decided to give the children an assignment about representing addition of fractions. According to her, she was generally *"very curious to see what would happen when she gave the children the same assignment as part of their own Project."* (Throughout the Project we never gave any assignments or told the children what to represent. We were not sure how the children would react to the idea of an assignment within this open-ended and free Project.) She also initiated it because she *"wanted to see how they thought about addition"* and also *"wanted to create a base-line for talking about representations for fractional operations."* In fact, the teacher realized that many of the students had not created representations for fractional operations, and felt that, if she introduced one fractional operation (addition), they would start thinking more about representing other fractional operations.

This was an interesting experiment within the framework of ISDP. In the focus session, the children generated several ideas on how to represent addition of fractions. What was amazing was that all the children except two clearly stated in their Plans For Today (on May 14) that the teacher had given them an "addition assignment." On May 14, Debbie, for example, wrote in her Notebook: *"Today my teacher gave us an assignment. We did adding fractions. Bye!!!"*

This is an interesting statement for Debbie, because she always called all her representations "my project," or "my new scene." But in her writings, she referred to the addition representation as "the addition assignment." Beside this question of ownership, Debbie had no problems understanding the assignment or fulfilling it. On May 14 she designed two representations in her Notebook (Figure 62).

The differences between the first and second representations are interesting. The first is the one that the teacher had drawn on the blackboard after her conversation with the class. Most of the children copied it in their Notebooks. The second one was generated by Debbie, after the teacher told the children: *"Now, after we did this one together, try to do one representation for addition on your own."* In the second representation, I find that Debbie was more sensitive to the instructional purpose of the representation than her teacher was. She created a clear correspondence between the two pictures on the left side of the equation (one-fourth and one-half) and the one on the right (three-fourths). Debbie very clearly stated her reasons for doing it this way:

Debbie: *The first one* [number 1] *is true and correct but it is not really good for teaching. Because in the second one that I did, they* (the users) *can really see*

Name _Debbie_

Today's Date _May 4, 1987_

MY PLANS FOR TODAY

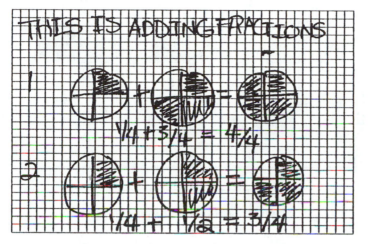

Figure 62.   May 14 Hand-drawn Designs for Representing Addition of Fractions.

> *that the one-fourth goes here* [she points to the top-left fourth at the three-fourth representation] *and that the two other fourths goes here* [she points to the top-right and bottom-right fourths in the three-fourths representation]. *It's much much much better.*

Debbie's mindful instructional approach was implemented by her on the computer as shown in Figure 63.

Debbie worked on that screen in parallel with working on her equivalent fractions screen. She never appropriated the addition screen and never thought of it as "her own thing"; for example, in her Reflections form on May 18 she wrote: *"Today I didn't have any problems. I didn't do adding fractions assignment. But I did not do my equivalent fractions project yet, but I have to finish it soon. . . . I made sort of little changes* [in her other procedures] *but thank you and goodbye!!!"*

Debbie writes about two things she did not do, but describes each of them in a different tone: *"I didn't do adding fractions assignment,"* as opposed to *"I did not do my equivalent fractions project, but I have to finish it soon."* Although she felt uncomfortable about this assignment being imposed on her, she still managed to complete it. The following is Debbie's first version of Logo code for her representation of an addition of two-fourths:

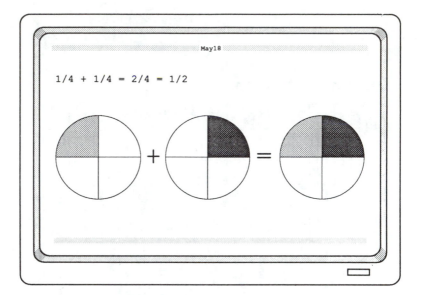

Figure 63.   The Screen Representing Addition of Fourths.

TO ADD   **[THE SUPER-PROCEDURE]**
ADDINGFR   [calls the left side of the equation]
HALF   [calls the right side of the
                                            equation]
PR [1∨4 + 1∨4 = 2∨4 = 1∨2]   [prints the instructional
                                            statement, translating the pictorial
                                            representation into symbolic
                                            operation.]

END

TO ADDINGFR   [FIRST VERSION]
SETC 1+RANDOM 14   [the computer randomly selects a
                                            color for the pen]
PU SETPOS [-100 0]   [positions the Turtle at the left side
                                            of the screen]
PD REPEAT 36 [FD 5 RT 10]   [draws a medium-sized circle]
RT 90 PD FD 57   [cuts the circle horizontally into
                                            halves]
PU BK 28.5 LT 90 PD FD 29 BK 55   [cuts the circle again vertically, so
                                            that it shows fourths]
PU HOME
PU SETPOS [-80 10]   [positions the Turtle at the circle's
                                            top-left fourth]
SETC 4 PD FILL   [shades the top-left fourth in red]
PU HOME PU SETPOS [-25 0]   [positions the Turtle on the right
                                            side of the circle]

LABEL"+   [prints the sign + next to the
                                           circle, at its right]

PU HOME   [finishes drawing one fourth]

SETC 1+RANDOM 13   [the computer selects one color
                                           randomly]

PU SETPOS [-10 0]   [positions the Turtle on the middle
                                           of the screen]

PD REPEAT 36 [FD 5 RT 10]   [draws the same size circle as
                                           before]

RT 90 PD FD 57 BK 28.5 LT 90   [cuts the circle horizontally]
FD 29 BK 56 PU HOME   [cuts the circle vertically to four-
                                           fourths]

PU SETPOS [35 10]   [positions the Turtle on the top-
                                           right fourth of the circle]

SETC 12 PD FILL   [shades in purple the top-right
                                           fourth]

END   [finishes the pictorial
                                           representation of 1/4+1/4]

TO HALF [FIRST VERSION]
PU HOME PU SETPOS [60 0]   [positions the Turtle on the right
                                           of the second circle]

LABEL"=   [prints the sign = for the
                                           equation]

PU HOME
PU SETPOS [75 0]   [positions the Turtle on the right
                                           of the screen]

SETC 1+RANDOM 14   [draws the same size circle as the
                                           other two]

RT 90 FD 57 BK 28.5   [cuts the circle horizontally]
LT 90 FD 30 BK 56 PU HOME   [cuts it vertically]
SETC 4 PU SETPOS [85 10]   [positions the Turtle on the top-left
                                           fourth of the third circle]

PD FILL   [shades the top-left fourth in red]
PU HOME
SETC 12 PU SETPOS [110 10]   [positions the Turtle on the top-
                                           right fourth of the circle]

PD FILL   [shades the top-right fourth in
                                           purple]

END   [finishes the representation of a
                                           half]

Debbie's modification of her ADDITION PROGRAM during June:

TO ADD   **[THE SUPERPROCEDURE]**
ADDINGFR   [calls the left side of the equation]
PR [1∨4 + 1∨4 = 2∨4 = 1∨2]   [prints the instructional statement
                                           which is a translation of the

	pictorial representation into symbolic operation]
END	

TO ADDINGFR   [SECOND VERSION with a subprocedure for the circle]

SETC 1+RANDOM 14	[the computer randomly selects a color for the pen]
PU SETPOS [-100 0]	[positions the Turtle at the left side of the screen]
CIRCLE.ADD	[Calls the subprocedure for drawing the circle]
PU SETPOS [-80 10]	[positions the Turtle on the top-left fourth of the circle]
SETC 4PD FILL	[shades the top-left fourth in red]
PU HOME PU SETPOS [-25 0]	[positions the Turtle on the right side of the circle]
LABEL"+	[prints the sign + next to the circle, at its right]
PU HOME	[finishes drawing one-fourth]
SETC 1+RANDOM 13	[the computer selects one color randomly]
PU SETPOS [-10 0]	[positions the Turtle in the middle of the screen]
CIRCLE.ADD	[calls the subprocedure for drawing the circle]
PU SETPOS [35 10]	[positions the Turtle on the top-right fourth of the circle]
SETC 12 PD FILL	[shades the top-right fourth in purple]
END	[finishes the pictorial representation of 1/4 = 1/4]

TO HALF   [SECOND VERSION]

PU HOME PU SETPOS [60 0]	[positions the Turtle on the right of the second circle]
LABEL"=	[prints the sign = for the equation]
PU HOME	
PU SETPOS [75 0]	[positions the Turtle on the right of the screen]
SETC 1+RANDOM 14	[the computer randomly selects a color for the circle]
CIRCLE.ADD	[calls the subprocedure for drawing the circle]
SETC 4 PU SETPOS [85 10]	[positions the Turtle at the top-left fourth of the third circle]
PD FILL	[shades the top-left fourth in red]

```
PU HOME
SETC 12 PU SETPOS [110 10]              [positions the Turtle on the top-
                                        right fourth of the circle]
PD FILL                                 [shades the top-right fourth in
                                        purple]
END                                     [finishes the representation of a
                                        half]

TO CIRCLE.ADD                           [THE NEW SUBPROCEDURE]
PD RETREAT 36 [FD 5 RT 10]              [draws a medium-sized circle]
RT 90 PD FD 57                          [cuts the circle horizontally into
                                        halves]
PU BK 28.5 LT 90 PD FD 29 BK 55         [cuts the circle again vertically, so
                                        that it shows fourths]
END
```

To summarize my observations during the addition assignment, this experiment revealed several things. On one hand, although Debbie felt that it was "an assignment" and not one of her own projects, she still invested her thought into its instructional designing and worked at improving the screen so "*it would teach better about addition.*" She worked at combining a pictorial representation of the addition operation with the symbolic representation of the operation. In her instructional statement, we saw that she even emphasized the addition algorithm of $1/4 + 1/4 = 2/4$ and then reduced it to $1/2$. Debbie was concerned that the algorithm should be emphasized in the pictorial representation as well, which she did by consistently showing a red fourth in the top-left of the circle and a purple fourth in the top-left. She learned several important things from creating this screen.

On the other hand, the major difference between this assignment and the other representations that the children worked on during the project was the fact that, during this week, all the children worked on the *same* thing; and since the *teacher* showed own example on the blackboard, the children felt they had to follow her example (as in all their other school assignments). Students were not strongly motivated to change or build on this representational framework. Although many of them really wanted to work on their own screens, they felt they needed to complete this particular representation because it was "an assignment." Unlike the other screens they had worked on during the project, this one was imposed on them and interrupted their ongoing work. On the whole, I do not think this assignment was as valuable to the children's learning as the creation of their own representations. The dominant flavor of this project was its diversity. One could walk around the class during the computer sessions and observe 17 different children working on 17 different screens and representations. But during the week of the 'addition assignment,' all the children produced almost the same thing and did not seem very excited or eager about it. It was something that they were *required* to complete, and not something they *wanted to* complete. This is clear from their writings in the Designer's Notebooks and also from the fact that many of them did not include this screen in their final piece of software.

JUNE

2.11. FINISHING UP: AN OVERVIEW OF DEBBIE'S WHOLE PIECE OF INSTRUCTIONAL SOFTWARE

In this last section of the case I shall describe Debbie's entire software and its Logo programming components. Debbie worked on these long pieces of code throughout the project, but, during the month of June, her goal was to work on all the pieces *simultaneously*, find ways to fit them together, and add connections and instructions for the user. We shall see in this section that Debbie's software and her use of Logo grew into a very large and complex undertaking, amazingly so when one considers her age and her initial lack of experience, interest, and apparent capability. And although much could be said about her procedures and thinking processes, we will refrain, at this stage, from comment and deep interpretation, and allow Debbie's piece of software, by its very length, to speak eloquently for itself.

From May 29 onward, all of Debbie's plans in her Designer's Notebook were concerned with finishing her project. As examples, let us look at two entries from her designer's notebook which were very typical of Debbie's writing throughout June:

- June 2, Plan:
  Today I'm going to try and finish my fractions project. Bye!!!
- June 2, Reflections:
  I had not one problem except finishing. I made no changes except the usual!
- June 12, Plan:
  Today I am going to try and finish my fractions project. Bye!
- June 12, Reflections:
  I had plenty of problems today and I didn't get my goal for today done. The problems I had were in fractions, logo, programming, and design.

Let us now look at Debbie's Logo pages one by one:

DEBBIE'S SOFTWARE PART 1: THE LOGO PAGE FRACTION

TO FRACTIONS

[THIS IS THE MAIN SUPER-PROCEDURE, THE USER TYPES "FRACTIONS" AT THE COMMANDS CENTER AND THE SOFTWARE BEGINS . . .]

HT CT CG
INTRODUCTION WAIT 50

["hello my name is Debbie . . . I teach you half of the screen" etc.]

HALF WAIT. FOR.USER
CG CT CC
CALF WAIT. FOR.USER

[representing half of the screen]

[multiple representations for halves using four geometrical shapes]

CG CT CC
TWO WAIT. FOR.USER

[the representation for two-thirds, and quiz]

CG CT CC
GETTOOLS "FRACT1

[get procedures from the third (new) Logo Page "Fract1]

QUEST

["Do you know how to do fractions? . . ." etc., and quiz]

WAIT. FOR.USER CC CG CT
HOUSE WAIT. FOR.USER
CG CT CC
EXAM

[the House Scene about halves]

[The "Do you remember what you learned? . . ." Screen, where Debbie provides a "going over," or a set of new representations]

SUPER

[connects this page with "Fract2, includes equivalent fract.]

END

TO INTRODUCTION
pr [Hello, my name is Debbie. I am going to teach you how to do fractions.
The first thing that I am going to teach you is the half of the screen.
The scene is a half or two-fourths.]
END

TO HALF
SETC 9 FD 250 — [cuts the screen horizontally]
PU HOME RT 90 SETC 1 — [goes back home and changes the pen color]

PD FD 320 — [cuts the screen vertically]
PU SETPOS [40 45] — [goes to the center of the top-right fourth]
LT 90 SETC 4 PD FILL — [fills it in red color]

```
PU SETPOS [40 -45]              [moves to the center of the bottom-right
                                fourth]

PD SETC 3 PD FILL               [fills it in pink color]
PR [This is my fraction project]  [prints instructional sentence at the top]
PR [This is 1/2 or 2/4]
PR []                           [skips a space]
PR [By Debbie]                  [prints her name]
END

TO CALF
HT SETC 1+RANDOM 14             [sets the pen color randomly]
PD FD 200                       [draws a vertical line across the screen]
PU HOME
RT 90
SETC 1+RANDOM 14                [sets the pen color randomly]
PD FD 320                       [draws a horizontal line across the screen]
PU HOME
PU SETPOS [30 50]               [moves Turtle to position of circle]
SETC 12 P. REPEAT 360 [FD.3 RT 1]
                                [draws a circle on the top right]

RT 90
PD FD 33                        [divides the circle in half]
PU SETPOS [45 40]
PD FILL                         [shades in the bottom half of the circle]
PD HOME
PR [ALL THESE FRACTIONS ARE 1/2]
                                [prints the instructional statement]
SETPOS [-60 50]                 [moves the Turtle to position of square]
SETC 1+RANDOM 14
PD REPEAT 4 [LT 90 FD 40]       [draws the square on the top left]
PU LT 90 FD 20 LT 90
PD FD 40                        [divides the square in half]
RT 90 FD 10 RT 90
PU FD 5 PD FILL                 [shades in the left half of the square]
PU HOME
SETC 1+RANDOM 14
SETPOS [35 -70]                 [moves Turtle to position of rectangle]
PD REPEAT 4 [FD 50 RT 90 FD 100 RT 90]
                                [draws a rectangle on the bottom right]
RT 90 FD 50 LT 90 PD FD 49      [divides the rectangle in half]
PU RT 90
FD 25 RT 90 FD 10 PD FILL       [shades in the right side of rectangle]
PU HOME
SETC 1+RANDOM 14
PU SETPOS [-105 -55]            [moves the Turtle to position of triangle]
RT 45 PD FD 50                  [creates a triangle]
RT 90 FD 52
```

```
RT 135 FD 73                              [moves the Turtle to position of cutting
REPEAT 2 [RT 90]                          the triangle into two equal parts]
FD 36 LT 90 PD FD 35                      [divides the triangle]
PU SETPOS [-55 -40] PD FILL               [shades the half on the right side of the
                                          triangle]

END


TO WAIT.FOR.USER
TYPE [PRESS ANY KEY TO CONTINUE]          [types a message on the bottom of
                                          the screen]
IGNORE READCHAR                           ["sends" the character that was typed by
                                          the user as the input for the IGNORE
END                                       procedure]

TO IGNORE :KEY                            [the procedure IGNORE takes one input,
                                          a character, but does nothing with it, so
END                                       the program simply goes on]


TO TWO
PU HOME SETC 1+RANDOM 14
PD REPEAT 360 [FD 1 RT 1]                 [creates a big circle]
PU SETPOS [60 5]                          [positions the Turtle in the middle of the
                                          circle]

SETC 1+RANDOM 14
PD FD 53                                  [draws lines for dividing the circle into
                                          thirds]

PU BK 53 RT 135 PD FD 57
PU BK 57 RT 90
PD FD 62 PU BK 62 RT 45 PU FD 20
SETC 1+RANDOM 14
PD FILL                                   [fills in one-third]
PU BK 40 PD FILL                          [fills in the second third]
PU HOME
WAIT 100 PR [THIS FRACTION IS 2\/3 ! IT
IS ONE OF THE FRACTIONS TEACHERS USE MOST
                                          [prints her instructional statement]
FOR EXAMPLES TO TEACH THEIR STUDENTS.]
WAIT.FOR.USER CG CT CC
QUESTION1
END


TO QUESTION1
PR [IS THIS FRACTION, 1\/2, 3\/4, 2\/3, OR 1\/26 ?]
NAME READLIST "ANSWER
IFELSE (ANSWER =[2\/3]
[PR[GREAT!!]][PR[PLEASE TRY AGAIN] CT WAIT 30 QUESTION1]
END
```

TO QUEST [one of the procedures that she modified in June]

PR [Do you know how to do fractions?]
name readlist "answer
ifelse :answer = [no] pr [Well, that's what I'm here for, to teach you about fractions!]]
[pr [That's fine. Now you will understand this work better!]]
pu home pd repeat 8 [setc 1+random 14 rt 45 fd 50]
pu bk 25 rt 90 pd fd 120
bk 60 lt 90 pu bk 60 pd fd 121 bk 70 rt 45 pu fd 20
setc 1+random 14
pd fill pu home rt 90 pu fd 20
setc 1+random 14 pd fill
pr [WHAT PART IS COLORED? IS IT 2∨3, 2∨4, or 4∨4?]
name readlist "answer
ifelse (:answer = [2/4] [pr [great!!!]] [pr [sorry, that's incorrect.] wait 35 quest]
END

TO OKAY [This is the "going over" for the procedure "EXAM"]

HOUSE WAIT. FOR.USER CG CT CC
HALF WAIT. FOR.USER CG CT CC
CALF WAIT. FOR.USER CG CT CC
TWO WAIT. FOR.USER CG CT CC
END

TO SUPER [This procedure is called by the "Fractions" super-procedure. It connects Debbie's two Logo Pages]

GETTOOLS "FRACT2
CT CG CC
PR [PLEASE WAIT A MINUTE OR TWO, THE TURTLE IS SLEEPING.
I'LL GO WAKE HIM UP. (WAKE UP YOU SILLY JERK.
WE HAVE A BIG AUDIENCE OUT THERE!!!)]

[this is an interesting note that Debbie prints on the screen as Logo searches for the other Page "Fract2.]

WAIT. FOR.USER
INTRODUCTION
WAIT. FOR.USER
EQUIV
WAIT. FOR.USER
MORE
WAIT. FOR.USER
UNDERSTANDING
END

DEBBIE'S SOFTWARE PART 2: THE LOGO PAGE "FRACT1"

TO HOUSE
[THE HOUSE, THE DOOR, AND THE ROOF:]

pu home setc 4 pu setpos [-65 25] rt 45 pd fd 100 rt 90 fd 100 rt 135 fd 140 lt 90 setc 1 fd 100 setc 13 lt 90 fd 140 lt 90 setc 10 fd 100 pu setpos [10 0] setc 11 pu bk 75 pd fd 100 pu home pd fill pu setpos [10 25] setc 12 pd fd 68 pu setpos [20 35] pd fill pu setpos [25 -75] setc 5 pd fd 60 setc 9 rt 90 fd 30 rt 90 setc 4 fd 60 pu setpos [25 -40] pu bk 3 rt 90 pd fd 30 pu setpos [36 -33] pd fill

[THE LEFT WOODEN WAGON:]

pu home pu setpos [-150 -40] pd repeat 2 [fd 30 rt 90 fd 60 rt 90] pu home

pu setpose [-155 -50] setc 1+random 14 pd repeat 360 [fd .2 rt 1] pu home

pu setpos [-120 -40] setc 4 pd fd 30 pu rt 90 fd 20 rt 90 fd 10 pd fill pu home pu setpos [-145 -50] pd fill pu home setc 1+random 14 pu setpos [-90 -50] pd repeat 360 [fd .2 lt 1] setc 4 lt 90 pu fd 10 pd fill

[THE RIGHT WOODEN WAGON:]

pu home pu setpos [85 -45] pd repeat 2 [fd 30 rt 90 fd 60 rt 90] rt 90 fd 30 lt 90 fd 30 pu lt 135 fd 15 pd fill pu home

setc 1+random 14 pu setpos [80 -55] pd repeat 360 [fd .2 rt 1] setc 4 pu rt 90 fd 10

pd fill pu home pu setpos [155 -55] pd repeat 360 [fd .2 rt 1] setc 4 lt 90 pu fd 10 pd fill

[THE SUN:]

pu home pu setpos [95 65] setc 14

pd repeat 360 [fd .3 rt 1] rt 90 pd fd 35 pu home pu setpos [115 75] pd fill

[THE INSTRUCTIONAL SENTENCE:]

pr [This is a house. Almost every shape is 1/2! I am trying to say, that you use fractions, almost every day of your life!]
END

TO EXAM
PR [DO YOU REMEMBER WHAT YOU LEARNED?]
NAME READLIST "ANSWER
IFELSE (:ANSWER = [YES]) [PR [GREAT!!! I WILL TEACH YOU MORE THEN ON FRACT2] WAIT 50] [PR [WELL. LET'S REVIEW IT!] WAIT 100 CT CG CC OKAY]
END

DEBBIE'S SOFTWARE PART 3: THE LOGO PAGE "FRACT2"

TO BIG
QUEST WAIT. FOR.USER CG CT CC
HALF WAIT. FOR.USER CG CT CC

HOUSE WAIT. FOR.USER CG CT CC
TWO
END

TO FRONT   [Remained empty at the end of the
                                          Project]

END

TO W   [Was never completed because Debbie did
                                          not like it. See Section 7 in the Case]

pu setpos [-85 55]
rt 135
setc 1+random 14 pd fd 20
lt 100
setc 1+random 14 pd fd 19
rt 100
setc 1+random 14 pd fd 20
rt 100
sect 1+random 14 pd fd 20
rt 100
setc 1+random 14 pd fd 19
END

TO INTRODUCTION   [Appears on the other Page as well]]

pr [Hello, my name is Debbie. I am going to teach you how to do
fractions.
The first thing I'm going to teach you is the half of the screen. The scene
is a half or two-fourths.]
END

TO QUEST   [Appears on the other Logo Page as well]
pr [Do you know how to do fractions?]
name readlist "answer
ifelse (:answer = [no]) [pr [Well, that's what I am here for, to teach you
fractions!]]
[pr [That's fine. Now you will understand this work better!]]
pu home pu repeat 8 [setc 1+random 14 rt 45 fd 50]
pu bk 25 rt 90 pd fd 120 bk 60 lt 90 pu bk 60 pd fd 121
bk 70 rt 45 pu fd 20 setc 1+random 14 pd fill
ct pr [what part is colored? Is it 2∨3, 2∨4, or 4∨4?]
name readlist "answer ifelse (:answer = [2∨4]) [pr [Great]] [pr [Sorry,
that's incorrect] ct cg QUEST]
END

TO TOPO   [Another super-procedure, was planned
                                          during April, and finally implemented
                                          during June]

INTRODUCTION   [In TOPO, Debbie included her two
                                          opening screens. She QUEST realized that

each serves a different instructional purpose]

```
WAIT. FOR.USER CG CT CC
WARNING@LETTER
```
[A very interesting "letter," look below . . .]

```
EQUIV
WAIT. FOR.USER CG CT CC
EQUIV2
WAIT. FOR.USER CG CT CC
TOGETHER
```
[This procedure was planned in April and implemented during June, look below]

```
END
```

```
TO INTRODUCTION
```
[Another Introduction, or an opening screen for her second part of the software]

```
PR [HELLO AGAIN! HAVEN'T YOU LEARNED ENOUGH?]
NAME READLIST."ANSWER
PR [NO MATTER WHAT, I GUESS YOU WANT TO LEARN MORE!]
WAIT 50 CT
END
```

```
TO WARNING@LETTER
PR [DEAR STUDENT,
   THIS IS VERY SERIOUS. I AM GRADING YOU ON IT ALSO!
   SINCE YOU FINISHED LEARNING 'WHAT A FRACTION IS' SO I
   THINK YOU'LL UNDERSTAND EQUIVALENT FRACTIONS.
   I HAVE GREAT GRAPHICS TO SHOW YOU WHAT IT IS.
                     SINCERELY,
                     YOUR TEACHER DEBBIE D.
WARNING; DANGER!]
END
```

```
TO TOGETHER
```
[CONNECTS THIS PAGE WITH THE FIRST PAGE]

```
GETTOOLS"FRACTION
WARNING@LETTER
PR [PLEASE WAIT A WHILE. GET IT? LET'S WAIT A WHILE.
I'M SERIOUS I'LL NEED A MINUTE OR TWO.]
HT CT CG
HALF WAIT. FOR.USER CG CT CC
CALF WAIT. FOR.USER CG CT CC
TWO WAIT. FOR.USER CG CT CC
HOUSE CG CC WAIT 1—CT
EXAM
INTRODUCTION
END
```

TO WAIT.FOR.USER

[EXIST ON OTHER PAGES AS WELL]

type [PRESS ANY KEY TO CONTINUE]
IGNOREreadchar
END

TO IGNORE:key

[was created on March 31]

END

TO EQUIV   [THE REPRESENTATION FOR
                                EQUIVALENT FRACTIONS]

PU HOME SETC 13
PD FD 190 PU HOME
RT 90 PD FD 320
PU SETPOS [20 10] SETC 1 PD
REPEAT 2 [FD 60 RT 90 FD 120 RT 90]

LT 90 BK 20 RT 90 FD 60
RT 90 FD 20 RT 90 FD 60 LT 90 FD 20
LT 90 FD 60 RT 90 FD 20 RT 90 FD 60
LT 90 FD 20 LT 90 FD 60 RT 90 FD 20
RT 90 PU FD 30 RT 90 PD FD 120

[cuts the rectangle horizontally, in the
middle, which creates twelve-twelfths]

PU HOME
PU SETPOS [30 30] SETC 9 PD FILL
REPEAT 2 [PU FD 20 PD FILL
RT 90 PU FD 20 PD FILL]
PU RT 90 FD 20 PD FILL   [shades six-twelfths in blue]
PU HOME
PU SETPOS [15 80] LABEL [6∨12 = 1∨2]

[prints over the rectangle 6/12 = 1/2 in
yellow]

PU HOME   [finishes the representation for six-twelfths
                                equals one-half]

PU SETPOS [-60 50] SETC 3
PD REPEAT 36 [FD 7 LT 10]
LT 90 FD 80
BK 40 RT 90 FD 43 BK 80
PU HOME
SETC 11
PU SETPOS [-75 65]
PU BK 10 PD FILL
PU BK 20 PD FILL
PU HOME
PU SETPOS [-65 80]

```
LABEL [1∨2 = 2∨4]                      [prints the equivalence one-half equals
PU HOME                                two-fourths]

SETC 4 PU SETPOS [25 -80]

PD REPEAT 4 [FD 50 RT 90]
FD 25 RT 90
FD 50 BK 25 LT 90 FD 25 BK 50 FD 25

RT 45 FD 32 BK 64 FD 32 LT 90 FD 32
BK 64
PU HOME
SETC 12 PU SETPOS [60 -35] PD FILL
PU BK 5 RT 90 PU FD 10 PD FILL
RT 90 PU FD 30 PD FILL                 [shades four-eighths in orange]
PU HOME
PU SETPOS [45 -15] LABEL [4∨8 = 1∨2]
                                       [prints the equivalence, four-eights equals
                                       one-half]

PU HOME
SETC 2 PU SETPOS [-140 -85]
PD REPEAT 2 [FD 60 RT 90 FD 120 RT 90]
PD REPEAT 10 [SETH 90 FD 12 LT 90 PD FD 60 BK 60]
FD 30 LT 90 FD 120
PU HOME
SETC 10 PU SETPOS [-135 -40]
PD FILL PU RT 90 FD 10 PD FILL
PU FD 15 PD FILL PU FD 10 PD FILL
PU FD 10 PD FILL PU FD 15 PD FILL
PU FD 10 PD FILL PU FD 10 PD FILL
PU FD 12 PD FILL PU FD 15 PD FILL
                                       [finishes shading ten-twentieths in light
                                       green]

PU HOME
SETPOS [-105 -15] LABEL [10∨20 = 1∨2]
                                       [prints the equivalence, ten-twentieths
                                       equals one-half]
```

END

TO EQUIV2 [The second representation for Equivalent Fractions. Was never completed]

```
SETC 11 PD FD 200 PU HOME              [divides the screen vertically in light blue]
RT 90 SETC 10 PD FD 320
PU HOME                                [divides the screen horizontally in light
                                       green]

SETC 4 PU SETPOS [15 55]
PD REPEAT 4 [RT 90 FD 50]              [draws a red square]
RT 90 FD 25 RT 90 FD 50 BK 25          [divides the square into two halves]
PU RT 90 FD 10 SETC 12 PD FILL         [shades the left half in orange]
```

```
PU HOME
SETC 12 PD REPEAT 4 [RT 90 FD 50]
```
[draws an orange square]
```
PU RT 90 FD 25 RT 90 PD FD 50
```
[divides it into fourths]
```
PU BK 25 LT 90 PD FD 25 BK 50
PU SETC 4 LT 90 FD 14.1/2 RT 90
PU FD 5 PD FILL
```
[shades the top-left fourth of the square]
```
PU RT 90 FD 15 PD FILL
```
[shades the bottom-left fourth of the square]
```
PU HOME

PR [ALL THESE SHAPES ARE EQUIVALENT
FRACTIONS. THIS IS WHAT I AM GOING TO
TEACH YOU!]
```
[prints the instructional statement]
```
PU HOME
SETC 5 PU SETPOS [-155 35]
PD REPEAT 180 [FD 1 RT 2]
```
[draws a purple circle]
```
PU RT 90 PD FD 56
```
[divides the circle into halves]
```
BK 28 LT 90 FD 28 BK 56 FD 28 RT 45
```
[divides the circle into fourths]
```
FD 28 BK 56 FD 28 LT 90 FD 28 BK 56
```
[divides the circle into eighths]
```
PU HOME SETC 13
```
[changes the pen color to pink]
```
PU SETPOS [-120 50]
```
[position the Turtle in one of the circle's eighths]
```
PD FILL RT 90 PU FD 10 PD FILL
```
[shades in pink two of the eighths]
```
PU BK 20 PD FILL
```
[shades in pink another eighth]
```
END
TO ADD
```
[THE SUPER-PROCEDURE FOR ADDITION]
```
ADDINGFR
```
[calls the left side of the equation]
```
HALF
```
[calls the right side of the equation]
```
PR [1∨4 + 1∨4 = 2∨4 = 1∨2]
```
[prints the instructional statement which is a translation of the pictorial representation into symbolic operation.]
```
END
TO ADDINGFR
```
[THE SECOND VERSION, with a sub-procedure for the circle]
```
SETC 1+RANDOM 14
PU SETPOS [-100 0]
CIRCLE.ADD
PU SETPOS [-80 10]
SETC 4 PD FILL
PU HOME PU SETPOS [-25 0]
LABEL"+
PU HOME
SETC 1+RANDOM 13
PU SETPOS [-10 0]
```

```
CIRCLE.ADD
PU SETPOS [35 10]
SETC 12 PD FILL
END

TO HALF
PU HOME PU SETPOS [60 0]
LABEL"=
PU HOME
PU SETPOS [75 0]
SETC 1+RANDOM 14
CIRCLE.ADD
SETC 4 PU SETPOS [85 10]
PD FILL PU HOME
SETC 12 PU SETPOS [110 10]
PD FILL
END

TO CIRCLE.ADD
PD REPEAT 36 [FD 5 RT 10]
RT 90 PD FD 57
PU BK 28.5 LT 90 PD FD 29 BK 55
END

TO SQUARE :NUM
REPEAT 4 [FD :NUM RT 90]
END

TO CIRCLE :NUM
REPEAT 36 [FD :NUM RT 10]
END

TO CIRCLE :NUM1
REPEAT 360 [FD :NUM1 RT 1]
END

TO RECT :NUM1 :NUM2
REPEAT 2 [FD :NUM1 RT 90 FD :NUM2 RT 90]
END

TO TALK
```

[She created this procedure during the last week of May]

```
HT PR [WHAT'S YOUR NAME?]
MAKE "NAMES READLIST
PR SE [HELLO] :NAMES

PR [HOW OLD ARE YOU?]
MAKE "AGES READLIST
PR SE [THAT'S GOOD FOR YOU!] :NAMES

PR [WHAT'S THE NAME OF YOUR SCHOOL?]
MAKE "SCHOOL READLIST
PR SE [THAT SCHOOL SOUNDS FAMILIAR!] :SCHOOL
```

```
PR [WHAT GRADE ARE YOU IN?]
MAKE "GRADE READLIST
IFELSE :GRADE = [4][PR[THAT'S REALLY GREAT!]]
[PR [I HAVE NOTHING TO SAY ABOUT THAT ...]]

PR [HOW MANY SISTERS DO YOU HAVE?]
MAKE "SISTERS READLIST
IF :SISTERS = [0] PR SE [THAT'S GOOD] :NAMES STOP]
PR SE [TOO BAD ...] :NAMES
END
```

In her three Logo Pages, FRACTION, FRACT1, and FRACT2, Debbie created so many combinations of procedures and super-procedures, several introductions, quizzes, and instructions for the user; it is almost impossible, on my part, to construct one comprehensive flowchart that would represent the structure of the software as a whole. A further analysis of Debbie's final code and its internal structure is required. In fact, Debbie wrote several other procedures in her project which were not reported in this context, because they require much longer and deeper analyses.

To my mind this—the software's complexity and length, and the fact that many procedures remained unfinished—is the beauty of her project. Debbie enjoyed the idea of modularity to the utmost, and so, to use her own words, "created many pieces of software, all in one." Every day during the month of June, she figured out a new combination for her "building blocks."

Another beautiful of Debbie's project lies in the fact that she never really finished it. Debbie was willing to go on and on and continue working on new screens, and on screens or procedures she never completed. But the school year ended on June 23, 1987, and since Debbie did not have a computer home, she never had a chance to continue working on her project during the summer. Instead (and unfortunately for Debbie) I took her many procedures and all of her writings and drawings to continue what she had started: to try and make sense of this Project, and to understand what fractions are, what Logo is, and what software design means for fourth-grade children.

(THE RESULTS FROM DEBBIE'S PRE- AND POSTTESTS WILL BE PRESENTED IN THE LAST SECTION OF CHAPTER III.)

Chapter III

Results from the Comparative Evaluation

The difference between math groups before and after the experiment

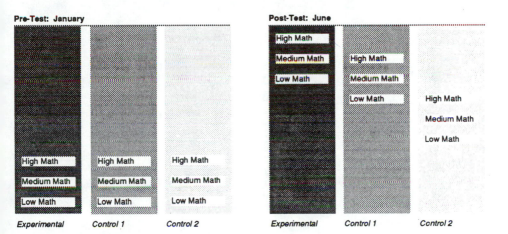

Pre-Test: January

Post-Test: June

Experimental   Control 1   Control 2

Experimental   Control 1   Control 2

INTRODUCTION

This chapter presents selected results from the evaluation of the ISDP Experiment. These are the results of the Fractions and Logo tests that were conducted with the experimental and two control classes ($n = 51$) before and after ISDP was implemented.

1.1. The Design of the Evaluation

The evaluation was designed to examine in what ways the knowledge of children who learned fractions and Logo by designing a piece of instructional software differed from the knowledge of children who learned fractions and Logo through other pedagogical methods, rather than through software design. Figure 1 shows the differences between the experimental and the other pedagogical approaches that were assessed for this evaluation:

Three fourth-grade classes from the same inner-city public school in Boston were selected for this evaluation ($n = 51$: in the experimental class $n = 17$, and in the two control classes $n = 18$, and $n = 16$). The reasons for their selection, and a detailed description of the characteristics of the pupils, their teachers, and their different fractions and Logo learning approaches were presented in Chapter I, Section 4. In brief, during January 1987, all three classes were pretested on specific skills and concepts in fractions and Logo. After the pretests were completed, the 4-month ISDP experiment was conducted with one of these classes (represented in the shaded overlap on the left side of Figure 1, and described in Chapter I). In June, all 51 pupils were again tested (when ISDP ended) on their knowledge and specific skills in fractions and Logo.

This evaluation procedure is represented in Figure 2, with a brief recapitulation of the differences between the three classes.

- *"Fractions Unit"* means that, for all three classes, the teaching of fractions was conducted starting at the end of February, through strictly regular math lessons and by following a traditional teaching method. The experimental class was not provided with any additional formal instruction on fractions (besides the material they covered in their regular math lessons) during the project.

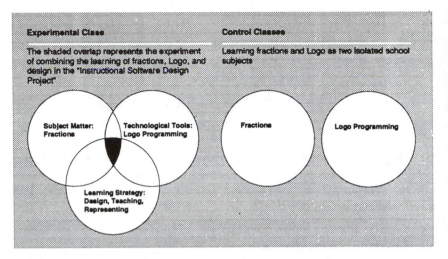

Figure 1.   An Illustration of the Experimental Approach.

- *"Isolated Logo"* (in control class 2) means that (a) the children programmed once a week in the school's computer laboratory; (b) they followed a conventional approach to Logo programming, using worksheets, exercises, and so on, as part of the City of Boston Computer-Literacy Program; and (c) the programming activities resulted in children's completion of short programming exercises.
- *"Integrated Logo"* (in control class 1) means that (a) the children programmed every day under Project Headlight conditions; (b) they integrated the Logo projects into various topics of the curriculum; and (c) the programming activities resulted in children's completion of various small-scale creative programming projects, each lasting approximately 1 to 3 weeks.
- "Software-Design Logo" (in the Experimental Class) means that (a) the children programmed every day; (b) they integrated Logo into the curriculum, but in the context of designing and programming instructional software for teaching about fractions; and (c) each child worked on the project for 4 months, and the programming activities resulted in a long and complex product—their Fractions software.

1.2. The Evaluation Objectives and Questions

The evaluation focused on the children's knowledge of fractions and Logo. Using the set of pretests, the differences between the experimental and the control children's knowledge of fractions and Logo *before* the experiment began were investigated; a base line was established, and no significant differences

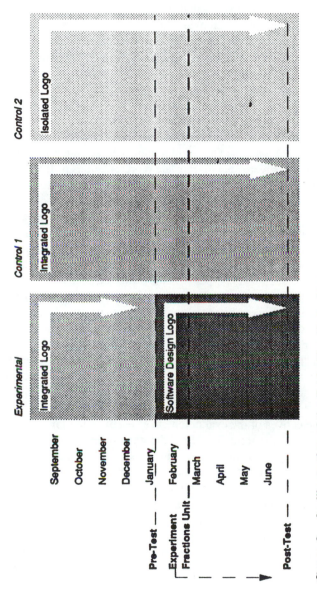

Figure 2.   An Illustration of the Evaluation Procedure.

were found. Four months later, using the set of posttests, the way in which these children differed in their knowledge and understanding of fractions and Logo *after* the Experiment were investigated in detail.

One part of the postevaluation aimed at assessing how much better the children from the Experimental class were at understanding fractions. Within this domain, emphasis was placed on one particular aspect of the children's knowledge of fractions: their ability to translate between various modes of fractional representations. As discussed in Chapter I, this aspect has been shown to be a crucial part of rational-number knowledge, and particularly difficult for young children (e.g., Lesh et al., 1983; Behr et al., 1983).

By giving specific attention to the children's knowledge of fractional representations, the evaluation aimed at examining how much better the children from the experimental class were able to translate representations of fractions after the experiment. For example, to see whether or not they got better at translating symbols into words, words into pictures, pictures into symbols, and so on; whether they showed improved flexibility in recognizing and understanding fractional representations, and an improved ability in identifying and giving examples for representations for fractions in nonschool situations (e.g., finding representations for fractions in rooms and stores, in money, clocks, calendars, or other manipulative aids, such as clay, pegs, Pattern-Blocks, etc.).

These Fractions test were also designed to assess whether the children from the experimental class were better at constructing their own representations for fractions after being involved in designing the instructional software; and what were the differences between the ways the children from the experimental and the control classes "talked about" fractions (i.e., assessing whether the experimental students were more flexible and articulate in their explaining of fractions and in their solutions or comments on fractions problems posed to them by the researcher).

The other objectives of the evaluation gave specific attention to the children's knowledge of Logo programming after the experiment. For this purpose, the evaluation was designed to investigate the ways in which the children from the experimental class differed from those of the control classes in their knowledge, use, and understanding of Logo programming commands, instructions, and operations. More specifically, it assessed whether the children from the experimental class knew and understood more programming commands and operations than the control children once the experiment was over.

The evaluation also investigated whether the experimental children could understand, implement, debug, transform, optimize, and modify someone else's programming code better than the children from the control classes; and whether they understood and used some of the Logo commands and operations, such as REPEAT, IFELSE, SETPOS, variables, and inputs in their projects, and became better at these skills than the children in the two control classes. Finally, the evaluation assessed whether the experimental children were able to construct

Logo routines for someone else's design or picture and whether they were better at this than the children in the two control classes.

In addition, given the breadth of the learning experience and the mixed methodology of assessments—including the extensive case studies of several children (i.e., examination of the children's progress, designer's notebooks, daily Logo files, finished products, interviews with participants during and following completion of the project), as well as the objective pre- and posttests—it was also possible to draw inferences regarding acquisition of metacognitive skills, and to trace in detail the microgenesis of Logo and fraction skills and concepts, exploring different approaches taken by children with different personal and learning styles.

1.3. The Evaluation Procedure

A series of tests, computer tasks, and interviews on fractions and Logo programming was administered to the experimental and the control classes before and after the experiment. A short description of each of the testing items is given below (and samples of these tests and interviews can be found in Appendix B in Harel, 1988).

The "task analysis" of each item in the tests is presented beside the results themselves, so that the reader can relate the tasks, their requirements, and their underlying conceptual scope, to the actual results. There were two versions for most items, one for the pretests and one for the posttests. However, the pre- and posttests were generally identical in terms of their underlying conceptual requirements. The posttests were usually longer and more demanding with several difficult questions added on. But in most cases, the prequestions also appeared in the posttests.

Instruments. The following is a list of all the tests and interviews that were used for the evaluation of ISDP.

1.   *THE RATIONAL-NUMBER PENCIL-&-PAPER TEST:*
     A set of 43 multiple-choice questions in the pretest, and 65 questions in the posttest—including written language, written symbols, and several types of pictorial representations—was used to assess the children's understanding of rational-number concepts before and after the experiment. This paper-and-pencil test was taken from a collection of tests developed for the Rational-Number (RN) Project by Behr, Lesh, and Post (see Lesh & Hamilton, 1981; Lesh, Landau, & Hamilton, 1983). The researchers of the RN Project discovered and documented many of the problems young children encounter when translating these representations of rational numbers (as described in Chapter I). The researchers of the RN Project had developed these tests for investigating the nature of children's ideas about

rational numbers in the second through eighth grades. The particular questions selected for this evaluation were geared towards exploring children's ability to translate within and between representational modes (written language, written symbols, pictures) on sets of structurally related tasks. All tasks in the selected test assess children's basic concepts of fractions and ratios; they also assess children's ability to translate representations, ordering, equivalent fractional forms, and simple proportions. The test was administered to each class separately but on the same day. Children were given 60 minutes to complete their tests.

2. *WHAT IS A FRACTION? INTERVIEW:*

A 30–45-minute clinical interview was conducted with each of the 51 pupils before and after the experiment. This interview was designed by the researcher to investigate the children's concept of what a fraction is, their "favorite" representations of fractions, their way of "talking about" fractions, and their ability to link or translate representations given by themselves or by the researcher, using various materials and manipulative aids. During the interview, children answered general questions, such as "What is a fraction?" or "Can you learn about fractions outside of school?" "How?" "When you close your eyes and think about fractions, what do you see, what images do you have?" "Do you like fraction?" "Why/Why not?" They were also asked to solve more specific problems such as "Please use this set of pegs (clay, paper, blocks, and other materials in the room) to show an example of the fraction 2/3." While the children constructed the required representations, the researcher probed the solidity of their knowledge by posing problems ("One child told me that this red block and this yellow block together equal one-half; what do you think?") and investigated their concept of fractions more deeply.

The interview was open ended. However, while the children were following their personal routes, the researcher, using a Piagetian technique, intervened with a predetermined set of questions. Several more structured tasks were added in the postinterview. Most of the added tasks required that the children manipulate several objects such as Pattern-Blocks and answer questions such as: "If this yellow block is the unit, what are these two yellow blocks and three red blocks together (one red block being half the size of the yellow block)?" After the child had 'constructed' an answer, the researcher could ask, "But one child told me that all of them together equal five, because there are five pieces here. What do you think?" These interviews were videotaped and transcribed, and a set of categories was developed in order to analyze and describe the results.

3. *BOSTON PUBLIC SCHOOLS MATH TEST, LEVEL-4:*

The Math Level-4 Curriculum Referenced Test, which is given to all fourth graders in the City of Boston at the end of each year, was used in the present study as a posttest only. The test included 40 multiple choice questions, of which 15 were about fractions. Children had up to 60 minutes to complete this test.

4. *LOGO PENCIL-&-PAPER TEST:*

This test included two open-ended tasks and three well-defined tasks. It was designed by the researcher to assess: (a) the children's understanding and use of Logo instructions and commands, (b) their ability to follow and execute a given code, and (c) their ability to 'chunk' a given program using sub-procedures, repeats, or variables. The posttest includes all of the pretest with additional, more difficult subtasks. These tasks require that children: (a) generate a Logo code for a given picture, (b) follow and execute (draw) a given code, and (c) manipulate the inputs for circles, half-circles, rectangles, and squares. Each of these pencil-and-paper logo pre- and posttests lasted approximately 45 to 60 minutes.

5. *LOGO COMPUTER TESTS:*

This test was designed by the researcher to assess the children's knowledge and ability to use Logo while working at the computer. This task required that they debug a program given to them online, by analyzing the picture created when the bugged program was executed. In addition, the children had to modify the debugged program according to the researcher's requests ("Make it modular," or "Try to use variables now," etc.). The Logo posttest was the same as the pretest, using a slightly more complex graphics. However, the underlying structure and the requirements of the pre- and post-Logo Computer Tests were identical. Each of the tests lasted approximately 45 to 60 minutes.

Figure 3 is a summary of the Logo and Fractions tests and interviews that were conducted with the 51 pupils from the experimental and the control classes, before and after the Instructional Software Design Project.

1.4. The Structure of Chapter III

No significant differences between the three classes were found in the pretests. The scores of control class 1 were slightly higher than those of the other two classes. For this reason, this chapter emphasizes and presents in detail only the results of the posttests. This chapter is divided into three major sections: Section 2.1. describes the results of the *Logo posttests*. Within this section there are two subsections. Section 2.1.1. describes the results from the pencil-&-paper Logo test; and Section 2.1.2. describes the results of the Logo computer tasks. Thereafter, Section 2.2. describes the results of the *Fractions posttests*. Within this section there are two subsections as well. Section 2.2.1. describes the results of the Rational-Number pencil-and-paper test, while Section 2.2.2. describes the results of the Boston Public Schools Math Referenced Test Level-4. Finally, Section 2.3. describes the results from Debbie's Fractions and Logo posttests, and compares her results with those of the children from the three classes.

Most of the results are presented in simple numbers according to the

	Name and Purpose of Test	Length	No. of Items
Pre-Tests			
Fractions	• Rational Number Pencil & Paper	60 minutes	43 questions
	• What is a Fraction? Interview	30-45 minutes	10 questions
Logo	• Logo Pencil & Paper	50 minutes	5 questions
	• Logo Computer Tasks	50 minutes	3 tasks
Post-Tests			
Fractions	• Rational Number Pencil & Paper	60 minutes	65 questions
	• What is a Fraction? Interview	30-45 minutes	15 questions
	• Boston Public School Level-4	60 minutes	40 questions
Logo	• Logo Pencil & Paper	50 minutes	10 questions
	• Logo Computer Tasks	50 minutes	4 tasks

Figure 3.   A Summary of the Pre- and Posttests and Interviews.

children's percentage of correct answers to a given question, a subset of questions, or the test as a whole. The quantitative and qualitative analyses focus on all of the 51 children's answers for each question in each of the tests. However, in the presentation of the results, consideration is given to specific questions, according to the children's class (experimental vs. control 1 vs. control 2), and to their math group (high vs. medium vs. low).

For establishing reliability, the quantitative and qualitative analyses of all the tests were conducted by the researcher, and in parallel, by an objective research assistant who worked independently at home. Following the researcher's requests, categories, and guidelines, the assistant also created a large database for all the results, so that searches and printouts of individual questions, subsets of questions, or the scores of whole tests—for each child, group of children, math-groups, or a whole class—could be performed.

The researcher and assistant were each very careful to follow the guidelines and categories for the analyses, and at the end of their analyses systematically compared their uses of the categories, and the scores and evaluations they had come with. Only rarely (on approximately six occasions) were discrepancies found and discussed; in these cases, final decisions were made in collaboration (usually according to the research assistant's opinions).

In addition, a description of how the different results related to the task's requirements and underlying conceptual requirements, to the researcher's objectives and questions, and to previous findings in other studies of Logo and fractions reported by existing literature (as described in Chapter I), will be presented throughout this chapter, with their relevancy to the findings.

RESULTS FROM THE POSTTESTS

In general, the 17 children of the experimental class did better than the other 34 children on all posttests (Fractions and Logo). Particular trends were revealed from analyzing the posttests data on fractions and Logo and relating them to the children's classes and their divisions into the three math groups. The experimental children from the *high-math* group were consistently better than all the other children. Similarly, the experimental children from the *medium-math* group, in many cases, were better, or at other times were the same as the high-math children from the two control classes—and consistently better than the control children from the medium or low-math groups. As for the *low-math* children from the experimental class, they were usually better than, or the same as the medium-math children of the two control classes, and consistently better than the control children in the low-math group.

In other words, the differences between the pre- and posttests were much greater for the experimental children (on all math-levels), than for those in two control classes. These trends had been originally predicted and were quite consistent in all the results from all the Fractions and Logo posttests. These trends are sketched in Figure 4.

2.1. RESULTS FROM THE LOGO POSTTESTS

The evaluation raised several points regarding fourth-grade children's learning and understanding of basic concepts of Logo programming, such as procedures or modularity, variables or inputs, repeat or recursion, conditionals, and other Logo commands and operations. It also investigated these children's abilities to understand processes in programming, such as generating codes, debugging codes, and manipulating and modifying codes written by themselves or by other people.

During January, at the time of the Logo pretests, the 51 tested children were on approximately the same level in terms of their knowledge of Logo commands and operations, their ability to generate codes, debug codes, and understand given codes. Control class 1 (C_1) scored slightly better in the Logo pretests than

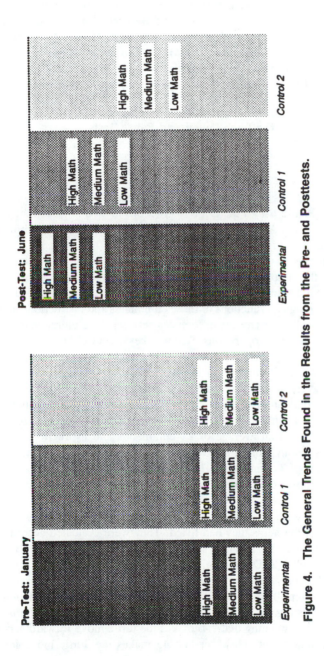

Figure 4.   The General Trends Found in the Results from the Pre- and Posttests.

the other two classes, and the experimental class scored slightly better than control class 2 (C_2). But it appears that the experimental children (the ISDP class) became far better programmers than those of C_1 (the "Integrated-Logo" class), and C_2 (the "Isolated-Logo" class). The following results will demonstrate in what ways the experimental children, working under the ISDP conditions, most successfully improved in their programming knowledge and skills.

2.1.1. Results from the Logo Pencil-and-Paper Tests

This test included seven questions which covered many aspects of the children's knowledge of Logo (see Figure 5).

Knowledge of Logo commands and operations. In Question 1 the children were asked: "Please list all the Logo instructions and commands that you know and use—in column A; then, write an explanation and given an example for each one—in column B."

The results for this question were divided into two major groups of findings. The first are the simple findings that relate to how many instructions and commands each child actually listed. The second relate to the children's understanding of the meaning and functions of these commands and instructions in the Logo language. Table 1 represents the differences between the children in terms of how many Logo commands, operations, function keys, control keys, and so on, they listed in the posttest.

For example, each child from the high-math experimental class listed and explained an average of 32 commands and instructions; while high-math students from C_1 listed only an average of 16 commands, and in C_2 high-math an average of 8 commands. Each child from the low-math experimental class, for example, listed and explained an average of 21 commands and instructions; while low-math students from C_1 listed an average of 11, and C_2 low-math students listed only an average of 7 commands. The advantages of the experimental children of all math groups over the children from the two control classes become clear from examining Table 1.

The children were also evaluated on the quality of their definitions and examples for each of the items they had listed. They were evaluated according to the following categories: (1) Did they spell or abbreviate the item correctly? (i.e. "FD means FORWARD"); (2) Did they give a reasonable example? (i.e., "for example FD 20"); (3) Did they describe clearly what it did? (i.e., "FD 30 makes the Turtle go forward 30 steps"); and (4) Did they use some kind of a combination of 1, 2, 3, above (i.e., listing the Logo command "FD," giving an example for how to use it, "FD 45," and explaining that "FD makes the turtle move forward according to the ~pecified number of steps," or "FD 45 makes the Turtle move forward 45 steps," etc.).

Questions: Skills Assessed

Question 1:
Basic knowledge and understanding of the Logo language commands, and their uses

▼

Question 2:
A classification task of the Logo commands; examined what relationships children perceived between different Logo commands and whether they thought about them as general classes or families, or as loose functional and more task-specific

▼

Question 3:
Read a linear Logo code, understand its flow of control, and draw the picture accordingly

▼

Question 4:
Modularize and optimize the code given to them in Question 3

▼

Question 5:
Understanding of inputs

▼

Question 6:
Transform several given procedures according to specified requests

▼

Question 7:
More deeply investigated the children's ability to read and understand short but quite confusing Logo routines and execute them through drawing

Figure 5. List of Questions in the Logo Pencil-and-Paper Test.

Table 1.   Contingency Table Analysis, Comparing the Average Number of Listed Logo Commands between the Experimental and Control Classes.

Experimental Class	Control 1 Class	Control 2 Class
25.6	12.0	8.3

$\chi^2 = 10.8426$

In C_1 no one was evaluated as "vg" (Very Good), whereas in the experimental class, three students who wrote over 40 commands and instructions and gave a very good example and definition of each, were evaluated as "vg." No one was evaluated "l" (low) or "vl" (very low) in the experimental class. However, four children in C_2 were evaluated as "l," since they listed less than five commands and instructions and did not provide examples or definitions for all or most of those. An example of these results is shown in the Table 2.

The right part of this table shows the evaluation given to each of the subjects in the high-math group of the three classes. For example, subject 4 of the experimental high-math group was evaluated "G" (i.e., Good). The left side of the table shows how many "goods" or "mediums" etc. were in the high-math group of children of each class. For example, in C_1 no one was evaluated as "vg," whereas in the experimental class, three students who wrote over 40 commands and instructions and gave a very good example and definition of each, were therefore evaluated as "vg." No one was evaluated "l" or "vl" among the high-math students of the experimental class. However, four children in C_2 were evaluated as "l," since they listed less than five commands and instructions and did not provide examples or definitions for all or most of those.

The classification task. In Question 2 of the test the children were asked: "Look at your list of Logo instructions and commands, and please classify, group, or categorize the list. Give a title, a label, a description to each one of your groups."

The wording of this question was prepared by the teachers, who felt that each child would understand the task through recognizing a different word; they thought that some children would be more familiar with the word *categorize*, others with *classify*, some with *label*, and others with *titles*.

The purpose of this classification task was to examine another aspect of children's understanding of the meaning and roles of the Logo commands; more specifically, to get a better idea of the relationships children perceived between the different commands, and see whether or not they thought about them as general classes or families, or in loose, functional, and more task-specific type of categories.

Table 2. Results from the Qualitative Evaluation of All High-Math Students to Question 1.

Exper.	sub. 1	sub. 2	sub. 3	sub. 4	sub. 5	sub. 6	sub. 7	sub. 8	VG	G	M	L	VL
evaluation	G	G	VG	G	VG	VG	G	M	3	4	1	0	0
Ctr. 1	sub. 1	sub. 2	sub. 3	sub. 4	sub. 5	sub. 6	sub. 7						
evaluat.	M	G	G	M	G	G	L		0	4	2	1	0
Ctr. 2	sub. 1	sub. 2	sub. 3	sub. 4	sub. 5	sub. 6							
evaluat.	L	L	VL	L	M	L			0	0	1	4	1

Class / Evaluation of the HIGH-MATH Subjects / Total per Class
KEY: VG = Very Good, G = Good, M = Medium, L = Low, VL = Very Low; sub. 1 = Subject No. 1.

This task furthermore, was *not* one of concrete classification. The children had to imagine the possible relationships between the different commands they knew, and group them according to their own experiences, as well to their more general ideas of the properties, functionalities, similarities, and differences between the different commands. This was a rather complex task for children of that age. However, I was interested in examining whether the experimental children had a more flexible understanding of the Logo language in general; and whether or not, because of their involvement in a project that by its very nature required "decentration" (in the Piagetian sense), they would be generally better at understanding this hypothetical task, as well as at creating more abstract and mutually exclusive groups than the other control children.

The results revealed three things: the first relates to who was able to perform this task in the first place; the second to how many groups and classes each child created; the third to the content of the groups in terms of their labels and members or components. Similarly to the Piagetian approach to his classification tasks, the children were not evaluated according to how large or small in number were the lists of components in the various classes they made up.

There was a correlation between being in the experimental class and being able to perform this task. Many children in the control classes (especially in C_2) wrote in their tests "I don't know," or listed several arbitrary commands on the page. During the test, I tried to help some of them; I asked: "Is this your group?" or incited them to create a title for their lists of commands. However, on most occasions, the children insisted that there was "no title for that group." Other children asked me, "Do I have to write that whole list again?" (i.e., the list of commands and operations in Question 1): They saw all of the Logo commands they knew as being members of one large group called "Logo," or in their words, "a group of Logo things." Thirty-nine percent of the control children (9 out of the 34 children) were not able to perform this task, while 100% of the experimental children were able to do it.

The experimental children also generated more groups or classes. Tables 3, 4, and 5 show the actual number of groups created by each child, and the average number of groups per child in each of the three classes and math levels.

Table 3.   The Number of Groups Created by the Low-Math Students in Each Class, in Question 2.

	EXPERIMEN LOW	CONTROL 1 LOW	CONTROL 2 LOW
NO. OF GRPS PER CHILD	5,5,5,5	3,2,1,0,0	2,1,1,0,0
AVERAGE	5 per child	1.2 per child	0.8 per child

Table 4. The Number of Groups Created by the Medium-Math Students in Each Class, in Question 2.

	Experimen Medium	Control 1 Medium	Control 2 Medium
No. of Grps per Child	5,5,4,3,2	3,2,1,1,0,0	4,1,1,0,0
Average	4.8 per child	1.2 per child	1.2 per child

The numbers in each slot of this table show the average number of groups created by each child in each math level and class (the number 0 means that the child did not generate any groups at all). For example, the low-math experimental children created an average of 5 groups per child, while the low-math children of the two control classes created 1.2 groups per low-math child in control class 1, and 0.8 groups per low-math child in control class 2. This resulted in an average of 4.85 groups per child in the whole experimental class, 2.6 per child in C_1, and an average of 1.2 per child in C_2.

As for the classification categories, all children from the three classes came up with very interesting ideas. On the whole, two major schemas were found:

1. "Abstract" classification. Here children constructed general or abstract relationships between the Logo commands, gave abstract reasons for including certain elements and giving certain labels or tiles, classified the items according to their properties, and created mutually exclusive groups (in the Piagetian sense). Here are some examples of the "abstract groupings" taken from the children's tests:

a. *Things that change the color"*
    setc, setbg, setc 1+random 14, repeat 10 [setbg :num +1 wait 15]
b. *"Opposites"*
    fd-bk, lt-rt, pu-pd
c. *"Things that turn the turtle to different sides"*
    rt, lt, seth (setheading)

Table 5. The Number of Groups Created by the High-Math Students in Each Class, in Question 2.

	EXPERIMEN HIGH	CONTROL 1 HIGH	CONTROL 2 HIGH
NO. OF GRPS PER CHILD	6,6,5,5,5,4,4,3	3,3,3,3,2,2,2	3,2,2,2,1,0
AVERAGE	4.75 per child	2.6 per child	1.6 per child

d. *"Things that erase"*
PE (Pen Erase), DEL, CG, CT, CC, BACKSPACE

e. *"Things that go to another page"*
Gettools, Getpage, Escape goes to Content

f. *"Things that write on the screen in a Logo program"*
Print, Type, Label, stamp (the shapes of my letters)

g. *"Function keys"*
fn.1, fn.2, fn.3, fn.4, fn.5.
(the latter a problematic case, since all of these are indeed function keys, but the problem is that each key is very different in its function from the other).

In this classification schema we can look at the title and predict the content of the list of Logo items in the group; or we can look at the list of items, and predict the title. "Things that erase" is the common factor of group (d) above; and "changing the color" is that of group (a). All members of each group share some conceptual similarity in terms of the Logo language characteristics, and defining the properties of each element of a given class determines what other items could also be placed within it.

2. "Loose" or "functional" classification. Certain children constructed loose, confused, or functional groups, where the properties of the group, such as those expressed by its title and elements, did not determine the elements of that group.

a. *"Things to make a boat"*
fd, lt, rt, repeat, setc, pu, pd, bk, fill.
(other examples of this type: "things to make a house," "a heart," "a circle," etc.)

b. *"Things to make a procedure"*
To Square
REPEAT 4 [fd 15 rt 90]
End

c. *"A lot of things to do in Logo"*
fd, bk, lt, rt, pu, pd, repeat, setc, setbg, seth.

d. *"Things used in REPEAT"*
repeat, fd, rt, lt, bk, pu, pd, fill.

e. *"Things that make the Turtle move on the screen"*
fd, bk, rt, lt, setpos, home, repeat

In this classification schema we cannot look at the title and predict the content of the list of items in the class, for there are many other options; and we definitely cannot look at the list of items and predict the title. The similarities between the individual members of each group are vague, although it is understandable that a 9-year-old child should have put certain items together under some of these titles.

The classification task in the Logo test was a hypothetical one by nature (i.e., it was a conceptual, imaginary, or a nonconcrete classification situation for the children). There was a correlation between being in the experimental class and creating more of the abstract, general mutually exclusive groups and labels, and less of the "loose" and "functional" groups or classes (in fact, the abstract examples above are taken from the Experimental children's tests).

Piaget's early and late studies of young children's reasoning (2–11-year-olds) show that the preoperational child has a tendency to group together various different events into a "loose and confused whole" (i.e., "syncretism"); that he or she sometimes fails to see the relationships between separate events ("juxtaposition"); and that he or she cannot deal with the relations between a part its a whole. All of these types of reasoning reveal common deficiencies: an inability to reverse a situation, to compensate one aspect of the situation for another, or to think about or perceive several aspects of a situation simultaneously.

According to Piaget, as children grow older and come into contact with opposing points of view, their thinking goes through the process of "decentration." In speech, they consider both what they want to express and the listener's needs; in games, they consider the other child's interests and rules as well as their own; in moral judgment, they consider both the outcomes of a person's behavior and his or her intents; and in reasoning and in classification tasks, they try to consider the complexities of the problems—the differences and similarities between the same event, the part–whole relationship, and the reasons for the part's being connected with the whole and vice versa.

In his later work on classification, Piaget found that children from about 7 to 11 years of age (the children in my experiment were 9 to 10 years old) are both capable of creating hierarchical classifications and of comprehending inclusion (i.e., stage 3 in the developmental stages of classification) of *concrete* objects (flowers, beads, etc.); but when a child of the same age is asked similar questions about *hypothetical* objects, he or she often fails to give an adequate answer. Apparently, at that age, the child does not understand that the same relationships can exist between imaginary items in classification, as in cases where concrete items are involved. This gap between hypothetical and concrete reasoning is one example of the "vertical decalage."

The analysis of this task reveal that Logo programming is not strictly a "concrete" material, or a "formal" one in the traditional sense, but rather that it combines aspects of the formal and of the concrete; and that many Piagetian ideas and experiments, such as the one of classification, could be extended to this Logo programming domain. Furthermore, these results suggest that Logo can be further used (as both concrete and formal material) to conduct studies about children's cognitive development within the Piagetian framework; and that children who were working with the Logo conceptual objects were similar in their thinking and stages of development to children involved with concrete materials (i.e., beads, flowers) or formal concepts (imagining flowers, or imagining animals). In fact, the experimental children probably developed a cognitive mechanism that allowed them to perceive the more abstract relations between the Logo commands and operations, and to generate more mutually exclusive groupings and titles. This finding requires further investigation.

Executing Logo graphics commands according to someone else's programming code. In Question 3 we focused on the children's ability to analyze a given programming code and to execute it on paper. A long, linear Logo code composed of short strips of Logo primitives was given to the children, and the children were asked to draw the graphics (Figure 6). This task required that children read the given linear code, comprehend it, understand its flow of control, build a mental model of what the computer would do when each of the lines in this program was executed, and draw the picture accordingly, step by step (Figure 7).

Tasks: Skills Assessed

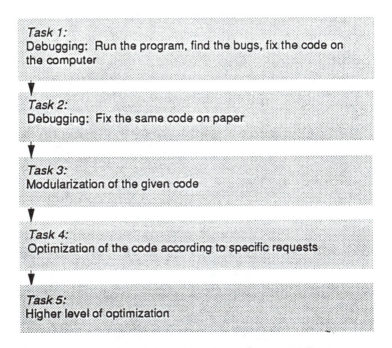

Task 1:
Debugging: Run the program, find the bugs, fix the code on the computer

Task 2:
Debugging: Fix the same code on paper

Task 3:
Modularization of the given code

Task 4:
Optimization of the code according to specific requests

Task 5:
Higher level of optimization

Figure 6.   Skills Assessed in the Logo Computer Test.

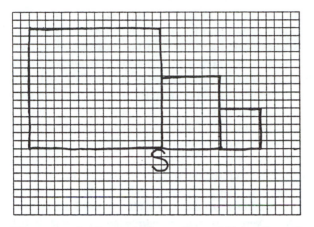

Figure 7.   An Example for a Correct Execution of the Logo Code given in Question 3.

Many researchers in the field of programming distinguish between writing a linear program and a modular program. These researchers consider a linear program as one which emphasizes the generating of effects without any consideration and understanding of the inner structure of the code (e.g., Kurland et al., 1987; Carver, 1987; Soloway, 1984; and others); on the other hand, a modular program emphasizes elegant and efficient programming and is accompanied, they claim, by a higher-level of understanding of programming in general, and of the programming language characteristics in particular. These researcher also claim that children usually find it quite difficult to write modular programs, and that children should learn very early on in their process of programming how to write them, since, "programs that consist of long strips of Logo primitives [i.e., linear programs] . . . are nearly impossible to read, modify, or debug, even for students who have written them" (Kurland et al., 1987).

The results from Question 3 show that the more knowledgeable children (and those who, during their process of learning to program, had written linear as well as modular programs), the better they were at understanding and correctly executing this confusing linear program, whereas the children who only knew how to write linear programs were not able to solve this problem accurately. We should note that experimental children often introduced structure into their programs (e.g., subprocedures and functional naming) only after a long period of purely linear programming. They introduced it when they themselves saw the need; it was not imposed on them from the outside.

Another interesting aspect of these results came to view in the "number of trials" category. Many of the experimental children tried more than once to draw the picture and finally found the right solution; but the children in the control classes who had gotten it wrong in their first trial were apparently not motivated or determined to try again or to find the right solution. Many of them simply wrote "I don't know how to do it," and went on to the next task on the test.

Each child was evaluated according to three categories: (a) the number of squares in the final picture (there were supposed to be three); (b) the number of times they tried to draw the picture (assessing the child's stamina and determination in solving the problem); and (c) the correctness of the picture in terms of the child's use of correct proportions (i.e., 4:2:1), and the child's use of a consistent unit throughout the picture (i.e., consistently using one small square on the grid to represent 10 Turtle Steps, or two squares for 10 Turtle Steps, etc.). We can see these results in Tables 6 and 7.

All the experimental children but one, from both the high-math and medium-math groups, understood the given code and executed it correctly. And when they actually drew the three squares, they always used the appropriate scaling and proportions and were consistent in their selection of the unit. On the other hand, the control children had a more difficult time finding how many squares were in the code: Most of them drew one or two, and even when they "discovered" the three squares and drew them, their scaling and units were not consistent or accurate.

Figures 8, 9, 10, and 11 show the most typical incorrect pictures that the children in the Control classes produced as they tried to solve this problem. It is not in the scope of this chapter to analyze these problematic versions in detail, but I shall describe some of the problems involved in these incorrect versions, so that the reader can infer what problems the experimental children solved, or did not encounter at all, while working on this complex task.

These two versions (Figure 8) are very interesting because they clearly demonstrate several problems encountered by the children who produced the pictures. The children who produced these two versions had problems understanding the relationship between the squares. These were the closest versions to the correct one, since the children identified the three squares but were not able to understand the relationship between them through the use of the rt 180 degrees

Table 6.   Results from the Medium-Math Children's Execution of the Logo Graphics on Paper, in Question 3.

Subject	Number of Squares in Final Picture						Number of Trials of Drawing the Picture						Correct Scale & Consistent Unit					
	S1	S2	S3	S4	S5	S6	S1	S2	S3	S4	S5	S6	S1	S2	S3	S4	S5	S6
Exp. Med.	3	3	3	3	3	x	2	1	1	3	3	x	y	y	y	y	y	x
Cot1 Med.	0	3	2	1	3	1	1	1	1	1	1	1	n	n	n	n	y	n
Cot2 Med.	0	1	4	0	0	x	1	1	1	1	1	x	n	n	n	n	n	x

Table 7. Results from the High-Math Children's Execution of the Logo Graphics on Paper, in Question 3.

Subject	Number of Squares in Final Picture								Number of Trials of Drawing the Picture								Correct Scale & Consistent Unit							
	S1	S2	S3	S4	S5	S6	S7	S8	S1	S2	S3	S4	S5	S6	S7	S8	S1	S2	S3	S4	S5	S6	S7	S8
Exp. high	3	3	3	3	3	3	3	5	1	2	1	1	1	2	2	1	y	y	y	y	y	y	y	n
Cot1 high	3	2	3	3	3	3	3	x	1	1	1	1	2	1	1	x	y	n	y	y	n	n	y	x
Cot2 high	2	1	1	1	3	3	x	x	1	1	1	1	1	1	x	x	n	y	n	n	y	y	x	x

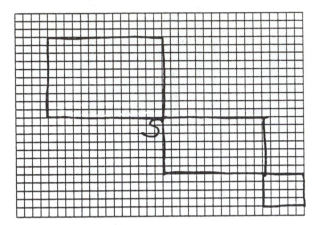

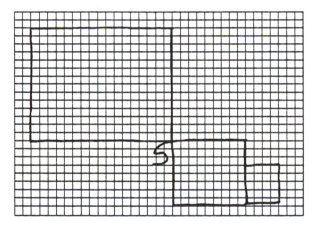

Figure 8.   Incorrect Versions 1.1 and 1.2.

between the first two squares (line 10 in the code), or the bk 20 rt 40 rt 50 between the second and third (lines 19, 20, and 21 in the code).

Version 1.1 shows that the child at least used appropriate scaling and propor-

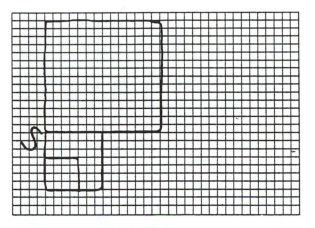

Figure 9.   Incorrect Version 2.

tions and was consistent in the use of the unit, and his only mistake was in the rt 180 between the first and the second square; Version 1.2. shows that the child was not accurate in the proportions of the squares, in his use of unit, or in understanding the connections between the first and second squares, or between the second and third.

The child who produced Version 2 (Figure 9) used the correct proportions and was consistent in his use of the unit for all three squares. However, he did not at all understand the relationships between the squares, and did not pay attention to

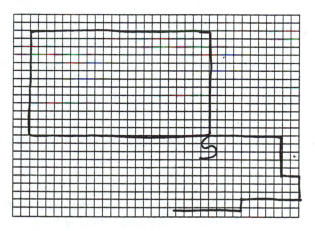

Figure 10.   Incorrect Version 3.

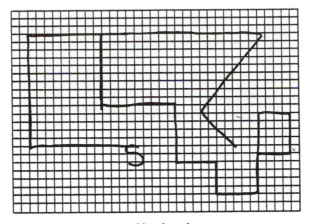

Figure 11.   Incorrect Version 4.

line 10, the rt 180, or to lines 19, 20, and 21, the bk 20 rt 40 rt 50. Instead he got confused and invented a new set of relationships between the squares.

The child who produced Version 3 (Figure 10) discovered that there was one square in the code, but was not able to figure out the other two. Although he did not use one unit consistently and followed the first nine lines of code correctly, the rest of the code was executed erratically.

The child who produced Version 4 (Figure 11) followed the first six lines of code correctly, then lost control for a while, came back to life in the last seven lines of code, producing the small square correctly, although not in the right spaces of the grid.

What we see from these results is that the "brute-force" programmers (in all the classes) did not find it very easy to follow and execute someone else's code; although in their regular ongoing programming experiences they had been able to produce a linear code quite well, they were not able to read one given by someone else; they were not determined to try and solve the problem more than once; and, as has been shown in previous findings in the field, they did not fully understand the flow of the program, the relationships between the parts, or such simple things as executing angles, fd's, or bk's correctly and accurately. In general, however, the experimental children, though some of them in their ongoing experiences could not write very elegant or efficient modular programs (in the hard, computer-science sense of the word *modular*), were still better able to follow the code given by someone else. They used appropriate scaling and kept the correct proportions between the squares, they were careful about being consistent in the use of their unit, and, above all, they demonstrated their stamina in trying to solve the problem more than once. Many of them tried two or three times, checked and rechecked their picture by rereading the code line by line, until they had found the correct answer. They believed that they would eventually find the solution if they worked hard on it.

Ability to simplify and modularize a given linear code. Question 4 assessed the children's abilities to modularize and optimize procedures. The children were asked: "After you finish your drawing (from Question 3), try to simplify this program, or clean it. In other words, think about other ways to write a Logo program that will produce or make the same drawing. Are there Logo commands that will make this program shorter? (Also, think about creating subprocedures.).''

In order to answer this question, the children had to make the program clearer and shorter, stop operating on the individual command level, and start thinking in a procedural mode, using repeats, subroutines, or procedures. This task was administered in order to examine how different children would approach a program that already worked well, and produce a different program for the same purpose by using higher-level units. In other words, when asked to read this program again, the child had to rescan the code and mentally simulate what the program was doing overall, rather than line by line, see how the goals of the original program were achieved, and how the program could be written in another way.

This is a very important aspect in analyzing children's knowledge of programming. Pea and Kurland (1984), for example, believe that just as we cannot expect students who can barely decode or comprehend text to be proficient writers, we also cannot expect students with a low-level ability in reading, decoding, and understanding programs to be able to write functional higher-level programs or gain insights into other domains.

On the whole, the experimental children were more flexible than the others and attempted to explore several different ways for producing the same drawing. They reached a more modular level of code, and most of them used repeats, subprocedures and variables.

Three levels of modularization or optimization of the given code were found among the tested children. Many versions were found among the children for each level of simplification. Many children (especially from the control classes) were in transitional stages between the first two levels. However, *all* the children were always evaluated according to the higher level of their transition. The three levels are described below.

Simplify level 1. On this level, the child combined all the fd 20 and fd 20 into fd 40, or rt 50 and rt 40 into rt 90, etc., which indeed made the program shorter and clearer, and was a first step towards optimization. One hundred percent of the experimental children produced Level 1 modifications, while only 78% of C_1 (i.e., four children were not able to do it all), and 69% of C_2 (i.e., five children were not able to do it) produced Level 1 modification to the procedure DESIGN.

Simplify level 2. On this level, the child simplified the code according to Level

1, but also tried to use REPEAT for the squares. A correct and consistent simplification in Level 2 resulted in the following procedures.

```
TO DESIGN (Version 1)
REPEAT 4 [fd 40 rt 90]
rt 90 fd 40 lt 90
REPEAT 4 [FD 20 rt 90]
rt 90 fd 20 lt 90
REPEAT 4 [fd 10 rt 90]
END
```

```
TO DESIGN (Version 2)
lt 90
REPEAT 4 [fd 40 rt 90]
rt 90
REPEAT 4 [fd 20 rt 90]
lt 90 bk 20 rt 90
REPEAT 4 [fd 10 rt 90]
END
```

A common trend on this level was to use the REPEAT correctly, and keep the right proportions between the squares (i.e., the proportion of 4:2:1 was kept by using three Repeat statements as follows: REPEAT 4 [fd 40 rt 90], REPEAT 4 [fd 20 rt 90], REPEAT 4 [fd 10 rt 90]). However, they connected the REPEAT parts incorrectly by copying the "connection commands" from the original program, which resulted, for example, in the following incorrect procedure:

```
TO DESIGN
lt 90   REPEAT 4 [fd 40 rt 90]
rt 180 REPEAT 4 [fd 20 rt 90]
bk 20 REPEAT 4 [fd 10 rt 90]
END
```

Some children on this level who used the REPEATs for creating each of the squares did not even attempt to connect the squares, and simply answered by writing three REPEAT statements, one for each square. One hundred percent of the high-math and medium-math children, and 75% of the low-math children of the experimental class, simplified the given procedure on Level 2. Only 20% of C_1 (i.e., only four children), and 25% of C_2 (again, only four children) worked on Level 2 in these two control classes.

Simplify level 3. On this level the child simplified the code according to Levels 1 and 2 above, but also used a subprocedure for the square with a variable for the size of the square's side. A correct and consistent simplification on Level 3 resulted in the following procedures:

```
TO SQUARE :num
REPEAT 4 [FD :num rt 90]
END

TO DESIGN
LT 90
SQUARE 40
rt 90
SQUARE 20
lt 90 BK 20 RT 90
SQUARE 10
END
```

It was also possible to make the procedure DESIGN even more generic, by keeping the proportions constant, but creating an option for drawing the whole design in different sizes:

```
TO SQUARE :num
REPEAT 4 [FD :num rt 90]
END

TO DESIGN :num
LT 90
SQUARE :num
rt 90
SQUARE :num/2
lt 90 BK 20 RT 90
SQUARE (:num/2)/2
END
```

This program will result in Figure 12:

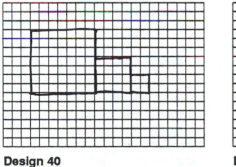

Design 40
(40:20:10)

Design 30
(30:15:7.5)

Figure 12. The Procedure Design in a more Generic Form, keeping the Proportions Constant, but Creating an Option for drawing the Whole Design in Different Sizes.

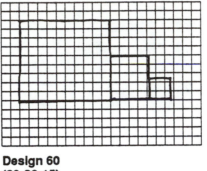

Design 60
(60:30:15)
Figure 12.   Cont.

A total of 13 children from the experimental class tried to write the program on Level 3; out of those, seven succeeded in writing it correctly, and the other six children were almost correct. Four children got some of the variable calls confused, and were not very consistent in their use. For example, one child wrote the following program:

```
TO SQUARE
REPEAT 4 [FD :num rt 90]
END

TO DESIGN
LT 90
SQUARE :num
rt 90
SQUARE :Num
lt 90 BK 20 RT 90
SQUARE :num
END
```

However, *none* of the children from Control class 2 even attempted to approach this problem on Level 3, and only one child in control class 1 worked on Level 3, but he did not write a fully accurate program.

Table 8 summarizes these results from Question 4. The numbers in the slots of this table show how many children in each group simplified on a specific level (1, 2, or 3): the number 4/5, for example, means that 4 out of the 5 children in the low-math group simplified the given program on Level 1. On the whole, the experimental children were more flexible than the others and attempted to explore several different ways for producing the same drawing. They reached a more modular level of code, and many of them tried to use repeats, subprocedures, and variables.

Table 8.   The Number of Children within each Math-Level and Class Who Simplified the Given Logo Code in Levels 1, 2, and 3.

	Simplify Level 1			Simplify Level 2			Simplify Level 3		
	Exp.	Cot.1	Cot.2	Exp.	Cot.1	Cot.2	Exp.	Cot.1	Cot.2
Hi	8/8	7/7	6/6	8/8	1/7	1/6	7/8	1/7	0/6
Med	5/5	3/6	3/5	5/5	2/6	1/5	5/5	0/6	0/5
Lo	4/4	4/5	3/5	3/4	1/5	2/5	1/4	0/5	0/5

These particular data require further investigation for at least one reason. It was assumed that many of the children would approach this problem in a more flexible way while working at the computer than they would on the written test. A similar problem was given the children to be solved while working at the computer; still, it was important to examine which children could also reach a high level of sophistication away from the computer by using their mental models of Logo, and by reflection. We shall see later in this chapter that the experimental children performed even better on a similar task while working at the computer, whereas the control children, especially those from C_2, performed much lower than they did here, on a similar task given to them while at the computer.

Understanding inputs. In Question 5 the children were asked a set of eight subquestions; each read, for example:

HOW MANY INPUTS DOES REPEAT TAKE?___

GIVE AN EXAMPLE:_____

They were asked the same question about the following Logo commands, and in the following order: FD (*I.E., FORWARD, WHICH TAKES ONE INPUT, FOR EXAMPLE,* FD 56); BK (i.e., Back, one input, for example, BK 97); SETC (i.e., Set Color, one input, for example, SETC 12); HOME (no inputs, one just types "home"); REPEAT (two inputs, one being the number of times to repeat, the other the list of things to repeat, for example, REPEAT 4 [fd 50 rt 90 fd 15 rt 90]); SETPOS (i.e., Set Position, one input, a list of two numbers, the X, Y coordinate points on the screen. For example, SETPOS [1 4]; LT (i.e., Left, one input, for example LT 45); and CG (i.e., Clear Graphics, no inputs, one just types CG).

This question was asked in order to assess the children's understanding of the structure of the commands they had most often used in their programming; whether they understood the meaning of the numbers attached to these commands, understood what inputs meant in general or in these different situations, and could give appropriate examples of their use in these contexts.

Table 9. The Average of Percenages of Correct Answers to "How Many Inputs" Question (Among the Low-Math Children from the Three Classes).

	FD	BK	SETC	HOME	REPEAT	SETPOS	LT	CG	AVERAGE
EXP LO	75%	75%	75%	75%	50%	50%	75%	75%	68.7%
CT1 LO	40%	40%	40%	60%	0%	40%	40%	60%	40.0%
CT2 LO	20%	20%	0%	0%	20%	0%	20%	20%	10.2%

Tables 9, 10, and 11 show the percentages of correct answers for all the children in each math level and class to the questions about inputs; the results clearly demonstrate the superiority of the experimental children over those from the two control classes in their understanding of inputs and how they were being used in these eight Logo commands.

Four of these subquestions were especially difficult for many of the control children: those on HOME, CG, REPEAT, and SETPOS. These four questions required a deep understanding of what inputs are, and also required from the children a higher-level generalization from their programming experiences.

The first two (HOME and CG) were difficult for the children who did not understand the concept of inputs in the first place. These children did not know that HOME and CG took no inputs. Only one child in the experimental class did not answer these two questions (on HOME and CG) correctly; 7 children in C_1 and 10 in C_2, gave the wrong answers.

The children who connected the concept of inputs with the idea that inputs are numbers, therefore inferring that the amount of numbers in a Logo statement is the amount of inputs, had difficulty answering the questions about REPEAT and SETPOS correctly.

The number of inputs used in REPEAT is rather difficult for children to understand. They came to understand it through a complex process of using REPEATs in various situations and for various purposes in their course of programming. In fact, the children knew, from their actual programming experiences, that most of the time, there are "many inputs" involved in a REPEAT statement. As one child from C_1, who answered that REPEAT TAKES "six or more inputs," told me during

Table 10. The Average of Percentages of Correct Answers to "How Many Inputs" Question (Among the Medium-Math Children from the Three Classes).

	FD	BK	SETC	HOME	REPEAT	SETPOS	LT	CG	AVERAGE
EXP MD	100%	100%	100%	100%	80%	60%	100%	100%	67.5%
CT1 MD	50%	50%	50%	34%	17%	17%	34%	50%	37.7%
CT2 MD	40%	0%	0%	0%	0%	0%	20%	0%	7.5%

Table 11.   The Average of Percentages of Correct Answers to "How Many Inputs" Question (Among the High-Math Children from the Three Classes).

	FD	BK	SETC	HOME	REPEAT	SETPOS	LT	CG	AVERAGE
EXP HI	100%	100%	100%	100%	100%	56%	100%	100%	94.5%
CT1 HI	100%	100%	100%	100%	27%	13%	87%	100%	78.3%
CT2 HI	34%	34%	34%	66%	0%	0%	28%	50%	30.7%

the exam, "it's because there are so many FD's and RT's and many other numbers in REPEAT." The most common answer for many of the Control children was "REPEAT takes three inputs"; as an example, they gave: REPEAT 4 [FD 50 RT 90].

Children with minimal experience and understanding of Logo programming understood the REPEAT statement in its local and limited use for the square. However, the children who accumulated a variety of experiences with the RE-PEAT statement were better able to generalize the number of inputs and on a higher level of understanding. They came to understand that, as one girl in the experimental class told me during the exam, "everything that is in the brackets is being repeated the amount of times you tell it to. And it doesn't matter what is in the brackets or how many things are in the brackets, the whole thing [that is in the brackets] will repeat itself." Seventy-five percent of the experimental children answered this question correctly; only 14% in C_1 and 6% in C_2 gave the right answer.

SETPOS posed another difficulty to the children who did not understand inputs very well or did not use SETPOS often. When a child uses SETPOS, he always has to type in brackets one number for the x point in the coordinate system and another for the y point. Together, these two points (or numbers), x and y, specify one location on the computer screen. The children from all classes found it difficult to understand that the two numbers in brackets next to SETPOS represented only one input (one list of two numbers), rather than two. Fifty-five percent of the experimental children answered this question correctly; 20% in C_1 and no one in C_2 gave the right answer.

Ability to transform given Logo precedents. In Question 6 the children were asked to create three transformations: (a) to transform a given procedure of a *circle* into a procedure of a *bigger circle;* (b) to transform the same given procedure of a *circle* into a procedure for *half a circle;* (c) to transform a given procedure of a *square* into a procedure for a *rectangle.* It had to be done in the following way:

1.   TO CIRCLE
    REPEAT 360 [FD 1 RT 1]
    END

1.1   CAN YOU MAKE A BIGGER CIRCLE? (Fill in the blanks)
      TO BIGGER.CIRCLE
      REPEAT_[FD_RT_]
      END
1.2   CAN YOU MAKE A HALF CIRCLE? (Fill in the blanks)
      TO HALF.CIRCLE
      REPEAT_[FD_RT_]
      END
 2.   *TO SQUARE*
      REPEAT 4 [FD 50 RT 90]
      END
2.1. CAN YOU MAKE A RECTANGLE? (Fill in the Blanks)
      TO RECTANGLE
      REPEAT[_____]
      END

This question assessed several things: the children's understanding of the role of each input in the given procedures; their ability to understand the properties of these basic geometrical shapes, which are often used in Logo graphics, and how these properties are expressed in the Logo language; their flexibility in understanding the structure and properties of these procedures as general templates, rather than specific or local ones; and their ability to manipulate the inputs and transform them in order to create new graphical effects required by another person.

Table 12 shows how many children of each math level and class were able to transform the procedures correctly (i.e., 3/5 means that three out of five children of a particular math level answered the question correctly; 0/6 means that zero out of six answered the question correctly).

Only one low-math child in C_2 was able to transform the circle into a bigger circle. The rest of the children in the class were not able to perform any of the three transformations. Out of the seven high-math children in C_1, only 5 knew

Table 12.   Results from the Children's Transformations of the Given Logo Procedures in Question 6.

	Circ to Bigger Circ			Circ to Half-Circ			Square to Rectangle		
	Exp.	Cot.1	Cot.2	Exp.	Cot.1	Cot.2	Exp.	Cot.1	Cot.2
Hi	8/8	5/7	0/6	7/8	5/7	0/6	7/8	2/7	0/6
Med	3/5	2/6	0/5	4/5	0/6	0/5	4/5	0/6	0/5
Lo	3/4	3/5	1/5	2/4	0/5	0/5	2/4	0/5	0/5

how to transform the circle into a bigger circle or a half-circle, and only two of these were able to transform the square into a rectangle. Only two medium-math, and three low-math children in this class, were able to transform the circle into a larger circle; the rest of the children in this class were not able to perform any of these tasks.

Although several of the experimental children were not able to perform these transformation, on the whole, most the experimental children on all math levels answered these questions correctly and were able to perform all the three transformations.

Two typical inaccurate answers in the transformation of the square into a rectangle were found: (a) REPEAT 2 [FD 50 RT 90]; or (b) REPEAT 4 [FD 50 RT 90 FD 20 RT 90].

In his first version, the child remembered the template of the rectangle's "REPEAT 2," but was not able to fill in the brackets correctly; in the second version, the child knew the elements in the brackets, but was not aware that these should be repeated only twice (instead of four times). Both versions demonstrate the child's inability to free himself or herself from the rigid and local "square template" of "REPEAT 4 [FD 50 RT 90]," and his or her misunderstanding of the properties of a rectangle and how they are expressed in Logo.

Summary of the results from the Logo pencil-&-paper test. The experimental children performed significantly better than the control children on all the items of this test. If knowing Logo programming means understanding the language's basic vocabulary and of its basic concepts and processes such as procedures, variables, and transformations of programs; and if it also means knowing how to generate code as well as to read, understand, interpret, and optimize a given code—then the results of this test demonstrate the experimental children's superiority over the control children in their knowledge of programming.

The children's learning of Logo under the Software-Design-Logo conditions was an unusually effective way for: (a) their learning of the language (its vocabulary, its structure, and its concepts and processes); and (b) their acquiring reflective and sophisticated knowledge and skills that were essential for solving the pencil-and-paper Logo test while *away* from the computer. In the following section we shall contrast the experimental children's abilities to debug and optimize a program given to them on the computer (i.e., in a hands-on task) with those of the control children.

2.1.2. Results from the Logo Computer Tests

This test included five related subtasks: subtasks 1 and 2 were about debugging; 3 and 4 were about modularity and optimization of the given procedure; and 5 was on an even higher level of optimization. The purposes of this Logo computer test were very similar to those of the Logo pencil-and-paper test, but assessed similar skills and knowledge of Logo while the child was actually using the computer. In the following pages the results from the different subtasks are described.

Debugging ability. In Tasks 1 and 2 of the Logo Computer Test the children were asked to solve problems related to debugging in the following way:

TASK 1) THIS IS WHAT I WANTED TO DRAW ON THE COMPUTER; THE NAME OF IT IS *"FLAGS."*

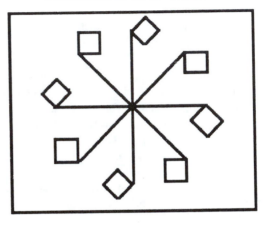

THIS WAS MY GOAL. **I THINK I HAVE *2 BUGS*, AND THIS IS WHAT APPEARED ON MY COMPUTER SCREEN:**

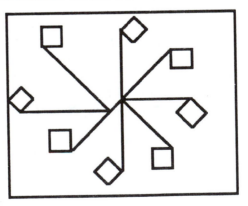

YOUR TASK IS TO:

RUN **THE PROGRAM "FLAGS" (WHICH IS ON YOUR DISKETTE)**
FIND **THE 2 BUGS**
FIX **THE PROGRAM**
DO IT UNTIL YOU GET IT TO LOOK LIKE THE *TOP PICTURE*.

TASK 2) THIS IS THE PROGRAM WITH THE TWO BUGS. PLEASE MARK YOUR CORRECTIONS HERE:

[Note: The following comments in the brackets, and the location marks of the bugs, were not included in the test form that the children received. These are provided here for clarity.]

TO FLAGS

ht home

fd 45   [draws the first stick of the first flag. It is the top vertical stick]

rt 45

fd 10   [the next 9 lines draw the first flag]

rt 90

fd 10

rt 90

fd 10

rt 90

fd 10

rt 90   [finishes drawing the first flag]

lt 45   [turns left 45]

bk 45   [goes back to home position]

rt 45   [turns right 45 degrees, preparing for the second stick . . .]

fd 30 fd 15 rt 45   [draws the second stick]

fd 10 rt 90   [starts drawing the second flag]

fd 10 rt 90

fd 10 rt 90

fd 10rt 90   [finishes drawing the second flag]

lt 45 bk 30 bk 15   [goes back to home position]

rt 45

fd 12 fd 12 fd 21   [draws the third stick]

rt 40 rt 5

fd 10 rt 90 fd 10 rt 90   [starts drawing the third flag]

fd 10 rt 90 fd 10 rt 90   [finishes drawing the third flag]

lt 45 bk 45 rt 45   [goes back to home position and turns 45 degrees]

fd 40 fd 5 rt 45   [draws the fourth stick]

repeat 1 [fd 10 rt 90 fd 10 rt 90   [starts drawing the fourth flag]

fd 10 rt 90 fd 10 rt 90]   [finishes drawing the fourth flag]

lt 45 rt 45 bk 45   [turns and goes back to home position]

fd 45 rt 45   [draws the fifth stick]

fd 10 rt 90   [starts drawing the fifth flag]

fd 10 rt 90

fd 10 rt 90

fd 10 rt 90   [finishes drawing the fifth flag]

lt 45 bk 45 rt 30 rt 15	[goes back to home position and turns 45 degrees preparing for next flag]
fd 45 rt 45	[draws the sixth stick]
repeat 2 [fd 10 rt 90	[starts drawing the sixth flag]
fd 10 rt 90]	[finishes drawing the sixth flag]
lt 45 bk *30* rt 30 rt 10 rt 5	[goes back only 30 steps instead of 45 to home position. This is the *first bug*. Then it turns right 45 degrees preparing as usual for the next flag]
fd 65 rt 45	[draws the seventh stick. This is the second bug, it goes fd 65 instead of 45 steps]
fd 10 rt 90	[starts drawing the seventh flag]
fd 10 rt 90	
fd 10 rt 90	
fd 10 rt 90	[finishes drawing the seventh flag]
lt 45 *bk 65* rt 45	[goes back to beginning of stick. This is a *sub-bug,* related to the second bug. Once one has discovered the second bug, this one is easy to find.]
fd 65 rt 45	[draws the eighth stick. But goes fd 65 instead of 45, a *sub-bug* to the second bug]
fd 10 rt 90	[starts drawing the eighth flag]
fd 10 rt 90	
fd 10 rt 90	
fd 10 rt 90	[finishes drawing the eighth flag]
lt 45 *bk 65* rt 45	[goes back 65 steps. This *sub-bug* is also related to the second bug]

END

Tasks 1 and 2 of the computer test were designed to assess: (a) the children's method and ability to debug a program given to them by someone else; (b) their understanding of the Logo-code structure on the computer; and (c) their understanding of the same Logo-code structure given on paper.

Debugging is a very complex skill. One central aspect of learning to program "is learning how to debug faulty programs . . . this aspect has been identified as one of the 'powerful ideas' that can generalize far beyond the programming context in which it is acquired" (Carver & Klahr, 1986, p. 2).

In their systematic analysis of the debugging processes, Carver and Klahr distinguishes between a *discrepancy,* that is, the difference between the original goal ("what I wanted to draw") and the program's output ("what came out on the computer screen"), and the *bug* itself (the error in the program that caused the discrepancy). They found four phases in the debugging process, which I also used for the analysis of this computer test. The four phases are described in detail in Carver and Klahr (1986, pp. 3–6), and I briefly summarize them here:

- *Phase 1:* "Program Evaluation." In this phase, a knowledgeable child (in terms of his or her debugging skills) is expected to *run* the program and *compare* the goal drawing with the actual output. When these two (the goal and actual output) do not match perfectly, then the child needs to *identify* the bug, *locate* the bug, and *correct* it.
- *Phase 2:* "Bug Identification." In this phase, the child must pay attention to the *pictorial features* of the output, *generate a description* of the discrepancies between the goal and the output, and think about several possible *types of bugs* that might be responsible for the discrepancy. After considering all possible options, the child hypothesizes on *one* specific bug (the reason for each discrepancy).
- *Phase 3:* "Bug Location." In this phase, the child *enters the Logo code* and, through identifying the structure of the code, investigates the probable *location* of the bugged command in the code.
- *Phase 4:* "Bug Correction." In this phase, the child *replaces the bug* with a *correction,* and re-evaluates the program (retracing the steps described in the "Program Evaluation," Phase 1 above).

Carver and Klahr created a related production-system model called GRAPES. They also specified in detail two sets of debugging heuristics, one for identifying bugs and one for locating them in a given code, and identified several operators that used in the process of debugging, whether done by humans or by the computer-program they had developed (i.e., the MATCH, CONTRAST, EXAMINE, INTERPRET, GENERATE, RUN, ENTER, SKIP, READ, DELETE, and INSERT operators, all of which are subskills necessary for processing information and performing actions in the process of debugging). They used this very detailed and *formal* task analysis of Logo debugging skills (based on an expert's skills of debugging) to assess children's performances of debugging, and found that children were not able to develop these sophisticated skills, follow the four phases, or use the needed operators and heuristics in what they called, "a normal Logo course" (p. 12). As a result, Carver (1986, 1987) developed an intensive Logo course that explicitly and directly teaches children the four phases, the operators, and the heuristics used in the process of debugging. Through the use of several evaluative tests with experimental and control children, Carver found that her debugging course was very effective and resulted in children's developing very sophisticated and systematic debugging skills that were even transferred to other more or less related debugging tasks in situations other than Logo programming. In the context of my research, none of the tested children (from the three classes) were formally instructed as were Carver's pupils. Also, unlike Carver in her research goals, I was not interested in the transfer of the debugging skills; rather, I was interested in investigating children's ability to learn these skills through their unique, open-ended, and intensive programming experience in the Instructional Software Design Project. However, I was strongly inspired by Carver's (1987) debugging tasks when I created these particular computer tasks for my research (all the ones described above and below), and I was also interested in using her debugging-process model in analyzing the children's knowledge of debugging.

Results (for tasks 1 and 2). On the whole, it appears that the experimental children developed the debugging skills required for solving Parts 1 and 2 during their processes of designing and programming instructional software, because they performed much better on these two subtasks, were faster at identifying the bugs, were able to locate the bugs in the given program on the computer and on paper, then reevaluated the program and created an output that corresponded perfectly with the original goal given to them in that task.

Tables 13 and 14 show the results for Parts 1 and 2, which required that the children run the given program; analyze the features of the picture (or defaulted output); identify the discrepancies; enter the Logo code on the computer; locate, one by one, the different bugs that were causing the discrepancies; fix the program on the computer; and finally, add the corrections on the program that was written on the paper.

The results revealed in these two tables speak for themselves. The superiority of the experimental children (on all math levels) over the other pupils is clear, as is that of C_1 over C_2 (the former having programmed more intensively and integratively than the latter).

The first thing all the experimental children did was to change the HT (Hide Turtle), which was at the very beginning of the procedure, to ST (Show Turtle), so that they could follow the Turtle as it executed the code. This was one of the strategies that helped them to analyze the program's features and identify the

Table 13.   Results from the Debugging Task from All 51 Children.

	No. of Bugs Found and Fixed	Identify & Fix Bugs in *Computer* Prog.	Identify & Fix Bugs in *Paper* Program	Average Time for Solving 1&2
Experimen. class N = 17	16—all bugs 1—one bug	17 children—yes 100% succeeded	17 children—yes 100% succeeded	15 minute per child
Control 1 N = 18	9—all bugs 4—one bug 5—none	13 children—yes 5 children—no 70% succeeded	8 children—yes 10 children—no 44% succeeded	35 minutes per child
Control 2 N = 16	2—all bugs 4—one bug 10—none	6 children—yes 10 children—no 37% succeeded	2 children—yes 14 children—no 12% succeeded	55 minutes per child

Table 14.   Contingency Table Analysis, Comparing the Number of Bugs Found in the Debugging Task between the Experimental and Control Classes.

	Experimental Class (%)	Control 1 Class (%)	Control 2 Class (%)
Bugs found:			
2	94	50	13
1	6	22	25
0	0	28	62

$\chi^2 = 138.92$

repeated pattern of the picture, its units, and the way these units related to each other, which resulted in their finding the bugs rather quickly.

On the other hand, the first strategy that most of the children in C_2 and many of those in C_1 used, rather than running the program several times, analyzing it, and trying to identify its structure and bugs, was to *copy* the program given to them on paper (in subtask 2) into the Logo Command Center and execute it line by line. This strategy worked well until they reached the repeat statements, which were written on more than one line. Then, the children got confused, because it did not work, and they were sure that they had located a bug; they "fixed the bug" but, of course, with little success. The procedure then became very different from the original one. Instead of trying a new strategy, these children erased everything and started to copy the procedure into the direct mode again, which resulted in the same thing happening again, and so on.

Carver and Klahr (1986) list three reasons why children usually fail to acquire debugging skills" "a) Debugging is a complex skill; b) it requires extra capacity; and c) it is rarely taught directly" (pp. 27–30). I definitely agree with the first two reasons but believe the third should be revised.

To my mind, children who study programming under exceptionally rich learning conditions should be able to acquire basic debugging skills. First and foremost, they should acquire these skills by frequently exploring and experiencing debugging situations in the course of their learning how to program, rather than just being taught these skills directly and beforehand. One should not necessarily assume that a deficiency in children's debugging skills is a direct result of their not having received instruction in the subject. It also seems that, though explicit teaching of debugging might be needed in some cases, it does not always needed to take place before a child has experienced and acquired some of these skills on his own.

ISDP offered another method for helping children to acquire these skills, a method that is radically different from Carver's (1987) instructional method. During their course of designing and programming instructional software, the experimental children went through many phases of debugging. There were many situations when a child designed something in his or her Designer's Notebook in one way, but, when he or she actually programmed it, there were discrepancies between his or her original drawing and the program's actual output. In some cases the child took advantage of the unexpected outcome, reevaluated his or her original plan or design, and decided to go on with whatever had appeared on the screen (in other words, the child modified his or her plan instead of treating the output as a result of discrepancies or bugs). However, in other cases, the child felt a strong need, for various reasons, to find the discrepancies between the program and its plan, and reevaluate the program's output, rather than the plan; in other words, he located the bugs and fixed them so that the program's output would match the original design drawn in his or her Notebook.

I find these two aspects equally important in children's programming processes. For various reasons related to children's developing creative skills or their breaking away from rigidity into developing flexible strategies in their thinking, designing, and programming, it would seem desirable to put them in situations where they might sometimes break away from their original plans and designs and learn how to benefit from unexpected outcomes or from programming constraints. However, children should also learn how their plans can be followed and implemented precisely, and how to locate and correct the discrepancies between their hand-drawn picture and the program that has been created for drawing that picture on the computer.

It appears that, through this combination of thinking and programming strategies, the experimental children learned to become good debuggers, as well as creative and flexible problem solvers (we will see evidence for this in the children's solutions to subtasks, 3, 4, and 5). I therefore suggest that children who learn under the Carver conditions will probably develop excellent debugging skills and will be able to transfer them; but I am not quite sure how creative these children will be in their ongoing problem-solving or programming processes, or how flexible they will become in terms of their cognitive development.

To summarize, in contrast to Carver and Klahr's (1986) and Carver's (1987) assumptions and findings, the children of the experimental class, who were not directly taught debugging but instead experienced a variety of debugging situations during their course of learning how to program, were able to learn basic debugging skills.

What will remains unknown and requires further investigation is the experimental children's ability to transfer these skills. It was not in the scope of my research to gather information about transfer in the same way that Carver did in her very systematic studies; however, I feel safe in saying that the experimental children would probably be able to transfer these skills better than those from C_1 and C_2.

Ability to optimize and modularize Logo programs on the computer. Tasks 3 and 4 of the Logo computer test were designed to assess, through the use of the same procedure FLAGS, the children's understanding of the Logo-code structure and their ability to modularize and optimize someone else's procedure, which was given to them on the computer. The tasks read as follows:

3) NOW, TRY TO *SIMPLIFY* THIS PROGRAM, OR *"CLEAN IT."*
IN OTHER WORDS, THINK ABOUT *OTHER WAYS* TO WRITE A LOGO
PROGRAM THAT WILL PRODUCE THE *SAME PICTURE*
CAN YOU MAKE IT *SHORTER?*
(THINK ABOUT CREATING SUB-PROCEDURES)

WRITE YOUR SHORTER VERSION ON THE ATTACHED PAGE
AND ON THE COMPUTER, CALL IT *"FLAGS1"*
[TO FLAGS1]

4) NOW, TRY TO WRITE THE SAME PROGRAM WITH *INPUTS* (IF YOU DID
NOT DO IT ALREADY), SO YOU CAN TYPE: *FLAGS 45 10* AND IT WILL
DRAW THE PICTURE OF 8 FLAGS AS BEFORE. OR IF YOU TYPE:
FLAGS 65 20 IT WILL MAKE THE SAME PICTURE BUT *BIGGER.*

WRITE YOUR PROGRAM ON THE ATTACHED PAGE
AND ON THE COMPUTER, CALL IT "FLAGS2"

(Note: For these two subtasks, the wording was prepared with the assistance of the three teachers, who thought that, for fourth-grade pupils, these would be the best words to use for this purpose, instead of *modularity* or *optimization*, etc.)

In other words, in Tasks 3 and 4, the children were asked to optimize the code given to them in Tasks 1 and 2 of this test. In order to solve these subtasks, the children had to make the procedure clearer and shorter by ceasing to operate on the individual command level and starting to think in a procedural mode, using repeats, subroutines, and procedures; and later, they also had to think about inputs. They had to think about how to make the procedure FLAGS more modular, useful, and flexible. They had to think about what functions the different parts of the program served, and how the different parts were lined up and connected together (some of these issues they had already had to think about while working on Parts 1 and 2 above).

These tasks were also administered in order to examine how the different children would approach a procedure that already worked well, and produce a different program for the same purpose by using higher level units. As in Question 4 of the Logo pencil-and-paper test, the children, when asked to read the FLAGS program again, after having debugged it, had to rescan the code and mentally simulate what the procedure was doing overall, and what its whole structure was (rather than each separate line), and see how the goals of the original procedure were achieved and how it could be written in more sophisticated way.

Results (for tasks 3 and 4). As we saw from the findings of Question 4 in the Logo pencil-and-paper test, three levels of modularization or optimalization of the given code were found among the tested children.

Simplify Level 1. On this level, the child combined all the fd 20 and fd 25 into fd 45, or rt 30 and rt 15 into rt 45, etc., which indeed made the program shorter, and clearer, and was a first step towards optimization. One hundred percent of the experimental children produced Level 1 modifications, but only 66% of C_1 and 25% of C_2 produced Level 1 modification for the procedure FLAGS (i.e., complete failure of six children in C_1 and 12 children in C_2).

This finding is very interesting since in the Logo pencil-and-paper test many more children from the control classes were able to simplify the given procedure DESIGN (Question 3 in that test) on Level 1. This might be a result of two things. First, DESIGN was an easier procedure to simplify than FLAGS; second, many of the children, especially from C_2, had already become confused during their process of debugging, and changed the original procedure given to them in Tasks 1 and 2 in such a way that it was later difficult to identify the procedure's structure and units for Tasks 3 and 4. In fact, many of these children who worked in direct mode and tried to copy, line by line, the procedure given to them on paper, made many mistakes while typing it into the computer and got rather lost in the process.

Simplify Level 2. On this level there were two versions, which I call Level 2.1 and 2.2. On Level 2.1, the child simplified the code according to Level 1, but also tried to use REPEAT for the flags at the ends of the sticks. A correct and consistent simplification in Level 2.1 resulted in the following procedures.

```
TO FLAGS1 (Version 1)
home fd 45 rt 45
REPEAT 4 [fd 10 rt 90] lt 45 bk 45 rt 45
fd 45 rt 45
REPEAT 4 [fd 10 rt 90] lt 45 bk 45 rt 45
fd 45 rt 45
REPEAT 4 [fd 10 rt 90] lt 45 bk 45 rt 45
fd 45 rt 45
REPEAT 4 [fd 10 rt 90] lt 45 bk 45 rt 45
fd 45 rt 45
REPEAT 4 [fd 10 rt 90] lt 45 bk 45 rt 45
fd 45 rt 45
REPEAT 4 [fd 10 rt 90] lt 45 bk 45 rt 45
fd 45 rt 45
```

```
REPEAT 4 [fd 10 rt 90] lt 45 bk 45 rt 45
fd 45 rt 45
REPEAT 4 [fd 10 rt 90] lt 45 bk 45 rt 45
END
```

No one in C_2 was able to systematically revise the FLAGS procedure on this Level. Most of these children used repeats in some places but not in others; in other words, they did not understand the structure of the procedure or the units that needed to be repeated in full. Many children in C_1, who managed to reach Level 2.1 stopped there, not realizing that a higher level of repeats could be used (i.e., nesting a repeat within a repeat). Ninety percent of the experimental children succeeded in simplifying the procedure on this level.

```
TO FLAGS1 (Version 2)
REPEAT 8 [fd 45 rt 45 REPEAT 4 [fd 10 rt 90] lt 45 bk 45 rt 45]
END
```

Simplify Level 3. On this level there were also two possible versions, which I call Level 3.1 and 3.2. On Level 3.1 children simplified the code according to Level 1, 2.1, and 2.2 as described above, but also used a subprocedure for making a FLAG.

```
TO FLAG
fd 45 rt 45 REPEAT 4 [fd 10 rt 90]
END
```

```
TO FLAGS3
REPEAT 8 [FLAGG lt 45 bk 45 rt 45]
END
```

Or, still on the same Level, other children wrote:

```
TO FLAG
fd 45 rt 45 REPEAT 4 [fd 10 rt 90] lt 45 bk 45 rt 45
END
```

```
TO FLAGS
REPEAT 8 [FLAG]
END
```

A total of 15 out of the 17 experimental children were able to write the procedure FLAGS on this Level; only 5 out of 18 children in C_1 succeeded, but no one in C_2.

On Level 3.2 children used variables, one for the stick and another for its flag. Twelve experimental children were able to do it:

```
TO FLAG :num1 :num2    [num1=stick's length, num2=flag's size]
fd :num1 rt 45
REPEAT 4 [fd :num2 rt 90]
lt 45 bk :num1 rt 45
END

TO FLAGS4 :num1 :num2
REPEAT 8 [FLAG :num1 :num2]
END
```

Ability to use variables. In Task 5 the children were asked to use variables. The children were asked:

"CAN YOU MAKE A PROGRAM THAT DRAWS THE *SAME PICTURE*,

BUT *EACH* FLAG WILL BE IN A *DIFFERENT COLOR?*"

A total of 10 experimental children, and 2 children from C_1, managed to solve this task. They did it as follows:

```
TO FLAGS5 :num1 :num2
REPEAT 8 [FLAG :num1 :num2 SETC 1 + random 14]
END
```

A total of 5 experimental children used a variable even for color (instead of using random). Their reason was: "When I used the random I sometimes got the same color twice, and you wanted each flag to be in a different color, right?" Here is what these 5 children did:

```
TO FLAGS6 :num1 :num2 :num3    [num1=stick's length, num2=flag's
                                size, num3=pen color]
REPEAT 8 [FLAG :num1 :num2 setc :num3+1]
END
```

Summary of the results from the Logo computer test. On the whole, the experimental children were more flexible and attempted to explore a greater variety of ways for producing the same drawing. They understood and reached a more modular level of code, and many of them tried to use repeats, sub-procedures, and variables. Interestingly enough, all the experimental children, who had already performed much better than the control children in the similar task (Question 4) of the Logo pencil-and-paper test, performed even better here, using the computer. But the children from C_2 got more confused at the computer, and performed less well than they had on the pencil-and-paper task. C_1 was somewhere in between: the high-math children, like those from the experimental class, performed much better at the computer, and the medium- and low-math children performed similarly to those from C_2, that is, far less successfully than they had in the pencil-and-paper task.

2.2. RESULTS FROM THE FRACTIONS POSTTESTS

All the teaching of fractions, for all the three classes, was conducted for 2 months, during regular math lessons only and following the City of Boston's requirements and traditional teaching methods. While the Instructional Software Design Project was being conducted, the experimental class was *not* provided with any additional instruction on fractions besides the material they had covered in their regular math lessons with the other control children. In the following subsection, selected results from the two fractions posttests, the Rational-Number pencil-and-paper test, and the Boston Public Schools Curriculum Referenced Math Test are presented. The results of the interviews are not available in this chapter. They were documented and presented in detail in a video entitled "What Is A Fraction?" (Harel & Stein, 1989).

2.2.1. Results from the Rational-Number Pencil-and-Paper Test

The posttest included 65 multiple-choice questions. Out of these, 60 were taken from the Rational-Number Project (RN Project, Lesh et al., 1983, pp. 309–336). The remaining 5 were designed by the researcher and included word problems and construction of representations. Of the 60 RN Project questions, 43 were given to the students in the pretest, then again in the posttest. As an example, Table 15 shows the children's average percentages of correct answers on the fractions pre- and posttests; Table 16 shows the table of results for the two-way factor analysis of variance with repeated measurement for the fractions pre- and posttests scores; and Figure 13 shows the interaction diagram of the two main factors. In general, the difference in pre- and posttest scores of the students from the experimental class was almost twice as great as that achieved by the students from class C_1, and $2^{1}/_{2}$ times as great as that of class C_2.

Table 15. The Average Scores on the Fractions Pre- and Posttests.

	Fraction Knowledge	
Treatment	Pre-Test (%)	Post-Test (%)
Experimental Class	52	74
Control Class 1	54	66
Control Class 2	47	56

Table 16.   The Two-Way Factor Analysis of Variance.

Source	d.f.	F-Statistics
A (Groups)	2	15.31**
Subjects between samples	48	
Within Subjects	50	
B (Pre-Post)	1	110.99**
A × B	2	8.29**
B × Subjects	48	
Between Subjects	51	
Total	101	

Specific attention is given to the analyses of the most difficult translation modes between rational-number representations that the students had to carry out in the test. Some of these translations were the most difficult for students of all ages in previous studies, and were equally so for all students in the present study's pretests. In the posttests, however, these translation modes were still relatively difficult for the control students, but dramatically less so for the experimental students.

Lesh et al. (1983) tested their subjects on different "translation modes" between representations of fractions. In their large-scale testing program they found that some translations were more difficult to process than others. These translations are presented in Figure 14 (from the easiest translation, Level 1, to the hardest translation, Level 9).

In the following sections, the results from the last four modes of translations

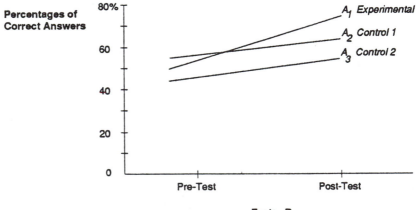

Figure 13.   An Interaction Diagram of the Two Main Factors.

Level 1

Translating number representation into word representation (for example, three-sixths equals six-twelfths: this was the easiest translation for the children in the RN Project conducted by Behr et al. 1983, and Lesh et al., 1983).

Level 2

Translating symbols into symbols (for example, 3/6 = 6/12).

Level 3

Translating symbols into words (for example, 3/6 equals six twelfths).

Level 4

Translating words into symbols (for example, three-sixths = 6/12).

Level 5

Translating a picture into a picture, for example:

Level 6

Translating words into a picture, for example:

Three-sixths =

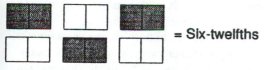

Level 7

Translating pictures into words, for example:

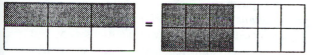 = Six-twelfths

Level 8

Translating symbols into pictures, for example:

3/6 =

Level 9

Translating pictures into symbols, (the hardest for children of ages 9-14):

 = 6/12

Figure 14.   The Different Translation Modes Between Representations of Fractions, Presented from the Easiest (Level 1) to the Hardest (Level 9).

will be presented (i.e., Levels 6, 7, 8, and 9 in Figure 14), since they were the most difficult for children of all ages in the Lesh et al. (1983) and Behr et al. (1983) studies, and were equally difficult for all the children in this study's pretests. In the posttests, however, these four translation modes were still relatively difficult for the children from C_1 and C_2; but the experimental children dramatically improved on these four modes in their posttests.

From this point forward, the scores of the children in the RN Project will be considered as *standard* scores (in their percentage of correct answers). In this way, the children from the experimental group ($n = 17$) will be compared, not only with those from the two control classes ($n = 18$, $n = 16$), but also with the fourth-grade children from the RN Project ($n = 43$). In other words, the 17 experimental children will be compared from here on with 77 other children on all the selected questions from this posttest.

Translating written representations of into pictorial representations (i.e., sixth level of difficulty in Figure 14). In order to answer questions 4, 5, 7, 11, 13, and 24 in the posttest, the children were required to translate a written representation of a rational number into pictorial representations of a rational number. The questions are listed here according to their level of difficulty for the children in the RN Project (Lesh et al., 1983, pp. 309–336). Table 17 shows the scores of all 51 children on these questions. The children are grouped according to their class (experimental, C_1, and C_2) and math level (high, medium, or low). Table 17 demonstrates the advantages gained by the children from the experimental group over those from the two control classes and the RN Project, once the experiment was completed.

Question 7, for example, was the most difficult in this subset, and the 51st most difficult in the whole set of 60 questions (see Figure 15).

In order to answer this question, the children had to translate the word *fourths* into the four options of discrete pictorial representations. Option (b), for example, was confusing, since a measurement was imposed on the picture but was not applicable. Option (c), which was the correct answer, included a perceptual distraction. The children first had to identify the number of parts in each option,

Table 17. Results from the Subset of Words to Pictures Translations.

	EXPER.	CTR 1	CTR 2	STAND.
HI	88%	80%	75%	
MD	84%	66%	80%	
LO	75%	66%	63%	
AVE	82%	70%	72%	67%

7) **Which picture shows fourths?**

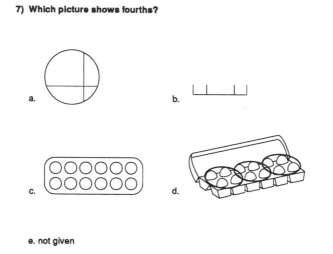

e. not given

Figure 15.   Question #7.

then compare the sizes of the parts in each object and see if the parts within each object were equal. This process of finding the right answer for Question 7 was rather complex. The options given as answers were definitely not "standard" ones (such as one circle divided into four equal parts). Option (a), considered to be the most basic and familiar representation of a circular region, assessed the children's knowledge of "the parts must be equal" schema. Table 18 shows the posttest scores for Question 7.

The experimental children scored significantly higher than those in the two control classes and in the RN Project. The medium- and low-math children from the experimental class scored higher than the medium- and low-math children from the two control classes, higher than the C_2 high-math children, and also higher than the RN Project children.

Table 18.   Average of Percent Correct on Question 7 (Translating the Word "Fourth" into a Picture Representation).

	EXPER.	CTR 1	CTR 2	STAND.
HI	78%	70%	32%	
MD	40%	32%	25%	
LO	50%	0%	20%	
AVE	56%	34%	25%	30%

In the pretests, the average of percentages of correct answers for this question was 12% for the experimental children from the medium- and low-math groups taken together. The other children had similar results in the pretest. However, the experimental children made far more progress than the other children in the period between January to June.

Translating pictorial representations into written representations (i.e., seventh level of difficulty in Figure 14). In order to answer questions 2, 8, 22, 23, 25, 30, 32, 35, 36, 37, 38, 49, 50, and 60 in the posttest, the children were required to translate a pictorial representation of a rational number into written representations of a rational number. The questions are listed here according to their level of difficulty for the children in the RN Project (Lesh et al., 1983, pp. 309–336). Table 19 shows the score of all 51 children on these questions, and the score of the fourth graders in the RN Project.

This subset (Level 7) was much more difficult than the previous one I discussed (Level 6). Questions 38, 50, and 60 were particularly complex. Therefore, the differences between the groups in this subset, as a whole, were not as significant as those in the previous subset. However, there were differences, and the experimental children did have an edge over the rest of the children. The differences between the experimental children of all three math groups and those of C_2 are very high: between the high-math children from the experimental and C_2, the difference is 28%, between the medium-math children, 14% and between the low-math children, 9%. In addition, the low-math children of the experimental group did better than all the children in C_2. When analyzing specific questions of this subset (pictures into words translations), we can see more dramatic differences.

Question 50, for example, is considered to be so complex that it was not given at all to the fourth graders in the RN Project, only to sixth-, seventh-, and eighth-grade children (Lesh et al., p. 326). It is shown in Figure 16.

This question was one of the two most difficult in this subset, and the 55th most difficult in the whole set of 60 questions. It presented children with a polygonal region representation, with a numerator that was higher than 1, a

Table 19. Results from the Subset of Pictures to Words Translations.

	EXPER.	CTR 1	CTR 2	STAND.
HI	85%	80%	57%	
MD	60%	60%	46%	
LO	59%	56%	50%	
AVE	68%	65%	51%	56%

50) What is the denominator of the fraction that tells us what part of the picture below is shaded?

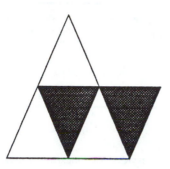

a. five-thirds   b. five   c. three   d. two   e. not given

Figure 16.   Question #50.

denominator, a representation of a rational number lower than 1, in a discrete object that included a perceptual distraction (i.e., one part was "outside" the triangle area). In order to choose one of the options, the children had to (a) translate the given picture into symbols or words (two-fifths are shaded in); (b) read the question again and realize that the question referred to the denominator of the shaded fraction; and (C) find the correct answer, which was (b). Option (a) is confusing because it is written like a spoken symbol and includes "relevant" numbers—five and thirds. Option (b) is confusing because it do not mention "fifths," but rather "five" (the denominator is "five"). Tables 20 and 21 show the

Table 20.   Average of Percent Correct on Question 50 (Translating a Picture of Three-Fifths into Words).

	EXPER.	CTR 1	CTR 2	STAND.
HI	88%	78%	16%	
MD	60%	16%	25%	Not given to 4th.
LO	50%	0%	40%	7th gr. got 26%
AVE	66%	31%	27%	

Table 21.   Contingency Table Statistics, Comparing Performance of the Study Sample with Performance of RN Project Sample (Lesh et al., 1983, Average of Grades 6–8), for Question 50.

	(%) Correct in Study Sample	(%) Correct in Background Sample
Experiment Class	66	33
Control Class 1 & Control Class 2 (Average)	29	33

$\chi^2 = 33.49$

scores in their percentage of correct answers for Question 50, and compares the performance of this study's sample with the performance of the RN Project sample.

The experimental children's scores were twice as good as those of the control children, and even twice as good as those of the *seventh* graders from the RN Project. The low- and medium-levels of the experimental group did much better in this question than the low- and medium-level of C_1 and all the levels of C_2. The average percentage of correct answers for the experimental low- and medium-levels taken together was 55%. The average of C_1's low- and medium-math levels, taken together with all three math groups in C_2, was only 32%. This finding is significant to this study because Question 50 was a rather complex question according to Lesh et al. (1983) and Behr et al. (1983).

In addition, my assumption here regarding this particular question is that the children who were better at Logo programming were probably better at answering this question correctly. What Lesh et al. (1983) and Behr et al. (1983) consider as a "perceptual distraction" (i.e., the one little triangle that was "outside" the big triangle area) was probably not a distraction for the children, who looked at the picture with "Logo eyes" and decomposed it into its five geometric components. Decomposing a given picture into its geometric components is a common process in Logo programming, and a skill children usually acquire in their ongoing programming experiences.

Question 22 (Figure 17) was another rather difficult question in this subset. This question was based on the number-line subconstruct of a rational-number. It was the 10th most difficult question in this subset, and the 49th most difficult in the whole test of 60 questions.

Only 17 out of the 60 questions in the posttest required translations of number-line representations. Question 22 was the 14th most difficult among them. In order to answer this question correctly, the children had to identify all the lines between the heavier lines (of number 1 and 2), see if the distances between these lines were equal, and carefully read the options given to them. The diagram below shows how many of the children selected option (a) as the correct answer.

22) This ruler measures Inches by:

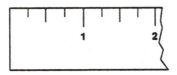

a. wholes, halves and fourths

b. wholes and halves only

c. wholes, halves, and thirds

d. wholes and fourths only

e. not given

Figure 17.   Question #22.

Again, we can see how much better the experimental class as a whole per-formed than the control classes. The experimental children's scores are almost three times as great, in fact, than those of the fourth graders from the RN Project. It is important to note, however, that *none* of the experimental children had previously used a number-line representation in their instructional software. In other words, they had not practiced using this particular rational-number sub-construct while involved in the experimental project. Moreover, *all* the children in the three math groups solved several number-line problems in their worksheets in the course of their regular math curriculum. These results show that the children's learning from worksheets alone was unsatisfactory.

Table 22.   Average of Percent Correct on Question 22 (Translating a Pictorial Number-Line into Words).

	EXPER.	CTR 1	CTR 2	STAND.
HI	100%	72%	16%	
MD	50%	32%	25%	
LO	50%	20%	20%	
AVE	66%	41%	20%	23%

However, as in Question 50, the low- and medium-math levels of the experimental class did much better on this question than the low- and medium-math levels of C_1, and all the levels of C_2. The average of their percentage of correct answers for the experimental low- and medium-math levels, taken together, was 50%. The average of C_1's low- and medium-math levels, taken together with all the three math groups in C_2, was only 22%.

Translating symbolic representations into pictorial representations (i.e., eighth level of difficulty in Figure 14). In order to answer Questions 6, 12, 14, 21, 27, and 51 in the posttest, the children were required to translate a symbolic representation of a rational number into pictorial representations of rational numbers. The questions were listed above according to their level of difficulty for the children in the RN Project (Lesh et al., 1983, pp. 309–336). Table 23 shows the scores of all 51 children on these questions, as well as those of the fourth graders in the RN Project. The advantage of the experimental children over the RN Project fourth graders and the children from C_2 is clear. There are differences between experimental and C_1, but they are not very dramatic in this subset.

Translating pictorial representations into symbolic representations (eighth level of difficulty in Figure 14). In order to answer Questions 1, 3, 16, 19, 29, 31, 33, 34, 39 41, 42, 43, 44, 45, 46, 47, 48, and 53 in the posttest the children were required to translate a pictorial representation of a rational number into symbolic representations of a rational number. Again, the questions are listed here according to their level of difficulty for the children in the RN Project (Lesh et al., 1983, pp. 309–336).

For example, Question 42 of this subset (Figure 18) required translating a ratio represented by a picture into its symbolic representation. This question was the 13th most difficult of the 18 asked in this subset. It was the 44th most difficult in the whole set of 60 questions given in the RN Project to children from fourth through eighth grades (Lesh et al., 1983, p. 323). It included a discrete object representation in which the represented rational number was less than 1; moreover, parts of this object were not congruent and were visually distracting. Tables 24 and 25 show the results from this question.

Table 23.   Results from the Subset of Symbols to Pictures Translations.

	EXPER.	CTR 1	CTR 2	STAND.
HI	78%	72%	55%	
MD	66%	64%	54%	
LO	51%	50%	45%	
AVE	65%	58%	31%	52%

42) **What fraction of the balls are tennis balls?**

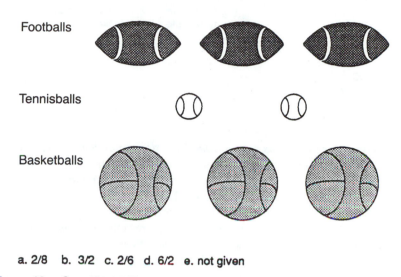

a. 2/8   b. 3/2   c. 2/6   d. 6/2   e. not given

Figure 18.   Question #42.

In this complex question none of the high-math experimental children made any mistakes. The medium-math experimental children scored like the high-math children in the two control classes. The experimental class as a whole did twice as well on this subset than the children in the RN Project, and 14% better or 27% better than C_1 and C_2, respectively.

Table 24.   Average of Percent of Subjects Responding Correctly to Question 42 (Translating a Ratio Represented in a Picture into its Symbolic Representation) by Treatment and Methematical Ability.

	Mathematical Ability		
Treatment	**Low (%)**	**Medium (%)**	**High (%)**
Experimental Class	50	72	100
Control Class 1	40	68	72
Control Class 2	20	50	72

Table 25.   Contingency Table Statistics, Comparing the Performance of the Study Sample with the Performance of the RN Project Sample (Lesh et al., Grades 4).

	(%) Correct in Study Sample	(%) Correct in Background Sample
Experiment Class	74	36
Control Class 1 & Control Class 2 (Average)	53.5	36

$\chi^2 = 42.62$

Summary of the results drawn from the rational-number concepts and their representations pencil-and-paper test. Specific attention has been given to the most difficult translation modes between rational-number representations. These were: translating words into pictures (i.e., Level 6 in Lesh et al., 1983); translating pictures into words (i.e., Level 7); translating symbols into pictures (i.e., Level 8); and the most difficult, translating pictures into symbols (i.e., Level 9). These four levels of translations were the most difficult for children of all ages in previous studies, and were equally difficult for all children in the present study's pretests. In the posttests, however, we have seen how these four translation modes were still relatively difficulty for the control children, but the experimental children dramatically improved in these particular translations (and even more significantly in other translations that were not reported here). We have examined more deeply the most difficult questions in these subsets; they were Question 7 in Level 6, Questions 50 and 22 in Level 7, and Question 42 in Level 9. In these difficult questions, the experimental children consistently scored much higher than the control children as well as dramatically better than those from the RN Project.

On the whole, the trends that were found in the results of the Logo posttests were also found in the results of this posttest: The experimental children constantly scored higher than the other two classes, and control class 1 usually scored higher than control class 2.

The high-math children from C_1 were an exception to the rest of the control children and to those from the RN Project (Behr et al., 1983; Lesh et al., 1983). They were never as good as the high-math experimental children, and most of the time they were as good as the experimental medium-math children. Yet their scores are often higher than those of the children from the RN Project and of the rest of the control children.

These findings are interesting if, and only if, there exists some kind of correlation between being a part of Project Headlight and having the ability to understand the relationships between different rational-number representations. This is all the more interesting because, if the correlation exists, it only does so in the case of the high-math children from C_1. It seems as though only the high-math C_1 children strongly benefited from Project Headlight (see Chapter I, Sections 1.2 and 4.2). This is probably due to the fact that their ongoing programming projects, which consisted in manipulating graphics and text, contributed to their ability to translate picture representations into written ones, and vice versa. The other children from the same class, however, who were also part of Project Headlight did not score significantly higher than those of C_2. This phenomenon requires further investigation. It is an interesting one, since it suggests a correlation between the child's level of understanding and involvement in Logo programming, and his or her ability to understand and use different representational systems. This could also give an indication of the child's level of readiness. Perhaps the high-math children of C_1 were cognitively more developed and therefore had a better understanding of these complex translations between fractional representations—or were better at automatically transferring their knowledge from Logo programming into fractional representation tasks. It is important to note that, by the time these posttests were given, all the children from the experimental class had both a higher level of programming and of experience in creating representations for their instructional software. These two factors combined resulted in the consistently and significantly higher scores across the board. Still, it seems as though the combination of being relatively bright and a good programmer (like the high-math children in C_1) might also result in being able to understand representational systems quite well.

2.2.2. Results from the Boston's Public Schools Curriculum Referenced Test, Math Level-4

On June 15 and 16 all the pupils were tested in math, as part of their end-of-year public school series of referenced tests.

This mathematics test included 40 multiple-choice questions. The average of incorrect answers per child on the whole test (i.e., for all 40 questions) was 5.06 incorrect answers per child in the experimental class; 6.27 incorrect answers per child in C_1; and 9.45 incorrect answers per child in C_2.

Out of those 40 questions, 6 were specifically on fractions ordering and equivalence; 4 on decimals; 4 on measurement of distance and time that included fractions; and 1 on understanding geometrical shapes (i.e., this was the subset of 15 questions directly related to rational-number concepts, their representations, and their computation). The average of incorrect answers per child on this subset of *15 rational-number questions* was only 1.60 in the experimental class; 3.16 in C_1, and 4.62 in C_2.

Several conclusions can be drawn from analyzing these results. The first is that the experimental children, in general, did much better on the entire conventional school test than the other two control classes (i.e., the experimental's average of incorrect answers per child was 5.06, as compared with 6.27, and 9.45 in C_1 and C_2, respectively).

The second conclusion is related to the children's incorrect answers in the rational-number concepts subset of this test. In the experimental class, only 29% of the average incorrect answers per child in the whole test (40 questions) were incorrect answers about rational-number concepts (i.e., an average proportion of 1.60 incorrect per child in fractions, to 5.06 incorrect per child on the whole test). But in both C_1 and C_2, approximately 50% of the incorrect answers per child were, in fact, about rational-number concepts (i.e., in C_1 the average proportion was 3.16 to 6.27; in C_2 it was 4.62 to 9.45). Table 26 shows the proportion of incorrect answers in this rational number subset to the whole test.

The third conclusion is related to "transfer." By subtracting the average of incorrect answers on the fractions subset from the average of incorrect answers on the whole test, we can examine the children's average of incorrect answers to all the nonfractions questions: for the experimental class, $5.06 - 1.60 =$ an average of 3.46 incorrect answers per child on nonfractions questions; for C_1 $6.27 - 3.16 = 3.11$; and for C_2, $9.45 - 4.62 = 4.83$. It seems, however, that the differences between the experimental class and C_1 are not significant, but that the differences between these two classes and C_2 are. This finding is interesting, because it might be that the Project Headlight children's (experimental and C_1) experience with Logo programming contributed to their general mathematical ability.

Let us briefly focus on some specific questions in this test. Questions 19, 20, 21, 25, and 31 were about fractions or mixed fractions equivalence and ordering, and they were also the most difficult for many of the children. Many children in all three classes answered these questions incorrectly, but *fewer* children answered them incorrectly in the experimental class.

- In *Question 19* the children were asked:

    19. Which sign makes this number sentence true?

    $$\frac{1}{5} \; ? \; \frac{1}{3}$$

    a)> b)= c)≥ d)<

In order to answer this question, the children had to have a conceptual understanding of fractions ordering. Behr et al. (1984) found that fourth-grade children do not have a strong quantitative notion of fractions for dealing with problems of ordering fractions such as this one, for their whole-number concepts get in the way. In this question, for example, most children probably looked at the denominators 5 and 3 and thought that, because 5 was bigger than 3, therefore option (a) was the correct answer. The idea that, when the two numerators are 1 (as in the case of 1/5 and 1/3), the larger the denominator is, the smaller the

Table 26. Contingency Table
Analysis, Comparing the Proportion
of the National-Number Subset
to the Whole Test in the Boston
Schools Math Test between the
Experimental and Control Classes.

Experimental Class (%)	Control 1 Class (%)	Control 2 Class (%)
29	51	48

$\chi^2 = 6.631$

fraction, is a very very difficult concept for children to understand in ordering fractions, because it conflicts with their concept of ordering whole numbers.

Also, in order to compare two fractions that have nothing in common, such as one-third and one-fifth, children must reason about two groups at once: the internal relationship between the numerator and the denominator within each fraction, and the external relationship between the two fractions and their denominators and numerators (see also Tierney, 1988). Piaget and Inhelder found that this comparison between two groups or "families" of numbers required performing formal operations, an ability which, according to them, does not usually develop before age 12 or 13 (the children in my study were 9 to 10 years old). In the experimental class, only 3 children answered this question incorrectly; in C_1, 9 children, and in C_2, 10 children.

- In *Question 20* the children were asked:

20. Write as a mixed number: $\dfrac{13}{7}$

    a) 2   b) $\dfrac{7}{13}$ c) $1\dfrac{6}{7}$ d) $1\dfrac{6}{13}$

In order to answer this complex question, the children had to understand both the concept of ordering and equivalence of fractions, and of mixed fractions. A child's ability to link the written symbols with the words representing them could help in this situation as well. In this question, in fact, the children could choose the right answer without actually calculating it, by paying attention to the word *sevenths* as the denominator, then eliminating the wrong options. If a child understood that he or she had to look for a number that had "sevenths" in it, he or she would choose option (c) right away. He or she might try to consider option (a), but by using his or her equivalence concept he or she would realize that 2 wholes would need 14 sevenths, not 13. The other two options were confusing for the children who did not have a clear concept of ordering, equivalence, or mixed fractions.

In the experimental class, only 5 children answered this question incorrectly; in Control class 1, 8 children; and in Control class 2, 11 children.

- In *Question 21* the children were asked:

21. Which fraction equals $8\frac{2}{3}$

    a) $\frac{19}{3}$ b) $\frac{13}{3}$ c) $\frac{48}{3}$ d) $\frac{26}{3}$

This question requires the same conceptual understanding as Question 20, but in reverse. However, unlike Question 20, the correct answer requires a precise computation. In order to answer this question, the children needed to understand the algorithm of how to translate a number composed of wholes and fractions into a mixed fraction. Option (b) was selected by several children who added 8 + 3 + 2 = 13, and therefore selected 13/3 as the correct answer. Option (c) was selected by several others who multiplied 3 * 8 = 24, and then, instead of adding 2, multiplied 24 * 2 = 48, and selected 48/3 as the correct answer. All together, only 6 children answered this question incorrectly in the experimental class, 9 in C_1, and 12 in C_2.

- In *Question 25* the children were asked:

25. Which of these fractions equals $\frac{1}{2}$?

    a) $\frac{5}{10}$ b) $\frac{2}{5}$ c) $\frac{2}{3}$ d) $\frac{1}{4}$

This question required a very basic concept of equivalency of halves. Although Smith (1987) found evidence of children's great "ease of movement" within the half-equivalence class, by use of the Halving Operator (p. 9), 4 children answered this question incorrectly in C_1, and 10 in C_2. Only one child in the experimental class did not answer this question correctly; in fact, for an unknown reason, he did not answer it at all.

- In *Question 31* the children were asked:

31. Aaron starts his gymnastics class at 3:15. The class lasts $1\frac{1}{2}$ hours. What time is class over?

    a) 4:45   b) 4:30   c) 4:00   d) 3:45

This question required that the children first translate the symbol 1/2 into minutes, then add 1 whole hour, and 1/2 of an hour in minutes, to the number 3:15 (i.e., 3:15 + 1 = 4:15, and 4:15 + 0.30 = 4:45). The children's concept of a whole number got in their way when they had to figure out that a whole hour equaled 60 minutes (not 100), and that half an hour therefore equaled 30 minutes. The correct answer (option a), was *not* selected only by 3 Experimental, 6 C_1, and 12 C_2 children. Table 27 summarizes the total incorrect answers in each class for the above five most difficult questions in the school math test.

Summary of the results from the curriculum referenced math test. In this section we have seen how much better the experimental children did on this whole conventional school test than those from the other two control classes (i.e., the experimental's average of incorrect answers per child was 5.06, as compared with 6.27, and 9.45 in control class 1 and 2, respectively). Moreover, in the experimental class, only 29% of the average incorrect answers per child in the whole test (40 questions) were incorrect answers about rational-number concepts (i.e., an average proportion of 1.60 incorrect per child in fractions, to 5.06 incorrect per child on the whole test). But in both C_1 and C_2, approximately 50% of the incorrect answers per child were in fact about rational-number concepts. Furthermore, in giving specific attention to the subset of the five most difficult questions (Questions 19, 20, 21, 25, and 31), we have seen even more dramatic

Table 27.   A Summary of the Total Incorrect Answers in each Class for the Five most Difficult Items from the School Math Test.

Class:	Ques. 19 Incorrect per Class	Ques. 20 Incorrect per Class	Ques. 21 Incorrect per Class	Ques. 25 Incorrect per Class	Ques. 31 Incorrect per Class	Total of Incorrect Answers per Class
Experimental class	3 children	5 children	6 children	1 child	3 children	18 incorrect ans. an average of 1.05 per child
Control class 1	9 children	8 children	9 children	4 children	6 children	36 incorrect ans. an average of 2.01 per child
Control class 2	10 children	11 children	12 children	10 children	12 children	56 incorrect ans. an average of 3.50 per child

differences between the experimental and the control children: a total of only 18 incorrect answers in the experimental class, but a total of 36 in C_1 and 56 in C_2.

On the whole, these results are very important to this study, because the experimental children did not spend more time than the others in being directly and formally instructed on how to perform such algorithms as those needed for solving Questions 20 and 21. They had not been given more formal instruction than the other children in the control classes on fractions or mixed fractions ordering and equivalence, or the algorithms involved. But they did do better on this test, and especially on the subset of the most difficult questions on fractions. My reasoning for these results, as well as my discussion of the results of the other posttests, will be presented in Chapter IV.

2.3. DEBBIE'S RESULTS FROM THE EVALUATION

In this section I shall briefly summarize some of Debbie's scores from the posttests. A detailed description of these tests, their objectives, purposes, and content was provided to the reader in the previous sections of Chapter III as well as in Chapter I. For this reason, the results will be presented without task analyses or deep interpretations. The purpose of this section is to highlight Debbie's exceptional progress between January (pretests) and June (posttests), and to compare her progress with that of the other children. In subsection 2.3.1., I compare Debbie's scores on the Rational-Number pencil-and-paper test with those of her peers; in subsection 2.3.2., I do the same with her scores on the school's math test; in subsection 2.3.3., with her answers in the written Logo test; and finally, in subsection 2.3.4., with her accomplishment on the Logo computer tasks. The results from Debbie's pre- and post- "What Is A Fraction?" interviews are not provided here; many of them were described in Debbie's Case (Chapter II). A further analysis of Debbie's interviews, and how the data from the interviews relates to her processes and progress during ISDP is documented and described on a video entitled, "The Story of Debbie: A Case Study of a Young Software Designer" (Harel & Stein, 1989).

2.3.1. The Results from Debbie's Rational-Number Test

Debbie's score on the Fractions pretests on translations among representations was 50% correct. This was a typical score for this pretest among the tested fourth-graders from the medium-math group (i.e., Debbie's math-group); the experimental medium-math group's average percentage of correct answers on this pretest was 51%; it was 51% for the medium-math children from C_1, and 46% for the medium-math children from C_2. Most of the children in this study, as well as the children from the RN Project (Behr et al., 1983; Lesh et al., 1983) had many difficulties with the questions that required translations from pictures to symbols, symbols to pictures, and pictures to words. Debbie's posttest scores show that she overcame many of these difficulties. Debbie's score on this Rational-Number posttest was 84% correct. This was a very high score compared with those of the other children in her math group, and even compared with most children of the high-math group. The average posttest score of the experimental's medium-math group was 71% correct; the average score of C_1 was 62%, with 59% correct for C_2. Debbie's posttest score was not only much higher than those of her medium-math peers, but also higher than the average score of the children in the high-math group. In the posttest, the experimental high-math children's average score was 82%; the high-math of C_1 scored an average of 78% correct, and the high-math children from C_2, and average of 55% correct. Figure 19 compares Debbie's pre- and posttest scores with those of her 15 peers from her medium-math group. Figure 20 compares Debbie's pre- and posttest scores with those of the 21 children from the high-math group.

Figure 19 and 20 demonstrate Debbie's exceptional progress in the period of time between the pre- and posttests. Before the project started, Debbie was on the average level of the medium-math children (50%); however, after the project ended, Debbie's answers were far better than those of the children in the medium-math group. The average of percentages of correct answers for the whole medium-math group taken together (i.e., the children from experimental, C_1, and C_2 classes taken together), was 64%, while Debbie's was 84% correct.

Moreover, the comparison between Debbie's pretest score and those of the high-math children shows that, before the project started, Debbie scored quite a bit lower than the high-math children from the three classes (50% for Debbie, as opposed to 60% for all the high-math children taken together); in the posttest, however, we saw that she progressed much more than many other children of the high-math group. She scored 84% correct, whereas the high-math experimental children scored an average of 82%, and the three classes' high-math children, taken together, an average of 71% correct.

2.3.2. The Results from Debbie's Curriculum Referenced Test, Math Level-4

Debbie answered only two questions incorrectly out of the 40 given to the children in this test. One of her wrong answers was on Question 21 (see Section 2.2.2 in this chapter). Table 28 compares Debbie's answers on the most difficult subset of questions (about fractions) in this test.

Debbie was one of the six children in the experimental class who answered Question 21 incorrectly. However, the other questions that posed great difficulty to many children from the medium-math group were not difficult for Debbie, and she answered them correctly.

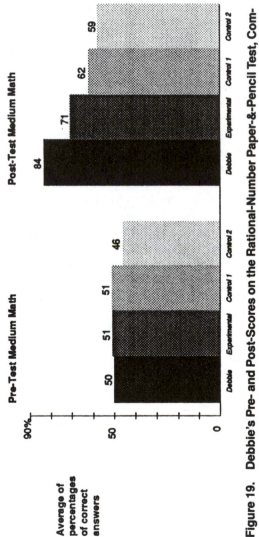

Figure 19.   Debbie's Pre- and Post-Scores on the Rational-Number Paper-&-Pencil Test, Compared with those of her Peers from the Medium-Math Group.

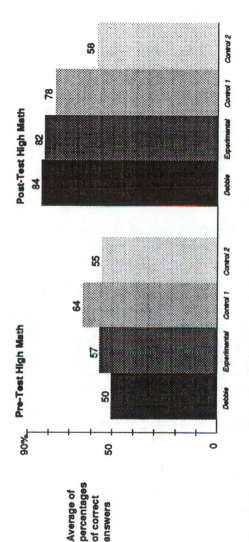

Figure 20. Debbie's Pre- and Post-Scores on the Rational-Number Paper-&-Pencil Test, Compared with those of Students from the High-Math Group.

Table 28.   Comparing Debbie's Incorrect Answers on the Five Most Difficult Items on the School Test with those of the Children from the Three Classes.

Class:	Ques. 19 Incorrect per Class	Ques. 20 Incorrect per Class	Ques. 21 Incorrect per Class	Ques. 25 Incorrect per Class	Ques. 31 Incorrect per Class
Debbie	(+)	(+)	(−)	(+)	(+)
Experimental class	3 children	5 children	6 children•	1 child	3 children
Control class 1	9 children	8 children	9 children	4 children	6 children
Control class 2	10 children	11 children	12 children	10 children	12 children

2.3.3. The Results from Debbie's Logo Pencil-and-Paper Test

In *Question 1* of this test, the children were asked to list all the Logo instructions and commands they knew, to define them, and to give examples of how they were used in Logo programming. In the pretest, Debbie listed only 9 Logo commands and did not define exactly what they did, whereas in the posttest she listed 29. In the posttest, Debbie correctly abbreviated all the 29 commands she listed. Also, out of these 29 commands, she gave good examples for 27 of them, and for 26 of them she gave excellent and accurate descriptions for what they did and how they should be used in Logo programming. In short, for her math level, she performed extremely well on this task.

Table 29 compares Debbie with the high-, low, and medium-math children from the three classes, on the average number of commands listed by each child in the posttest.

In *Question 2,* the children were asked to classify their lists of Logo commands and instructions. In the pretest, Debbie did not list any group (her page in

Table 29.   The Number of Logo Commands and Instructions that Were Listed by All Children and by Debbie in the Logo Post-Test.

	EXPER.	CTR 1	CTR 2	DEBBIE
HI	32	16	8	
MD	24	9	8	29
LO	21	11	7	

this pretest shows that she listed one arbitrary group which she classified as "Logo things," but she erased it and wrote "I don't know" next to it). In the posttest, Debbie created only two groups; however, both of her groups were mutually exclusive, and of the abstract kind; whereas no one in C_2 (among the medium-math children) created abstract groups, and only two children in C_1 did so (each of these two children created one "abstract" and one "loose" group). The two groups that Debbie created in the posttest were the following:

Group number 1. Title: "'Things that Erase.' Members: "PE, DEL, BACKSPACE."

Group number 2. Title: "Things that go to another page (or connect pages together)." Members: "GETTOOLS, GETPAGE, ESC (goes to content."

Table 30 summarizes the results on Debbie's ability in this nonconcrete classification task, and how she compares with her peers from the medium-math group.

In *Question 3,* the children were asked to execute a given linear Logo code given to them on paper. Table 31 shows that Debbie (Subject 5 in the Exp. Med.) executed this code accurately, found the three squares, and used a consistent unit and correct scaling (4:2:1). Her handwritten scribbles on this page indicate that she tried it three times and did not give up after she had made mistakes the first time; she checked and rechecked her drawing until she was sure she had found the right answer, which she finally did.

In *Question 4,* the children were asked to simplify (or optimize) the code given to them in Question 3. All the medium-math children from the experimental class, and Debbie among them, managed to reach Level 3, which was a high level of modularization (i.e., using procedures, subprocedures, a variable for the square's size, and REPEATs). Table 32 shows that not one of the medium-math children from C_1 or C_2 reached that level of sophistication.

In *Question 5,* the children were asked how many inputs certain basic Logo commands took (i.e., FD, BK, LT, SETPOS, REPEAT HOME, CG, and SETC). In the

Table 30. Debbie's Results from the Logo Classification Task in Relation to her Peers.

	EXPERIMEN MEDIUM	CONTROL 1 MEDIUM	CONTROL 2 MEDIUM
NO. OF GRPS PER CHILD	5, 5, 4, 3, 2 Debbie 2 grp.	3, 2, 1, 1, 0, 0	4, 1, 1, 0, 0
Abstract vs. "loose"	Debbie 2 Abs. groups.	2 children each created 1 Abst.	No abst. grps in all children.

Table 31.   Debbie's Ability to Execute a Logo Code on Paper, Compared to the Ability of her Peers.

Subject	Number of Squares in Final Picture						Number of Trials of Drawing the Picture						Correct Scale & Consistent Unit					
	S1	S2	S3	S4	S5	S6	S1	S2	S3	S4	S5	S6	S1	S2	S3	S4	S5	S6
Exp. Med.	3	3	3	3	3^z	x	2	1	1	3^z	3	x	y	y	y	y	y^z	x
Cot1 Med.	0	3	2	1	3	1	1	1	1	1	1	1	n	n	n	n	y	n

pretest, Debbie did not have a clear concept of inputs, what they meant, or how many each of the above Logo commands took. She answered 5 subquestions incorrectly in the pretests. She wrote that FD took "A lot of inputs," and wrote the same for BK. She wrote that REPEAT took "1 input," and gave as an example "Repeat 10[etc.]." She wrote that LT took "2 inputs," and gave an example "LT 45," than answered "I don't know" beside the subquestion about SETPOSITION. At the bottom of the page in the pretest (under Question 5) she wrote: "I can't answer it. I'm not so sure!" Her answers were typical; most children, from all the three classes and math groups, were very confused during that time about this item of the pretest, and many of them wrote "I don't know."

In the posttest, however, Debbie answered all of these questions correctly, and scored 100%. Table 33 compares Debbie's success in answering this question with that of the medium- and high-math children from the three classes. Debbie scored much higher than her peers from the medium-math group, was at the level of most of the experimental high-math children, and definitely superior to all the control children from the medium- and high-math groups.

In *Question 6,* the children were asked to transform three simple Logo procedures: to transform a given procedure for a circle into one for a larger circle, to

Table 32.   The Number of Children, in each Class and Math Group, that Reached Level 3 of Optimization in Question 4.

	Simplify Level 3		
	Exp.	Cot.1	Cot.2
Hi	7/8	1/7	0/6
Med	5/5	0/6	0/5
Lo	1/4	0/5	0/5

Table 33.   Results from Question 5 about Understanding Inputs.

	Med-math	Hi-math	DEBBIE
Experimen.	67.5%	94.5%	100%
Control 1	37.7%	78.3%	
Control 2	7.5%	30.7%	

change a given circle to half-circle, and to transform a square into a rectangle. This question was not given to the children in the pretest. In the posttest Debbie was able to create all the three required transformations. No control children from the medium-math group were able to transform a circle into half-circle or a square into a rectangle. Table 34 summarizes these results.

2.3.4. Results from Debbie's Logo Computer Test

Debbie accomplished the Logo computer task in both the pre- and the posttests. In both cases she scored higher than many of her peers from the medium-math group. However, the posttest was more difficult than the pretest, and many children from the medium-math were not able to perform all the debugging task or the optimization requirements. In the posttest Debbie, like all the members of her class, found all the bugs rather quickly and optimized the procedure according to all the requirements. No one from C_2, and only two children from the medium-math group of C_1, were able to locate all the bugs on paper and in the computer program, and to fix the program. No medium-math child in C_1 or C_2 reached Level 3 of optimization of the given code on the computer, and no medium-math control children knew how to change the colors (subtask 5) or how to use variables in this context.

Table 34.   The Three Black Sots Represent Debbie's Success in the Three Transformations in Question 6.

	Circ to Bigger Circ			Circ to Half-Circ			Square to Rectangle		
	Exp.	Cot.1	Cot.2	Exp.	Cot.1	Cot.2	Exp.	Cot.1	Cot.2
Hi	8/8	5/7	0/6	7/8	5/7	0/6	7/8	2/7	0/6
Med	3/5^z	2/6	0/5	4/5^z	0/6	0/5	4/5^z	0/6	0/5

2.3.5. Summary of Debbie's Results from the Evaluation

The preceding results demonstrate Debbie's exceptional progress in learning fractions and Logo through ISDP. The pretest scores indicate that Debbie's abilities in Logo and Fractions before the project began were average or low (before the project started she was one of the lowest pupils in her medium-math group); however, her scores at the end of the year after the project ended (in the posttests), were of a high-math child, often at the top 10th percentile of all the 51 tested children. In the posttests, as we have just seen, she constantly scored higher than all the medium- or low-level children in the experimental and control classes.

These findings are particularly interesting because, before the project started, Debbie had been far less proficient in her math than in her writing skills. After the project ended, Debbie continued to progress in her acquisition of high math skills as well. Such quantitative findings must be considered in relation to the many qualitative aspects of Debbie's learning, thinking, and development during the project, which have been described in detail in Chapter II. Further interpretations of these findings are presented in Chapter IV as well as in Harel and Papert (1990).

Chapter IV

Discussion of Conclusions

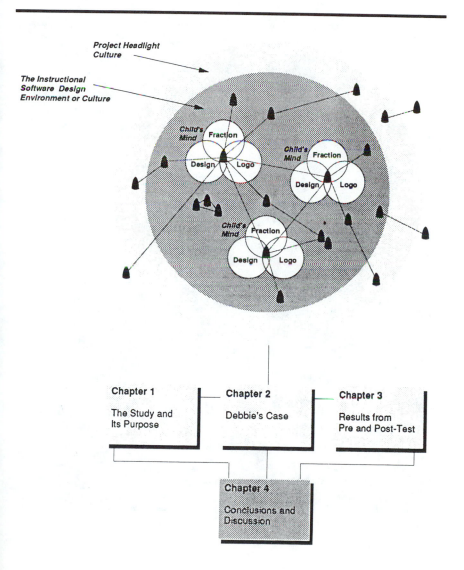

(Stephen Sherman Photography)

CHILDREN DESIGNERS: WHAT WAS ACCOMPLISHED?

The overall goal of this study was to implement, assess, and describe an experiment called the Instructional Software Design Project. In the first chapter of this book, I analyzed the new conditions for learning fractions, Logo programming, metacognitive skills, and software design which were explored in ISDP, and indicated that this in-depth study had several goals. A review of these goals follows.

The two general theoretical goals were to construct a *holistic picture* by using Papert's theories (e.g., 1980, 1986) and Perkins' theories (e.g., 1986) as well as Vygotskian's and Piagetian's perspectives. I asked what it meant for a child to learn and be involved in an open-ended, complex, and unusually long problem-solving process related to the learning of mathematics, designing, and computer programming I used instructional software design as a *vehicle* for analyzing (a) a child's *total learning* in this "extreme" environment and over an extended period of time; (b) an activity involving several theoretical perspectives and many variables (many which could be considered ill defined); and (c) how and what students learned through their complex solution processes.

Using ISDP as a model, I wanted to experiment with one prototypical activity in order to understand how students can learn several topics or subject matters at the same time, and to consider how the learning of one domain (or set of skills) can contribute to the learning of another. I asked, for example, what major changes can ISDP offer to educational practice? I also considered whether it reveals any information that might lead to changes in the way fractions and Logo are now being taught and learned in elementary schools.

In addition, my study had specific objectives based on the above theoretical goals and on previous research in the relevant fields. First, I wanted to investigate the ways this project enhanced students' learning and understanding of basic concepts of Logo programming such as procedures or modularity, variables or inputs, repeat or recursion, conditionals, and other Logo commands and operations. I aimed at investigating the students' ability to learn Logo through the project, their ability to generate, debug, manipulate, and modify codes, written by themselves or by other people. But, I was *not* interested in investigating the learning of Logo for the sake of learning Logo as an isolated piece of knowledge;

neither was I interested in a microcausal investigation of which instructional method would result in the transfer of specific Logo skills into other specific domains. Instead, I used Logo as a tool for *reformulating and manipulating other kinds of knowledge* (e.g. instructional design, software production, or rational-number representations), assessed the learning of Logo as *one aspect* in the child's whole learning experience, and investigated whether or not students who learned programming by designing and programming instructional software for other would become better programmers than those who, meanwhile, were learning programming in more limited situations (such as the ones reported in existing literature).

In addition, I assessed the students' knowledge of fractions. The focus was on students' understanding of the rational-number representational system, and their ability to translate and combine representations. By giving specific attention to rational-number representations, I investigated whether or not the students' designing and programming representations of fractions, and their creating of graphical displays for equivalence and operations of rational numbers, influenced their thinking and learning about representations of fractions and the relationships between them. I studied in what ways students' experiences of representing and explaining fractions to other students helped them overcome their own difficulties in understanding fractional representations—a problem that had been reported in other studies.

With this in mind, I also looked at the ways the project enhanced students' metacognition: their cognitive awareness (i.e., students' thinking about their own thinking), their cognitive control (i.e., planning, reflecting, self-management, and thinking about these cognitive processes), and their metaconceptual thinking (i.e., students' thinking about their own knowledge and understanding of concepts).

I had several methodological goals as well. They were related to data collection and analysis and consisted in conducting several kinds of investigations:

- Gathering daily data on the microgenetic process of an individual creating an interactive teaching device, that is, investigation on an *individual level*.
- Gathering data on the process of the whole class participating in this project, that is, investigation on a *classroom or "cultural" level*.
- Conducting a *comparative evaluation* with the experimental class and two other control classes, and contrasting the achievements of the participating students with those of nonparticipating students. The results of the evaluation were needed for investigating the progress of each individual child and the experimental class as a whole (see Figures 2, 4, 23, 24, and 25 in Chapter I for a summary of this study's goals and objectives, experimental design, and procedure).

In the second chapter of this book (Debbie's Case), I accomplished many of the abovementioned goals by analyzing Debbie's 70-hour-long problem-solving enterprise, and describing the day-by-day learning and cognitive processes involved as Debbie and her peers combined their learning of fractions and Logo programming. We realized how Debbie's knowledge was acquired through the planning, designing, programming, and using her own piece of software. In the third chapter, I showed the ways in which the students involved in the project became superior in their mathematical knowledge and programming expertise to students from two classes, who learned fractions and Logo by methods other than ISDP.

The case study and the results from the evaluation, taken together, demonstrated that fourth-grade students, placed beside one another to work on a common software-design project over a long period of time, were strongly motivated and fully in charge of their own learning. They also established sequences of learning and development that were an interesting mixture of Piagetian and Vygotskian processes and Papert's and Perkins's theories of knowledge construction and learning. The project resulted in different students' establishing different stage sequences in organizing and implementing their long-term projects. The use of Logo to design instructional software was an unusually effective way of learning Logo programming. The learning of fractions through the use of Logo, through teaching and explaining, and through designing instructional software on fractions involved students in creating and translating multiple representations for fractions and enhanced their mathematical understanding of what fractions are. The students' ongoing work during the project also seemed to enhance their metacognitive awareness and cognitive control strategies.

But why did they learn? The simplest description of the ISDP experiment reads like a "treatment" type of experiment: these subjects did something particular (made instructional software) for so many hours (close to 70 hours of work). In fact, because there were too many particulars involved, the situation is vastly more complex than anything that could be described as "changing one variable while keeping everything else constant." To make their pieces of software, the students used particular computers (IBM PCjrs) and a particular programming language (LogoWriter). The project included focus sessions where the specific content of fractions was discussed in a particular way—informally, and compared with school classes, briefly. The project took place in a particular part of the school where there is a particular "computer culture." And during the ISDP, the culture developed further in a particular way, with particular customs of interaction, attention, mutual help, secrecy, humor, and so on. The students and their teacher were aware of having a unique relationship with the experimental staff. They reacted in particular ways to the presence of video cameras, question-askers, and note-takers.

One can formulate innumerable conjectures about the "real" source of their learning about fractions. Did the simple fact of spending some seventy hours programming representations in Logo contribute? Was the "moral climate" in the project largely responsible? Or was the fact that the teacher felt she was part of something important significant? Some such conjectures, or aspects of such conjectures, we can, and do, try to check by studying control groups. But there are far too many!

What can be said here with some certainty is that we created a *total learning environment* in which some impressive learning took place. Teasing out the contributions of particular aspects of the environment is not a reasonable goal for any single well-defined experiment. Understanding will come only through the process of accumulation of many projects and a great deal of theory building (which is happening since this study was completed; e.g., Kafai & Harel, 1990, 1991). What I can do here is to share intuitions and, as part of the larger scientific enterprise, formulate and discuss some conjectures concerning these intuitions (many of these conjectures and intuitions were developed through discussions and re-analysis of the data with Seymour Papert; e.g., Harel & Papert, 1990).

I shall speculate that improvement in performance might be affected by factors related to the *affective side* of cognition and learning; to the children's process of *personal appropriation* of knowledge; to the children's use of *Logo-Writer,* to the children's constructivist involvement with a deep structure of fractions knowledge—namely *construction of multiple representations;* to the "*integrated-learning*" principle; to the "*learning by teaching*" principle; to the *power of design* as a learning activity. However, the main point I would like to make here is that each one of those conjectures, when considered alone, would give only *partial* information about the "why." Only by considering them together, and by speculating about their interrelationships, can we take a step towards understanding the holistic character of Constructionism in general, and of ISDP in particular.

Structure of this chapter. Eight major conclusions are presented in this chapter. Each conclusion is presented first, followed by a description of its evidence, meanings, and implications for research and educational practice.

In Conclusions 1 through 6, I will highlight the ways in which the study did or did not succeeded with respect to its major purposes, goals, and the interpretations of its data. Several questions for further research are also discussed in this context. What microgenetic phenomena could be further investigated in such an extreme leaning environment? What are the necessary conditions under which this project could be implemented? What other subjects could be learned by elementary-school students through the method of instructional software design?

The seventh conclusion summarizes the ways in which video was used as a research tool in this context, and the advantages of using video for this type of investigation.

Finally, in the eighth conclusion, I discuss what design tools or computer technologies could be further developed and used in learning processes similar to ISDP.

Conclusion 1. Growth and development through design.

A group of fourth-grade students, working side-by-side in front of computers over a 4-month period, were involved in a software design project in view of designing and using their individual software for teaching fractions to younger students. They were found to be strongly motivated and fully in charge of their own learning; they appeared to establish sequences of learning and development that were an interesting mixture of Piagetian and Vygotskian processes; and they bore out Papert's and Perkins's theories of knowledge construction and learning. Furthermore, the students treated their knowledge in a functional manner, designed and built meaningful products, and established deep relationships with the objects and ideas involved.

The first purpose of this study was to 'construct a picture' of what it meant to a fourth-grade child to learn and be involved in an open-ended, complex, and unusually long problem-solving process related to design, the learning of mathematics, and computer programming. ISDP proved to be a useful and informative vehicle for constructing this picture. Chapter III provided us with several straightforward results on what the project meant for students: becoming better programmers, growing better at understanding rational-number concepts and their representations, and even being more successful in the school-like tests. Chapter II provided us with a very detailed analysis of one experimental girl, Debbie and the impact of her being involved in this project. Through the analysis of Debbie's Case we examined many of the *reasons* that led to the results presented in Chapter III. We saw that, in fact, the project meant much more to the students than being successful in tests, acquiring more information of various kinds, or better understanding the related topics. It meant *being in charge of their own learning and enjoying their learning;* it also meant being productive, creative, and self-motivated. No one instructed them on what to do or how to do it. For four months, almost every single day, they worked hard on their products and invested a great deal of time and thought in their planning, replanning, designing, implementing, programming, and revising of an entity that would not be graded or evaluated in a conventional way. The rewards they received were their own enjoyment and satisfaction during the various phases of production, and the best evidence for this was their not wanting to cease working on it.

Changes in self-esteem and attitudes towards learning mathematics. One aspect of learning that was highlighted during the project was the impact of ISDP on students' *self-esteem and their attitude toward school learning in general.* Debbie's personality, for example, and her particular attitude towards school learning and socializing, have been discussed in detail in Chapter II. Debbie was a model case for an average inner-city public school fourth grader: a young black girl, very reserved and somewhat unhappy, who seemed wary of trying anything new. She was not academically or socially successful, but through the project she learned to be independent and was "discovered" by her peers and teachers, who often gave her positive comments about her work. Debbie grew to feel better about herself, opened up, and interacted more freely with the people around her.

The effects of affect on cognitive growth. From certain points of view one could see a paradox in the results obtained here. Here are a few example from the ISDP students' test scores: Debbie scored 51% correct on the fractions pretest and 84% on the post (33% difference); Casey scored 55% on pre and 83% on post (28% difference); Rachel, 55% on pre and 87% on post (32% difference); or Oai, 55% on pre and 97% on post (42% difference). Debbie's Oai's, Casey's, and other children's ability to work with fractions improved considerably from working on a project that was entirely self-directed, gave them no "feedback" in the form of marking responses right or wrong, and offered little guidance or information about fractions.

The "obvious" explanation, which surely has more than a little truth, is that the students developed a better attitude towards fractions, and perhaps even came to *like* fractions. We recall that Debbie was initially reluctant to have anything to do with fractions or software design but ended up with enthusiastic missionary zeal. One does not need any complex theory of affectivity to conjecture that she might therefore be more likely to engage her mind with fractions in the regular math class, where she would learn more about what she wanted to teach, and that, in test situations, she would receive better scores.

Pursuing the idea that Debbie changed her "relationship with fractions" leads to an area where the line between the affective and the cognitive becomes hard to maintain. We see something happening that is analogous to the development of a greater intimacy in relationships with people. Debbie becomes willing to take more risks, to allow herself to be more vulnerable in her dealings with fractions. As long as fractions-knowledge was the teacher's knowledge regurgitated, she was emotionally safe. In other words, the risk of poor grades is less threatening than the risk of exposing one's own ideas.

Papert's view of people like Debbie is strongly colored by the sense that, when they allow themselves to tap into personal knowledge, they allow knowledge about fractions to become connected with the personal sides of themselves. The conjecture is that improvement in performance is related to the extent to which the students respond to a problem about fractions by "digging around" in *their own* stocks of knowledge as opposed to trying to follow set procedures. This point could be formulated in Scribner's (1984) language by saying that their thinking about fractions shifts from *scholastic* intelligence, characterized by rigid, inflexible, externally imposed methods, to *practical* intelligence, characterized by the use of multiple, flexible, and personal methods.

Developing an ability for "breaking away." For these students, the project also meant *breaking away* from simplistic thinking and rigidity, becoming aware of several aspects of a situation simultaneously, learning to perceive and generate complexities, and being able to think more abstractly about fractions, Logo, and design. Debbie was an interesting case in this context, especially in the light of Piaget's theories on constructivism and on the underlying patterns of thought during the different stages of cognitive development. In her processes of thinking, designing, programming, and learning throughout the project, Debbie moved according to Piaget's progression scheme (although only *local aspects* of the Piagetian progression were studied here); furthermore, within each step or stage of her software design we saw a recapitulation of the Piagetian developmental stages. In her thinking and actions during the project, Debbie moved back and forth between being attentive to limited and static amounts of information and considering several aspects of a situation simultaneously; from concrete preoperational thought to more formal thought; from rigid thinking that focused on one dimension of a programming problem to more fluent and dynamic thinking related to several dimensions of her computer programs. Moreover, Debbie, who began by constructing very simple plans, designs, and screens, was later able to create more complex ones, moving back and forth between simplicity and complexity. In general, Debbie (like her other classmates) learned to free herself from rigidity and acquired more flexibility during ISDP.

Integration of constructivist and social visions in children's ways of working. Both Vygotsky's and Piaget's views on learning and intelligence were emphasized and combined in this study. Debbie's learning, for example, was interpreted as a clear combination of both perspectives. In several situations she was shown to be strong case for constructivist learning (e.g., the House Scene, or her writing of several superprocedures for the same purpose), and at the same time she demonstrated social-cultural learning (e.g., the design of her Introduction screen, many of her instructional statements, the Sesame Street screen, or her use of the Wait.For.User Logo procedure in her program). By studying Debbie's learning and cognitive development as a *total activity,* we realized that some aspects of her learning were influenced by the "scaffolding" of a guiding adult (e.g., imitating the teacher's approach in her screen about Thirds), a helpful peer (e.g., learning how to create a triangle in Logo), or by a probing researcher (e.g., understanding that the "empty" unshaded parts of divided shapes were also fractions). Those situations were interpreted according to Vygotsky's perspective:

> Every function in the child's cultural development appears twice, on two levels. First on the social, and later on the psychological level; first *between* people [as an] *intrapsychological* category, and then *inside* the child, [as an] *interpsychological* category. (Vygotsky, 1978, p. 57)

Other aspects of Debbie's learning were interpreted as a result of her own interaction with the specific learning tools and of her own thoughts and resulted in various spontaneous inventions (e.g., rhyming procedure names, or attaching symbols to a real-life fractional representation) and spontaneous constructions (e.g., discovering that she could connect procedures in a superprocedure only after she had spent a whole month constructing five separate ones). These situations were interpreted through Piaget's perspective of how a child must invent and reinvent the basic concepts and logical-thought forms that constitute his or her intelligence, then develop cognitively through being involved in spontaneous constructions and inventions of ideas for himself or herself:

> The development of intelligence itself—what the child learns by himself, what none can teach him and he must discover alone . . . it is precisely this spontaneous development which forms the obvious and necessary conditions for the school development. (Piaget, 1973, pp. 2–4)

These two different aspects of learning (i.e., imitating as opposed to inventing, or being guided by an adult as opposed to being guided by her own ideas), created an interesting *learning pattern* that repeated itself in Debbie's work, as well as in those of the other experimental students, throughout the project.

The role of objects-to-think-with. Papert's perspective on the important role of self-constructed, interactive objects in students' learning, thinking, and socializing (Papert, 1980; Turkle & Papert 1990) was emphasized throughout. In Debbie's case, for example, the role of her software construction in Logo was crucial to her change of attitude towards learning, her emerging self-esteem, her developing expertise in Logo, and her better understanding of fractional representations.

Building knowledge through design. Perkins' ideas of treating knowledge as design, or knowledge as an object whose meaning students construct through design, were emphasized throughout and were integral to this study. The processes of students' producing complex products, learning about large meaningful chunks of information through building instructional systems, identifying the purposes and structure of each component in that system, and creating interrelationships between components—processes that rarely exist in conventional education—had a crucial role in students' ability to establish strong relational networks between concepts, and to make their pieces of knowledge highly connected to each other. We examined how Debbie, for example, connected and related her knowledge of Logo to her knowledge of fractions, and how, during May and June, she also updated her "old" Logo knowledge with the "new" (updating and revising the existing parts of her program and connecting these to her new parts). Knowledge was manipulated and treated as functional, and as Perkins believes:

Knowledge should be seen and treated as functional, as something that gets put to use much as a screwdriver or a hammer. To do justice to knowledge and to the learner, we have to keep the learner doing something with the knowledge gained. . . *Knowledge as design holds that all knowledge has a tool-like character . . . some knowledge is explicitly tool-like, designed to manipulate other knowledge and facilitate thinking and problem solving activities of various sorts.* (Perkins, 1986, pp. 215–216, emphasis added)

Role of language and social communication. We examined the important role of language (natural language as well as the Logo language) in the students' processes of learning. We saw this in Debbie's writing and planning, in the way she sometimes "talked to" the Designer's Notebook (e.g., after she wrote her plans and drew her designs, she often seemed to be addressing her notebook directly: *"I hope this is clear. Bye now, and see you tomorrow!"*); or in her conversations with herself as she typed on the computer keyboard while talking to the computer (e.g., *"Why did you do it to me?!, Ah . . . I know there's a bracket missing there . . ."*), or in her explanations and comments to others (e.g., *"All these shapes are one half!"* or *"I am trying to say that you can use fractions almost every day of your life!"* or, *"Naomi, do you think these colors are o.k.?"*).

Because she was involved in thinking about teaching and explaining, and because she was thinking about *communicating knowledge to other students* through the use of language and via her software, she developed cognitively during the project as well. The path from the objects involved (i.e., the computer and the software or the notebook) to Debbie, and from Debbie to these objects, was one of language, either natural speech or Logo. Language was used intensively in this context: in students' teaching and explaining about fractions, in their planning and reflecting in writing, in their discussion of designs and screens with their peers, in their talking about Logo, and so on. This intensive use of language facilitated in many ways their ability to gain control over their actions and processes. As Vygotsky believes, speech acts as an organizer, unifier, and integrator of many disparate aspects of student's behavior, such as perception, memory, and problem solving. Words provide learners with ways to become more efficient in their adaptive and problem-solving efforts (Vygotsky, 1978, Chapter 4).

Complex relations among 17 minds. In Debbie's Case we also examined some of the complex relations between the 17 minds involved in the same job: how the students worked together, and how they influenced each other or resisted influence. We also examined the relationships between the internal and external knowledge of each child, and between all the experimental students and the other people, products, and knowledge which formed their "culture." The culture created within ISDP enhanced interactions, connections, reciprocal relations

with many of the following: *objects* such as computers, computer tools, Designer's Notebooks; *people* such as other students, the teacher, the researcher and
members of the MIT staff; and the *knowledge* of fractions, Logo, and design
which the students could observe and discuss by walking around and looking at
the various computers or plans and designs in the Notebooks. (Further analyses
and discussion of these issues are the focus of our current ISDP studies. See
Kafai & Harel, 1990, 1991a, 1991b.)

Exceptional progress. Finally, the ISDP students' exceptional progress in
learning fractions and Logo through the project was emphasized in Chapter III.
Debbie's pretest scores, for example, indicated that her abilities in Logo and
Fractions before the project began were average or low (she was a member of the
medium-math group, and was one of the low pupils in that group); however, her
scores at the end of the year (in the posttests) were of a high-math child, often at
the top 10 percentile of all the 51 tested students. In the posttests she consistently
scored higher than all the medium- or low-level students in the three classes. It
seems that *all* that was discussed above should be considered equally as important factors when we examine the results from the posttests or assess what the
project meant for Debbie, or for all the students in the ISDP class.

Conclusion 2. Computer programming as a learning power.

**The student's intensive and meaningful use of the Logo programming lan-
guage to design instructional software on fractions, over a long period of
time, was an unusually effective way to learn Logo programming concepts
and skills.**

A unique approach for learning programming. The "Software-Design-
Logo" learning approach that was implemented in this study was strongly inspired by and very similar in nature to Papert's approach to programming (e.g.,
1980, 1986), and radically different from the typical "Logo Course" or "Logo
Curriculum" approaches, which are predominantly used in schools today and in
Logo research over the last decade (e.g., Pea & Sheingold, 1987; Soloway,
1984; Carver, 1987; Perkins & Martin, 1985; Heller, 1986).

Software-Design-Logo took Papert's ideas one step further. It consisted in that
students use Logo for the purpose of designing and programming instructional
software. It involved students in programming something for others rather than
just for themselves, which seemed to enhance students' ability to think about a
target audience and to construct a program that would work for a younger pupil.
The usual Headlight Integrated-Logo projects lasted from a few days to three
weeks, whereas the Software-Design-Logo Project lasted four moths. We saw
that the *length, structure, and complexity* of the project enhanced the students'
learning of Logo, as well as their revisions, debugging, and maintenance of their
programs. In addition, the students in Software-Design-Logo had their minds on

other issues besides "a program that works." They worked on their project while thinking about teaching other pupils, about screen designs, about interactivity and feedbacks—much like professional software designers.

If knowing programming means understanding basic concepts such as procedures, variables, functions, conditionals, and transformations, then the students' software products, and the results presented in Chapter III, prove that the experimental students learned how to program. They demonstrated expertise in generating and interpreting both their own or someone else's code. Debbie's software provided us with an example of how she was able to generate a great amount of code in an open-ended way during her software production; but we also saw how she was able to do so very efficiently and precisely, following the predefined constraints and requirements of the Logo posttests. Through the Software-Design-Logo approach students also experienced a great variety of debugging situations; it seemed that they learned several general ideas about debugging. This was shown in the posttests by the ISDP students' superiority over the control students in their debugging strategies and achievements.

There is a difference between ISDP and a typical Logo curriculum. The great differences between the experimental class and control class 2 had been predicted from the beginning. The students from control class 2 learned programming once a week in the school's computer lab and were *not* involved in large-scale, meaningful, or complex programming projects; in the 5-month period between the pre- and posttests, these students programmed for a total of approximately 23 hours. It was therefore assumed that they had not developed understanding or expertise in programming as well as the experimental students, who had spent a total of 70 hours programming. Still, it was important to compare these two classes, since many studies in the Logo field are conducted with students of the "control class 2 type." Such studies have influenced many of the research and development projects used today and have determined the instructional strategies to be used in classrooms. These studies often link the students' low performances in Logo with the fact that they have not been taught Logo properly, if at all; they also recommend that students be explicitly taught what they should understand about programming concepts and instructed how best to approach different programming problems.

Many "Logo-programming courses" have been developed, and many Logo exercises and worksheets created, in view of an *isolated* "Logo curriculum" to be used in a class (such as control class 2). But many of these, in fact, miss the purposes and the major ideas rooted in Logo (or programming in general). They also reduce the creative learning possibilities offered to young students through Logo programming, and minimize the use of Logo as a thinking and learning tool, or as a "knowledge reformulation tool" (Papert, 1980) to be integrated into the learning of other subjects.

Why were there differences (in Logo learning) among the three classes? Although the differences between control class 2 and the experimental class had been expected from the start, this was not the case with control class 1 and the experimental class. Since both classes were part of Project Headlight (i.e., control class 1 was programming as intensively, and for the same number of hours as the experimental class, and was working on meaningful projects that were integrated into the curriculum), no one could predict whether they would show any difference in their knowledge and understanding of programming by the end of the experiment. However, there were many differences, which proved to be quite interesting. It seems that the experimental conditions (Software-Design-Logo) helped develop a higher-level knowledge and expertise in Logo programming for all the experimental students on all math levels. On the other hand, Project-Headlight conditions also developed some expertise among the students of control class 1, as evidence by the fact that they had consistently scored higher than those of control class 2. But when compared to the experimental class, only the high-math students of control class 1—and only occasionally—achieved the average level of Logo understanding of the experimental students, whereas the medium- and low-math students from control class 1 did not seem to benefit as much from the Project Headlight conditions. The same math-level students in the experimental class of the same level (i.e., medium- and low-math) did much better on the Logo posttests than those in control class 1. The results from the Logo posttests therefore demonstrate that the experimental students, working under ISDP conditions, were those who improved most dramatically in their Logo programming knowledge and skills.

Logo and the "cognitive effects" question. There is a body of literature that addresses the question whether "programming" in general or "Logo" in particular can induce cognitive effects, and, if so, to what extent. In this sense, Logo would be seen as a causal factor in the improvement of fractions-knowledge or cognitive skills seen in this study.

But Papert (1985, 1987a) has used the term *technocentrism* to warn against simplistic applications of this question. In different contexts the import of the phrase "learning Logo" can differ so greatly that the question can become meaningless. Nevertheless, in the particular context of ISDP, where Logo was not isolated from a total context, and where students programmed intensively and extensively, one can meaningfully *begin* to ask how various features of Logo contributed to the success of the children's work.

At least one important contribution of Logo in this study was *indirect*—having less to do with acquiring cognitive skills than with mastering a subject domain. Learning how to program and use Logo enabled students to become more involved in thinking about fractions knowledge.

But Logo, because of its structure (or ISDP, because of the unique way it used the structure of Logo), has a direct effect. The structure of Logo brings young students into direct and concrete contact with issues of *representation*—in the case of ISDP, the representation of fractions, as well as with the representation of objects, projects, structures, and processes in terms of subprocedures, LogoWriter pages, and other computational structures.

It is relevant to note that much of what the ISDP students accomplished could, in principle, be accomplished by other methods, such as using pencil and paper to draw representations, or using physical manipulatives for representation. This might seem to make the contribution of Logo quite incidental. But in practice, it is implausible that traditional media could equal the ease with which Logo allows students to save and connect concepts and their different representations, and to develop and modify them over long periods of time. Even more importantly, working in Logo on one's own machine, in a culture where everyone is working on a similar project, simultaneously reinforces: (a) the learner's contact with his or her personal knowledge that is expressed in a real product—a piece of software that can be used and reused, changed, and modified; and (b) the learner's process of growing with the knowledge of himself or herself and of the culture. Logo facilitates this ongoing personal engagement and gradual change of knowledge; and at the same time, it facilitates the sharing of the knowledge with other members of the design studio while allowing learners to continue and easily build upon their own and others' ideas. In short, Logo facilitates communication about the processes and acts of cognition and learning.

Of course we do not mean to maintain that only Logo could do this (Harel & Papert, 1990). Surely, many new media will develop that will do it better. But a careful look at the features of Logo that contributed here, and the ways it was used in the ISDP context, will be of use in guiding further developments. Pursuing such issues is a topic that requires further research. However, further research will not be well guided by the kind of questions that have often been posed in existing literature, like: "Does Logo have such and such a cognitive effect?" Rather, research needs to consider questions like, "Can Logo be used to amplify and support such and such a direction of children's intellectual development, or such and such a change in a learning culture?"

Conclusion 3. Connecting with representational issues.

The students' designing of software to teach third graders, using Logo, was an effective way for learning, creating, and translating rational-number representations, and for enhancing their mathematical understanding of what fractions and basic fractional representations are. This method also affected their success in the final posttests and interviews.

Whereas most school work touches only on the surface structure of rational-number knowledge, ISDP put students in touch with the deep structure. As stated in Chapter I, elementary-school children's processes and difficulties in learning fractions and understanding their representations have been well documented. Unlike whole numbers, the meaning of which students generally grasp informally and intuitively out of school, learning the rational-number system is confined almost exclusively to school. Because rational-number concepts and algorithms are so difficult for so many pupils, they figure prominently in school curricula beginning in the second grade, and appear mainly in the form of algorithmic tasks and in the solving of specific well-defined mathematical problems. Even so, several national assessments have found that children's performance on fraction ordering and computation was low and accompanied by little understanding (see Harel, 1988, 1989b, 1990a). *This is particularly unfortunate because fractions are ideal tools for learning about number systems and representational systems in mathematics.* Moreover, the understanding of the rational-number knowledge. Representations form part of the deep structure of rational-number knowledge, whereas algorithms put students in touch with only the surface structure (e.g., Lesh & Landau, 1983; Janvier, 1987; Harel & Papert, 1990).

Logo is a rich route for understanding fractions. Logo can be a direct route to the deep structure, enabling students to explore the concept of fractions through various on-screen representations of their own devising. By becoming designers of instructional software, the students gained distance and perspective in two ways. First, they were dealing, not with the representations themselves, but with a Logo representation of the representations. Moving between representations was subordinate to programming good examples of representations. Second, the students programmed, not for themselves, but for others. They had to step outside and think about other children's reactions. The depth and creativity of such an experience contrasts with the rote, superficial quality of what typically occurs when a student is taught by an externally conceived sequence of learning. ISDP consisted in students' working *between* several representational systems; *combining* the different islands of rational-number knowledge (e.g., connecting or *translating* between two different rational-number subconstructs such as 50% and 1/2); and *creating* and translating several representational modes (e.g., designing a screen that combined both graphical and written representations for 1/3).

Contrary to most existing curricula, ISDP did not attempt to identify the "best" manipulative aids for the fractions learning process. ISDP emphasized that, while working with Logo, students could decide for themselves which representations they wanted to create and manipulate. The computerized Logo environment proved to be rich in the representations that were potentially available (i.e., the representations were not there, in the computer, but the students created procedures for many representations) and in providing the ability for students to combine several representations on the same screen at the same time. Also, the Logo *code* itself became a new kind of rational-number representation, which the students generated and manipulated.

Success without "formal" instruction. It seemed that the ISDP students did well on the Fractions posttests, not because they were explicitly and formally instructed on fractions and their representations, but because—through designing and programming instructional software on fractions, creating representations of fractions through Logo, and explaining and teaching about fractions and their representations—they had the opportunity to think about, reflect upon, revise, and experience (although on a very small scale) the principles involved in the relationship between the different rational-number subcontructs and their representational systems. Hardly anyone in the experimental class was able to design or program more than a maximum of 15 representations during the curse of ISDP. In the process of learning fractions in the project, the students did not use any manipulative aids, cover a very wide range of rational-number sub-constructs, or translate or manipulate a large number of representations. How-ever, the posttests did include a large number of rational-number subconstructs, their multiple representations (in the pencil-and-paper test), and a variety of manipulative aids (in the interview). Therefore, these tests were assessing some kind of transfer, in the sense of "learning and understanding." The experimental students did well on these tests and transferred the knowledge they had gained from producing software about fractions to the tests quite successfully. Further-more, the students' goal of representing and explaining fractions to another person helped them to overcome their own difficulties in understanding fractional representations (which had been identified in the pretests and reported in other studies about fractions; e.g., Behr et al. 1983; Lesh et al. 1983; or Tierney, 1988).

Developing a language for talking about fractions. In addition to getting higher scores on the Fractions posttests, the experimental students also talked about, thought about, and related to fractions in a special way, both during their involvement in the project and in the interviews and tests that took place after-wards. From their point of view, they learned "*a lot*" about fractions through this project because, as one student commented, "*how can you teach it if you don't know it yourself?*" I found it exciting that 9- and 10-year-olds could discuss what was most difficult about fractions, how the same fraction could be represented in different ways, and how the equivalence or addition of fractions could be ex-plained both verbally and graphically. ISDP encouraged children to become epistemologists and helped them develop language for expressing their epistemo-logical concerns.

ISDP provided students with multiple perspectives and 'tools-to-think-with' about fractions. Logo, the computer, and the Designer's Notebooks all played very important roles in the students' thinking about fractions. It appears that the experimental students developed a concept of the role of the computer and the Notebook in their own learning of fractions and in that of their "users." One girl said, "*I love drawing the pictures in my Designer's Notebook. This way I know what I want to teach. But with the computer, you can see it or do it yourself. It's much more fun.*" One boy said: "*With the computer, I got answers to what I did wrong, and they [the users] get answers to what they do wrong. I give them the answers, show them things, like that 2/6 equal 1/3, and I tell them how to do things like that.*" Another girl stated: "*On the computer you learn better about fractions. They're [fractions] not boring anymore, 'cause I make them with colors and I use different shapes and pictures and I make stories about them [about fractions]. It's fun."* The ISDP experiment invited students to think about their own knowledge of fractions, and how this knowledge might become their own, or someone else's. They were also able to distinguish between what *they* learned from the process of creating instructional software, and what they saw *other* students learn from their interactive lessons on the computer. As one boy said, *"Some of my things* [fraction representations] *were very confusing at first. At least they were confusing to me. Now I know these things. But this* [my software] *is just a little demonstration with simple testing. It should be used with my good explanations before, during and after you use it."*

To summarize, ISDP recast fractions learning in essentially three ways: (a) it emphasized more *involvement with the deep structure* (representations) over the surface structure (algorithms) of rational-number knowledge; (b) it made learning simultaneously *incidental and instrumental to a larger intellectual and social goal,* that is, having students think about and explain what they think and learn, in an interactive lesson for younger children; and (c) it encouraged both *personal expression and social communication* of rational-number knowledge and ideas.

Conclusion 4. Learning to learn & thinking about thinking.

The students' working at representing, teaching, designing, and instructional designing enhanced their metaconceptual and metacognitive awareness. The Designer's Notebooks, among the other production tools that were used in this project, were very useful in the students' design processes, and seemed to enhance their planning, reflections, and other metacognitive and cognitive control skills. The students also acquired cognitive flexibility, control over their solution processes, and confidence in their thinking.

Another goal of this study was to find out whether design encouraged students' cognitive awareness (i.e., thinking about their own thinking and learning); cognitive control (i.e., managing and controlling their own learning, constructing their own plans and revisions, allocating their time throughout the project, accomplishing the task given to them, and reflecting on all the above); and metaconceptual understanding (i.e., thinking about the structure of fractions and their representations, reflecting on how they had come to perceive it, realizing how other students might learn to perceive it, understanding the meaning and purpose of Logo commands in various situations, thinking about the purpose of their screens and the reasons for designing them in particular ways, etc.).

ISDP seemed to enhance the Experimental students' metacognitive experiences, as well as to promote the growth of several cognitive executive processes and skills. According to Flavell (1979, in one of the first papers on metacognition the term *metacognition* generally refers to "metacognitive knowledge," that is, a cluster of competencies that have to do with people's understanding of their own thinking and other cognitive processes; and "metacognitive experience," that is, a cluster of experiences that occur before, during, or after a cognitive enterprise, and which stimulate highly conscious thinking and encourage the establishing of goals and the activating of metacognitive knowledge and strategies (i.e., executive or cognitive control processes). In a slightly different way, Schoenfeld (1985) specified three related but distinct categories of metacognitive intellectual behavior: (a) knowledge about one's own thought processes, (b) one's control or self-regulation and one's beliefs and intuitions about bodies of knowledge, and (c) ways of knowing them. In light of Flavell's and Schoenfeld's perspectives on what metacognition is, it is clear that this project encouraged the experimental students to undergo a great many "metacognitive experiences"; they learned and very often activated metacognitive knowledge and control strategies of various kinds; they also came to change many of their beliefs and intuitions about their abilities in math, programming, or problem solving in general. I shall now specify some of these well-known "meta" strategies and skills, and show how they were acquired and activated by the students during ISDP.

1. *Through the Project the students Developed Problem-Finding Skills.* For 4 months, the students were involved in day-by-day processes of self-generating or self-discovering problems to solve. No one specified the problems for them; rather, *they* were the ones in charge of deciding, for example, what was difficult about fractions, what screens to design in order to explain fractions, what Logo procedures to create, and so on. They were also involved in constantly targeting their ideas for possible solutions, and in redefining and revising the problems and the solutions they encountered.

2. *Students Developed an Awareness of the Skills and Processes Necessary for Solving Various Problems.* The Designer's Notebooks required that students design many of their screens in advance. The students' drawings and planning in their Designer's Notebooks demonstrated that they were aware of the Logo-programming and fractions knowledge and skills needed for accomplishing their designs, in that they rarely came up with a design that they could not manage to solve in Logo. In addition, they were aware of their knowledge of fractions, challenged it, and worked along the edge of their knowledge. They also had to be aware of their users' knowledge of fractions and to clearly explain the representations they had created on the computer.

3. *Students Learned how to Activate Various Cognitive Rules and Strategies.* The students' awareness of the strategies needed to solve a problem was one important aspect of the project, but activating these strategies was another. We have seen in the Logo posttests, for example, that the experimental students were aware of the skills needed to optimize or modularize a given Logo procedure, and also of the project's time constraints. Moreover, they were

able to activate the proper knowledge, rules, and strategies to solve problems given to them. We have also seen how, at the beginning of the project, Debbie was not fully aware that there might not be enough time to accomplish all of her plans; later in the project she wrote, *"I'll do this if I'll have time,"* or learned to plan less and to allocate her time better.

4. *The students Adjusted their Cognitive Efforts to Match the Difficulty of the Problem at Hand.* Often students would begin to implement their designs in Logo; but when they realized that too many efforts were needed to accomplish a rather simple or "unimportant" design, they ceased working on it and moved on to a more important screen for their software, or decided to redesign the problematic screen. We saw, for example, how Debbie designed one opening screen for her software that read: WELCOME TO FRACTIONS! She began to implement it, and when she decided that the time and effort needed was too great in relation to the general importance of that screen in her software. She then designed another opening screen instead, and concentrated her efforts on a problem that was more important to her, or on an instructional screen that had a more significant role in her software.

5. *Students Developed Cognitive Flexibility.* During the project, the students developed the ability to discard inefficient designs, plans, and solutions that were not working, and to search for better alternatives. We have seen, for example, the number of attempts of the experimental students' in the Logo posttests. They rarely gave up, were not rigid in their solution processes, and did not stop working on a difficult problem (whereas many of the control students simply answered "I don't know").

6. *Students Learned to Control Distractions and Anxiety.* In this open-ended project (and in Project Headlight in general), the students were working in an open area next to their classroom. Different students were working on various problems, with other students, teachers, and visitors often walking around. In spite of this, the students learned to keep their attention focused on the problems they were working on, and to resist being distracted by external stimulation (such as noises, other people's behavior, etc.). They also learned to control their anxiety when a problem was difficult. During the posttests I realized that the Project Headlight students seemed to be better at avoiding "test fears." They focused efficiently on the problems given to them and did not let external interference distract their productive thoughts and actions.

7. *Students Learned to Monitor their Solution Processes.* The experimental students were constantly relating their ongoing performances and implementation phases to the general goals of the task (i.e., designing instructional software); they also made appropriate changes if they decided that their performances were too slow or unclear, or if they thought they were unlikely to reach a successful solution to the task given them. They also evaluated their performances every day when they logged in and ran their software, or when other people used parts of their software.

8. *The students Developed Faith in their Thinking.* Because the students themselves were in charge of their own learning and production, they knew that, when they encountered difficulty, their own thoughts and actions might help them generate the needed solution. We saw by the posttests that, whenever an initial solution did not work for the control students, they stopped trying; however, most of the experimental students learned to appreciate that their own mental process could be useful in their being successful in the test.

The project did not involve any direct or explicit teaching of thinking skills; rather, it emphasized them as being completely integrated and interlaced with the learning of the subject matters involved. No formal instruments were used for measuring the success of this approach or for comparing it with other approaches. In other words, no systematic measurements were made of the students' metacognition and cognitive levels before the project started, or of their improvement in their metacognitive and metaconceptual knowledge of the topics involved after the project ended. Comparisons with control classes regarding these skills were not conducted in this context either, but several attempts were made throughout the project to encourage these higher-level cognitive processes, as well as to document them among the experimental students. I believe that all students had to develop some kind of expertise in terms of their cognitive control strategies because they were in charge of their own learning and progress throughout the project. They were the ones who decided what to do each day, what to teach, how to allocate the time they spent working at the computer, what to design, what to implement, how and when to revise their plans or programs, etc. Indeed, they managed to do these things quite well, since, after all, each one of them succeeded in understanding and solving the given task of software design, achieved a great deal through the project, and programmed a complex piece of software.

How was evidence gathered on the students' metacognitive skills. I followed and observed the software designers every day while they were working on their designs and programs, and often asked them questions which required that they reflect upon their own thinking. For example, I would ask why they were creating a particular thing on the computer or in their Designers's Notebooks, and what they thought about the issues they discussed with me or with their teacher and friends. During the course of the project they became quite good at answering these questions (i.e., they were able to think better about their own thinking and learning).

In addition, in this extreme learning environment, people's thinking—about design, mathematics, and programming—became integrated and overt. Metacognitive and metaconceptual thinking were facilitated and explicit in the culture. The records of the design and cognitive processes that were created by the students themselves benefited the *child,* the *teacher,* and the *researcher* at the same time.

Facilitating metaconceptual discussions of mathematical ideas. My conversations with the students, as well as the short classroom discussions that were conducted during the period of ISDP, were very useful vehicles for encouraging and gathering data about the students' metaconceptual thinking. These discussions and conversations focused, for example, on the difficulties of specific fraction concepts or of Logo programming techniques. They required that the students generate ideas on why some fractions concepts were difficult, and on how they might be explained, represented, or taught. In two of the classroom discussions, we hung two posters, one on each side of the blackboard. On one poster we wrote, WHAT IS DIFFICULT ABOUT FRACTIONS? and on the other, WHAT SCREENS OR REPRESENTATIONS COULD BE DESIGNED TO EXPLAIN THESE DIFFICULT CONCEPTS? We asked the students to generate ideas for both posters simultaneously, by asking them: *"Think about what was difficult for you, which concept you did not understand at first, and what it means to know this concept."* Long lists of ideas were generated by the students, meaning that, under these conditions, they were able to think about these issues, express them verbally in the classroom, and later incorporate them into their pieces of software.

Facilitating students' production process and their metacognitive development with the Designer's Notebook. We did not tell the students what to write, how much to write, what or how to plan or draw, or how to reflect or make changes. However, like professional software designers, they kept track of their ideas and changes, which helped their implementation, their concentration, and their not losing good ideas from one day to the next. Writing in the Designer's Notebook was a problem at first, since the students were not accustomed to a routine of planning, note taking, and reflecting in writing. But after 2 weeks into the project, the Designer's Notebook became an important personal element for the students and made them aware of the benefits of reflecting, keeping track of their own planning, note taking, and changes. Moreover, they realized that they did not necessarily have to implement what they wrote, that the Notebook facilitated their thinking of new ideas while implementing old ones, and that going back in their Notebooks to old drawings and notes was beneficial to them and very useful in their programming processes. We saw several examples in Debbie's case of her personal relationship with the notebook, and of her use of it for planning and reflecting on new ideas as well as on changes she made.

The importance of the Designer's Notebook for research on metacognition. The Notebook was found to be a useful and informative research instrument for assessing metacognitive growth among the students. In Debbie's case we saw many examples of this. Thanks to the Notebook, I was able to accumulate records on her design and reflection processes, her plans, drawings, changes, problems, etc. At this stage, I can only offer a brief analysis of the Designer's Notebooks and Logo files of the 17 Experimental students, but it is clear that the Notebooks themselves reveal precious information on the differences and similarities in the students' higher-level cognitive and metacognitive skills. Through them, I realized that some students liked to plan in writing in detail, while others preferred to write less and draw more screens and create more story-board scripts. Some students reflected in detail on the problems they had encountered during the sessions, while others did not see the problems they had solved as problems and therefore did not report them. Some students, as they progressed in the project, created more complex and detailed plans, while others planned less, since they "already knew what they wanted to do." A deeper investigation and analysis of these Notebooks would probably reveal very important information about the students' processes of planning, designing, and reflection, and about how they became more adept at these during the project, and what they gained from them. Another investigation should be aimed at relating the 17 students' plans and reflections to their actual programs in Logo (their implementation). And while Debbie's case revealed to us very important information in that regard, 17 cases, constructed and interpreted like Debbie's, would allow us to generalize and build more detailed models for these processes.

Researcher's metareflections on metacognition research. In order to find more information about the students' metacognitions, a more systematic questioning method could be developed for use in this context: the researcher, for example, could ask all the students a predetermined set of "metacognitive" questions every day, compare the students' answers, and measure more precisely their metacognitive development. However, we should not forget that these questions might also lead the students to follow different routes from those they would spontaneously choose to take.

My philosophy during this project was not to ask too many questions, to let the students work as they wished, and to ask them metaquestions only *after* I saw something that captured my interest. When asked, many of these students spoke of the importance of their thinking process about the future users of their programs. They often commented on, and were aware of, what they had learned about fractions and Logo from their creation of a particular screen, and what was or was not interesting for them or for their users. They were ready to describe why they had designed a screen in a particular way, which problems they had encountered; why they had selected certain colors or shapes; why they had provided particular instructions, explanations, or introductions; why they had given certain feedback; and when and why they had combined graphics and text, and so on. These observations as well as others that have been made in my pilot study (Harel, 1986), demonstrate that the students were involved in a higher-level and reflective form of thinking. To my mind, placing students in a learning situation where these issues were actually raised in the first place, as well as discussed and shared, is a powerful and appropriate measure of metacognition in its own right.

Often, during my project, I would wonder how much "scaffolding" I needed to provide, whether I was asking children too many questions, or interrupting them rather than helping them along. I also wondered how much problem-solving modelling should I do. These are great dilemmas for people who believe in constructivist-discovery types of learning and are interested in what children can construct and invent on their own; and who are also interested in "what is going on inside the child's mind," in the development of the child's metacognitive awareness and control, and in how children have developed their abilities to think about or answer the "metaquestions" posed to them by the researcher.

Conclusion 5. A paradigm shift in research on learning.

The activity of instructional software design proved to be manageable by fourth-grade students and a vehicle for their learning of problem solving in general. Through the intensive and constructive experience of software design, the students experienced complex and productive problem-solving processes and simultaneously came to learn and understand different subjects, concepts, and skills. The analyses reached through the study of one individual pupil suggest new methods and models for analyzing students' different styles of instructional software design, as well as the different stage sequences in their organization and implementation of long-term projects. More comprehensive and global models of the processes involved in students' design could be developed by analyzing several other cases, as was Debbie's Case here.

"Design for learning" suggests a paradigm shift from existing "problem-solving-research" in regard to both focus and methodology. In Chapter I, I described several of the studies which aimed to examine the processes involved in software design (e.g., Adelson & Soloway, 1984a,b; Guindon, 1987; Guindon, Krasner, & Curtis, 1987; or Jefferies et al., 1981), and I concluded that these studies provided a detailed description of very specific cognitive processes in software designers with various levels of expertise who performed very logical and well-defined tasks over a short period of time. Because of this, I suggested that only a few generalizations could be drawn from these researchers' work that were strongly relevant to my study.

Furthermore, aside from the collection of verbal protocols and the use of videotaping, only a few models existed that could be directly adopted for ISDP, since the problem given to my subjects was open ended and presented in the following manner: "Design a program that teaches a younger child about fractions." The students/designers' processes toward solving the problem took approximately 70 hours of programming, and within this long and complex context, each child established his or her own route, goals, and subgoals, which could not be predicted in advance in a production-system model or later analyzed by the researcher—in the sense of "good" or "bad" designs, or of "expert" as compared to "novice" approaches.

In the present study I placed great emphasis on what was *learned* through the long solution process, and how it was learned. In Debbie's case, I emphasized these aspects throughout. I paid careful attention to the skills the problem solver gained in the solution process rather than limit myself to analyzing her solution processes per se or the qualities of her final product. Unlike the participants studied in the literature mentioned above, the students in my project learned about the a computer language (i.e., their major software design tool) during their actual processes of software design. And whereas the existing studies emphasized the role of prior domain experience and prior knowledge of designing software, the students I studied learned the domain while producing the software for it. My study focused on the processes of learning, rather than on the relationships between knowing more about fractions or Logo and producing better software. The relationships I stressed were quite different.

In ISDP, new research methods were used for studying students' open-ended and prolonged problem-solving processes, and proved to be successful for the students; for the researcher too, these methods were very informative on many levels. This experiment aimed at shifting away from what has been most predominantly emphasized in problem-solving research over the last decade, concentrating instead on students' problem-solving and cognition in a richer and much more complex learning environment, and over a longer period of time.

In short, the project suggested two major methodological changes for studying students (or even software design): the first was to study an open-ended problem-solving enterprise; the second was to study students solving the same problem over a long period of time (70 hours, rather than in various short and well-defined problem-solving sessions—the most common approach in the field).

Software design proved to be a great vehicle for students' learning and problem solving. This study indicates that, through the intensive and constructive experience of software design, the students learned many Logo operations and commands and wrote long and complicated programs that students of that age are not usually able to manage. The students also demonstrated expertise in the understanding, interpreting, and modifying of their own Logo programs, as well as the programs of others (in the posttests). At the same time, the integrative approach of the software design activity (as shown in Figure 1) was a challenging way for the students to learn basic rational-number concepts. Their experience in this complex task, which is rarely mastered in school mathematics, encouraged them to engage in difficult academic constructs such as relationships between fractional representations. Throughout ISDP, the students were constantly involved in metacognitive acts: learning by explaining, creating, and discussing knowledge representations, finding design strategies, and reflecting on all the above.

The process of design encouraged epistemological pluralism. All the experimental students succeeded at the same job—producing a piece of instructional software, each student in his or her own way. As shown in previous findings on Logo and learning (e.g., Turkle, 1984; Turkle & Papert, 1990; Weir, 1986; Lowler, 1985; Papert, 1980, 1984a,b), software design also proved to be a learning activity that allowed for individual differences in learning, mastery, and expression. New microgenetic phenomena were seen in this extreme environment. This was shown, for example, in the way the different students went through different stage sequences in organizing and implementing their long-term projects, in the different fractions they chose to represent on their computer screens, and in their choices regarding how to teach others about fractions. New methods would have to be developed for identifying, analyzing, and describing the individual differences between participating students, their various styles of expression, and the different ways they created their products. These phenomena are worth further exploration, especially because *the complicated ISDP learning environment touches upon the complexities of the everyday world in which students and adults learn and live.* A further comprehensive analysis of more students/software-designers cases would probably reveal an interesting model, or several models, of the processes involved in students' software design; these models could be used later and more systematically in future studies of this kind. Better strategies for studying the processes could also be revealed by interpreting all 17 cases as I interpreted Debbie's. The data exist, and more cases like Debbie's should be constructed in future studies as well (e.g., already underway in Kafai & Harel, 1991a and b).

Conclusion 6. Implications for educational practice.

The project offered major changes for educational practice in general, and for the teaching of fractions and Logo in particular. The techniques developed in this study could be used for teaching fractions and Logo programming, as well as other subjects, in other schools. However, these techniques must be implemented within an umbrella or educational philosophy that is child centered, open ended, dynamic, and oriented towards working on common projects and on students' construction of meaningful products. They should also be oriented toward connecting various aspects of students' knowledge, and integrating them into an environment that is rich in computers that are fully integrated into the school's curriculum and culture. All these criteria were established in the ISDP site, the Project Headlight's model school.

The experimentation in this prototypical project aimed at exploring what major changes the project offered in educational practice in general, and in the teaching of fractions and Logo in particular. In Debbie's case I investigated many of these issues. In Chapter III, I described in what ways the experimental students succeeded in the posttests. Their consistent superiority over the control students revealed that the changes offered to the existing curriculum by the project were very effective for the students' learning and understanding of fractions and Logo, among other things.

The "Integrated Learning" Principle. The first change this project offers to educational practice relates to the fact that different subject matters and skills were found to be mutually supportive of one another, were learned by the students at the same time, and contributed to each other in many ways. This idea has been highlighted throughout this book. The project was a rare pedagogical approach, difficult to implement in educational practice. Still, we saw that the experimental students did not find it difficult or confusing to learn different skills or subject matters at the same time; in fact, they benefited from this pedagogy, which resulted in the learning of one skill's contributing to the learning of another. Chapter II provided us with Debbie's processes of parallel learning: She learned fractions and Logo at the same time, and often the learning of Logo contributed to her understanding of fractional representations. Similarly, the learning of fractions contributed to her acquiring new Logo skills. Chapter III provided evidence that the learning and understanding of the topics and skills involved did occur in Debbie's case, as well as in the experimental class in general. On the whole, this was a Logo-based and fractions-based project that promoted and integrated thinking and learning among fourth-grade students on many levels and in several domains at the same time. As Perkins wrote,

> What does one school subject have to do with another? Whatever answers there might be, it is clear that conventional schooling pays little heed to them. The several subjects run their courses as separately as rivers on different seaboards. Yet *building connections is not hard. . . . the usual subject matters need not stand so distant from one another. In fact, it might be said that they only stay so because they are left there.* Instruction based on knowledge as design need not, indeed should not, accept this status quo. Knowledge as design is a natural bridge builder, pointing up commonalities and inviting contrasts between the various disciplines. (1986, pp. 221–222; emphasis added)

However, there are certain problems with integrating instructional software design activity into a school's curriculum. Software design is a time-consuming and complex enterprise for a teacher to handle, and it is not yet clear how it can fit into the average class schedule. Also, at the present time, it is not very clear which subjects would lend themselves best to this process of learning.

But, and as Papert believes, because it has a reflexive synergistic quality, knowledge about computation (such as programming) and the sciences of information (involving control over one's own processing, metacognition, and information construction) has a special character in this respect—it facilitates other knowledge. In ISDP, the learning of fractions and the learning of complex skills (programming, design, etc.) did not compete for time; rather, each took place more effectively than if they been taught separately. The reflexive quality of information science offers a solution to the apparent impossibility of adding another component to an already full school day. If some knowledge facilitates other knowledge, then, in a beautifully paradoxical way, more can mean less!

The idea that learning more science and math necessarily means learning less of something else illustrates an incorrect conception (Papert, 1986). If these domains are properly integrated into an individual's knowledge and into learning cultures, they will be supportive, not competitive, with other learning. The possibility of integrating science, mathematics, art, writing, and other subjects could help to make them mutually supportive. In ISDP this principle of integration—which meant that young students learned fractions, Logo programming, instructional designing, planning, story-boarding, reflection, self-management, and so on, all at the same time and in a synergistic fashion—greatly contributed to the results.

Special merits to learning by teaching and explaining. As educators or teachers, producers, computer programmers, software developers, and professional people in general, we are rarely encouraged to draw on our own learning experiences in order to better understand the reasons, purposes, and processes of learning and teaching our subject matter. Too often we forget what was really difficult for us to understand, or why one learning experience was more or less valuable for us than for others in the course of our own intellectual and professional development.

It has been observed by students and educators in our group as well as by many "experts" that the best way to learn a subject is to teach it. In Chapter I, I considered some experiences that are common to professional people in many fields in the course of their everyday work or professional training. Teachers, professional computer programmers, university professors, pilots, architects, therapists—and even software designers—very often comment on their learning-while-teaching experiences.

In addition to this type of evidence from 'everyday cognizers,' the intellectual benefit of generating one's own explanations have been stressed by a number of theorists such as Piaget and Vygotsky. And among contemporary researchers, Ann Brown (1988), for example, has done many studies elucidating the ways in which explanatory processes, as part of reciprocal teaching activities, motivate learners and encourage the search for deeper levels of understanding and subject mastery. Brown characterizes these explanatory-based interactive learning environments as ones that push the learners to explain and represent knowledge in multiple ways and therefore, in the process, to comprehend the subject more fully themselves. The interactions could be supported by computers, teachers, or other learners. Hatano and Inagaki (1987) also argue that comprehension and interest is enhanced when students have to explain their views and clarify their positions to others. Their studies demonstrate how persuasion or teaching requires the orderly presentation of ideas and better intraindividual organization of what one knows. It also invites students to commit themselves to some ideas, thereby placing the issue in question in their personal domains of interest.

Fourth-grade children seldom have such opportunities. Peer teaching or reciprocal teaching can be used to take a small step in this direction. ISDP took a much larger step.

Integrating the learning of subjects with the learning of cognitive strategies and problem-solving skills. Another change that the project suggests is that the learning of thinking skills and cognitive control strategies completely integrated into the subject matters involved. In ISDP they were integrated to such an extent that it was difficult for the researcher to study and document these skills as separate from the content knowledge involved. However, in conventional schooling, thinking skills are usually taught in separate courses, outside the normal curriculum (in the same way that Logo is taught separately). ISDP argues for integrating the learning of these skills into the learning of subjects, because, "without integration into subject matters, thinking skills are not as likely to empower the active use of knowledge for critical and creative thinking" (Perkins, 1986, p. 217); and, to use Papert's well-known expression from *Mindstorms,* "we cannot think about our thinking without thinking about thinking about something."

Learning through producing. Other points this project stressed were the students' learning through producing products, and the teacher's focusing on her pupils' processes of learning. In addition, the teacher favored a variety of complex, large, nonunified, and creative products, rather than unified short "right" answers as the outcomes of her pupils' learning activities. We must remember that

> Outside of school almost all worthwhile activities involve products rather than short answers, whether the product is a plan for an advertising campaign, a poem, or a well-crafted chair . . . [learning through the processes of design and construction of products] reveals designing to be the paradigmatic human activity, and designing anything invariably involves producing some sort of extended product rather than a brief answer. Although some might think that students do not know enough to deal with products, [a Project of this kind, and many other tasks which are mentioned in Perkins' book shows] how appropriate tasks can be found and [offers] numerous examples for a range of subject areas. (Perkins, 1986, p. 217)

In summary, this project, with its approach of learning through designing and programming instructional software, offered new conditions for learning. This means that young students learned fractions, Logo programming, designing, instructional designing, planning, story-boarding, reflection, explaining, self-management, and so on, all at the same time and in a synergistic fashion. In the context of the project, and through the use of the computer, these different kinds of knowledge and disciplines were integrated and proved to be mutually supportive of one another while the child was in the process of learning them.

Is ISDP a "curriculum?" ISDP points towards to a more general pedagogical approach. It offers specific changes in the approach to learning and teaching Logo and fractions (and several more general thinking and problem-solving skills), but it also proposes a more general approach that could be implemented with other topics in the elementary-school curriculum. Further experiments should be conducted for investigating which topics lend themselves best to this approach, and how this method contributes and changes students' understanding of these topics and their ways of thinking about them. In fact, several teachers have already approached me, requesting curriculum materials that would guide them in implementing this project and in adopting a specific pedagogical approach in classrooms. Researchers have also requested these materials in order to implement similar studies on students' cognition and problem-solving processes. The latter are accustomed to reading long and complex papers and research reports (such as the one presented here) and might perhaps find answers to their questions, concerns, and interests. Educators and teachers, on the other hand, are usually less accustomed to, and have less time for, this form of presentation. They tend to request clear and precise guidelines and directions.

In working with teachers within Project Headlight, I grew to be very sensitive and respectful regarding this issue. I learned to admire teachers for their very difficult task of teaching and educating students, and for "covering" all the subjects and concepts they are required to teach throughout the year. It would be an easy thing for me to say to a teacher: "Try it and see," or "Experience it and learn." However, I learned that these are not appropriate approaches for involving teachers in innovative educational methods. Teachers are part of a very complex and rigid system that does not very often allow them to try new things and explore new pedagogies—even when they strongly wish to learn innovative approaches and seek changes in their curricula.

We saw how interesting, informative, and successful this project was, and how effective the changes were for educational practice and for research in the fields involved. Clearly, curriculum materials are very important for the dissemination and distribution of ideas and instructional methods, for making teachers and educators rethink their curricula, and especially for making educational policy makers understand the ideas behind ISDP and other projects, and helping them see these ideas as models for change in educational practice. I have given a great deal of thought to what strategy might be used in writing these materials, but I find it quite difficult to develop concrete, written materials for an open-ended, integrative, and complex project of this kind. It is difficult to develop a curriculum that would provide teachers with a clear model they could follow but without step-by-step, well-defined guidelines, worksheets, or exercises. The holistic characters of the project, the scope of students' learning and thinking in this project, as well as the complex structure of the project's culture—are all difficult to transmit in a written curriculum package. Here are some interesting questions regarding these issues.

Could the project be implemented without my being there? I do not know the answer to this question. I am aware that the individual attention I gave to each pupil was crucial. However, the teacher I worked with played a very important role throughout this project, and I am sure that she will be able to carry on many projects of this nature in the future, and in the most wonderful way. But, in order for her to learn the process, she had to experience it and work very intensively with me and with her pupils. We collaborated and constantly discussed various issues of implementation, as well as the various steps in the students' progress. This, to my mind, was the best approach for her (and for me) to learn how to implement and manage a project of this kind. It should also be emphasized that this teacher had participated in Project Headlight for approximately 20 months before we started to work on my project. She was very familiar with our philosophy of integrative, child-centered projects, and had the opportunity to talk with other MIT members, including Papert, and to work on various other projects during that period.

The experimental students also played a very important role in this project. We had to collaborate, and we constantly shared our problems and ideas with one another. As I stated previously, I did not have a well-defined plan for the project as a whole, or for the classroom discussions (the focus sessions). These were generated according to the students' requests, as needed. Many times it was difficult to decide what to discuss with the students and when, since each child took his own personal route in the project, and at any given time in the project, different students were involved with different fractional concepts, instructional design concerns, and programming problems.

Could this project be implemented outside of Project Headlight? I doubt it. It is my belief that computers must first be generally integrated into a school, in the way that is done with Project Headlight, so that a project of this kind to become a natural element in the environment. This project could probably not stand alone in a conventional school curriculum, for it needs to be rooted in a culture that uses computers very intensively and extensively for other projects of various kinds, which are integrated into other domains through various methods.

Could this project be implemented with students who have never used the computer or Logo before? My answer to this is YES. In fact, we saw how this project became a great tool for both the teacher and her students to learn about Logo and to experience its "original" philosophy (of Papert, 1980). This project provided us with evidence and support for the many benefits of integrating the learning of Logo immediately into the curriculum, and for allowing students to explore and construct meaningful products with Logo over a long period of time. This study has shown us that such an approach resulted in students' learning Logo on a very high level.

Could this project be implemented with students of various ages? I conducted my first pilot study with fifth graders (Harel, 1986), at the end of their school year. They were quite knowledgeable in Logo and fractions at the time they worked on their projects. But by examining the effects of this pedagogy on these fifth graders, I decided to conduct this study with younger students, from the fourth grade, who knew much less about Logo and fractions at the time the project began. In fact, many of my colleagues had warned me that, because of the students' young age and particular stage of cognitive readiness, they might not be able to handle this complex project, be capable of writing in the Designer's Notebooks, or manage to accomplish the sophisticated tasks that were given to them. But we have seen how successful these students were, and how much this project meant to them in terms of their learning, cognitive development, etc. The data given in this study speaks for itself in that regard.

Is the long time-frame necessary? My answer to this is straight YES. However, the fact that Debbie, for example, spent a great deal of time on halves (one month) poses an interesting dilemma: How can a teacher detect who "needs" to spend more time on something, as opposed to who "needs" a broader learning experience? This is a very difficult question to answer. In fact, because of the long time-frame in the context of ISDP, the students *themselves* were in charge of "solving" this dilemma. We could not foresee that Debbie would actually spend so much time on the concept of halves; nor could we predict in what ways her particular activities during the project would affect her knowledge of fractions or Logo, or how well she would finally do on the school math tests, or the posttests. However, Debbie's case, as well as the experiences of other experimental students, demonstrate that the long period of time they were able to spend on one concept affected their total learning in a positive way.

The point I therefore wish to make is that we should consider creating learning contexts that are rich and complex and prolonged enough to allow students to make relevant decisions and experience "conceptual principles" even when dealing with one concept. The students' creation of a 'home base' as they worked on this new task (the 'home base' or 'entry space' was one aspect that I highlighted in Debbie's case) should probably be considered an important aspect in their learning, or in our designing learning environments for them. Also, the project lasted long enough so that Debbie was eventually able to 'free' herself from her obsession with halves and go on to explore other concepts and algorithms.

In addition, the students in this project were quite independent, so that the teacher was able to walk around the computers, help her students, consult, and advise them according to their needs. In this prolonged project, the teacher found the time to give individual attention to everyone, so that each child's talent was cultivated in a particular way (see also Weir, 1986). This, of course, contributed greatly to the students' success. I assume that any teacher (or researcher), after experiencing several projects of this nature, would become sensitive to this issue of time, and capable of making decisions about students' needs of this kind.

High and low students within the same learning environment? Another challenge this project poses for educational practice is how to create constructively oriented learning settings in which a great deal of learning would occur for both high- and low-ability pupils. In ISDP we clearly realized that the typical separation of students into math groups was completely unnecessary. In fact, the ongoing interactions among students with different abilities and thinking styles is a crucial factor in the process of learning in ISDP (this feature of ISDP is further expanded and investigated by Kafai & Harel, 1991). However, several more important questions could be raised regarding this issue: What are the crucial elements in a learning environment that would allow low- and high-level pupils to "blossom?" Was it important that ISDP occur near the beginning stage of learning of Logo or fractions? What will happen in these students' next Fractions Project? How can we take a pupil who is at the "top" of his or her learning curve and put him or her at a beginning of another learning curve? How can we "renew" the subject matter for students so that, when they become sophisticated on "level 1," they still have a great deal to learn in order to be sophisticated on "level 2?"

What are some of the characteristics of learning activities that, by their nature, involve students in connecting new knowledge with old? How can we encourage students to *not* "put aside" their finished work and old knowledge, but to constantly integrate these elements with new ideas and pieces of knowledge?

It seems to me that we must differentiate between learning activities that foster an attitude among students towards treating their work as a *static* entity that can be finished and put aside, and those that foster an attitude towards treating their work or knowledge as a *dynamic* entity that can be continually revised, manipulated, and integrated with new knowledge and new ideas. But do we always want students to integrate old knowledge with new? Or do we sometimes want them to learn how to "finish" something, leave it aside, and go on to another, in order to gain new perspectives or skills? All these questions require further investigation.

ISDP is constructionism. In *Mindstorms* (1980), Papert discussed computers, Logo, and computer cultures in a way that was both very influential and controversial and that often resulted in people's rethinking education, reflecting on their own learning, reconsidering uses of technologies for learning, and reexamining students' cognition and development through using Logo.

In 1980, Papert wrote about the computer (or Logo) as being

Not a culture unto itself but [as a thing which] can serve to advance very different cultural and philosophical outlooks. (p. 31)

And to the teachers and researchers who consulted (or criticized) him about "Logo curriculum," classroom organization, scheduling problems, pedagogical issues, and the way Logo "really" conceptually related to the rest of the curriculum, Papert answered:

I have thought about it [Logo] as a vehicle for Piagetian learning, which to me is learning *without* a curriculum. (p. 31)

This statement raised a great many debates in the field, especially among people who had not carefully read the paragraph immediately following the sentence just quoted:

But 'teaching without curriculum' does not mean spontaneous, free-form class-rooms or simply 'leaving the child alone.' It means *supporting* students as they build their own intellectual structures with materials drawn from the surrounding culture. In this model, educational intervention means changing the culture, plant-ing new constructive elements in it and eliminating noxious ones. This is a *more ambitious* undertaking than introducing a curriculum change [or a new curriculum package], but one which is feasible under conditions now emerging. . . The educa-tor as an anthropologist must work to understand which cultural materials are relevant to intellectual development. Then, he or she needs to understand which trends are taking place in the culture. Meaningful interventions must take the form of working with these trends"; emphases added. (pp. 31–54)

ISDP was a *project,* not a curriculum. It could, however, be integrated into, and change, many of the existing curricula. It implied revision in the learning of "old" information (fractions), but also offered new subjects and matters for the students to learn and think about (computation, instructional software design in Logo, designer's notebooks, etc.); it certainly did not imply learning each of the subject matters involved as isolated pieces of information. It would be a poor idea, in my opinion, for a school to decide to teach a new "instructional software design curriculum."

This project meant "learning without a curriculum" in the Papertian sense described above. Moreover, it meant learning fractions without a curriculum, learning Logo without a curriculum, and learning planning, reflection, design, or software design—all at the same time—without a step-by-step, well-defined curriculum, but with a great deal of integration and structure, and with many rituals and activities that *supported* the adults' and the students' learning and functioning in that culture. What remains to be explored is how to describe and transmit the ideas in this study to teachers, educators, and policy makers, in a way that would not destroy the holistic character of the project, or the manner in which the teacher, the students, and the researcher learned and thought about it, and interacted and worked together because of it.

Conclusion 7. Video as a research tool.

Four approaches for using video were tested for documenting the ISDP research. In what I named VideoMode1, I utilized video as a *holistic interview-recorder.* In VideoMode2, I utilized video as a *silent observer.* VideoMode3 was used as a *video-based note taker.* VideoModes 1, 2, and 3 contributed greatly, but differently, to the data-collection process, and espe-cially to the quantitative, qualitative, and comparative analysis of the study's results. VideoMode4 was a process of conducting *research and observation of phenomena through video chunking and editing.*

Both the quantitative and qualitative research techniques that were used for this study involved the extensive use of videotaping. The videotaping was done for several purposes: first, for an assessment of children's learning of mathematics, programming, and software design; second, for a documentation of the development of the project's culture in the whole class, among particular students, and in relation to the teacher; and third, for a comparison of the experimental class's knowledge with that of two control classes.

I must admit that video making was not one of my primary research goals, and I do not value my video data as being "beautiful" or "good" in the conventional artistic senses of film and video production. I only wish to highlight here how video was used for my *specific* research. I do not claim that certain uses of video as a researcher's tool are better than others. Also, I was not concerned with creating a hierarchical ranking of various uses of video. Rather, I wished to explore how the implementation of various video techniques in ISDP contributed to the data collection and research analysis. I found that each of these different uses of a videocamera captured certain aspects of the research better than other research tools could have done. Video assisted me in systematically capturing conceptual, learning-related, and developmental phenomena. I claim that certain data on such complex phenomena could only be captured, and later analyzed in detail, through video.

VideoModel: Using video for a holistic documentation of interviews with research participants. The holistic characteristics of video documentation was utilized in several contexts during the ISDP research. For establishing a base line about children's knowledge of fractions and Logo programming before ISDP had begun, 51 children from three classes (one experimental and two control classes) were given written and computer-based tests, and were also interviewed at length on video, using the Piagetian clinical method. The camera was placed on a tripod during these interviews focusing sometimes on both the researcher and the child, and at other times, only on the child.

Today, the most common piece of technology researchers use in interviewing is the audiotape. It is usually used for recording interviews when a word-by-word transcript is crucial for the research. The audiotape is preferred over handwritten notes because it records the data in a more "objective" way and frees the researcher from taking careful notes during the interview. This approach enables him or her to focus on the person being interviewed—which makes the process of interviewing much more "friendly and comfortable" for all participants. In addition, audiotape allows for postinterview replay and reanalysis of any given moment in the interview—an advantage it has in common with the videocamera. A disadvantage of the videocamera in comparison with the audiotape is the effect it can have on the ambiance of the interview. Most people feel more comfortable and less intimated in front of an audiorecorder than in front of a camera. However, this was not a problem for most children in my study, who had become

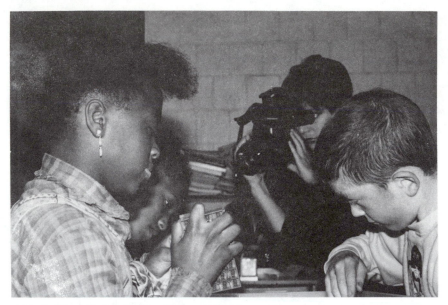

(Jacqueline Karaaslanian Photography)

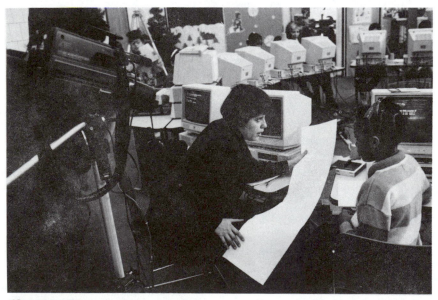

(Stephen Sherman Photography)

Different Modes for Video Use as a Researcher's Tool.

(Jacqueline Karaaslanian Photography)

(Jacqueline Karaaslanian Photography)

(Stephen Sherman Photography)

Conducting Research through Videotaping and Video Editing.

accustomed to the several videocameras used by various researchers at Project Headlight.

Any advantages in terms of comfort would in this case have been offset by the importance of being able to view the students' facial expressions and body language, which, for the purpose of answering certain research questions, were as important as what was actually said (or not said) during the interview sessions. Since most of these interviews focused on the idea of constructing and talking about representations of fractions, children often used movement and facial expressions for expressing their ideas. They were also asked to work with some manipulative materials (blocks, clay, drawings, pegs)—activities that could only be captured in detail on video. I therefore opted for what I considered a superior method of recording children's conceptual understanding and their multiple ways of expressing their knowledge and ideas to me.

After the preinterviews and tests were done, ISDP started. All three classes (experimental and controls) followed the regular mathematics curriculum, including a two-month unit on fractions. However, the control classes differed from the experimental class, and from each other, in their computer learning experience. When the ISDP project ended, posttests and interviews were conducted with the experimental and control groups to document the differences in their performances and knowledge. All these interviews were again recorded in VideoMode1. These pre- and post-videodata allowed me to view segments back-to-back, and to capture, for example, any growth or change that occurred in children's understanding of fractions and their representations, or in their attitudes towards mathematics in general. I could measure response time when needed, look for regulations, and code the information systematically according to categories of interest. As I watched the videos over again, new categories for analyses emerged. Some aspects of the qualitative and quantitative analysis of each child, and the cross-analysis of several groups of children, could not have been done through the use of notes or audiorecorded interviews.

Finally, VideoMode1 was often used *during* the period of ISDP as well. For example, if I had certain questions I wanted to ask the teacher or the children about their projects and learning, I videotaped the person in the process of answering and reacting to my questions. The camera was placed on a tripod for these interviews. In summary, close to 80 hours of video data in the form of VideoMode1 was collected for the ISDP research.

VideoMode2: Using video as a "silent observer" for documenting participants' development during a project. In VideoMode2, the videocamera was placed on a tripod in one position for an entire session and simply allowed to run (often for an entire hour). VideoMode2 was used to capture classroom discussions, brainstorming sessions, one or two children working on their software projects at their computer, and the teacher's or the researcher's interactions with her students. VideoMode2 was my *major* way of using video in ISDP. Since

ISDP lasted close to 4 months, VideoMode2 captured a great quantity of developmental phenomena. It was used much like another observer who takes extensive notes about children in action. However, it was different from a human observer, since it captured data more "objectively" and more comprehensively than even the most experienced human researcher could do by hand.

VideoMode2 not only captured data in an objective and holistic way, but also "freed" me as a researcher. I needed to be an active participant in this environment. With the use of VideoMode2, I did not have to be concerned about the camera, and I was able to devote my full attention to my work with the children. Therefore, from the children's and teacher's point of view, I became more of a helper in the culture than an observer.

I collected close to 60 hours of video in VideoMode2, which allowed me to later observe children and teacher learning, designing, and interacting—often in situations when I was not directly present.

I found that VideoMode2 was the most objective way of documenting children at work. Whatever happened in front of the camera was taped, without preplanning or any fixed agenda. The only "agenda" I had was, for example, to "capture Tim and Monica once a week in VideoMode2." But I did not ask them questions, nor did I tell them what to do, or how to act, at the times when the camera was there to record them. I therefore believe that using the camera in VideoMode2 was the least intimidating for the research participants. Since no person carried the camera, the participants felt quite free to act the way they usually do. In certain situations, however, the participants did react to the camera. They approached the camera and spoke to it, demonstrated things to it, or joked with it. These situations, in fact, revealed very important ideas that were present in children's minds on a given day, revealed information about their projects, and captured moments related to social to social play. I believe that such moments could not have been so beautifully captured if a person, not a tripod, had been holding the camera. Here is an example.

The importance of VideoMode2 in investigating Tim's case. Tim, one of the most successful children in what we describe as "school mathematics," usually scored high on school tests and was a very proper, self-disciplined, and organized student. Not surprisingly, Tim developed much greater knowledge of fractions and Logo after ISDP. Although he scored high in the posttesting, it turned out that the most important revelation, captured by video, was not the effect of ISDP on "how he got better in solving school-like problems," but closely related to what I discovered about other aspects of his experience. In the video, I saw new facets of Tim's personality and observed how they affected his style of involvement in ISDP and hence his learning. VideoMode2 recorded the many occasions when Tim spoke spontaneously to the camera about what he was doing at that time. Tim was never asked to speak to the camera, but he liked very much to do so. He would often turn around, look straight into the lens, and say things such as: "This is the six o'clock news. And we focus today on Tim's Fractions Software . . ." He would then demonstrate his piece of software, step-by-step, to his imaginary "six o'clock news audience," explaining his fractions representations, and his Logo-related discoveries. At other times, he would say to the camera, "Wait, I will return shortly after I help Cassina with her programming, and will tell you more about my very, very cool project."

At times, Tim also introduced his partner Micky to his imaginary "news audience": "This is my friend Micky. We work together every once in a while. His project is cool, too. Let's look at what he has accomplished so far . . ." Tim and Micky presented each other's progress to the camera, told jokes to it, and socialized in front of, and with it. They "collected" a great deal of data for me about their own processes and progress in the project.

First, I believe they would not have done all that if I had been carrying the camera. Second, with 17 children around me, I was not able, even if I wanted to, to invest a great deal of time with any one child. I could not play and joke with children in the same way they did with my camera. I could never have recorded such detailed reports of their projects as they voluntarily presented to the camera.

To summarize, VideoMode2 captured two important aspects of Tim's personality. It revealed a "playful Tim," very different from the "successful, proper, shy, quiet" Tim familiar to his teachers and me. The camera on a tripod did not intimidate him. The opposite occurred: He was captured as a free, spontaneous, uncensored, and much more joyful child who blossomed in the absence of adults. Tim expressed himself very differently when he was left alone, or with a couple of friends with whom he could fool around and exchange ideas. In this playful mode, Tim did extremely creative, yet disciplined, work on a project that was meaningful for him.

Another aspect of Tim's work that was captured in VideoMode2 was his relationship with Micky. They sat next to each other during the 4 months of the project. Much like professional adults, they worked together, had fun together, and helped each other on fractions and Logo programming. Individually and collaboratively they were trying to accomplish the same job. The camera recorded their unusually relaxed and non-competitive relationship. Yet, it also recorded how each of them was very concerned about his own processes and product, which later resulted in two different pieces of instructional software.

VideoMode3: Using video as a note-taking tool. In VideoMode3, the videocamera was carried by me and directed at taping interesting events. Certain aspects of VideoMode3 are the closest to conventional video-making techniques. When certain events occurred that seemed to me to be significant for answering my research questions, I videotaped them instead of taking notes by hand. VideoMode3 was used mostly for capturing something that was interesting *con-*

ceptually. Although the quality of the image and sound were not necessarily my first priority, I did sometimes use it for capturing a "good shot" of a child at work, "a close up" of someone's laugh, joy of accomplishment, frustration; or an interesting interaction among children or between a teacher and a child. However, much like VideoMode1, these shots were more purposeful and subjective, and were directed at recording certain things that were important for me personally, as the researcher—for later observation and analysis.

VideoModes 1, 2, and 3: their importance to the analysis of the quantitative, qualitative, and comparative results. By the time I had completed my study, I had accumulated close to 100 hours of video in the form of VideoMode1. This data included about 80 hours of pre- and postinterviews with 51 fourth graders, 5 hours of interviews with the teacher during the project, and 2 hours of interviews with her a year after the project ended. In addition, my colleague Carol Stein (a professional editor who collaborated with me on the editing project) interviewed me about the project, and together we interviewed Seymour Papert as well. I also had close to 60 hours of video in the form of VideoMode2, which showed children working at their computers, giving classroom presentations, and brainstorming (Goldman Segall's, 1990, footage was available to me as well). And finally, I had images of the Headlight computer pods, including close-up shots of the children's computer screens, as well as close-ups of the Designer's Notebooks showing explanations of their story boards, designs, and plans and how these related to the final pieces of software.

These video data were used in the analysis of the study's results to supplement my personal handwritten observations, the children's daily Logo files, the contents of their Designer's Notebooks, and their written fractions and Logo tests. Video made significant contribution to the analyses of individual children's work in ISDP, as well as to the comparative analysis of the three classes of children. Although the other data (nonvideo) I collected were as important, I cannot imagine conducting and analyzing a constructionist research project of this kind without the video data I collected. Here are two examples.

The contributions of VideoModes 1, 2, and 3 to the investigation of Debbie's case. As I analyzed Debbie's case, I often had to consider the video data. My data in the form of VideoMode2, for example, enabled me to observe Debbie, often sitting by herself as the back of the classroom. She looked self-conscious and insecure. The video captured how rarely she participated in classroom discussions, and how seldomly she interacted with the other children outside of the classroom.

I had not expected ISDP to transform Debbie's personality and social life. However, I discovered in my video segments that her particular style of involvement and her thinking and learning did change in ways that I had not anticipated. On camera during ISDP, she appears deeply engaged in her designs and programming work, which convinced me that something in the ISDP approach had "clicked" for her. My earlier video segments demonstrated that she didn't connect with the regular classroom activities. However, later video data showed that she connected powerfully to this particular project. For example, as I observed her independence and her stubbornness on video from the ISDP period, I realized that these characteristics were probably a strength for her in a project of this kind. She was able to work on her own, in a private manner—but she could also share her ideas via the computer screens without being concerned about direct communication with others. The video I had in VideoMode3 showed that Debbie developed ideas about teaching and explaining which she applied in a direct, sometimes stern, manner that contrasted with her usual intimidated and isolated stance.

Another change that was captured on video in VideoMode1 was the way in which Debbie's initial lack of excitement about fractions in the preinterviews gave way to a growing interest and comprehension. The extent of this appropriation is evidenced in the general knowledge of fractions Debbie displayed in the videotaped interviews conducted before and after the project. As stated previously, like most children in the preinterviews, her fractions knowledge was limited, and she was insecure and vague. After the project ended, the video helped me compare her language, performance, and definitions with those of 50 other children. It showed that Debbie felt much more comfortable when talking about fractions than other children did, and that she overcame many of the rigid notions she had demonstrated in the preinterview.

The video also captured for me how Debbie came to be known for her good ideas and how she enjoyed feeling creative and successful. Other children wanted to see or play with her software, and gave her positive comments: "I love it!" or "This is fresh!" Then, they would ask her to teach them how to do things: "How did you ever make these colors change?" In VideoMode3, I also taped how Debbie's representation of the house became part of the general classroom culture. A few weeks after Debbie completed her representation of the house and the wagons, Tim's house appeared on video, and then Paul's. Of course, all these video data complemented the school test scores and the results from Debbie's written test.

In retrospect, Debbie's case was extremely rich. Yet she did not have the "ideal" personality for participating in the type of experimental investigation that required a great deal of collaboration with the researcher and a continual sharing of personal ideas, thoughts, knowledge of various kinds, designs, and programming problems. Interacting with Debbie was sometimes difficult, and I often felt I had to play games with her to elicit a meaningful response. VideoMode2—such as the "silent observer"—was crucial for collecting data on a child like Debbie. Such children are often ignored by researchers in favor of children whose personalities and attitudes make them easier or more enjoyable to work with. (In fact, I did not plan to focus on Debbie at first, and I had much more data about other children in her class.) With the assistance of my video as the "silent observer and note taker," I was able to develop a sense of who Debbie was. It was the reviewing of all my data (video and nonvideo) in integration that made me decide that I should choose to investigate—and more importantly, to present her case to teachers and researchers, not only because of its intrinsic interest, but also because of the general importance of gathering and presenting data on children who are socially and academically at risk.

The contribution of VideoModes 1, 2, and 3 to the investigation of Sherry's case. Another demonstration of the high value of video data is the case of Sherry. Sherry was a slow worker, easily distracted, and quite disorganized in her thinking and writing. Her concentration was intermittent, and she was rarely fully engaged in her regular school work, as was captured in the earlier video segments. However, the camera later captured Sherry's ways of enjoying ISDP. In VideoMode2, I was able to record her *processes* of designing one of the more interesting pieces of software in this class. Given her personality and style of work, organizing a project of this kind was in itself an important learning experience. Her Logo program was not as large or complex as some of the other children's, but the video data made me realize that it was quite an accomplishment for her. My video data emphasized, for example, that, for Sherry, the *length* of the project was a crucial factor in enabling her to become engaged in it and see it through to a finished product. The video shows that she did not accomplish much during any individual session. Still, it was rare to see her as involved with her other school work as she was in ISDP. Moreover, the videocamera captured Sherry's unique body language, which made me realize that Sherry's style was to move and dance as she thinks and solve problems—behaviors that are certainly not encouraged in other classroom settings, but which enabled her to function effectively.

Sherry did not write much in her Designer's Notebook (unlike Debbie). But even the little that was videotaped about her notes and designs provided a window into her progress. She started with what she described as "fractionizing shapes." And later, she created in her Notebook a "generic design" for all the screens that show "fractionized shapes." The camera also recorded how the month of April (i.e., the second month of the project) was a transitional period for her. Sherry then stopped working on shapes and started to think about a very different kind of representation: *The Clock*. The video data allowed me to capture this process of transition and to explore "with her" the discoveries she made as she was moving her fingers on the computer screen, calculating angles, taking notes, and programming her animation of the Clock.

Sherry did well on most items in the videotaped postinterview, but the most interesting moment in the postinterview occurred when she looked around the room and chose to talk about the clock as a representation of a fraction. Only the camera could capture how she "struggled" at this part of the interview. Although

Sherry had spent an entire month programming a clock in Logo, during the interview it seemed she was still at a transitional level of understanding the different properties of this representation. A great deal of information was non-verbal in this interview: her shy smile, her animated big eyes, and her use of her hands to express and explore many of her thoughts. Videotaping was crucial for understanding and analyzing what was going on with her. Sherry was thinking of what the clock represents in relation to fractions. The clock as an object is quite confusing, since it represents both fractions as area (in its shape divided by the clock's hands), as well as fractions in time (days, hours, minutes, seconds, etc.). This segment of the interview raised many epistemological questions in my mind in the same way it did for Sherry. But I could always observe Sherry on video, again and again, and ask: What is really going on in Sherry's mind?

VideoMode4: Doing research through video chunking and editing. After I completed writing my thesis (Harel, 1988), the large amount of raw audiovisual information collected for the original research purposes in VideoModes 1, 2, and 3 was reanalyzed, chunked, and/or edited to produce several short segments that would be useful for documenting the project. What do I mean by "useful?" Why was editing an important research project in itself?

Often teachers request curriculum materials from our group. They need materials that will guide them in implementing Constructionist projects with computers, and they seek ways of adopting the Epistemology and Learning Group's pedagogical approach in their classrooms. As stated previously, this presents a dilemma: the open-ended and Constructionist character of ISDP (as well as of other projects in the E&L Group) does not easily lend itself to conventional step-by-step guidelines, worksheets, or exercises. In addition, teachers are part of a complex and rather rigid system that often does not allow them to try new things or explore new pedagogy even when they want to be innovative.

Therefore, one goal of VideoMode4 was to create a series of video segments with which to document several aspects of ISDP and—at the same time—to situate it within the theoretical framework of Constructionism.

In VideoMode4, I wanted to explore whether video can be a flexible medium that conveys complexity. I attempted to create a series of videotapes that could inform and inspire teachers and researchers alike without destroying the holistic character of the project, which we thought we could do most effectively by capturing on video, for example, someone who was a "real" teacher speaking about her own experiences in the project.

To summarize, in ISDP I was able to experiment with using video as a research tool in the following ways: VideoMode1 was utilized as a *holistic interview recorder,* VideoMode2 as a *silent observer,* and VideoMode3 as a video-based *note taker.* I gave examples of how each of these three approaches contributed greatly, but differently, to the data collection and analysis. Some examples demonstrated how all VideoModes together—when combined with handwritten notes, the participants' project-portfolios, and other data—contributed to the investigation of the case studies about the children and their teacher, and to the documentation of the project.

I found that video, which is usually considered to be a qualitative data-recorder, assisted me, not only in the qualitative analysis of the results, but also in the quantitative and comparative analysis. Video is a medium which has a great potential for comparing individual children's and groups of children's learning and development over time and in detail. Although good ethnographic research can also be conducted without the use of video, in my examples I attempted to show that certain *kinds* of data could only be captured through video.

In addition, I described VideoMode4 as a process of *conducting research through video chunking and editing*. Video is a holistic and multidimensional medium that could play a great role in teacher's development and in the presentation of Constructionist ideas that do not readily lend themselves to a step-by-step presentation.

I must make some remarks about the "objective" and "subjective" aspects of video recording. I see all VideoModes as *subjective* in one sense: In VideoModes 1, 2, and 3, I placed the camera and "framed" what *I* wanted to capture, and in VideoMode4, I edited the segments for communicating ideas that *I* wanted to convey about the project and its theoretical approach. However, I do see VideoMode2—the silent observer—as the most objective of these four modes for two reasons: first, because I did not have direct control over what was going on in front of the camera; second, because I think children behave differently if the "camera's eye" is operated by a person as opposed to operating by itself on a tripod. In all four cases the participants reacted to the presence of the camera. However, my data revealed that I was only able to collect certain kinds of information via VideoMode2—information related to social play, freedom of expression, and uncensored behaviors of the participants. Therefore, the data I collected in VideoMode2 often revealed precious insights about the participants which I could never have gathered otherwise.

Yet, to some degree, all VideoModes are also *objective,* since one can always go back to the video data, reobserve them, retrieve more information, replay segments, and look at the same data in many different ways. One can also present such data to various researchers and get their opinions about the meaning of any given recorded moment—something I often took advantage of during my data analysis.

Finally, I hope the "video cases" I described above (of Tim, Debbie, and Sherry) will inspire the readers' thinking about the potential power of video as a researcher's tool. My explorations of video as an information-recording medium and as an information-analysis medium were quite preliminary and specific to ISDP. A great deal of exploration about video is taking place within our research group (e.g., Granott, 1990; Goldman Segall, 1990; Strohecker, 1990) and elsewhere. Further investigation of these issues is needed for developing the field in relation to the modification and refinement of the techniques described in this section, and the development of additional techniques that could be used for different types of research.

Conclusion 8. Programmable design and production tools for children's learning.

The findings of this thesis revealed the need to create an integrated environment that would allow children to program, design, reflect, plan, take notes, and make changes. This environment must also allow the information produced by one child or by a group of children to be presented, simply and efficiently, within the same computer system. More sophisticated and dynamic tools could be developed and used for this purpose. Computerized Designer's Notebooks, for example, would encourage children's reflections *during* the design and implementation phases, rather than after; a specially designed computer interface, including online designer's cards and links, could assist the children during the different phases of their software presentation or execution; videodisc technology could enhance their thinking of many more real-life representations of rational numbers. My preliminary ideas for a Logo-based, integrative, software development environment for children are briefly presented below.

The Experimental children's day-by-day copying of their Logo files, their saving of them on a special diskette, and their ongoing writing in the Designer's Notebooks was unique, because these tools not only represented the children's processes, but also kept track of their ideas, actions, and thoughts while solving the software design task. In this way, a child's software design process and its history became objects of study for the children, their teacher, and the researcher. Although a great deal of rich data were gathered by the use of these tools (the Logo files and the writing in the notebooks, supplemented by videotaping and the researcher's notes), other, more sophisticated and dynamic tools could be developed and used for this purpose. While working on this study, I realized that more sophisticated methods for organizing and presenting the software were needed to encourage higher levels of metacognition in children and a clearer metaconceptual understanding of the topics involved (Logo, design, and fractions). In this section I outline my preliminary ideas for an integrative computer environment for software design, production, and presentation.

A system for facilitating young children's learning. The system I shall outline here is aimed at facilitating young children's learning through software design and programming, rather than the developing of software by experts. It is based on many of the findings and observations, and seriously takes into consideration the learning and cognitive (or metacognitive) processes, that were (or could be) involved in students' software design. It is based on children's constructionism, rather than on the premise of using of the system for better mediation processes, such as tutoring and intelligent promptings. It is based on the philosophy of Logo programming, rather than on the philosophy of intelligent tutoring systems (e.g., Anderson et al., 1986; Collins & Brown, 1985). In fact, when a sophisticated system is developed, the children themselves could construct intelligent tutoring systems through the use of this system.

In other words, the system proposed here would not provide the child with "better" or more varied representations of fractions, with sophisticated instruction and modelling for solving fractional algorithms, or with sophisticated links between representations and processes; rather, through using this proposed system, the child himself or herself would be able to construct these representations and links in the system. Furthermore, the system would not produce process records for the children, but would instead allow them to produce their own records and written comments on their processes of software design and production. Finally, the system outlined here is Logo-based, but it is aimed at making Logo more flexible, and integrates Logo with other online design and production tools.

Electronic Designer's Notebook. The computer is a very dynamic medium, much more so than the Designer's Notebook, which was, after all a linear, nonintegrative, and difficult medium for children to appropriate. For example, the Notebook made it difficult for students to establish interrelations between the Notebook's parts, and to efficiently keep track of the history of their ideas, to understand the dynamic relations between these ideas, and grasp their own conceptual development during the project.

In the area of cognitive sciences, "computational techniques have proved to be powerful tools for both theoretical and experimental investigations of mind" (e.g., Collins & Brown, 1985, p. 1). The computer has an ability to record and represent processes as well as products of thought, and also allows the organization of topics, materials, and concepts, in different ways. It therefore makes sense to create an integrated environment that would allow children to program, design, reflect, plan, take notes, make changes, and present the information within the same computer system.

A computerized Designer's Notebook, for example, could become a very useful tool in children's software production; and once it was computerized and strongly integrated with Logo, it would encourage children's reflections *during* the design and implementation processes. Moreover, it should be linked to the actual programming and production environment for various other reasons that are listed below.

The Designer's Notebook was found to be a very important medium in the children's planning, designing, and reflections. However, one problem lay in the Notebook's being rather large in size, so that, because of space constraints at the computer table, the children usually put their Notebooks on their laps when they used them, or on top of the computer monitor, or under their chairs when they did not. This was not a very practical solution for the children, and it resulted in their using the Notebooks only infrequently while working at their computers. Perhaps the problem lay in the fact that, when the children were typing at the computer, they were obviously not able to freely shift from using the computer keyboard to using a pencil, or vice versa. Many children took notes on fractions, Logo concepts, and algorithms during their processes of programming; but in order to do this, they had to look for their pencil, move the computer keyboard aside, and, in this peculiar way, somehow manage to write in their Notebooks during their production phases. This may explain why the children often did not write in detail about the problems they encountered during their production phases, or forgot new ideas that occurred to them during their implementation processes.

A tool for integrating several pieces of software. Towards the end of the project, when the third graders were trying out many of the fourth graders' products, or when we attempted to connect some children's pieces of software together into one larger piece (which we called a *package*), we encountered several other difficulties. These difficulties were mainly related to questions of organization and presentation, the Logo interface, its memory space, and its slow program-execution pace (i.e., when it had to move from one Logo page to another and search for procedures in other Logo pages). Other difficulties were related, for example, to two children's giving similar names for their two different procedures, and to all the children's wanting their piece of software to appear first in the package. A more sophisticated system could be developed for solving some of these problems. This system should be developed for the purpose of assisting the children during different phases of software design and programming, as well as for improving software presentation or execution. A tentative computer interface for this purpose is sketched in Figure 1.

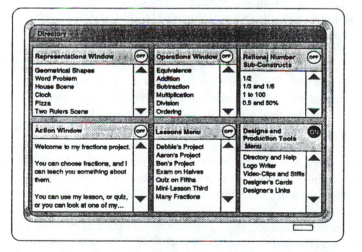

Figure 1.   A model Interface for an Integrative Software-Design-and-Production Tool for Young Children.

The appearance of this interface might look familiar; however, a major difference between this proposed system and others is that the content of each window would be written *by the children* rather than by the system's developer. This interface would be suitable for children's designing, programming, executing, and evaluating processes. It would also be useful when several students were connecting their pieces of software together. This particular model screen demonstrates the system's capabilities and features in the context of fractions (this particular subject being relevant to my thesis), but the system could be also used for any other topic.

A child can activate a window by clicking on the "ON/OFF" button. Then he or she can select any option offered at any given window. It is important to note that the content of all the windows (excluding the Design & Production Tools Window) are defined and created *by the child* or by a group of children during or after their software designing.

The only window of which the content is predefined by this system's developer is the Design & Production Tools Window. In this window, the child/software-developer can choose whether he or she wishes to work in the Logo Writer environment, use Video Clips or Stills that are stored in an integrated videodisc environment, use the Designer's Cards environment, or the Designer's Links (the latter two environments I am proposing here are for assisting children's ongoing planning, designing, and reflections, and are based on the role of the Designer's Notebook in the project). Furthermore, when a child is in one of these environments (Logo, Videodisc, Designer's Cards, or Designer's Links), the other three are always available for interaction and use.

The following screen is an example of how the interface might connect Logo with the plans and designs a child has created on Designer's Cards. The child would be able to call up his or her Designs Cards, Story-Board Scripts, Plans Cards, Reflections Cards, Notes Cards, Grid Cards, and so on, while working in LogoWriter.

This screen shows the LogoWriter environment being activated and enlarged over the whole screen. Designer's Cards is also activated on the top right of the screen. In this example, a child has chosen to work on one particular plan he or she has created and, while working in Logo, has decided to cross out the bottom part of his or her original plan (i.e., not implementing it) and briefly sketch a new design instead. Designer's Cards gives the child an option to *Enlarge* the Card he or she is working with to any desired and comfortable size, and to look at his or her *Cards Directory* for other plans and designs. Video Clips and Stills and Designer's Links are not activated in this particular example, but they are available for the child's use while he or she is in the Logo environment or in any other of these four.

As a further example, while programming in the Logo Writer environment, children might select "Video Clips and Stills." A library of discs would be available in the classroom so that children could select whatever appropriate

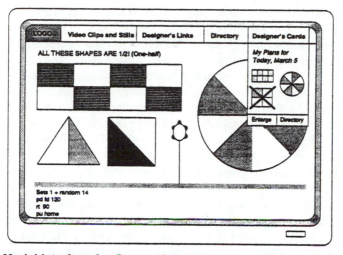

Figure 2.   A Model Interface for Connecting LogoWriter with Designer's Cards Online.

video clips or stills they needed for the particular fractional representation they were working on, or for any other purposes such as an opening scene or a feedback (a reward for a correct answer in their testing procedure, for example). During their processes of programming or of viewing visuals from the videodisc, they could also click on Designer's Cards, examine their prewritten plans for that day and their designs from the day before, or annotate their reasons for having made certain changes and choices while developing their product.

Designer's Cards would allow children's online, day-by-day planning, screen designing, story boarding, note taking, or other written reflections, in the same way that the Designer's Notebook was used by the children during the Instructional Software Design Project. The advantage of having Designer's Cards online is that children would be able to take notes and reflect more freely *during* their process of designing, programming, and production. They would be able to more easily compare their original designs and plans (goals) with their outcomes (the screens they had implemented) and decide whether to revise the plan or the program's output.

Designer's Links would allow children various options. (a) To create links in their computerized Designer's Notebook (i.e., their personal Designer's Cards). As we remember, Debbie would sometimes design a screen and not implement it for several days or weeks: Designer's Links would allow Debbie to keep better track, online, of her ideas, and to establish interrelations between her various designs and plans. (b) To create links between the various Logo or videodisc files and screens that had already been programmed. We saw how Debbie got confused when her program became long and complex: Designer's Links would allow her to keep better track of all the superprocedures or routines in which a particular procedure was used, or to create interrelations between the various parts of her software and Logo pages. (c) To plan links between procedures even before they fully existed. We saw how Debbie sometimes created lists of "empty" procedures (i.e., To Show. . . To Test. . .To Again), which were her plans for a teaching unit, or parts of her software. On several occasions, a day or two after she had created these "empty" procedures, she would lose track of where these should fit within her whole project, and sometimes decide not to implement them: Designer's Links would allow Debbie to sketch connections and relations, and to keep track of where these procedures should or could fit into or relate to her existing product.

During and after the programming of their software in Logo, a child, or a group of children, could place in the *Rational-Number Subconstructs Menu* all the rational numbers they had created representations for. In the *Operations Window,* they could place the operations they had made representations for; in the *Lessons Menu,* the titles of the lessons or quizzes they had created; and in the *Representations Window,* the titles of the representations they had made for specific rational-number concepts, and/or operations.

As a concrete example let us examine what Debbie could do by using a system of this kind (as presented in Figure 1).

> Debbie could list 1/2 in the Fractions Menu Window, list HALF-THE-SCREEN, GEOMETRICAL-SHAPES, and HOUSE-SCENE, in the Representations Window; she could also list EQUIVALENT FRACTIONS in the Operations Menu, and her EQUIVALENCE-SCENE in the Representation Window. In the Lessons Menu, she could list DEBBIE'S FRACTIONS PROJECT, that is, her whole piece of software, or choose to list each meaningful part of it separately, such as ON HALVES, THE ADDITION LESSON, THE EXAM, and so on. She could also pre-select to put her INTRODUCTION in the Action Window, and use this space for giving instructions to the user on what to do.

Debbie would be the one in charge of creating the items that appeared in the windows; she would also be in charge of establishing (programming) the links between items and windows. This organization would probably help Debbie develop a better mental model of her product and its parts (i.e., its part–whole relationship). It could also encourage her thinking about the differences between various rational-number concepts, operations, representations, and to organize those in minilessons, quizzes, projects, and so on. The programming process itself would remain similar to the one she went through during the project. However, the organization of her finished or partially finished procedures and superprocedures would be much facilitated by the use of this system.

A Logo-based system. I have already given some of my reasons for integrating the Designer's Notebook online in the form of Designer's Cards and Designer's Links. I shall now briefly explain why I recommend a Logo-based system, and why I wish to integrate it with a videodisc system. The various reasons for this are related to the cognitive processes involved and to children's experiences in learning this programming language. Again, I wish to stress the fact that my study revealed that children felt very comfortable programming in Logo, enjoyed it a great deal, and learned how to program quite rapidly. In my project, which was based on the learning of fractions, Logo was ideal for creating fractional representations and links or translations between them.

Integrating video technology into the children's productions process. Many interesting representations could be created by children with real-life images, and by relating Logo graphics and text to them. In the case of fractions learning, this might involve children in thinking more about real-life rational-number situations. It could make Logo a more flexible tool, since it is quite difficult to program in Logo real-life images of people, animals, food, nature, shops, movement, and so on—all of which are easy to store on the visual database of a videodisc (or by using DVI technology directly in the computer's memory; see Benenson, 1990). Logo could also be used for highlighting various features of these pictures, creating interesting patterns, or superimposing text and graphics on the visual (or with two separate monitors, in parallel with the visuals). The use of a video input could also bring into play the use of narrations and music in the children's products; with sound and narrations, children could explore many more rational-number representations related to words, poems, and musical rhythms.

Another reason for integrating video technology is that digital video and videodisc developers and researchers have recently investigated how these have great potential and are very powerful in the way they help children to learn through *exploration and manipulation of visual and auditory material.* It is not in the scope of this section to review these interesting and valuable findings. However, one problem I shall mention is that this type of technology requires very expansive hardware and very complex, time-consuming, and expensive software development. Educational institutions and school systems, so far, have not been able to afford to invest in the research and development of computer-based video and videodisc systems and software of this kind. To my mind, one way we could incorporate this technology into education is by making it as *generic* as possible (like word processors or the Logo programming language, which can be incorporated into the learning of many domains). Children should be able to use video and videodiscs in their processes of programming (and computer programming already exist in many schools) once an appropriate interface between Logo and video or a videodisc player had been developed. While almost no such systems existed at the time I worked on my dissertation (1987–1988), several are out there and under development as I write this section (Harel, 1990c). But my emphasis remains on "letting children do it"—such as, let them experience and learn from design, production, and multimedia programming with computer systems that incorporate video and videodisc materials.

These were only a few ideas, on a very superficial level, for creating a system for children's software development and production. They are based on my finding that, even through Logo alone, the experimental children learned a great deal from their processes of software development. I invite the reader to begin to imagine what these same children could learn from using a system integrating Logo with Designer's Cards, Designer's Links, and Video Clips and Stills (offered for their use through videodisc technology). It goes without saying that children's intensive use of this kind of a system could open up many new areas to researchers for investigating children's minds, cognitive development, problem-solving processes, and their processes and ability to learn several mutually supportive topics and skills at the same time.

SUMMARY OF CONCLUSIONS

Software design for learning. ISDP offers changes in the approach to the learning and teaching of Logo and fractions concepts and skills, and of several important and more general thinking and problem-solving skills. But it also proposes a more general approach that could be implemented with other topics in mathematics (e.g., proportional reasoning), as well as many other topics in the elementary school curriculum. Children should be able to learn areas of science, geography, literature, art, and social studies through this method of instructional software design. Further experiments should be conducted for investigating which topics lend themselves best to this approach, and how this method contributes to and changes children's understanding of these topics.

A shift in research methodologies. As shown in previous findings on Logo (e.g., Turkle, 1984; Weir, 1986; Lawler, 1985), programming and software designing also proved to be a learning activity that allowed for individual differences in learning, mastery, and expression. New research methods are needed for identifying, analyzing and describing these differences. Such methods could, for example, trace similarities and differences in individual learning processes and production strategies, and relate them to different technological tools and learning theories.

A mixture of traditional research methods with an extensive use of videotaping was used to systematically study this open-ended and extended problem-solving process and to trace individual differences within it. This marked a shift away from standard methodology in the field, which concentrates on analyzing shorter and more narrowly defined problem-solving sessions. I was able to collect many different kinds data (on cognitive as well as social phenomena; on individuals as well as social phenomena; on individuals as well as on groups; written data, and video data, as well as textually based data; informal data, as well as formal data from standardized tests; researcher's observational data, as well as children's own writings, programs, and portfolios; and quantitative, qualitative, as well as comparative data). All these pieces of data taken together were informative at many levels.

Dissemination of ideas to educators. Several teachers have requested curriculum materials that would guide them in implementing this project and in adopting a similar pedagogical approach in classrooms. This presets a dilemma. On the one hand, the open-ended character of the project does not easily lend itself to step-by-step guidelines, worksheets, or exercises. On the other hand, teachers are part of a complex and rather rigid system that does not often allow them to easily try new things or explore new pedagogy. The use of video, for example, could facilitate teachers' appropriation of the ideas embedded in this project. However, there is a need to experiment further with constructive dissemination of the ideas and principles of ISDP (and other projects of this kind). At MIT we are working with teachers, in classrooms and at workshops, in an ongoing effort to find more constructive ways of communicating our ideas to the educational community.

Programmable tools for software design. We could imagine several technological tools that would facilitate the implemention of ISDP or any similar design-oriented projects. A tentative computer interface for this purpose was sketched in Conclusion 8 of this chapter. However, there is a need to investigate what programming will mean in the world (inside and outside education) during the 1990s and beyond. In the 1970s, when Logo was developed, researchers and educators thought that the main purpose in children's programming was the "cognitive gains" from the programming activity itself and the transfer of those "thinking skills" into areas outside of programming. However, ISDP points in another direction—towards programming as a means for learning and building other things, formulating ideas, and constructing knowledge. Researchers and tool developers will need to investigate this issue deeply as they think about the next generation of programmable tools.

Children, mathematics, and multimedia technology. Multimedia design and production tools are now in use (they were not really in use at the time the ISDP study was conducted). Adults are already working with and enjoying them, and Mitterer (1989), for example, lists 537 recent writings in which adults describe their research experiences with hypermedia. As two of them, HyperCard and Intermedia, become more popular, we begin to think about how they could be integrated into mathematics education, and what new learning and thinking experiences could become possible for the students using them. We know that we can now produce wonderful interactive, nonlinear designs that were not previously possible—for various reasons related to hardware, software, or our level of expertise as programmers and producers.

The degree to which these designs can advance educational goals is still to be investigated. However, it will surely depend on whether the lessons learned in the last decade about how to use Logo are applied to this new technology.

If used by children in constructivist way, these new tools could provide new ways of learning—as the constructionist approach to Logo has done. But if used in an instructionist way, there are likely to yield poor quality results that would reflect—inaccurately—on the medium itself. Good hypermedia educational materials will result when conventions for their use become more highly developed, and when thoughtful and creative researchers, developers, and educators have learned enough about the new medium to use it effectively.

While tool developers in the multimedia and hypermedia fields need to think about how to create better interfaces or tools for children's use, and how to make the programming and design languages more accessible and powerful to young children, educational researchers and teachers need to think about ways of making constructivist pedagogy possible for children. This could mean, for example, figuring out ways of integrating these tools—in the ISDP spirit—into the students' explorations of existing curricular topics in mathematics. In order to avoid repeating the mistakes made in the use of Logo in many classrooms, educators need to think about these systems as constructive tools for *knowledge reformulation*. They must structure projects in such a way that *children* become the explorers, the designers, and the builders with these tools. Mathematics and Science are ideal subjects for such multirepresentational explorations.

ISDP as a model for constructionist learning. This book had a dual intention: To describe ISDP, and to situate this particular project in a general theoretical framework called Constructionism. ISDP offered a realistic and comprehensive model for our constructionist vision of education in general, and for the use of computers in education in particular. It also offered a model for the kinds of research that we find insightful and beneficial to our understanding of learning and development, thinking, teaching, and education, and of the use of computers to facilitate these processes.

We saw how the participant ISDP class, comprised of 17 fourth-grade students, integratively learned mathematics, design, and programming, and so on, in the course of using LogoWriter to develop pieces of instructional software for teaching third graders. I illustrated various aspects of our evaluation—quantitative and comparative results, as well as qualitative ones. The evaluation showed that the ISDP students achieved greater mastery of both Logo and fractions and improved metacognitive skills, better than either control class. The ISDP approach of using Logo programming as a tool for reformulating fractions knowledge was compared with other approaches to using Logo. In particular, it was compared to the traditional learning of programming per se in isolation from a content domain, and to other approaches of learning fractions. The ISDP experiment showed that simultaneously learning programming and fractions was more effective than learning them in isolation from each other.

ISDP recast fractions learning in essentially three ways: (a) it emphasized more involvement with the deep structure (representations) over the surface structure (algorithms) of rational-number knowledge; (b) it made fractions learning instrumental to a larger intellectual and social goal, that is, having students think about and explain what they think and learn, in an interactive lesson designed for younger children; and (c) it encouraged both personal expression and social communication of rational-number knowledge and ideas.

I emphasized the fact that ISDP had little to do with the idea that learning Logo is in itself either easy or beneficial. We discussed how, in different contexts, the importance of the phrase "learning Logo" can differ so greatly that the question borders on meaninglessness. Nevertheless, in the particular context of the ISD project, where Logo was integrated into a total context, and where students programmed intensively and extensively, one can meaningfully begin to investigate the question of how various features of Logo contributed to the success of the children's work.

Logo facilitated the ongoing *personal engagement* and gradual evolution of different kinds of knowledge; and at the same time, it also facilitated the *sharing* of that knowledge with other members of the community, which in turn encouraged the learners to continue and build upon their own and other people's ideas. In short, Logo facilitated communications about the processes and acts of cognition and learning. I do not maintain that only Logo could do this. But looking carefully at which specific features of Logo enhanced individual cognition and social learning can help guide us in future technological developments. And indeed, ISDP provided us with many insights (cognitive/developmental as well as technological) into what kinds of learning tools we want to develop for constructionist learning.

ISDP should not be read like a "very controlled treatment" type of experiment. The pedagogical situation was quite complex, and one could formulate innumerable conjectures about the "real" source of the experimental children's learning. I conclude that ISDP allowed us to create a total learning environment in which some impressive integrated learning took place. It was beyond the scope of this study to single out the contribution of the individual aspects of that environment. A more complete understanding of this learning process can come through an integrative and cumulative process of experimentation and theory building (and there are several projects of this kind within our group at the Media Laboratory). This study is also intended as a contribution to that process, in which I presented some conjectures and the bases on which I formulated them. I hypothesized, for example, that improvements in performance among ISDP students could have been affected by factors related to the affective side of cognition and learning, the children's process of personal appropriation of knowledge, the children's use of LogoWriter, the children's constructivist involvement with the deep structure of fractions knowledge, the integrated-learning principle, the learning-by-teaching principle, and the power of design as a learning activity.

However, the main point is that each one of those conjectures, when considered alone, would give only very partial information about the meaning of the results. By considering them together, and by speculating about their interrelations, we are endeavoring to make use of the very kind of holistic approach—to knowledge and cognition, and to the development of learning technologies—that we believe informs and characterizes Constructionism in general, and ISDP in particular.

Finally, ISDP demonstrated that children—given a context of adequate structure and control over their learning—can function much like a community of adult professionals. The experimental children shared ideas, criticized each other's products, and often provided help to their peers; yet, in the end, they each produced their own product. An interface system similar to the one proposed above, combined with hypermedia and multimedia technology, would further encourage children along this path of greater responsibility for their individual work and enhanced collaboration with others—such as, supporting individual and social constructionism.

However, no "technological fix" can bring about the evolution of a learning community. Children in the ISDP, and in Project Headlight generally, had free access to computers they could use and appropriate as tools in flexible ways for exploring ideas of their own as well as for exploring different school subject areas—mainly through design, building, and programming (ISDP explored the learning of mathematics, other projects focus on other topics). Many factors, including the complexity and open-endedness of the project, the children's independent work styles, the project's length, and the enthusiastic and constructive working relationship among researcher, teacher, and students combined to create an essentially new approach to learning.

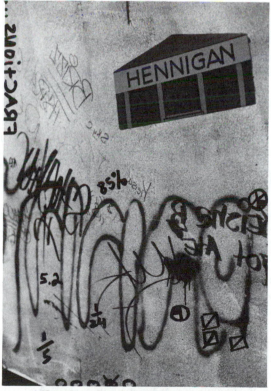

(Stephen Sherman Photography)

CODA:
Situating *CHILDREN DESIGNERS* in the Current Research Scene

Integrating learning through design into the culture of schools is a research area now beginning to emerge in several research centers in the United States. During the recent Annual Meeting of the American Educational Research Association (AERA, April 1991) I was struck by how much more sympathetic the atmosphere is to this kind of work. "Design for learning" did not really exist as an object of study six years ago when many of us within Papert's group, at the newly formed Media Laboratory, were looking for ways to implement the first constructionist "children designers" research program (Papert, 1986; Harel, 1986).

In the mid-1980s *precisely defined studies on cognitive skills, their acquisition and performance in children and experts,* within the paradigms of the "teaching of thinking," "studies in metacognition," "problem-solving skills," and the like were most dominant in the field (e.g., L. Resnick, 1987, 1991; see also the literature review in Chapter 1 of this book). It was particularly true within the mathematics and science education research, the technology and education research, the framework of artificial intelligence in education, and the experimental studies of computer programmers (e.g., Chipman, Segal, & Glaser, vol. 1 & 2, 1985; Collins & Brown, 1985, 1987; Soloway & Iyengar, 1986; and others). Even Perkins' conceptualization of the " Knowledge as Design" theory back in 1985–1986, which inspired my work, was conceived primarily within the framework of teaching thinking. The act of learning through designing and producing (in the ways expressed in Papert's vision and writings during that period, and prior to that) was secondary. For Perkins, "thinking about knowledge and information as designs" represented an effective strategy for thinking, rather than for learners doing and building educational artifacts. His studies on programming (1986, 1987) are examples of that methodology.

These days, however, one can notice the emergence of an interesting trend, or even a *paradigm shift,* in both methods of research and educational practice within the *same* community of researchers. Several presentations during the 1991 AERA conference are evidence of this paradigm shift. And while *I am not sure where it leads,* I find it important enough to note and raise some related questions. This may help us situate Papert's work, the work I presented in this book, and our work in progress (see Appendix), in the current research scene.

My personal and informal "ethnographic survey" of researchers and presentations during the 1991 AERA leads to identifying trends towards several of the themes presented in ISDP: the general constructionist approach; the particular emphasis on design; the casting of children in the role of media producers rather than consumers; and the enthusiasm towards—and multiple presentations of—students' products. Here are several examples. Five years ago, Elliot Soloway, then at Yale University, invested most of his efforts in developing various programming and debugging tools, and in investigating the learning (and instruction) of programming from the point of view of helping students develop planning and debugging skills. He also investigated how expertise is attained by moving from problems to goals—to plans—to implementation in "an expert's style." In the past two years, with his colleagues at the University of Michigan, Soloway has investigated and developed tools for supporting learning through design. Their research projects with MediaText in the context of high school classrooms are good examples of this current, very different, research enterprise.[1] Roy Pea from the Institute for Research on Learning, who in the mid-1980s was known for his Bank Street studies on planning, debugging skills, problem solving, and cognitive transfer with Logo and other tools, started to run a multimedia production club for children's learning in January 1991. This rich design-based learning environment plays an important role in Pea's current research. It is epistemologically very different from the kinds of environments he chose to study in the past.[2] During 1986–88, at Carnegie-Mellon University (CMU), Sharon Carver studied debugging abilities and programming misconceptions in children, and came up with a set of well-defined instructional strategies to foster and strengthen debugging and problem solving in children's programming (see my review of this work in Chapter III of this book). Today, at the University of Rochester, Carver designs learning environments of a very different kind, where students learn problem solving through their design and production of HyperCard-based software.[3] In Richard Lehrer's recent studies at the

---

[1] a) *HyperText Environments Expand the Bandwidth of Interactivity;* b) *The Promise of Technology for Promoting Change;* and c) *MediaText Demonstration,* Elliot Soloway, Advanced Technology Center, University of Michigan. All three papers were presented at the Annual Meeting of the AERA, April 1991, Chicago IL. Compare these to his studies in Soloway E. & Iyengar, S. (Eds.). (1986). *Empirical Studies of Programmers.* Norwood, NJ: Ablex.

[2] See, *Students Learning through Design with Multimedia Tools for Collaborative Research, Composition, and Presentation.* Pea, R. D., Allen, C., Chertok, M., Godreau, E., Shaw, J., & Velrum, N. Institute for Research on Learning (IRL). Paper presented at the Annual Meeting of the AERA, April 1991, Chicago IL., (Compare this work to earlier Logo studies by Pea and his colleagues, in Pea R.D., & Sheingold, K. (1987). *Mirrors of Mind.* Ablex.)

[3] See, *Interdisciplinary Problem Solving,* Sharon Carver, University of Rochester. Paper presented at the Annual Meeting of the AERA, April 1991, Chicago IL. (Compare that to Carver, 1986, 1987.)

University of Wisconsin-Madison,[4] we see students learning about historical topics, such as the Civil War, by designing software about the Civil War for other students in the school. Lehrer has also recently adopted a design approach, which he did not use in his Logo studies of the 1980s. Likewise, Bill Tally and Kathy Wilson from Bank Street College recently entered a new phase in their work. Wilson, a multimedia designer of sophisticated instructional materials for schools and museums, is now passing the authorship power to the hands of her NYC students.[5] Ann Brown and Michael Jay at UC-Berkeley also use HyperCard-based tools to study children's design and production process, and social construction of knowledge in their Scientific Literacy Project.[6] At OISE Canada, to take another example, Marlene Scardamalia[7] and her colleagues have been developing computer environments that support *children's design and construction* of scientific databases. Andy diSessa, who, during the past 10 years, built some of the most exciting microworlds for learning with Logo, and later with Boxer, *for* children, is now beginning to implement Boxer in classrooms in a slightly different way—as a design learning environment for children. In the ISDP spirit—of children constructing representations about a mathematical domain for other children—diSessa's research subjects are beginning to use Boxer for representing their knowledge and arguing with other students about it.[8] The image of the "child as a designer" is so dominant in his current work, and, in the near future, we may be able to see studies of *children* designing and programming microworlds for physics and mathematics similar to the ones that diSessa once constructed for them.

There are several other holistic projects in the spirit of ISDP that are beginning to emerge in the field. The ACOT Projects (Apple Classrooms of Tomorrow) is another larger example. ACOT began its operations about four years ago

---

[4] See, *Knowledge Design in History,* Richard Lehrer, University of Wisconsin-Madison. Paper presented at the Annual Meeting of the AERA, April 1991, Chicago IL. (Compare that to Lehrer, 1987, 1988.)

[5] See, *Multimedia Authorship in the Classroom,* Bill Tally and Kathy Wilson, CCT, Bank Street College. Paper presented at the Annual Meeting of the AERA, April 1991, Chicago IL.

[6] See, *The Scientific Literacy Project,* Ann Brown and Michael Jay, UC-Berkeley. Paper presented at the Annual Meeting of the AERA, April 1991, Chicago IL.

[7] See, *Computer Environment for Group-Based Knowledge Construction: CSILE Computer Supported Intentional Learning Environments,* Marlene Scardamalia, OISE Paper presented at the Annual Meeting of the AERA, April 1991, Chicago IL. Scardamalia and her colleagues have been working in this framework for the past three years. Therefore, this is not a clearcut example of a paradigm shift in their work. Yet, they now choose to emphasize certain aspects of "learners as designers and builders" in ways not explicitly expressed in previous years.

[8] Personal communication; and his paper, *Images of Learning,* Andrea diSessa, UC-Berkeley. diSessa's vision and writings in the past 10 years have been promoting the image of the "child as designer." However, it is only recently that we can see these visions actually *implemented* in the studies conducted by him and his research team at Berkeley. See, for example, diSessa, A., Hammer, D., Sherin, B., & Kolpakowski, T. (in press). Inventing Graphing: Children's Meta Representational Expertise. *Journal of Mathematical Behavior.*

by placing many computers and ready-made software for children to use. Their initial reports were about various ways of existing software use in computer-rich classrooms. However, some of their current reports[9] indicate that in some ACOT classrooms, they begin to observe how students learn by building their own software and expert systems for their classes, their schools, and their larger community.

With the emergence of these holistic, "messy" design-based projects on thinking and learning, several papers at AERA explicitly reflected the need for a shift in research methodology (in similar ways to the shift proposed in the section on methodological issues in Chapter I of this book). Edith Ackermann, for example, presented how clinical interviews in the Piagetian spirit can be stretched to become design environments for learning—for both the researchers and their subjects.[10] In the talk for the Award for Distinguished Contributions to Educational Research, Lauren Resnick provided her fascinating personal accounts about this shift in methodology from 1985 to 1990, and how this shift expressed itself in her own research, theorizing, and writing about the learning and thinking situations she chose to investigate in the laboratory or implement in educational settings.[11] And Ann Brown gave an explicit talk about the current need to shift in methodologies, and reflected on changes in the kinds of environments she currently designs and studies.[12]

It is important to note that research and projects of the kind listed above did not exist before. When some of us at the Epistemology & Learning Group began to develop Lego/Logo design projects (e.g., Resnick, Ocko, & Papert, 1986) and software design projects (as described in this book), these ideas on children's learning through complex, integrative, and messy design projects did not exist much in the literature, or even in the air.[13] Why? What does this mean?

---

[9] See, *Trading Places: When Teachers Utilize Student Expertise in Technology-Intensive Classrooms*, Judith Haymore Sandholtz, Cathy Ringstaff, and David Dwyer, Apple Computer, Inc. Paper presented at the Annual Meeting of the AERA, April 1991, Chicago IL.

[10] See, *Who is Designing What for Whom, and Who is Learning What from Whom?* Edith Ackerman, MIT Media Laboratory. Paper presented at the Annual Meeting of the AERA, April 1991, Chicago IL. For Ackermann, however, this paper does *not* represent a current shift in research methodology. She has been writing and researching in this spirit for the past 10 years.

[11] See, *Situations for Learning and Thinking*. Lauren Resnick, University of Pittsburg, Learning Research and Development Center (LRDC). Paper presented at the Annual Meeting of the AERA, April 1991, Chicago IL (as the Award for Distinguished Contributions to Educational Research-1990). Compare that to *Education and Learning to Think*. (1987). Washington DC: National Academy Press.

[12] See, *On Paradigms and Methods: What Do You Do When the Ones You Know Don't Do What You Want Them To?* Ann Brown, UC-Berkeley. Paper presented at the Annual Meeting of the AERA, April 1991, Chicago IL (in a session with Allan Schoenfeld from UC-Berkeley, and Geoffery Saxe from UCLA).

[13] To a certain extent they were "in the air" at MIT of 1985: in Papert's vision, and in some of his writings, as well as in Jeanne Bamberger's and Donald Schon's work. But even within the MIT Logo community, there was a strong need to develop the idea of constructionist learning further and in

During this AERA conference, as I realized (with excitement) the emergence of this important shift in the field, I decided to ask people at the conference whether they too noticed this shift, and why they thought it was happening.[14] I was asking myself and others: Why weren't researchers willing to put children in the "driver's seat" before? Why weren't they interested in dealing with messy design environments? Why is it that what is happening now in research methodology did not widely exist before? What brings these researchers much closer to the constructionist end of things?

Let me share with you only one aspect of my limited "findings"—the aspect that was the most upsetting. It was upsetting for me to find that most people's answers were: *"What do you mean why now?! We simply couldn't do it before!" "Well, it's the technology that we didn't have before. Now we can do stuff like that with children." "The Macintosh." "It's the Mac. And HyperCard too. That made it possible for me." "Now we have great tools that are finally so accessible to children. Tools that can make children do such things." "I am fascinated with the multimedia capabilities of current technology. Children love video, and so it makes sense to start projects like this now."*

This is only some of what I heard from within the community of people who were creating and studying design environments like this, or from their audiences.[15] And I ask: Is it really the *Macintosh* that created this shift? Does *HyperCard* have an intrinsic quality in itself for changing researchers' methods of investigation in such a radical way? Does *multimedia technology* have this quality of giving children the power of design for the first time? Does *it* give researchers the power to lose their power and control?

I don't think so. (See Papert's 1985 and 1987 papers on technocentric thinking). In many of our studies we implemented design-based learning environ-

---

richer ways (see Papert, 1986, 1987), and to develop methods for building even stronger models (or cases) in educational practice for "Constructionism" and for "Design for Learning." Today we have accumulated a large collection of cases to support this paradigm from a variety of perspectives. See, for example, Harel, I., & Papert, S. (Eds.). (1991). *Constructionism.* Norwood, NJ: Ablex.

[14] In fact, many of the names I listed above are names of colleagues with whom I worked, interacted, and discussed research in the past seven years. (And many are also ex-Logo-community people, who I also quoted throughout my book, people who "argued" with about research methods and results.)

[15] I must note that these are the initial, first reactions to my questions. From people whom I had a chance to talk with at greater length, I heard "deeper" and less technocentric reasons for their decisions to conduct such design studies in constructionist holistic style. Some people, for example, explicitly told me that they were influenced by the work presented in this book, and of other researchers at MIT's Epistemology & Learning Group. For other people, the shift toward studying learning and thinking in design environments is a result of a deeper shift in the theoretical framework within which they now prefer to work (e.g., the "Situated Cognition Movement"). As they shift their theoretical framework, beliefs, and practices, they come closer and closer to the constructionist ideas and conceptualizations about research and practice as they were presented in Papert (1971, 1980, 1986), in Harel & Papert (1990, 1991), and in this book, see Papert's Preface, the Overview, and the discussions in Chapter I and IV.

ments which were not using the technological forefront as its main models (e.g., encompassing simple IBM PCjr's and Logo). (In other words, back in 1985, when we first started our work at Project Headlight, the IBM PCjr was not the most advanced technology, and the Logo version we used was not the most sophisticated programming environment. Moreover, Papert, more than 20 years ago, began to provide us with particular visions of learning while Logo was running on slow and stupid computers with no screens, limited memory, no personal diskettes, and no multimedia capabilities! And many theorists and practitioners before Papert provided us with simlar visions and practices of this kind without the use of sophisticated technological developments.)

Nevertheless, it seems as if the constructionist design paradigm of computer-based activity in schools is emerging in many places and multiple forms now. Without denying the fact that certain technologies give rise to certain activities not possible before,[16] my assumption is that researchers and their theoretical frameworks changed, and not only the technological developments. We must try to understand this process: What is this trend about? What factors in our society could explain this trend? Can we see it happening in other areas? Which ones?[17]

"Constructionist Learning" and "Design for Learning," in the ways I only began to illustrate in this book, are examples of pardigms for empowering children. The *researchers and educators* who design environments and technology with the Constructionist "Design for Learning" framework in mind (with and without advanced technology) are empowering children. Nevertheless, there is a clear need for a better conceptualization of what "design," or "the child as a designer," could mean in the different studies I listed above and in educational practice, and what will be the implications of these images and experiments on theory and research about thinking and learning. There is also a need to refine and better define this shift in paradigms, and to implement and compare different learning environments and research enterprises of this kind.

Dewey, Montessori, and Papert, among others, have taught us to question our assumptions about children's limitations. ISDP was presented in this book as one way for freeing children from constrained images of themselves as learners; ISDP fostered children's mathematical thinking, intellectual excitement,

---

[16] For example, technological developments, such as car phones, computerized word processors, fax machines, Macintosh LogoWriter programming, object-oriented programming, parallel-processing programming, etc. However, see Falbel, 1991, for his elaboration of Papert's argument from *Mindstorms* (1980)—that good wood doesn't produce good houses. People do. Moreover, as researchers and educators we must remember that even the most powerful and flexible technology has the potential of being used in ways that limit children's thinking and learning power.

[17] Some reasons and need for the creation of such environments and studies (from both research methods and educational practice perspectives) were presented and discussed at length throughout this book (beginning with Papert's Preface, the book's Overview, and in the theoretical discussions of Chapters I and IV), and other publications at the E&L Group. But this process (or trend) requires further investigation and theorizing.

creativity, and a sense of social and individual commitment to their work. The small learning community that emerged over the four months of the project exemplified these qualities and simultaneously produced feelings of success among children and rich data among researchers, as measured in both conventional and nonconventional ways.

APPENDIX

The following is a brief summary of our "children as media designers" research projects during the past 6 years:

- **FIRST "Children as Fractions Designers" STUDY: Harel, 1986 (Pilot Study)**
  - The project lasted 1 month with 18 fifth-grade students.
  Five participants were studied in depth after the completion of the project.
  - The children were from Linda Moriarty's and Joanne Ronkin's classes at Project Headlight.
  - The results of this study are available in this book and in:
    Harel, I. (1986). *Children as Software Designers: An Exploratory Study in Project Headlight.* Paper presented at the LOGO-86 International Conference. Cambridge, MA: MIT Media Laboratory.

- **SECOND ISDP STUDY: Harel, 1987–1988 (Dissertation Study)**
  - The project lasted 4 months in Linda Moriarty's classroom.
  - 17 fourth-grade children participated in the Experimental class, and two other classes from the same school made the two Control Groups.
  - A description of this study and its results is available in this book and in:
    Harel, I. (1988). *Software Design For Learning: Children's Construction of Meanings for Fractions and Logo Programming.* Unpublished Doctoral Dissertation. Cambridge, MA: MIT Media Laboratory.
    Harel, I. (1990). Children as Software Designers: A Constructionist Approach for Learning Mathematics. In *Journal of Mathematical Behavior, 9* (1). Norwood, NJ: Ablex.
    Harel, I., & Papert, S. (1990). Software Design as a Learning Environment. In *Interactive Learning Environments, 1* (1). Norwood, NJ: Ablex.

- **THIRD & FOURTH ISDP STUDIES: Kafai & Harel, 1989–1990 (Two Reimplementations of ISDP Studies)**
  - The two projects lasted a whole year with three theachers and their classes.
  - The first implementation was in Marquita Minot's fifth-grade class with 15 students, lasted three months.

- The second implementation was in Gwen Gibson's fourth-grade class with 21 students, lasted three months.
- Fifth graders designed software for fourth graders in the Fall. Fourth graders designed software for third graders in the Spring, and the fifth graders became software-design consultants.
- A description of this study is available in:
    Kafai, Y., & Harel, I. (1990). Replicating the Instructional Software Design Project: A Preliminary Research Report. In I. Harel (Ed.), *Constructionist Learning: A 5th Anniversary Collection of Papers*. Cambridge MA: MIT Media Laboratory.
    Kafai, Y., & Harel, I. (1991a). Learning through Design and Teaching: Exploring Social and Collaborative Aspects of Constructionism. In I. Harel & S. Papert (Eds.). *Constructionism*. Ablex (Chapter 5).
    Kafai, Y., & Harel, I. (1991b). Children Learning through Consulting: When Mathematical Ideas, Programming and Design Knowledge, and Playful Discourse are Intertwined. In I. Harel & S. Papert (Eds.), *Constructionism*. Ablex (Chapter 6).

- **FIFTH ISDP STUDY: Children as Game Designers, 1990–1991 (Yasmin Kafai's Dissertation)**
    - The project is happening during Spring 1991, will last a whole semester within one fourth-grade class.
    - We added a new context: instead of instructional software design, we are now asking the children to design educational mathematical games (i.e., software games for teaching fractions concepts for third graders).
    - A description of this study will be available in Yasmin Kafai's Dissertation (Summer 1992).

Other related research on constructionist learning by design from the Epistemology & Learning Group:

- Papert, S. (1986). *Constructionism: A New Opportunity for Elementary Science Education*. A proposal to NSF. Cambridge, MA: MIT Media Lab.
- Papert, S. (1990). Introduction to Constructionist Learning. In I. Harel (Ed.), *Constructionist Learning: A 5th Anniversary Collection*. Cambridge, MA: MIT Media Lab.
- Papert, S. (1991a). Situating Constructionism: A Theoretical and Social Context. In I. Harel & S. Papert (Eds.), *Constructionism*. Norwood, NJ: Ablex (Chapter 1).
- Turkle, S., & Papert, S. (1991). Epistemological Pluralism and the Revaluation of the Concrete. In I. Harel & S. Papert (Eds.), *Constructionism*. Norwood, NJ: Ablex (Chapter 9).

- Resnick, M., Ocko, S., and Papert, S. (1988). Lego, Logo, and Design. In *Children's Environments Quarterly, 5* (4). New York, NY: Children's Environments Research Group, The City University of New York.
- Resnick, M., & Ocko, S. (1991). Lego/Logo: Learning Through and About Design. In I. Harel & S. Papert (Eds.), *Constructionism.* Ablex (Chapter 7).
- Resnick, M. (1991). Xylophones, Hamsters, and Fireworks: The Role of Diversity in Constructionist Activities. In I. Harel & S. Papert (Eds.), *Constructionism.* Norwood, NJ: Ablex (Chapter 8).
- Wilensky, U. (1991). Abstract Meditations on the Concrete and Concrete Implications for Mathematics Education. In I. Harel & S. Papert (Eds.), *Constructionism.* Norwood, NJ: Ablex (Chapter 10).
- Gargarian, G. (1991). Towards a Constructionist Musicology. In I. Harel & S. Papert (Eds.), *Constructionism.* Ablex (Chapter 16).
- Jackson, I. (1990). Children's Software Design as a Context for Studying Collaboration. In I. Harel (Ed.), *Constructionist Learning: A 5th Anniversary Collection.* Cambridge, MA: MIT Media Laboratory.
- Dickinson, S., & Schaffer, M. (1990). The Visual Telecommunication Workstation. In I. Harel (Ed.), *Constructionist Learning: A 5th Anniversary Collection.* Cambridge, MA: MIT Media Laboratory.
- Benenson, A. (1990). *VideoLogo: Synthetic Movies in a Learning Environment.* Unpublished Master's Thesis. Cambridge, MA: MIT Media Laboratory.
- Harel, I. (1990, June). Expanding the Logo Environment: A Review of Research & Development Projects of Multimedia Programming Environments for Young Learners. In D. Newman (Ed.) *AI & Education SIG News Letter* (pp. 9–14). Based on a Paper presented at the AERA-90 Symposium entitled, "Computers and Learning: Human Construction and Artificial Intelligence."

Acknowledgments

Many people have taught me throughout my lifetime, and many have helped and guided me during my graduate studies at Harvard and MIT and during my work on my doctoral dissertation—which formed the foundation for this book. I can only thank a few of them by name, but I would like to express my deep thanks to all the people by whom I was inspired and with whom I have worked over the years.

The Media Laboratory at MIT has provided me with a highly stimulating intellectual environment, with many talented people and many exciting state-of-the-art projects to learn from. I want to thank the director of the Media Lab, Nicholas Negroponte, and all my colleagues and friends from the Lab for inspiring me and discussing ideas and research with me, and for helping me at times when I was desperate for help and advice from a human being, rather than from a computer, a book, or a stimulating lecture.

I particularly wish to thank my professor, my mentor, and my colleague Seymour Papert. Much is owed to him for my education in most of the matters explored in this book. By accepting me into his Epistemology & Learning Group at the Media Lab about six years ago, and by allowing me to collaborate with him in Project Headlight, Seymour opened many new windows in my thinking, learning, and professional growth. He inspired me throughout, and still does so to this day. Many of his lectures, as well as our personal and group discussions, were invaluable and helped shape and re-shape my thinking, until I finally came up with this Project which I love and believe in, and which I continue to develop with other people in the Lab.

I also want to thank another group of people at "that other place" up along the Charles River, which happens to prove something that only a few MIT people believe: That other creative and productive lives exist outside of MIT. There is almost nothing I could have done on my own at MIT without the skills and knowledge I gained while studying for my Masters Degree at Harvard. I came to MIT after studying at the Harvard Graduate School of Education, and working with Judah Schwartz and other researchers from the Educational Technology Center, from the Special Telecommunication Services Department of Channel 2 (with which it was affiliated at that time), and from the Human Development

Department. From them I learned a great deal about conducting research, cognitive development, interactive technologies, software development, and videodisc design and production. I am deeply indebted to them for their help and advice, and for their allowing me to live in both worlds—of Harvard and MIT—and to maintain close working relationships with people and projects at both places.

Among the Harvard people with whom I worked, I wish to give special thanks to David Perkins and Sheldon White. David Perkins, whose work and ideas I was inspired by constantly, was the most systematic supporter and advisor during my years as a graduate student in Cambridge. He was there for me whether I was at Harvard or at MIT, was constantly available to discuss my research, and worked very hard at "pulling me up in my zone of proximal development" by his wonderful questions and insights. Sheldon White taught me that there are no limits to human thought . . . whatever I thought and wrote was never "crisp" enough for his very demanding taste. He taught me how to be more critical and careful in my analyses or syntheses of theories and data, and how to situate my ideas in the broader perspectives in the history of psychology. For this I am deeply grateful.

Seymour Papert, Sheldon White, and David Perkins (my dissertation committee) invested a great deal of their time in reading and commenting on all my thesis drafts. I never ceased to marvel at the constancy and abundance of their insightful and detailed comments. I am deeply grateful for their criticisms and reviews and hope that they believe in my studies as much as I believe in their theories and ideas. To a certain extent, my projects are their projects as well.

I thank all the members of the Epistemology and Learning Group and those from the other Research Groups at the Media Lab, as well as all my colleagues and friends from outside of MIT who worked with me during the years, inspired me, and read and commented on my papers. Sylvia Weir, Sherry Turkle, Brian Harvey, Edith Ackermann, Gabi Salomon, Tamar Globerson, Judy Sachter, Marlene Kliman, Tim Walker, Ricki Goldman Segall, Mitch Resnik, Steve Ocko, Terry Tivnan, Alan Kay, Sharon Carver, Jim Kaput, Elliot Soloway, and Roy Pea contributed their ideas and commented in detail on mine while I worked on my pilot studies and on the dissertation. For this I wish to express my gratitude. During the past two years, Carol Strohecker, Nira Granott, Greg Gargarian, Yasmin Kafai, Paula Hooper, Uri Wilensky, Fred Martin, Alan Shaw, Kevin McGee, Aaron Brandes, Issac Jackson, Hillel Weintraub, Carol Sperry, Marilyn Scheffer, David Chen, as well as the teachers from Project Headlight and the SWL Project—all contributed to my thinking and provided helpful comments on my ideas, studies and papers.

Throughout this book, I have sometimes used (without specific quotations or attribution) language, ideas, and statements that have become "common currency" in our Epistemology and Learning Group. These include language from Papert's writings, his discussion of my particular studies, as well as ideas from our proposals to the NSF to which several members of our group contributed; in particular, proposals that were written through the collaboration of Seymour Papert, Mitch Resnick, and myself. In research terms, we usually describe this act as "deep appropriation."

I would also like to express my gratitude to Mario Bourgoin and Harry Nelson for their tireless help in Logo programming and other computer-related and technological issues throughout my ISDP studies during 1986–1987; to Jacqueline Karaaslanian and Stephanie Hobart for providing administrative support and more during my graduate studies, and again to Jacqueline as well as to Philip Pardi, Mai Cleary, and Wanda Gleason for their ongoing administrative support.

I wish to express my deep gratitude to the institutions that supported my Ph.D research financially: the National Science Foundation (Grant # 851031-0195), the McArthur Foundation (Grant # 874304), the IBM Corporation (Grant # OSP95952), the LEGO systems A/S, and the Apple Computer Inc.

My current research and the preparations for this book were supported by the National Science Foundation (Grant # MDR 8751190), the Lego Company, and Nintendo Inc. Japan. The ideas expressed here do not necessarily reflect the positions of these supporting agencies.

I would like to thank all the teachers and students of Project Headlight and to Eleanor Perry, the principal of the Hennigan School; with my special thanks to Linda Moriarty and Joanne Ronkin, and to the 51 young participants for enthusiasm for my projects and experiments. Linda Moriarty was a wonderful person to collaborate with on my long and complex project. She was so much on top of all the theoretical and practical issues of the Instructional Software Design Project and helped me in its implementation throughout. I learned a great deal from her about what learning in the public schools of today is all about, and about what a great art teaching is. I thank her students for sharing their ideas and thoughts with me, for allowing me to ask them all these "strange questions," to look at their private computer files and writings, and for doing exactly what they did and in the way *they* really wanted to do it. From them I learned a great deal about children's learning, problem solving, cognitive processes, and about their inner worlds.

I wish to express special thanks to Eyal Salei, who was organized and so very precise in our intensive encoding processes of the thesis data. I thank Yasmin Kafai for her help in statistical analysis and in reading my drafts and reviewing the figures. I thank Marie-Claire Cournand, who was very helpful and creative in the ways she taught me how to write, edit, and revise while struggling through my thesis writing with me. And to Leah Osterman I thank for her editing assistance during the preparations of this book. Elisabeth Glenwinkle assisted me in redesigning and redoing most of the thesis figures for the book. Steve Sherman and Jacqueline Karaaslanian provided their great talents in photography, and I thank them for helping me with the book's pictures.

Among the people who helped me in transforming my PhD dissertation into this book, I wish to thank Barbara Bernstein and Carol Davidson from Ablex, and especially Elliot Soloway for inviting me to write a book for his series. Without Elliot's encouragement and argument my dissertation would never have been published as a book. Every time I met Elliot—even back in 1986 during my Pilot Study phase, and later as I was collecting the data for my dissertation—he was always so excited and encouraging, "very important studies!" he would say, "great stuff!" Elliot, in fact, invited me to give my very first talk about ISDP to his students at Yale, a day after I completed a year of intensive data collection. I shared with him and his group my very first insecure, and raw reflections about ISDP. Since then, ideas and concepts in ISDP are being refined and redefined through the work of the Epistemology and Learning Group and our affiliated teachers, and especially through the work of Yasmin Kafai—to whom I thank for being a wonderful research collaborator. As I put together this book, I know that several new ideas and projects in the ISDP spirit are happening out there—but not really mentioned here at great length. It was indeed difficult to draw the line. Many newer ideas and relevant projects got excluded in the process of preparing this book. At this point, I can say with certainty—To Be Continued . . .

Finally, and most importantly, my family has continually provided love, support and encouragement. The constant love and million great ideas that I receive from my best friend and husband David and from my two splendid children Anat and Ron—give me the power and will to keep up with the hard work. I also wish to thank my brother Eyal and his family: Maryrose, Sharon, and Daniel; Julie and Yossi Harel; Sharon, Ronald and Tamara Cohen; Alfred Noiman; Ronen Sever; and especially to my sister Tali and my mother Rachel, who proved that love and support could come in huge quantities and with very special qualities— from overseas by short visits and long long-distance phone calls. I thank my mother and all my family so much for their support and for believing in me. My mother was a great source of strength in writing this book. And to my father Yehuda, may he rest in Heaven, who I believe must be up there watching all of this happening: Thank you for being a wonderful father to me for eight years and three months, and for being with me and loving me from afar for the last 24 years. There is probably no one who would better be able to enjoy this work than you. I wish you were here.

Idit Ron Harel
Media Laboratory
Massachusetts Institute of Technology
Cambridge, MA
March, 1991

Many Thanks to the Teachers of Headlight Model School of the Future, who Taught Me a Lot More than I Could Express in this Book

Linda Moriarty, Teacher of the ISDP Experimental Class, Headlight Teacher 1985–1987. Presently, Assistant Principal of the John Holland School in Dorchester, MA. (Jacqueline Karaaslanian Photography)

Joanne Ronkin, Headlight Teacher of the Fourth- and Fifth-Grades Advanced Work Class with her Students (also the teacher of ISDP Control Class 1) (Stephen Sherman Photography)

Eleanor Perry, Principal of the James Hennigan School (Stephen Sherman Photography)

Robert Holland, the Vice-Principal of the Hennigan School, with Headlight Teacher Fran Streeter and her Regular Ed. Third-Grade Students. Fran's students participated in many ISDP experiments from 1986–1990. (Stephen Sherman Photography)

Headlight Teacher Gwen Gibson and her Regular Ed. Fourth-Grade Students, Participated in ISDP-II 1990. (Stephen Sherman Photography)

Headlight Teacher Nora Guzman with her Spanish-English Bilingual Ed. Fifth-Grade Students (Stephen Sherman Photography)

Headlight teacher Angela Arai with her students at the school's Resource Room (Stephen Sherman Photography)

Discussing a project with Gilda Keefe, Headlight teacher of the Spanish-English Bilingual Ed. Fourth-Grade Class (Jacqueline Karaaslanian Photography)

Marquita Minot, Headlight Teacher of the Fourth- and Fifth-Grade Advanced Work Class with her Student. Marquita participated in ISDP-II during 1989. (Stephen Sherman Photography)

With Seymour Papert and some Teachers from the Science and Whole Learning Project (SWL) at MIT (Stephen Sherman Photography)

BIBLIOGRAPHY

Ackermann, E. (1990). From decontextualized to situated knowledge. In I. Harel (Ed.), *Constructionist learning: A 5th anniversary collection of papers*. Cambridge, MA: The Media Laboratory.

Ackermann, E. (1991, April). *Who is designing what for whom, and who is learning what from whom?* Paper presented at the Annual Meeting of the AERA, Chicago, IL.

Adelson, B., & Soloway, E. (1984a). *A cognitive model of software design* (Cognition and Programming Project, Research Rep. No. 342). New Haven, CT: Yale University.

Adelson, B., & Soloway, E. (1984b). *The role of domain experience in software design* (Cognition and Programming project, Research Rep. No. 25). New Haven, CT: Yale University. (Also in *IEEE Transactions on Software Engineering, 11*(11), 1985).

Atwood, M. E., Jefferies, R., & Polson, P. G. (1980, March). *Studies in plan construction I and II* (Tech. Rep. NO SAI-80-028-DEN). Englewood, CO: Science Applications, Inc.

Behr, M. J., Lesh, R., Post, T. R., & Silver, E. A. (1983). Rational number concepts. In R. Lesh & M. Landau (Eds.), *Acquisition of mathematics concepts and processes* (pp. 91–126). New York: Academic Press.

Behr, M. J., Wachsmuth, I., Post, T. R., & Lesh, R. (1984). Order and equivalence: A clinical teaching experiment. *Journal of Research in Mathematics Education, 15*(5), 323–341.

Benenson, A. (1990). *VideoLogo: Synthetic movies . . . Movies in a learning environment*. Unpublished Master's Thesis, MIT Media Laboratory, Cambridge, MA.

Bennett, A. B. (1981). *Fraction bars: A step by step teacher's guide*. Durham, NH: University of New Hampshire & Scott Resources Publishers.

Bransford, J. D. (1985). *Computer, videodiscs, and the teaching of thinking*. Unpublished paper from the Vanderbuilt's Learning and Technology Center. (Also presented at the American Educational Research Association, Washington, DC.)

Brown, A. L. (1978). Knowing when, where, and how to remember: A problem of metacognition. In R. Glaser (Ed.), *Advances in instructional psychology*. Hillsdale, NJ: Erlbaum.

Brown, A. L. (1984). Reciprocal teaching: Comprehension-fostering and comprehension-monitoring activities. *Cognition and Instruction, 1*(2), 117–175.

Brown, A. L. (1988). Motivation to learn and understand: On taking charge of one's own learning. *Cognition and Instruction, 5*(4), 311–322.

Brown, A. (1991, April). *On paradigms and methods: What do you do when the ones you know don't do what you want them to?* Paper presented at the Annual Meeting of the AERA, Chicago, IL.

Brown, A. L., Bransford, J. D., Ferrara, R. A., & Campione, J. C. (1983). Learning, remembering, and understanding. In W. Kessen (Ed.), *Handbook of child psychology: Cognitive development* (Vol. 3). New York: Wiley.

Brown, A., & Jay, M. (1991, April). *The scientific literacy project.* Paper presented at the Annual Meeting of the AERA, Chicago, IL.

Brown, J. S., Collins, A., & Duguid, P. (1989). Situated cognition and the culture of learning. *Educational Researcher, 18*(1), 32–42.

Bruffee, K. S. (1984). Collaborative learning and the "conversation of mankind." *College English, 46,* 635–652.

Bruner, J. S. (1966). *Towards a theory of instruction.* New York: W. W. Norton.

Bruner, J. S. (1985). Vygotsky: A historical and conceptual perspective. In J. V. Wertsch (Ed.), *Culture, communication, and cognition.* Cambridge, UK: Cambridge University Press.

Burton, R. R., Brown, J. S., & Fischer, G. (1984). Skiing as a model of instruction. In B. Rogoff & J. Lave (Eds.), *Everyday cognition.* Cambridge, MA: Harvard University Press.

Carpenter, T. P., Coburn, T. G., Reys, R. E., & Wilson, J. W. (1976). Notes from the National Assessment: Addition and multiplication with fractions. *Arithmetic Teacher, 18*(4), 245–249.

Carver, S. M. (1987). *Transfer of LOGO debugging skill: Analysis, instruction, and assessment.* Unpublished doctoral dissertation, Carnegie-Mellon University, Department of Psychology.

Carver, S. (1991, April). *Interdisciplinary problem solving.* Paper presented at the Annual Meeting of the AERA, Chicago, IL.

Carver, S. M., & Klahr, D. (1986). *Assessing children's LOGO debugging skills with a formal model.* Pittsburgh, PA: Carnegie-Mellon University, Department of Psychology.

Case, R. (1985). *Intellectual development: From birth to adulthood.* New York: Academic Press.

Chipman, S. F., Segal, J. W., & Glaser, R. (1985). *Thinking and learning skills* (Vol. 1 & 2). Hillsdale, NJ: Erlbaum.

Clements, D. H. (1985, April). *Effects of Logo programming on cognition, metacognitives skills, and achievement.* Paper presented at the American Educational Research Association, Chicago, IL.

Clements, D. H., & Gullo, D. F. (1984). Effects of computer programming on young children's cognition. *Journal of Educational Psychology, 76*(6), 1051–1058.

Collins, A., & Brown, J. S. (1985, December). *The computer as a tool for learning through reflection.* Paper presented at the American Educational Research Association, Washington, DC.

Collins, A., & Brown, J. S. (1987, April). *The new apprenticeship.* Paper presented at the American Educational Research Association, Washington, DC.

Cooper, C. (1980). Development of collaborative problem solving among pre-school children. *Developmental Psychology, 16,* 443–440.

Daiute, C. (1985). *Writing with computers.* Reading, MA: Addison-Wesley.

Daiute, C. (1986). Do 1 and 1 make 2?: Patterns of collaboration in writing. *Written Communication, 3.*

Davidson, J. (1969). *Using the Cuisenaire Rods—A photo-text guide for teachers.* New Rochelle, NY: Cuisenaire Company of America.

Davidson, P. S. (1977). *Idea book for Cuisenaire Rods at the primary level.* New Rochelle, NY: Cuisenaire Company of America.

Dewey, T. (1974). *The child and the curriculum.* In R. D. Archambault (Ed.), *John Dewey on education.* Chicago: University of Chicago Press. (Original work published 1902).

diSessa, A. (1985). Learning about knowing. In E. Klein (Ed.), *Children and computers* (New Directions in Child Development 28). San Francisco: Jossey-Bass.

diSessa, A. (1988). Knowledge in pieces. In G. Forman & P. Pufall (Eds.), *Constructivism in the computer age.* Hillsdale, NJ: Erlbaum.

diSessa, A. (1991, April). *Images of learning.* Berkeley, CA: University of California Press.

diSessa, A., Hammer, D., Sherin, B., & Kolpakowski, T. (in press). Inventing graphing: Children's meta representational expertise. *Journal of Mathematical Behavior.*

Ellenbruch, L. W., & Payne, J. N. (1978). A teaching sequence from initial fraction concepts through addition of unlike fractions. In M. N. Suydam (Ed.), *Developing computational skills (Yearbook of the National Council of Teachers Of Mathematics)* (pp. 129–147). Reston, VA: The Council.

ETC. (1985). *"Pies are hard to find out about. . ." An inquire into children's understanding and nature of fractions* (Tech. Rep. No. 85-21). Cambridge, MA: The Educational Technology Center, Harvard Graduate School of Education.

ETC. (1985). *Seeing the unseen: The Science Videodisc Project.* Cambridge, MA: The New Technology Group, Educational Technology Center, Harvard Graduate School of Education.

Falbel, A. (1990). The computer as a convivial tool. In I. Harel (Ed.), *Constructionist learning: A 5th anniversary collection of papers.* Cambridge, MA: MIT Media Laboratory.

Feurzeig, W., Horwitz, P., & Nickerson, R. S. (1981, October). *Microcomputers in education* (Rep. No. 4798). Cambridge, MA: Bolt Beranek & Newman.

Feurzeig, W., Papert, S., Bloom, M., Grant, R., & Solomon, C. (1969). *Programming languages as a conceptual framework for teaching mathematics* (Tech. Rep. No. 1899). Cambridge, MA: Massachusetts Institute of Technology, and Bolt, Beranek, & Newman.

Flavell, J. (1979). Metacognition and cognitive monitoring: A new area of cognitive-developmental inquiry. *American Psychologist, 34*(10), 906–911.

Flavell, J., & Draguns, J. (1957). A microgenetic approach to perception and thought. *Psychological Bulletin, 54,* 197–217.

Flavell, J. H., & Wellman, H. M. (1977). Metamemory. In R. V. Keil & J. W. Hagen (Eds.), *Perspectives on the development of memory and cognition.* Hillsdale, NJ: Erlbaum.

Forman, G., & Pufall, P. (Eds.). (1988). *Constructivism in the computer age.* Hillsdale, NJ: Erlbaum.

Gargarian, G. (1990). Music composing as problem setting. In I. Harel (Ed.), *Constructionist learning: A fifth anniversary collection of papers.* Cambridge MA: MIT Media Lab.

Ginsburg, H., & Opper, S. (1978). *Piaget's theory of intellectual development.* Englewood Cliffs, NJ: Prentice-Hall.

Ginsburg, H., & Allardice, B. (1984). Children's difficulties with school's mathematics. In B. Rogoff & J. Lave, *Everyday cognition.* Cambridge, MA: Harvard University Press.

Goldman Segall, R. (1990). *Learning constellations: A multimedia ethnographic research environment, using video technology, for exploring children's thinking.* Unpublished Doctoral dissertation, MIT Medical Lab, Cambridge, MA.

Goldman Segall, R. (1989a). *Videodisc technology as a conceptual research tool for the study of human theory making.* Unpublished paper, Media Laboratory, MIT, Cambridge, MA.

Goldman Segall, R. (1989b). *Learning constellations: A multimedia ethnographic description of children's theories in a Logo culture.* Unpublished doctoral dissertation proposal, Media Laboratory, MIT, Cambridge, MA.

Granott, N. (1990). Through the camera's lens: Video as a research tool. In I. Harel (Ed.), *Constructionist learning: A 5th anniversary collection of papers.* Cambridge, MA: MIT Media Laboratory.

Gruber, H., & Voneche, J. J. (1977). *The essential Piaget.* New York: Basic Books.

Guindon, R., & Curtis, B. (1988). *Control of cognitive processes during software design: What tools are needed?* Austin, TX: Microelectronics and Computer Technology Corporation.

Harel, I. (1986). *Children as software designers: An exploratory study in Project Headlight.* Paper presented at the LOGO 86 International Conference, Cambridge, MA.

Harel, I. (1988). *Software design for learning: Children's construction of meaning for fractions and Logo programming.* Unpublished doctoral dissertation, Media Laboratory, MIT, Cambridge, MA.

Harel, I. (1989a). Tools for young software designers. *Proceedings of the Third Workshop of Empirical Studies of Programmers (ESP Society).* Austin, TX.

Harel, I. (1989b). Software design for learning. In W. C. Ryan (Ed.), *Proceedings Book of the National Educational Computer Conference (NECC).* Boston, MA: The International Council of Computers in Education.

Harel, I. (1989c). Software designing in a learning environment for young learners: Cognitive processes and cognitive tools. *Proceedings of the FRIEND21 International Symposium on Next Generation Human Interface Technologies.* Tokyo, Japan.

Harel, I. (1989d). Software design for learning mathematics. In C. Maher, G. Goldin, & R. Davis (Eds.), *Proceedings Book of the Eleventh Annual Meeting of Psychology of Mathematics Education.* New Brunswick, NJ: Rutgers University, Center for Mathematics, Science, and Computer Education.

Harel, I. (1990a). On realistic constructionism: Children learning mathematics through instructional software design. *Journal of Mathematical Behavior, 8*(3), 5–95.

Harel, I. (1990b). The silent observer and holistic note-taker: Using video for documenting a research project. In I. Harel (Ed.), *Constructionist learning: A 5th anniversary collection of papers.* Cambridge, MA: MIT Media Laboratory.

Harel, I. (1990c). *Expanding the Logo environment: A review of research & development projects of multimedia programming environments for young learners.* Paper presented at the Annual meeting of the American Educational Research Association (AGRA), Boston MA. (Also appeared in *Artificial intelligence and education newsletter, 3*(1), June 1990.)

Harel, I. (Ed.). (1990d). *Constructionist learning: A 5th anniversary collection of papers.* Cambridge, MA: MIT Media Laboratory.

Harel, I. (1991, April). *Why and how "design for learning"?* Paper presented at the Annual Meeting of the AERA, Chicago, IL.

Harel, I., & Papert, S. (1990). Software design as a learning environment. *Interactive Learning Environments, 1*(1), 1–32.

Harel, I., & Papert, S. (1991). *Constructionism*. Norwood, NJ: Ablex.

Harel, I., & Papert, S. (Eds.). (1991, in progress). *Headlight stories: Constructionist teaching in a computer culture.*

Harel, I., & Stein, C. (1989). *The instructional software design project: A video series.* Cambridge, MA: MIT, Media Laboratory.

Harrison, B. (1972). *Pattern blocks activities for children.* Weston, MA.

Harvey, B. (1985). *Computer science Logo style. Volume 1: Intermediate programming.* Cambridge, MA: MIT Press.

Hatano, & Inagaki. (1987). A theory of motivation for comprehension and its applications to mathematics instruction. In T. R. Romberg & D. M. Steward (Eds.), *The monitoring of school mathematics: Background papers. (Vol. 2): Implications form psychology, outcomes from instruction.* Madison, WI: Center for Educational Research.

Heller, R. S. (1986). *Different Logo teaching styles: Do they really matter?* Paper presented at the First Workshop of Empirical Studies of Programmers. Washington, DC.

Holdaway, D. (1979). *The foundations of literacy.* New York: Ashton Scholastic.

Inhelder, B., Sinclair, H., & Bovet, M. (1974). *Learning and the development of cognition.* Cambridge, MA: Harvard University Press.

Jackson, I. (1990). Children's software design as a collaborative process: An experiment with fifth graders at Project Headlight. In I. Harel (Ed.), *Constructionist learning: A 5th anniversary collection of papers.* Cambridge, MA: MIT Media Laboratory.

Janvier, C. (Ed.). (1987). *Problems in representation in the teaching and learning of mathematics.* Hillsdale, NJ: Erlbaum.

Jefferies, R., Turner, A. A., Polson, P. G., & Atwood, M. E. (1981). The processes involved in designing software. In J. R. Anderson (Ed.), *Cognitive skills and their acquisition.* Hillsdale, NJ: Erlbaum.

Kafai, Y., & Harel, I. (1990). The Instructional Software Design Project: Phase II. In I. Harel (Ed.), *Constructionist learning: A 5th anniversary collection of papers.* Cambridge, MA: Media Laboratory, MIT.

Kafai, Y., & Harel, I. (1991a). Learning through design and teaching: Exploring collaborative and social aspects of constructionism. In I. Harel & S. Papert (Eds.), *Constructionism.* Norwood, NJ: Ablex.

Kafai, Y., & Harel, I. (1991b). Children learning through consulting: When mathematical ideas, programming and design knowledge, and playful discourse are intertwined. In I. Harel & S. Papert (Eds.), Norwood, NJ: Ablex.

Kieren, T., & Nelson, D. (1978). The operator construct of rational numbers in childhood and adolescent: An exploratory study. *The Alberta Journal of Educational Research, 24*(1), 234–247.

Kurland, D. M., Clement, A., Mawby, R., & Pea, R. D. (1987). Mapping the cognitive demands of learning to program. In R. D. Pea & K. Sheingold (Eds.), *Mirrors of Minds* (pp. 103–127). Norwood, NJ: Ablex.

Kurland, D. M., & Pea, R. D. (1983). Children's mental models of recursive Logo Programs. *Proceedings of the Fifth Annual Cognitive Science Society.* Rochester, NY: Cognitive Science Society.

Lammer, S. (1987). *Programmers at work.* Redmond, MA: Microsoft Corp. Press.

Latour, B. (1987). *Science in action: How to follow scientists and engineers through society.* Cambridge MA: Harvard University Press.

Lawler, R. W. (1985). *Computer experience and cognitive development: A child learning in a computer culture.* West Sussex, UK: Ellis Horwood Limited.

Lehrer, R. (1991, April). *Knowledge design in history.* Paper presented at the Annual Meeting of the AERA, Chicago, IL.

Lesh, R., & Hamilton, E. (1981, April). *The rational number project testing program.* Paper presented at the American Educational Research Association Annual Meeting, Los Angeles, CA.

Lesh, R., Landau, M., & Hamilton, E. (1983). Conceptual models and applied mathematical problem-solving research. In R. Lesh & M. Landau (Eds.), *Acquisition of mathematics concepts and processes* (pp. 264–344). New York: Academic Press.

Lesh, R., & Landau, M. (1983). *Acquisition of mathematics concepts and processes.* New York: Academic Press.

Lesser, J. S. (1974). *Children and television: Lessons from Sesame Street.* New York: Vintage Books.

Linn, M. C. (1985). The cognitive consequences of programming instruction in the classrooms. *Educational Researcher, 14,* 14–29.

Mandinach, E. B. (1984). *Classifying the A in CAI for learners of different abilities.* Paper presented at the American Educational Research Association, New Orleans.

Markman, E. L. (1977). Realizing that you don't understand: A preliminary investigation. *Child Development, 48,* 986–992.

Meichenbaum, D., Burland, S., Gruson, L., & Cameron, R. (1985). Metacognitive assessment. *The growth of reflection in children.*

Milojkovic, J. (1985). *Children learning computer programming: Cognitive and motivational consequences.* Unpublished doctoral dissertation, Stanford University, Palo Alto, CA.

Minsky, M. (1986). *Society of mind.* New York: Simon and Schuster.

Motherwell, L. (1988). *Gender and style differences in a Logo-based environment.* Unpublished doctoral dissertation, Media Laboratory, MIT, Cambridge, MA.

Nachmias, R., Mioduser, D., & Chen, D. (1985). *Acquisition of basic computer programming concepts by children* (Tech. Rep. No. 14). Tel Aviv, Israel: Center for Curriculum Research and Development, School of Education, Tel Aviv University.

Nickerson, R. S. (1986). *Using computers: Human factors in information systems.* Cambridge, MA: MIT Press.

Nickerson, R. S., Perkins, D. N., & Smith, E. E. (1985). *The teaching of thinking.* Hillsdale, NJ: Erlbaum.

Newell, A., & Simon, H. A. (1972). *Human problem solving.* Englewood Cliffs, NJ: Prentice-Hall.

Papert, S. (1971a). *Teaching children thinking* (AI Memo No. 247, and Logo Memo No. 2). Cambridge, MA: MIT.

Papert, S. (1971b). *Teaching children to be mathematicians vs. teaching about mathematics* (AI Memo No. 249, and Logo Memo No. 4). Cambridge, MA: MIT.

Papert, S. (1980). *Mindstorms: Children, computers, and powerful ideas.* New York: Basic Books.

Papert, S. (1984a). *Microworlds transforming education.* Paper presented at the ITT Key

Issues Conference, Annenberg School of Communications, University of Southern California.

Papert, S. (1984b). *New theories for new learnings*. Paper presented at the National Association for School Psychologists' Conference.

Papert, S. (1985, July). Computer criticism vs. technoratic thinking. *LOGO 85 theoretical papers* (pp. 53–67). Cambridge, MA: MIT Media Laboratory.

Papert, S. (1986). *Constructionism: A new opportunity for elementary science education.* (A proposal to the National Science Foundation). Cambridge, MA: MIT Media Technology Laboratory.

Papert, S. (1987a). Computer criticism vs. technocratic thinking. *Educational Researcher, 16*(1), 22–30.

Papert, S. (1987b). *Using computers to combat illiteracy: Towards a constructionist theory of creative learning* (A proposal to the MacArthur Foundation). Cambridge, MA: Media Technology Laboratory, MIT.

Papert, S. (1991a). Perestroika and epistemological politics. In I. Harel & S. Papert (Eds.), *Constructionism*. Norwood, NJ: Ablex.

Papert, S. (1991b). New images of programming: In search of an educationally powerful concept of technological fluency. A proposal to the National Science Foundation (NSF). MIT Media Lab, Cambridge, MA.

Papert, S. (1991c). Situating constructionism: A theoretical and social context. In I. Harel & S. Papert (Eds.), *Constructionism*. Norwood, NJ: Ablex.

Papert, S. (1992, in press). New York: Basic Books.

Papert, S., Watt, D., diSessa, A., & Weir, S. (1979). *Final report of the Brookline Logo Projects. Parts I and II* (Logo Memo No. 53). Cambridge, MA: MIT.

Pea, R. D. (1984). *Symbol systems and thinking skills: Logo in context.* Paper presented at the LOGO 84 Conference, Cambridge, MA.

Pea, R. D. (1985, October). *Transfer of thinking skills: Issues for software use and design*. Paper presented at the National Conference on Computers and Complex Thinking. National Academy of Sciences, Washington, DC.

Pea, R. D. (1987). Cognitive technologies for mathematics education. In A. Schoenfeld (Ed.), *Cognitive science and mathematics education*. Hillsdale, NJ: Erlbaum.

Pea, R. D. (1988). Putting knowledge to use. In R. Nickerson & P. Zodhiates (Eds.), *Technology in education in 2020*. Hillsdale, NJ: Erlbaum.

Pea, R. D., Allen, C., Chertok, M., Godreau, E., Shaw, J., & Velrum, N. (1991, April). *Students learning through design with multimedia tools for collaborative research, composition, and presentation*. Paper presented at the Annual Meeting of the AERA, Chicago, IL.

Pea, R. D., & Kurland, D. M. (1983). *On the cognitive effects of learning computer programming*. New York: Bank Street College Center for Children and Technology.

Pea, R. D., & Kurland, D. M. (1984). On the cognitive effects of learning computer programming. *New Ideas In Psychology, 2*(2), 137–168.

Pea, R. D., & Sheingold, K. (Eds.). (1987). *Mirrors of mind: Patterns of experience in educational computing*. Norwood, NJ: Ablex Publishing Corp.

Peck, D. M., & Jencks, S. M. (1981). Conceptual issues in the teaching and learning of fractions. *Journal for Research in Mathematics Education, 12*(5), 339–348.

Perkins, D. N. (1985). The fingertip effect: How information-processing technology changes thinking. *Educational Researcher, 14*(7), 11–17.

Perkins, D. N. (1986). *Knowledge as design.* Hillsdale, NJ: Erlbaum.

Perkins, D. N., & Martin, F. (1985). *Fragile knowledge and neglected strategies in novice programmers* (Tech. Rep. No. 85-22). Cambridge, MA: Educational Technology Center, Harvard Graduate School of Education.

Perret-Clermont, A. N. (1980). *Social interaction and cognitive development in children.* London: Academic Press.

Piaget, J. (1955). *The language and thought of the child.* New York: New American Library.

Piaget, J. (1968). *Six psychological studies.* New York: Vintage Books.

Piaget, J. (1972). Intellectual evolution from adolescence to adulthood. *Human Development, 15,* 1–12.

Piaget, J. (1973). *The child and reality: Problems of genetic psychology.* New York: Grossman.

Piaget, J. (1976). *The grasp of consciousness: Action and concept in the young child.* Cambridge, MA: Harvard University Press.

Piaget, J., & Inhelder, B. (1967). *The child's conception of space.* New York: W. W. Worton.

Post, T. R. (1981). Results and implications from the National Assessment. *Arithmetic Teacher, 28*(9), 26–31.

Post, T. R., Wachsmuth, I., Lesh, R., & Behr, M. J. (1985). Order and equivalence of rational numbers: A cognitive analysis. *Journal on Research in Mathematics Education, 16*(1), 18–36.

Resnick, L. (1991, April). *Situations for learning and thinking.* Paper presented at the Annual Meeting of the AERA, Chicago, IL.

Resnick, M., & Ocko, S. (1990). LEGO/Logo: Learning through and about design. In I. Harel (Ed.), *Constructionist learning: A 5th anniversary collection of papers.* Cambridge, MA: MIT Media Laboratory.

Resnick, M., Ocko, S., & Papert, S. (1988). Lego, LOGO, and design. *Children's Environments Quarterly, 5*(4).

Rogoff, B., & Wertsch, J. V. (Eds.). (1984). *Children's learning in the "zone of proximal development."* San Francisco: Jossey-Bass.

Rubin, A., & Bruce, B. (in press). Learning with QUILL: Lessons for students, teachers, and software designers. In T. E. Raphael & R. E. Reynolds (Eds.), *Context for school based learning.* New York: Longman.

Sachter, J. (1987). *Children's development of spatial understanding through the use of a 3-D computer graphics system: An exploratory in Project Headlight.* Unpublished paper, MIT, Cambridge, MA.

Sachter, J. E. (1990). *Kids in space: Exploration into children's cognitive styles and understanding of space in 3-D computer graphics.* Unpublished doctoral dissertation, MIT Media Laboratory, Cambridge, MA.

Salomon, G. (1979). *Interaction of media, cognition, and learning.* San Francisco: Jossey Bass.

Salomon, G. (1986). *Information technologies: What you see is not always what you get* (Rep. No. 3). Tel Aviv, Israel: Unit for Communication and Computer Research in Education, Tel Aviv University.

Salomon, G., & Perkins, D. N. (1986, February). *Transfer of cognitive skills from programming: When and how?* (Tech. Rep. No. 2). Tel Aviv, Israel: Unit for Communication and Computer Research in Education, Tel Aviv University.

Sandholtz, J. H., Ringstaff, C., & Dwyer, D. (1991, April). *Trading places: When teachers utilize student expertise in technology-intensive classrooms (ACOT).* Paper presented at the Annual Meeting of the AERA, Chicago, IL.

Scardamalia, M. (1991, April). *Computer environment for group-based knowledge construction: CSILE computer supported intentional learning environments.* Paper presented at the Annual Meeting of the AERA, Chicago, IL.

Schön, D. A. (1987). *Educating the reflective practitioner.* San Francisco: Jossey-Bass.

Schoenfeld, A. H. (1985a). *Mathematical problem solving.* New York: Academic Press.

Schoenfeld, A. H. (1985b). *What's the fuss about metacognition?* Hillsdale, NJ: Erlbaum.

Scribner, S. (1984). Practical intelligence. In B. Rogoff & J. Lave (Eds.), *Everyday cognition: Its development in social context.* Cambridge, MA: Harvard University Press.

Shneiderman, B., Mayer, R., McKay, D., & Heller, P. (1977). Experimental investigations of the utility of detailed flowcharts in programming. *Communications of the Association for Computer Machinery (ACM), 20,* 373–381.

Siegler, R. S. (1983a). Five generalizations about cognitive development. *American Psychologists, 38,* 263–277.

Siegler, R. S. (1983b). Information processing approaches to cognitive development. In W. Kessen (Ed.), *Handbook of child psychology: History, theory and methods* (Vol. 1). New York: Wiley.

Siegler, R. S., & Klahr, D. (1982). When do children learn: The relationship between existing knowledge and the ability to acquire new knowledge. In R. Glaser (Ed.), *Advances in instructional psychology.* Hillsdale, NJ: Erlbaum.

Simon, H. A., & Chase, W. (1973). Skill in chess. *American Scientist, 61,* 394–430.

Smith, J. (1987). *What is fraction conceptual knowledge?* Paper presented at the annual meeting of the American Educational Research Association, Washington, DC.

Solomon, C. (1986). *Computer environments for children: A reflection on theories of learning and education.* Cambridge, MA: MIT Press.

Soloway, E. (1984). *Why kids should learn to program?* (Cognition and Programming Knowledge Research Rep. No. 29). New Haven, CT: Yale University.

Soloway, E., (1991, April). a) *HyperText environments expand the bandwidth of interactivity*; b) *The promise of technology for promoting change*; and c) *MediaText demonstration.* Papers presented at the Annual Meeting of the AERA, Chicago, IL.

Soloway, E., & Ehrlich, K. (1984). *Empirical studies of programming knowledge* (Cognition and Programming Knowledge Research Rep. No. 16). New Haven, CT: Yale University.

Soloway, E., & Iyengar, S. (Eds.). (1986). *Empirical studies of programmers.* Norwood, NJ: Ablex.

Steinberg, R. E. (1984). *Teaching computers to teach* (On creating CAI). Hillsdale, NJ: Erlbaum.

Sternberg, R. J. (Ed.). (1984). *Mechanisms of cognitive development.* New York: W. H. Freeman.

Strohecker, C. (1990). Knot-Tying: A constructionist Environment for Topology. In I.

Harel (Ed.), *Constructionist Learning: A Fifth Anniversary Collection of Papers*. Cambridge, MA: MIT Media Lab.

Suchman, L. (1987). *Plans and situated actions: The problem of human machine communication*. Cambridge, UK: Cambridge University Press.

Tally, B., & Wilson, K. (1991, April). *Multimedia authorship in the classroom*. Paper presented at the Annual Meeting of the AERA, Chicago, IL.

Tierney, C. C. (1988). *Construction of fraction knowledge: Two case studies*. Unpublished doctoral dissertation, Harvard Graduate School of Education, Cambridge, MA.

Turkle, S. (1984). *The second self: Computers and the human spirit*. New York: Simon and Schuster.

Turkle, S. (1990). Growing up in the age of intelligent machines: Reconstructions of the psychological and reconsiderations of the human. In R. Kurzweil (Ed.), *The age of intelligent machines* (pp. 68–73). Cambridge, MA: MIT Press.

Turkle, S., & Papert, S. (1990). Epistemological pluralism: Styles and voices within the computer culture. In I. Harel (Ed.), *Constructionist learning: A 5th anniversary collection of papers*. Cambridge, MA: MIT Media Laboratory.

Vygotsky, L. S. (1962). *Thought and language*. Cambridge, MA: MIT Press.

Vygotsky, L. S. (1978). *Mind in society: The development of higher psychological processes*. Cambridge, MA: Harvard University Press.

Watt, D. (1979). *Final report of the Brookline Logo Project. Part III: Profiles of student's work* (Logo Memo No. 54, A.I. Memo No. 546). Cambridge, MA: Artificial Intelligence LAB, MIT.

Wearn-Hilbert, D. C., & Hilbert, J. (1983). Junior high students understanding of fractions. *School Science and Mathematics, 83*(2), 96–106.

Webb, N. M., Ender, P., & Lewis, S. (1986). Problem-solving strategies and group processes in small groups learning computer programming. *American Educational Research Journal, 23*(2), 243–261.

Weir, S. (1986). *Cultivating minds: A Logo case book*. New York: Harper & Row.

Wertsch, J. V. (1985). *Culture, communication, and cognition: Vygotskian perspectives*. Cambridge, UK: Cambridge University Press.

White, S. H. (1978). Psychology in all sorts of places. In R. A. Kasschau & F. S. Kessel (Eds.), *Houston Symposium, Vol. 1. Psychology and society: In search of symbiosis*. New York: Holt, Rinehart & Winston.

White, S. H. (1980). Cognitive competence and performance in everyday environments. *Bulletin of the Orton Society, 30*, 29–45.

White, S. H., & Siegel, A. W. (1984). Cognitive development in time and space. In B. Rogoff & J. Lave (Eds.), *Everyday cognition: Its development in social context*. Cambridge, MA: Harvard University Press.

Author Index

Subject Index